Praise for *Highway Heist*

"In *Highway Heist*, James Bennett provides vital, new, intellectual infrastructure for a timely and authoritative critique of pork barrels, potholes, and political privilege."
> —**George Gilder**, bestselling author, *Wealth and Poverty*, *Life After Google*, *Telecosm*, *Knowledge and Power*, and other books

"James Bennett's indispensable book *Highway Heist* critically examines the corruption, waste, and runaway costs of government transportation infrastructure. He reveals how interest groups have long exploited infrastructure spending policies to enrich themselves while subjecting the public to such recurring failures as traffic congestion, dangerous conditions, crumbling roads and bridges, and pork scandals. Instead of such unnecessary problems from government monopolies, *Highway Heist* shows the viability of private, market-based, enterprising systems in directly serving transport needs, with real accountability, innovative benefits and enormous savings."
> —**Rand Paul**, U.S. Senator; Ranking Member, Senate Committee on Small Business and Entrepreneurship

"Whatever your views on highway construction, the remarkable and indispensable book *Highway Heist* will improve it. Who knew for example that Transportation Secretary John Volpe saved New Orleans' French Quarter in the 1970s? This fascinating book could not be timelier as state Departments of Transportation throughout America, keeping social objectives in mind, start ramping up infrastructure spending with new Federal funds."
> —**Diana Furchtgott-Roth**, former Deputy Assistant Secretary for Research and Technology, U.S. Department of Transportation; Adjunct Professor, George Washington University

"One can never know enough history. From Mancur Olson, we know that given enough time, there will be coalitions that prompt interest-group formation and success. So much for the 'public interest.' From James Bennett's book *Highway Heist* we now have a very readable and informative complement to Olson's insight, a lively account of how the U.S. highway lobby came to be and what it delivered. The good as well as the bad. We went from muddy roads to the Interstates. And back again. We now have potholed roads in too many places alongside pork projects and congested arteries. Political allocations seemingly end up that way. I cannot think of a better guide to U.S. transportation policy and politics than *Highway Heist*."
> —**Peter Gordon**, Emeritus Professor of Public Policy, University of Southern California; co-editor, *The Voluntary City: Choice, Community and Civil Society*

"James Bennett and the Independent Institute offer a provocative and timely challenge to state and federal policymakers. In the important book *Highway Heist*, we are treated to both a history lesson of how 'infrastructure policy' has evolved and the key question facing us as we look to the future: Can't a nation of innovators agree upon a better way to build, maintain and pay for necessary internal improvements? Bennett raises all the appropriate questions. Who will be willing to respond and lead?"

—**John M. Engler**, former Governor of Michigan; former President and CEO, Business Roundtable

"The fascinating and timely book *Highway Heist* provides a comprehensive account of the economics, politics and history of government 'infrastructure.' A true joy to read, this compelling book vividly shows how real economic, social and environmental progress requires innovative, market-based, entrepreneurial, transportation systems without the cronyism, corruption, boondoggles, profligacy and waste from the interest-group politics of Big Government. Highly recommended!"

—**Peter F. Schweizer**, President, Government Accountability Institute; bestselling author, *Clinton Cash, Red-Handed, Profiles in Corruption, Secret Empires*, and other books

"The lively and entertaining book *Highway Heist* underscores an important rule of thumb: the more government is involved in infrastructure, the more likely it is to be crumbling. The solution, the book clearly shows, is not to spend more government money on infrastructure, but to spend less of our tax dollars and rely instead on user fees and private ownership."

—**Randal O'Toole**, Director, Thoreau Institute; author, *Gridlock: Why We're Stuck in Traffic and What to Do About It* and *Romance of the Rails: Why the Passenger Trains We Love Are Not the Transportation We Need*

"Convenient, quality, efficient and inexpensive transportation infrastructure systems are irreplaceable for economic, social and environmental progress. However, the meaning of 'infrastructure' has been twisted politically into a deceptive buzzword to cover up massive and flagrant corruption, pork and waste that Americans are compelled to fund. James Bennett's timely and essential book *Highway Heist* now vividly exposes how today's government transportation boondoggles have come to dominate, but also how innovative, competitive, private, entrepreneurial systems can and should be adopted. *Highway Heist* is required reading for policymakers, business and civic leaders, educators and students, and the general public in order to secure our vital transportation needs."

—**Michael S. Lee**, U.S. Senator; Ranking Member, Joint Economic Committee; Member, Senate Committee on Commerce, Science, and Transportation

"In *Highway Heist*, Bennett makes sense of highway provision in America. Alexis de Tocqueville wrote in the 1830s, during the toll-road era, and celebrated local management, including voluntary financing and private management of toll-road companies. That approach continued through much of the 19th century and across the nation. But later the imperious Progressive mentality extended itself throughout public life.

Activists for 'Good Roads' showed little concern, Bennett writes, that 'centralizing the administration of roadwork would drain the lifeblood from the local body politic.' That, too, is Tocqueville to a T. American highways have traveled the road that Tocqueville foresaw. Into the 20th century, highways were almost thoroughly governmentalized. The ride up to the present day has been bumpy, but now in *Highway Heist* we have a guide that is a real delight even during the worst stretches of the journey."

—**Daniel B. Klein**, Professor of Economics; JIN Chair, Mercatus Center; George Mason University; co-author, *Curb Rights: A Foundation for Free Enterprise in Urban Transit*

"James Bennett's *Highway Heist* offers readers an excellent history of the politics and economics behind the development of the nation's transportation network. Everyone can see the roads. Bennett reveals the cronyism, corruption, boondoggles, and waste that accompanied their construction, and explains how entrepreneurial market-based transportation alternatives can improve the system."

—**Randall G. Holcombe**, DeVoe Moore Professor of Economics, Florida State University

"I betray no secret when I note that politics is the art of wealth redistribution, with all of the perverse incentives, massive resource waste, and absurd outcomes that are the inexorable features of the modern administrative state. Water projects that foul streams and rivers. Bullet trains to nowhere. Highway projects that destroy old and functioning communities. All so that the usual suspects can receive large subsidies: labor unions shielded from competition from minority firms, state and local governments in hot pursuit of 'free' federal dollars, government bureaucracies interested in budgets ever-larger, local interests pursuing enhanced economic activity at the expense of others. 'Infrastructure' projects—in principle, investments in public capital, but almost always far more, or, rather, less—lend themselves perfectly to this perverse game because infrastructure spending more-or-less is site-specific, and so can be used to buy the votes of specific politicians. But as James T. Bennett demonstrates in his important book, *Highway Heist*, infrastructure does not have to be this way. Investment in public capital can be achieved by harnessing the incentives inherent in entrepreneurial capitalism for the delivery of maximum value at a minimum of resource cost. This is a book that offers crucial lessons at a time when 'infrastructure' has come to be defined as 'anything that politicians can dream up.' It will stand the test of time."

—**Benjamin Zycher**, Resident Scholar, American Enterprise Institute

"In *Highway Heist*, Bennett concisely summarizes important US and European research indicating that taxpayers and users often receive considerably less infrastructure than promised and that megaprojects have a dismal record of attracting projected usage. He cites no less a public figure than former San Francisco Mayor Willie Brown who seemingly endorsed such results, suggesting that 'If people knew the real cost from the start, nothing would ever be approved.' It is no wonder that taxpayers and users have so little faith that their taxes and user fees are well spent."

—**Wendell Cox**, Principal, Wendell Cox Consultancy/Demographia; former Member, Los Angeles County Transportation Commission; former Member, Amtrak Reform Council

"James Bennett's book *Highway Heist* provides a most informative history of the politics and economics of how we got to where we are today where government dominates highway transportation. In America's early years there was considerable debate over whether the federal government should play any role at all. No such authority was granted in the U.S. Constitution save a power to establish post offices and post roads. Over time, though, a desire to improve communications across the land and the belief that the federal government ought to build and operate roads overwhelmed strict constructionist objections. However now, the inequities and inefficiencies of government ownership and operation of highways combined with technological solutions to how better match benefits with payments opens up an opportunity to improve things going forward. The most obvious evidence of the inefficiencies and inequities of government-owned highways is traffic congestion which inflicts an enormous waste of time on everyone who travels. As a result, market-based privatization of highways is now more feasible and necessary than ever. Bennett suggests that Americans and their political leaders should be reconsidering whether it has been wise to allow government to take over this vital sector of the economy when a more productive and equitable private-sector option is available. A useful next step for making this happen would be for as many of them as possible to read the incisive book *Highway Heist*."

—**John H. Semmens**, former Senior Planner, Arizona Department of Transportation

"*Highway Heist* is a fascinating, brilliantly written political history of government-built infrastructure (roads, bridges, canals) since the founding of the republic. The book's title tells the story: the lack of critical thinking, the frenzy for more building and spending, and the lamentable squandering of so much federal and state money to benefit the interest groups. Hope lies in growing public acceptance of express lanes, tolls, public-private partnerships, and private roads, along with opposition to eminent domain, massive government spending, and the idea that government must own, operate, and maintain highways."

—**E. S. Savas**, Presidential Professor Emeritus and former Director of the Privatization Research Organization, Baruch College, CUNY; co-author, *Privatization and Public-Private Partnerships*

"Although politicians and pundits often claim that 'crumbling' infrastructure is a major problem, James Bennett shows that our infrastructure problems run much deeper. Pork barrel politics influences the construction, financing, and placement of roads and other forms of infrastructure that users rarely pay market prices to access. The result is soul-crushing congestion in some places and bridges to nowhere in others.

Highway Heist traces these problems through more than 200 years of U.S. history but also shows us how increased reliance on privatization and market forces could 'build back better' a more efficient system of infrastructure in the future."

—**Benjamin Powell**, Professor of Economics and Executive Director of the Free Market Institute, Rawls College of Business, Texas Tech University

"James Bennett's book *Highway Heist* is a provocative and extensively researched book that makes a powerful case for more private-sector involvement in our nation's roads and highways."

—**Ronald D. Utt**, Founder, Potomac Renovations, Ltd.; former Associate Director of Privatization, Office of Management and Budget; former Senior Research Fellow, Heritage Foundation

"*Highway Heist* by James T. Bennett is a much-needed tell-all book about the ugly reality of transportation infrastructure policy in the United States. Even if one accepts, as Adam Smith did, that constructing roads and bridges is a legitimate role for government, we still have a problem. What kinds of roads and bridges? And where? Without authentic market prices to guide decision-making, we are left with a politicized process where the best-organized and loudest special-interest voices are heard—while the weakest and quietest among us get our homes and businesses condemned to satisfy the latest transportation fad favored by the elites. Meanwhile, those of us who simply want to drive to work are left to navigate roads that look increasingly like a moonscape as government fails to perform even its most basic functions."

—**Robert A. Lawson**, Clinical Professor, Jerome M. Fullinwider Centennial Chair in Economic Freedom, and Director, Bridwell Institute for Economic Freedom, Cox School of Business, Southern Methodist University; co-author, *Economic Freedom of the World: Annual Reports*

"In *Highway Heist*, James Bennett has written a comprehensive, informative, and entertaining history of federal infrastructure programs from before the Constitution through President Biden's massive infrastructure bill. Any American who pays taxes should read this book to find out how their money has been spent, and largely wasted, on infrastructure, which now includes far more projects and programs than it ever has in the past. Bennett does not just talk about the problems, he also prescribes solutions, including greater privatization and reducing the gas tax, which would quite properly give the states more responsibility for infrastructure spending."

—**Thomas A. Schatz**, President, Citizens Against Government Waste

"I have greatly enjoyed reading James Bennett's important book, *Highway Heist*. It describes, analyzes, and suggests policies for efficient and equitable investment and operation of highways, bridges, and canals. The book provides historical development of such facilities in the U.S. from the beginning of the 19th century until 2021. It explains the federal and state roles in funding and managing these infrastructures, and the need to implement user fees and private ownership to replace government funding and thereby to improve social performance. Interestingly, the author claims and proves that such a move is merely a return to 19th century practices.

"Privatization of highways is facilitated by tolling roads, and the fact now of electronically collecting tolls makes the transaction costs minimal. The direct relationship between the producers and consumers, and the funding by the users of the roads rather than by taxpayers, makes the provision and use of the roads both efficient and equitable.

"The author uses his immense knowledge of history, public finance, and public choice to blend it all into a coherent story which is widely supported by relevant examples. The historical review concludes with the description and analysis of President Biden's infrastructure bill, showing how interest groups benefit from it at the expense of taxpayers. Private toll roads serve better social welfare than government-funded free highways and cannot be objected on constitutional grounds. Indeed, the Republicans have suggested that a significant part of Biden's allocation for highways, bridges, be done via public-private partnerships instead of by taxpayers' money. By tolling, the benefactors of the roads pay for their use rather than the taxpayers. The users who are clearly identified, and where electronic collection of fees is cheap, should pay for their use like any other private good. Moreover, Bennett's examples show that congestion pricing is indeed common in private highways and such prices improve traffic flow and reduce pollution. Easy-to-read and very well-documented, *Highway Heist* is a must-read globally by transportation planners, policymakers in transportation, and by anyone concerned with improving efficiency and equity in government spending."

— **Simon D. Hakim**, Professor of Economics and Director, Center for Competitive Government, Temple University; editor, *Handbook on Public-Private Partnerships in Transportation*

"James Bennett's wonderfully readable book *Highway Heist* recites the history of controversy over transportation issues from the early controversies over roads and canals to President Biden's 2,700-page proposal to spend $1.2 trillion from the Infrastructure Investment and Jobs Act. Throughout this insightful book, one central point rings clear: government is a source of division and not unification. The philosophers of the Scottish Enlightenment recognized this property of political power at the time of our nation's founding, but this wisdom has been long erased through the fight for power and wealth within the federal political commons. Reading *Highway Heist* will help us both to understand better how those liberties have been lost and then to show us how to regain them."

— **Richard E. Wagner**, Holbert L. Harris Professor of Economics, George Mason University; author, *To Promote the General Welfare: Market Processes vs. Political Transfers*

"James Bennett's *Highway Heist* is a highly readable and engaging history of the arguments for and against federal involvement in infrastructure development from the founding era to the present. Those who enjoy a non-polemical review of American history, or who enjoy thinking about what is good policy instead of presuming they already know, will particularly enjoy it. In the founding era, the debate focused upon whether the federal government should support the construction of roads, bridges and canals—what the proponents and opponents of such spending called either 'internal improvements' or 'infernal improvements' depending upon which side of the argument they took. The book principally focuses upon the question of federal funding for roadways, as it has been a constant in American history for over two hundred years. (There was not a lot of discussion then on electric charging station infrastructure, just as there is not now a lot of discussion about canal building.) One learns that a strong case can be made that federal involvement in funding highways and other infrastructure is unconstitutional except in limited instances. We see that while some key founders were making the case against federal funding and arguing that it is unconstitutional, others, including Washington and Adams, were arguing that it was constitutional and were ardent in their advocacy. *Highway Heist* takes us through two hundred-plus years of American history to the present, and we note that while the particulars of what is being debated have changed, the essential framework of the arguments for and against federal involvement in highway construction—and infrastructure development more broadly—have remained the same. The pro-federal-spending interests have always had the financial edge. Just think about it in connection with the interests on the receiving end of Biden's $1.2 trillion infrastructure blowout. If to get their hands on a slice of this spending, these interests were willing to invest just 1% of their sought-for payout in advocacy, that would equate to $12 billion being made available for advertising, lobbying and political contributions to move the public and buy political support. Those on the other side of the argument had no resources to bring to the debate except their reason, voice and pen. Bennett allows us to hear the voices and arguments of those who saw there are other ways to do things: ways that could provide better infrastructural development, faster and cheaper for the public while being less corrupting of the federal government and its office holders."

— **Bret D. Schundler**, former Mayor, Jersey City, New Jersey; former New Jersey Commissioner of Education; former Chief Operating Officer, King's College in New York City

HIGHWAY HEIST

INDEPENDENT INSTITUTE is a non-profit, non-partisan, public-policy research and educational organization that shapes ideas into profound and lasting impact. The mission of Independent is to boldly advance peaceful, prosperous, and free societies grounded in a commitment to human worth and dignity. Applying independent thinking to issues that matter, we create transformational ideas for today's most pressing social and economic challenges. The results of this work are published as books, our quarterly journal, *The Independent Review*, and other publications and form the basis for numerous conference and media programs. By connecting these ideas with organizations and networks, we seek to inspire action that can unleash an era of unparalleled human flourishing at home and around the globe.

100 Swan Way, Oakland, California 94621-1428, U.S.A.
Telephone: 510-632-1366 • Facsimile: 510-568-6040 • Email: info@independent.org • www.independent.org

HIGHWAY HEIST

America's Crumbling Infrastructure and the Road Forward

JAMES T. BENNETT

INDEPENDENT
INSTITUTE

Independent Institute
100 Swan Way, Oakland, CA 94621–1428
Telephone: 510–632–1366
Fax: 510–568–6040
Email: info@independent.org
Website: www.independent.org

Cover Design: Denise Tsui
Cover Image: lightwise / 123RF

Library of Congress Cataloging-in-Publication Data

Names: Bennett, James T., author..
Title: Highway heist : America's crumbling infrastructure and the road forward / James T. Bennett.
Description: Oakland, CA : Independent Institute, [2022] | Includes bibliographical references and index.
Identifiers: LCCN 2022001760 (print) | LCCN 2022001761 (ebook) | ISBN 9781598133448 (cloth) | ISBN 9781598133462 (ebook) | ISBN 9781598133462 (mobi) | ISBN 9781598133462 (epub)
Subjects: LCSH: Infrastructure (Economics)--United States. | Transportation and state--United States. | Public works--United States.
Classification: LCC HC110.C3 B46 2022 (print) | LCC HC110.C3 (ebook) | DDC 363.0973--dc23/eng/20220322
LC record available at https://lccn.loc.gov/2022001760
LC ebook record available at https://lccn.loc.gov/2022001761

Contents

Acknowledgments

I **WANT TO** express my deep appreciation to the Independent Institute for having the exceptional vision and commitment in making this book possible throughout its development. In particular, the masterly work of its president David J. Theroux and his colleagues William F. Shughart II, Christopher B. Briggs and George L. Tibbitts have been invaluable.

I am also especially grateful to my editor, Bill Kauffman, for I am indebted to him for significant contributions to this book. I further thank Nicholas Pusateri and Stuart Paul for their conscientious research assistance.

Introduction

INTERNAL IMPROVEMENTS—altered by critics to the hellish-sounding *infernal improvements*—was the term used nearly conterminously with the republic's founding to denote public works, with an emphasis on those facilitating transportation. Thus roads, bridges, and canals were the most prominent early examples thereof, along with lighthouses and various improvements to waterways and harbors.

Deployed early, an especially useful polemical theme that persists to this day is the identification of internal improvements with progress and the branding of skeptics as mossbacks and reactionaries. Are you a progressive? Prove it by supporting state subsidy of our road, our bridge, our canal. Farmers, many of whom saw internal improvements as a racket, a scam by which mercantile interests pilfered the pockets of husbandmen while waxing grandiose about their big visions, magnificent dreams, and progressive mindset, saw only tax bills and, in the case of toll roads or waterways, charges to travel byways and waterways that they had theretofore traversed for free. But the narrative designed by the internal improvements crowd held that these carpers and cavilers were sticks in the mud, unimaginative rustic dolts, and, in the case of those who in the mid-twentieth century would object to the state seizing and demolishing their homes to make room for highways, *NIMBYs*—selfish embodiments of a *Not-In-My-BackYard* spirit.

That these improvements were artificial adornments to or offenses against nature was a theme that would not be played with any success by internal improvement opponents until the middle years of the twentieth century, when the destruction wrought by such highwaymen as Robert Moses—the obliteration of city neighborhoods, venerable structures, ethnic enclaves, and vital communities, all done with huge exactions of taxpayer money—aroused middle-class and college-educated reformers and set the government-subsidized engineers on their heels. *Infrastructure* is the rather unlovely term that replaced *internal improvements*; for in the twentieth century, the canals emptied and humble roads became highways, and the national government took on a larger—though not majority—share of spending thereon. Infrastructure in the form of roads and highways has often been seen as an economic boon, enabling producers to reach wider markets, get their products to market more quickly and cheaply, and expand their choice of suppliers; it also gives employees a broader range of choices in where to work and live, and expands options for consumers as well. It is, obviously, essential to a modern economy. But it is not so obvious that these avenues of conveyance need planning, building, and support by government, whether at the federal, state, or local level. Locating such responsibility in the public rather than the private sector means, perforce, their politicization, and consequently the misapplication of resources due to political pressures exerted by and on behalf of influential political actors—in other words, that porcine metaphor for all seasons, the pork barrel.

Moreover, there is a related definitional problem. Advocates of increased public spending on infrastructure love to use—in fact, they caress—the word *investment*. It sounds responsible, wise, above reproach. Yet governments are not like private enterprise: they do not keep capital budgets or assess rates of return for projects they may undertake. They "take no account of that which is not seen," to borrow a phrase from the nineteenth-century French economist Frédéric Bastiat; they do not consider alternative uses of taxpayer monies.[1] Their decisions are the result of political, and not economic, calculations, and thus to use the word *investment* in discussion thereof is a solecism.

The Congressional Budget Office has laid out seven infrastructure categories: highways, public transit, wastewater treatment, water resources, air traffic control, airports, and municipal water supply.[2] This book focuses on a broadened version of the first and, in many ways, most visible and historically significant category: roads and bridges, as well as their aquatic kin, the nineteenth-century canal. Also examined is US transportation policy from the Constitutional Convention through the presidency of Donald Trump—

that is, from "internal improvements" in antebellum America to the current trope of "crumbling infrastructure."

Concentrating on debates over government subsidies necessary to promote roads and canals, Chapter 1 explores the most contentious, and consequential, transportation issues of the early nineteenth century. These include the 1808 report of Thomas Jefferson's secretary of the treasury proposing a major expansion of government's role in facilitating the movement of goods and people; New York State's building of the Erie Canal, the first major state-level internal improvement; the contrasting visions of Presidents John Quincy Adams, who advocated the construction of magnificent, federally assisted public works, and Andrew Jackson, who insisted that any such works must pass strict constitutional muster; and the rise and fall of turnpikes, an early example of a mixed public/private roadbuilding venture.

Chapter 2 reviews the origin and growth of the "Good Roads" movement, which began as the project of bicycle enthusiasts grouped around the upper-crust League of American Wheelmen and expanded to include a coalition of progressives, engineers, and business leaders whose primary obstacle, once constitutional objections to their program were overcome, was persuading recalcitrant farmers to relinquish local control of road maintenance and cede authority to more remote centers of power, up to and including the new state departments of transportation. This chapter also surveys early efforts by the states and the federal government to extract taxes and fees from automobilists, as well as the formative experiences of such later architects of US highway policy as Dwight D. Eisenhower and Thomas H. MacDonald of the Bureau of Public Roads.

Chapter 3 outlines the genesis, development, and eventual enactment of the National System of Interstate and Defense Highways, which is commonly referred to today as the grandest public works project in the history of the nation, if not the world. Special attention is paid to the handful of often cogent and prescient critics of the aborning interstate, who ranged from budget-conscious conservatives to social critics and philosophers who cautioned against the massive destruction and displacement that construction of the interstate would entail.

Chapter 4 recounts the comparatively abrupt about-face in public attitudes toward the interstate and the roadbuilding project in the 1960s and 1970s. The cession of power from localities and small-scale democratic entities to centralized bureaucracies had produced not only the extraordinary achievement of a forty-one-thousand-mile system of impressively engineered roadways, but also the razing of hundreds of thousands of homes and businesses and the displacement or uprooting of over one million Americans, in many cases by the government exercise of eminent domain.

Chapter 5 documents the revival of the public works movement, which had taken to calling its bailiwick "infrastructure" and emphasizing both the alleged deterioration of America's physical plant, especially its roads and bridges, and the rosy employment possibilities of sharply increased federal spending thereon. The twists and turns of infrastructure politics and policy up through the Trump administration are followed, as are contemporary reform proposals, particularly the widespread tolling of highways and the prospects for their full or partial privatization.

And now, as a rhapsodist of the open highway once said, let us go on the road ...

I

Internal—or Infernal?—Improvements: A New Nation Confronts Infrastructure

THE CONSTITUTIONAL CONVENTION, meeting in the sweltering Philadelphia summer of 1787, agreed without debate that among the powers granted Congress in Article I, Section 8, would be "to establish post offices." Even the strongest critics of what they perceived as the centralizing tendencies of the new Constitution conceded that function to the national government. But the appendage to that grant, "and post roads," which was the hook on which internal improvements were hung (back in the day when constitutional limits were more scrupulously recognized than they are today[1]), made it into the final document by the skin of its teeth, or by the thickness of a postcard. Over the meanings and nuances of the terms *establish* and *post roads* would flare a constitutional dispute that would endure into the early twentieth century.

On August 16, 1787, as the convention was racing down the homestretch before its adjournment one month hence, Massachusetts delegate Elbridge Gerry, best known for lending his name to the manipulation of election districts ("gerrymandering"), offered an amendment to tack onto the congressional power to establish post offices the right also to establish—whether that meant to authorize, to finance, or to build was not made clear—post roads.

Two members of the small-government faction at the convention, New York's decentralist duo of John Lansing and Robert Yates, kept journals of the conclave's actions, but each had left Philadelphia long before August 16, suspecting its leading lights of harboring excessive ambitions for a powerful United States government. So James Madison, author of the Virginia Plan, which became the convention's mark-up document, left us the only account of what transpired on that date, and Madison's notes are, with respect to post roads, exceedingly sparse. We know only that Mr. Gerry made the motion and that it passed by the narrowest of margins, 6–5, with the quintet of nay votes coming from the two states whose delegations were most protective of state vis-à-vis national powers (New Hampshire and North Carolina) as well as Connecticut, New Jersey, and Pennsylvania.[2] (Two centuries hence, no congressional delegations were more avid, more ravenous, more rabid for federal highway construction money than those of Pennsylvania and New Jersey.)

In the waning hours of the convention, Benjamin Franklin, the *éminence grise* of the gathering, proposed to further stretch the power to "establish post offices and post roads" to include also "a power for cutting canals where deemed necessary."[3] Roger Sherman of Connecticut, a moderate who signed not only the Constitution but also the Declaration of Independence and the Articles of Confederation, objected that "the expence [*sic*] in such cases will fall on the U. States, and the benefits accrue to the places where the canals may be cut."[4] In other words, forcing the new union as a whole to pay for projects that aided only constituent parts. Was the Constitution to be a mechanism by which the largest and most politically influential states could shake down their smaller partners in union?

Rebutting Sherman was James Wilson of Pennsylvania, a fervent nationalist who was a dependable partisan on the side of expanding the central government's reach. "Instead of being an expence to the U.S.," said Wilson, canals "may be made a source of revenue."[5] Their subsidization might well be a wise and even profitable policy of the national government. This disagreement foreshadowed much of what was to come. Wilson emphasized "the importance of facilitating by canals, the communication with the Western settlements."[6] The triumvirate of Franklin, Wilson, and their supporter James Madison, so prepotent at other points of the convention, was soundly routed on the matter of federal subsidy of canals. They went down by a vote of 8–3, winning only Pennsylvania, Virginia, and far-flung Georgia, which was eager to ease communication with her sister states. (As was the case with the post roads issue, states voted as a unit, and New York lacked a quorum while independent-minded Rhode Island never sent a delegation.)

James Madison, fittingly, sponsored the federal government's maiden venture into the subvention of internal improvements: the Lighthouses Act of 1789, which the Father of the Constitution proposed in April 1789, just one week into the life of the First Congress. The act, as passed—it was just the ninth piece of legislation enacted under the new Constitution—provided for the transfer of the dozen extant lighthouses from the states to the federal government, which henceforth would be responsible for their "support, maintenance, and repair," as well as that of lighthouses yet to be built.[7] Because such aids to seafaring navigation were more common along the rocky coastlines of the Northern states, the measure enjoyed greater support in the North than it did among Southern members of Congress, who counted just two lighthouses—those at Charleston Harbor in South Carolina and Tybee Island in Georgia—within their region.[8] Nevertheless, it passed and was signed into law in August by President Washington. Internal improvements—infrastructure—had gained its first beachhead.

(In a classic 1974 paper, Ronald H. Coase made a powerful case for private provision of lighthouses, which had long been thought to be a public good that, of necessity, must be provided by government.[9] His examples were drawn primarily from the tradition of private lighthouses in Great Britain.[10])

Madison also moved to use the post roads provision that Elbridge Gerry had succeeded in adding to the document. In 1796, Madison proposed a survey of the main post road stretching the length of the eastern United States, from Maine to Georgia. He was chastised by none other than Thomas Jefferson, who, as the historian Joseph H. Harrison Jr. of Auburn University has written, "thought the power to establish post roads was merely that of choosing between roads already in existence."[11] Jefferson told Madison that a federal power to do anything with respect to roads beyond such choosing would be "a source of boundless patronage to the executive, jobbing to members of Congress & their friends, and a bottomless abyss of public money." Moreover, it would set off an "eternal scramble among the members who can get the most money wasted in their State; and they will always get most who are meanest."[12]

Jefferson, it seems, foresaw the pork barrel before the first stave was in place or the first pig had been slaughtered or even before the first log had been rolled. His archrival, Alexander Hamilton, had in his *Report on Manufactures* (1791) expressed his wish that "the National Government … lend its direct aid on a comprehensive plan" to assist "the transportation of commodities."[13]

Thus the battle lines were drawn early on, though they would often be blurred by sectional dustups, for when government funds were at stake, principles became unusually—though not inevitably—malleable.

Direction of the earliest appropriations for internal improvements went to projects in the territories, as the constitutionality of direct aid to the states was a matter of contention. In 1796, speculator Ebenezer Zane, eponym of Zanesville, Ohio, was granted three sections of land in the Northwest Territory through which he cut Zane's Trace, a horse trail and footpath running from Wheeling in what later became West Virginia to Limestone (later Maysville), Kentucky.[14] This seems to have been "the first instance of local subsidy by the Federal Government," according to that same federal government.[15]

American roads in the infancy of the republic were rude and primitive, often unfriendly to wheels, cleared of stumps and big rocks but seldom surfaced with the gravel or "pounded stone" that covered some of the busier roads near cities.[16] Such trails as Zane blazed, for horse and foot, carriage and wagon, would often become, over the generations, highways, rather as early documents, as they are written over many times, become palimpsests.

They were crude, rutted pathways from settlement to settlement trod by horses and oxen carrying wagonloads of the bounty of the harvest, or dry goods, or necessaries. They turned to slush in the springtime melt, then mud, then dust in summer, and quicksand in the rainy autumn, and returned to frozen and impassable, if not impossible, ruts in winter. Potholed, rutted, hard on horses, hard on oxen, hard on their drivers: a desire to improve such rudimentary roads surely was reasonable.

The states found that it was easier to issue edicts than it was to smooth the roads. The Ohio state legislature, for instance, handed down the difficult-to-enforce law that roads should not contain stumps more than one foot in height.[17] The leveling of the Buckeye State's paths, however, was left to men largely without any formal training in the viatical arts. They did the best they could.

In the early republic, West Point, established in 1802, was the only school in which engineering was taught, but its focus was war, not stump-cutting and path-blazing in order to get things to market. The first civilian "school of civil engineering, which has had a continuous existence, to be established in any English-speaking country" was an American academy, Rensselaer Polytechnic Institute in Troy, New York, founded in 1824 as the Rensselaer School.[18] Thus, passing few early American roads were built by trained engineers; they were the work of amateurs, relying on generations of received wisdom and practice. Some states appointed a principal engineer whose task was to send the most up-to-date information on methods, cost, and optimal location of road construction to the builders of roads, as well as best drainage practices. But, often, those in the field were on their own.

Gallatin and Jefferson Discover the Joys of Loose Construction

Thomas Jefferson and a considerable number of his namesake Jeffersonian Republicans shed their strict constructionist skin once the levers of power were in their hands. The Louisiana Purchase was the most spectacular example of this shift, though among the many smaller instances was Treasury Secretary Albert Gallatin's proposal that one-tenth of the revenue from public land sales within the soon-to-be state of Ohio be used to construct "a turnpike or other roads, leading from the navigable waters emptying into the Atlantic to the Ohio, and continued afterwards through the new state."[19]

Ohio was cash poor but land rich. So attached to her entry into the union was a provision that one-twentieth (rather than Gallatin's suggested one-tenth) of the proceeds of Ohio land sales be allocated to road construction, with 60 percent of this sum set aside for roads within Ohio and the remaining 40 percent dedicated to interstate roads going through Ohio. Using language previously associated with the consolidationist Federalists, Gallatin wrote of this venture "cementing the bonds of union between those parts of the United States, whose local interests have been considered as most dissimilar."[20] This was, charged the Federalists, a constitutionally dubious method of building roads at public expense in the Republican states of Virginia and Pennsylvania. How the tables had turned!

The Federalists were the party of loose, or expansive, construction, but in this instance, as would often be the case when it came to transportation policy, sectional interests trumped ideology. Thomas Jefferson, who barely a lustrum ago was deploring federal roads policy as containing the germ of rampant corruption, signed the Ohio legislation, as he also endorsed the Cumberland Road, the first major federal internal improvement, and one that would eventually receive almost $7 million from the federal treasury. His volte-face was almost complete when, in his Sixth Annual Message to Congress of December 2, 1806, President Jefferson proposed to apply the proceeds of the impost on foreign luxuries "to the great purposes of the public education, roads, rivers, canals, and such other objects of public improvement as it may be thought proper to add to the constitutional enumeration of federal powers. By these operations new channels of communication will be opened between the States; the lines of separation will disappear, their interests will be identified, and their union cemented by new and indissoluble ties."[21]

Note that while Jefferson now supported federal aid to such endeavors, he insisted that this aid be consistent with the enumerated powers in the Constitution. He was not unaware of the gap between his libertarian, strict constructionist philosophy and his presidential actions, and therefore he sought to at least justify his departures from principle with a constitutional amendment clarifying the federal government's power—"*in time of peace*"— to expend funds on "rivers, canals, roads, arts, manufactures, education, and other great objects within each State."[22] The proposed amendment came a cropper; as John Lauritz Larson writes, "Die-hard Federalists who would gleefully oppose such a gift to Jefferson's government abounded, while 'Old Republicans,' clinging to the original Spirit of '98, opposed any step toward 'consolidation.'"[23]

The amendment would never come close to being appended to the nation's charter, in part because the colorful strict constructionist John Randolph of Virginia, adamantine defender of a minimal federal government, chaired the committee to which the revision was assigned. And in time, advocacy of such an internal improvements–enabling amendment would be a sign of archaism and anachronism, as if a modern man took to wearing a peruke or pince-nez. It was at best an amusing affectation, but more likely a sign of odd, even eldritch, tendencies.

But in antebellum America, it was impossible to ignore the views of men such as Randolph. He scoffed at the anchorage of internal improvements on what he believed to be an exiguous constitutional hook; as Russell Kirk explained, the legendary Randolph of Roanoke condemned "latitudinarians of constitutional interpretation, who took the authority to *establish* post roads as signifying authority to *build* post roads."[24] Randolph lectured the US House of Representatives: "Gentlemen say we have the power, by the Constitution, to establish post roads, and, having established post roads, we should be much obliged to you to allow us, therefore, the power to construct the roads and canals into the bargain…. [S]upposing the power to exist on our part—of all the powers that can be exercised by this House, there is no power that would be more susceptible of abuse than this very power."[25]

The fiercest fighting over the Cumberland (aka National) Road concerned its course rather than its constitutionality. The Cumberland Road joined the Potomac with the Ohio Valley. It would be known by any number of names over the years, whether the Cumberland Road, the Great Western Road, Ohio's Road, Uncle Sam's Road, or the National Road.[26] It was to be built according to the most up-to-date specifications, beginning with the requirement that it must be four rods wide, with a roadbed of thirty feet, and surfaced with broken stone.

Over which territory would this National Road run? The Pennsylvanians and Virginians promoted routes beginning in Philadelphia and Richmond, respectively, but in December 1805, a special Senate committee chaired by Uriah Tracy (F-CT) endorsed a route that satisfied solons of neither the Old Dominion nor the Keystone State. Its starting point was to be Cumberland, Maryland, near one of the northern notches of the Potomac River, whence it would wend its way 156 miles to Wheeling, Virginia, on the Ohio River, from which it was envisioned, over subsequent years, to take a route through Ohio and the future states of Indiana, Illinois, and Missouri, to the apposite terminus of Jefferson City. The House passed the bill in March 1806 by a vote of 66–50, with heavy support from the West and from the Federalists, who approved of internal improvements on principle. As John Lauritz Larson notes, while Republicans split over the bill, "nearly all of the 38 Republicans voting nay came from Virginia or Pennsylvania."[27] Richmond and Philadelphia would not stand for this slight! Protecting the interests of one's state and district superseded ideology, not for the last time.

President Jefferson was pleased; he wrote Gallatin that the "road from Cumberland to Ohio will be an important link in the chain to St. Louis" from Baltimore.[28] The job-creating possibilities of road construction went unmentioned, as they would, by and large, until the 1930s. Construction of the road would span seven years, from 1811 to 1818; it would later be extended through Indiana and Illinois, stopping at the Mississippi River, before in 1838, Congress vouchsafed its final appropriation for the National Road.[29]

Big thinkers, visionaries, and grand conceptualizers, or at least those who fancy themselves such, go for overarching strategies. They scorn the piecemeal. And so in 1808, Secretary of the Treasury Gallatin eagerly and at great length responded to a Senate resolution of the year previous requesting him:

> to prepare and report to the Senate, at their next session, a plan for the application of such means as are within the power of Congress, to the purposes of opening roads, and making canals; together with a statement of the undertakings, of that nature, which as objects of public improvement, may require and deserve the aid of government; and also a statement of works of the nature mentioned, which have been commenced, the progress which has been made in them, and the means and prospect of their being completed.[30]

Gallatin's response bore the title *Report of the Secretary of the Treasury, on the Subject of Public Roads and Canals.* "The general utility of artificial roads and canals, is at this time so universally admitted, as hardly to require any additional proofs," declared the secretary of the treasury, seeming to shut off any discussion of first principles. The only debate, then, should center on who would build them and where. Large-scale works, he asserted, were beyond the ability of private enterprise to undertake, and yet their social and economic utility were so great as to be legitimate objects of public subvention. As Gallatin wrote, "Good roads and canals, [would] shorten distances, facilitate commercial and personal intercourse, and unite by a still more intimate community of interests, the most remote quarters of the United States. No other single operation, within the power of government, [could] more effectually tend to strengthen and perpetuate that union, which secures external independence, domestic peace, and liberty."[31]

Only the "General Government" has resources "amply sufficient for the completion of every practicable improvement."[32] Moreover, only that same government has the farsightedness, the ability to transcend the merely parochial, to choose projects based on merit rather than a grimy and venal political calculus. Echoing the hopeful theories of James Madison and Alexander Hamilton in *The Federalist Papers*, Gallatin averred, "The national legislature alone, embracing every local interest, and superior to every local consideration, is competent to the selection of such national objects."[33] This confident asseveration has not, to be charitable, been vindicated in later centuries.

Gallatin, with a contribution from Benjamin Henry Latrobe, the architect who designed the US Capitol, described the progress, challenges, cost, and other details of nearly two dozen canals, turnpikes, and river improvements. Some were going concerns; others were merely on the drawing board. They included canals in New York, Ohio, Massachusetts, Virginia, and elsewhere; "improvements" to such rivers as the Susquehanna, Potomac, James, and Santee; and roads connecting Nashville to Natchez, Cincinnati to St. Louis, and, most spectacularly, a "great turnpike," 1,600 miles in length, "extending from Maine to Georgia."[34]

There was nothing penny-ante or mingy in this lineup. The secretary admitted that "the expense seems to be the primary object of consideration" with respect to the Maine-to-Georgia road,[35] though the wonder of it all is that this Herculean feat of federal enterprise was being proposed by the administration of *Thomas Jefferson*, who in his first inaugural address extolled "a wise and frugal government, which shall restrain men from injuring one another, shall leave them otherwise free to regulate their own pursuits of industry and improvement, and shall not take from the mouth of labor the bread it has earned."[36] Seven years at the helm of a national government can alter one's view of the proper role of said government. While conceding that the consent of the states through which roads and canals pass is necessary before any work can be done, it was "highly probable," Gallatin assured the senators, that such consent would be obtained easily.[37] A constitutional amendment could render moot any other pettifogging objections.

Gallatin estimated the expense of these improvements at $16.6 million; throwing in an extra $3.4 million for "local improvements" in those states that do not figure prominently in the report's major projects, he came up with a nice round figure of $20 million, which, he pointed out helpfully, "would accomplish all those great objects in ten years" with an annual appropriation of just $2 million.[38] (To view this in perspective, total federal outlays in 1808 were $9.7 million, so this would require a more than 20 percent increase.[39])

As Larson recounts, the Gallatin report was translated into a bill offered by Rep. Peter Porter (R-NY) and Senator John Pope (DR-KY), which "committed the federal government to buying one-third of the stock of private companies chartered in the states to build every major project named in Gallatin's report," save the Potomac Canal.[40] Rep. Porter, who hailed from the frontier of western New York, argued that federal aid was essential if farmers were to find markets beyond the merely local; canals and roads would be incentives to increase production.

The Porter bill sank, done in by Federalist opposition as well as that of old Jeffersonians such as Rep. John Wayles Eppes (DR-VA). In any event, the impost revenue necessary to fund these projects had shrunk due to Jefferson's Embargo Act of 1807 aimed at Great Britain and France. Later, the War of 1812 put the quietus to Gallatin's plan. The secretary, as his biographer Henry Adams wrote, discarded "all his old hopes and ambitions, all schemes for discharging debts and creating canals, roads, and universities," and dedicated himself to "the single point of defending the Treasury," for Gallatin "regarded the habit of borrowing money with horror"; as war impended, he insisted that "expenditure should not exceed revenue" except in the direst circumstances.[41]

In his seventh annual message to Congress of December 5, 1815, President James Madison, who for three decades had vacillated between an expansive view of the powers of the federal government and a zealous regard to the rights of the states, sounded a Gallatin-like note:

> Among the means of advancing the public interest the occasion is a proper one for recalling the attention of Congress to the great importance of establishing throughout our country the roads and canals which can best be executed under the national authority. No objects within the circle of political economy so richly repay the expense bestowed on them; there are none the utility of which is more universally ascertained and acknowledged; none that do more honor to the governments whose wise and enlarged patriotism duly appreciates them. Nor is there any country which presents a field where nature invites more the art of man to complete her own work for his accommodation and benefit.
>
> These considerations are strengthened, moreover, by the political effect of these facilities for intercommunication in bringing and binding

more closely together the various parts of our extended confederacy. Whilst the States individually, with a laudable enterprise and emulation, avail themselves of their local advantages by new roads, by navigable canals, and by improving the streams susceptible of navigation, the General Government is the more urged to similar undertakings, requiring a national jurisdiction and national means, by the prospect of thus systematically completing so inestimable a work; and it is a happy reflection that any defect of constitutional authority which may be encountered can be supplied in a mode which the Constitution itself has providently pointed out.[42]

Perhaps sensing an opening, a weakening of old Jeffersonian rhetoric or even conviction, Rep. John C. Calhoun of South Carolina made a bold move. In 1817, Calhoun, an ardent War of 1812 hawk who would later be known as the prophet of disunion, proposed to "bind the Republic together with a perfect system of roads and canals" by means of the Bonus Bill of 1817.[43] This legislation would have dedicated $1.5 million that the federal government was set to receive from the Second Bank of the United States, as well as future bank dividends due the government ($650,000 annually, or so it was estimated), to the purpose of funding unnamed internal improvements. The assumption was that the Gallatin plan might offer a useful guide.

Calhoun, who apparently held more benign views of nationalism early in his career than later, exulted over the cohering possibilities of extensive federal subsidy of internal improvements. Constitutional permission to embark on this adventure he discovered in the general welfare clause. And the Cumberland/National Road was nearing completion; wasn't that a substantial precedent? "Let us conquer space," Calhoun enthused metaphysically, sounding like an antebellum version of Newt Gingrich or Jerry Brown.[44]

Again, those loyal to the old Jeffersonian faith revolted. Louisiana Republican Rep. Thomas Bolling Robertson charged that the Bonus Bill would lead to "one grand, magnificent, consolidated empire."[45] He succeeded in attaching an amendment to Calhoun's Bank Bonus Bill, apportioning the aid to the states according to population and ensuring that the states, and not a grasping federal government, made the spending decisions. Speaker of the House Henry Clay of Kentucky, like Calhoun an 1812 hawk, but unlike Calhoun a partisan of what would become the National Republican, and then the Whig Party, reluctantly accepted these modifications to ensure passage. Timothy Pickering, a Jefferson-hating old Federalist, attached a very Jeffersonian amendment allowing a state to veto any federal project within its borders.

Others denied that the Constitution granted the federal government the authority to subsidize the building of roads, bridges, or canals. John Randolph spoke for three hours in opposition, and Senator Nathaniel Macon, who was to cut a profile as one of the foremost foes of internal improvement legislation, opined that this was an unconstitutional exercise of power.[46] Moreover, some in the established states—New Englanders, New Yorkers, Virginians—suspected that this bill was a way to transfer Eastern wealth to the upstart West. The Bonus Bill squeaked by in the House, 86–84, and passed the Senate, 20–15, amended (or watered down) by the Robertson and Pickering provisions disbursing funds on the basis of state population rather than national needs and requiring the consent of the states before effectuating any putative improvements. But the unpredictable constitutional precisian James Madison would have the last word. On his final day in office, President Madison unsheathed his veto quill. He did so despite a last-minute plea from Speaker Clay, who wrote, "Knowing that we cannot differ on the question of the object of the Internal Improvements bill, however we may on the Constitutional point, will you excuse me for respectfully suggesting whether you could not leave the bill to your successor?"[47] No go.

Madison had long vacillated between the supporter of a vigorous central government that he had been at the Constitutional Convention and the Jeffersonian suspicious of federal overreach that he had been during the administration of President John Adams. In the Bonus Bill veto message, the latter manifestation roared. This exercise fell outside the enumerated powers, he insisted; displaying a restraint that seems almost bizarrely archaic in light of the imperial presidency that has held sway since the mid-twentieth century, Madison wrote plaintively:

> I am not unaware of the great importance of roads and canals and the improved navigation of water courses, and that a power in the National Legislature to provide for them might be exercised with signal

advantage to the general prosperity. But seeing that such a power is not expressly given by the Constitution, and believing that it can not be deduced from any part of it without an inadmissible latitude of construction and a reliance on insufficient precedents; believing also that the permanent success of the Constitution depends on a definite partition of powers between the General and the State Governments, and that no adequate landmarks would be left by the constructive extension of the powers of Congress as proposed in the bill, I have no option but to withhold my signature from it.[48]

Henry Clay exclaimed that "not even an earthquake that should have swallowed up half this city, could have excited more surprise than when" Madison's veto had been communicated.[49] There was insufficient time left for Congress to attempt an override of Madison's veto. The Bonus Bill was dead. And if anyone knew just what fell within/without the bounds of constitutional propriety, it was the primary author of that charter, James Madison. Right?

The Canal Cometh

Canals captured the imaginations of the earliest paladins of government-sponsored improvements. Robert Morris, the "financier of the Revolution," was an advocate for an "expensive canal diverting traffic to Philadelphia, where nature did not intend it to go," as John Lauritz Larson puckishly noted in his acclaimed *Internal Improvement: National Public Works and the Promise of Popular Government in the Early United States*.[50]

Elkanah Watson, an indefatigable promoter of canals and turnpikes in New York State, was a veritable *Publius* in his authorship of letters, articles, and broadsides in favor of internal improvements. But the man whose surname would become synonymous with the canal era, DeWitt Clinton, had bloodlines that were Republican, Jeffersonian, and strict constructionist. In 1793 he had denounced attempts to "enlist the passions of party on the side of hydraulic experiments."[51] But time, and political opportunity, are teachers.

Gallatin's 1808 report had envisioned a trans–New York canal, but its realization awaited the exertions of the teachable DeWitt Clinton. He was a nephew of George Clinton, the Revolutionary wartime governor of New York, a robust Anti-federalist, two-term vice president of the United States, and strict constructionist. Nephew DeWitt had more protean views. He slipped off his familial Republican skepticism of internal improvements and instead embraced them with a passion.

Though derisively called Clinton's Big Ditch, the Erie Canal was conceived, or at least limned in greatest detail, in, of all places, a prison. While in debtors' prison, a Finger Lakes–area flour miller and dreamer named Jesse Hawley, writing under the pen name Hercules, published a series of fourteen essays in 1807 proposing the construction of a canal "connecting the waters of Lake Erie and those of the Mohawk and Hudson rivers by means of a canal."[52] This was no job for private concerns, said Hawley, but rather a "patriotic government."[53] Even in debtors' prison, apparently, the benevolent possibilities of energetic government could inspire. The state legislature was impressed. It authorized a survey of the "most eligible and direct route for a canal" linking the Hudson River with Lake Erie.[54] The 1808 Gallatin report, which had advocated public subsidy of canals, suggested that perhaps New York might receive aid from the federal government for this project, though when New York assemblyman Joshua Forman raised the matter with Thomas Jefferson, the president, incredulous, replied that "you talk of making a canal 350 miles through the wilderness—it is little short of madness to think of it at this day."[55]

As indeed it was. For the challenge was daunting. At the time of the Erie Canal's conception, only three American canals were more than two miles long, and the longest canal in America (the Middlesex in Massachusetts) ran just 27.25 miles, or three miles for every year it took to dig. The Erie Canal, connecting the Great Lakes to the Hudson River (and thus to New York City), would stretch for 363 miles.

Nevertheless, in 1810, the New York legislature appointed seven members to the newly created Commission to Explore a Route for a Canal to Lake Erie. Commissioners included such eminences as DeWitt Clinton, mayor of New York City; the laird and patroon Stephen Van Rensselaer; Gallatin report advocate and congressman Peter Porter; and Gouverneur Morris, the one-legged rake whose facile pen had been responsible for the style, if not content, of the US Constitution. Morris was a buoyant Federalist, a believer in the bountiful possibilities of government encouragement of business. In

1800, he had a premonition of an inland waterway that would connect the Hudson and Lake Erie. He envisioned an American empire of vast riches and stretch: "The proudest empire in Europe is but a bauble, compared to what America will be, must be, in the course of two centuries, perhaps of one."[56]

After examining the competing routes, the commission did what enjoined government commissions always do: it endorsed the project. Gouverneur Morris acted, once more, as the penman. Not only was the canal possible, he wrote in a report submitted to the legislature in March 1811, but "too great a national interest is at stake" to leave this job to private enterprise. The commissioners asserted with an eye to this first (but not last) American Big Dig, "large expenditures can be made more economically under public authority."[57] The state legislature appropriated $15,000 to further the exploratory work on the canal.

The canal was a casualty of the War of 1812, in which the New York–Canada border was a scene of conflict. Nevertheless, its proponents, especially canal commissioner and head cheerleader DeWitt Clinton, never stopped rowing the boat. He and other influential supporters sponsored a gathering on December 30, 1815, at the City Hotel in Manhattan, where Clinton, dipping into hyperbole the way that other attendees were dipping into the sauce, told the assembled that the canal was "without parallel in the history of mankind."[58] At rallies across the state, supporters then gathered thousands of petitions from New Yorkers assenting to Clinton's claim that the canal would also be "a work more stupendous, more magnificent, and more beneficial than has hitherto been achieved by the human race."[59] Whatever else they were, the canal's backers were not modest.

Furious lobbying ensued, for if the canal were a success, the nodes along the construction route would surely spring up and prosper. In the parlance of a later time, the New York state legislature was going to be picking winners— and, by implication, leaving losers unpicked. Foes from other parts of the state carped. What was in this for southern New York, for the Adirondack region, for Long Island? Their taxed farmers would subsidize cheaper transportation to market for produce from other sections of the state. As one Samuel Beach, writing under the name Peter Ploughshare, protested, "I should like to know whether my little farm in the county of Jefferson has got to be taxed from year to year, for the purpose of enabling the farmers on the shores of Lakes

Erie, Huron, and Michigan to bring their produce to market for nothing."[60] Well, Peter … yes!

The state legislature approved, not without opposition, $20,000 for surveys and estimates in 1816. The next spring, the die was cast. By a vote of 64–36 in the state assembly and 18–9 in the state senate, the New York state legislature authorized the construction of what was at first known as the Western Canal and created a Canal Fund with which to pay for construction. It was a pool to which many revenue streams contributed: a state loan, land sales, a tax on auction sales and lands lying within twenty-five miles of either side of the canal, lottery proceeds, and taxes on salt and steamboat tickets.[61] The anticipated cost of the canal's construction was $6 million.

Support and opposition to the canal cut across party lines. DeWitt Clinton, by now something of a renegade Republican, was its most prominent sponsor, and influential Federalists could be counted among its advocates. Naysayers included anti-Clinton Republicans and Federalists whose districts were distant from the canal. Among the foes was State Senator Peter R. Livingston of Dutchess County on the lower Hudson River, who feared that the canal would devastate domestic industries by flooding the inland of the country with imports. "You will find it a ditch that will bury you all," he prophesied.[62]

Weeks later, the voters in the state of New York elected DeWitt Clinton as governor. The stupendous, magnificent gift to humanity approached parturition.

Madison's Bonus Bill veto, which DeWitt Clinton called "totally indefensible," dealt a blow to the Ditch's champions; New York had expected a federal subsidy of "$90,000 a year for twenty years, which amounted to a fourth of the total expense of the canal, or enough to pay all the interest on a loan for the purpose."[63] With Madison's veto of the Bonus Bill, the prospect of federal subsidy disappeared.

Joseph Ellicott, canal commissioner and agent of the Holland Land Company, which vended much of the land in western New York, resorted to threat, writing Rep. Micah Brooks (R-NY) that if the Bonus Bill monies did not fill New York's coffers for the canal, "the State will unquestionably retain the jurisdiction, police, and supreme control over it, and may exercise that control in such a manner as to be extremely injurious to the US territories, and exclusively beneficial to the State."[64] The warning was vague (what was New York going to do: throw in with Canada in the next war?) and barely veiled—yet it was ignored, and New York never followed through on this blackmail.

Bonus Bill or no, on April 10, 1817, the New York legislature passed "an Act respecting Navigable Communications, between the great western and northern lakes, and the Atlantic ocean."[65] With predictable symbolism, on July 4 of that year, digging began near the New York community of Rome—an aptly chosen site for those who foresaw the canal as a pillar of a new empire.

Construction of the canal required extensive takings, not always compensated. Some land was donated by landowners who expected an economic boon from the canal—the canal commission reported that 90 percent of those in western New York State complied with a request to cede land—but other times it was simply seized by the state.[66] If state appraisers determined that "the benefit a landowner would receive from proximity to the Canal outweighed the value of the land appropriated," then no compensation was owed.[67]

Construction damaged miles of privately owned land. Laborers destroyed trees, fences, and crops. Farms were cut in two, with no way for the farmer to cross from one section of his land to the other without at times using a far-away bridge. The bypassing of a town could be devastating; in 1827, a man in Manlius, which was several miles south of the chosen route, remarked on his town's "old, dilapidated, forlorn look ... The construction of the Erie Canal had a very injurious effect upon the business of the village."[68]

Digging started in the middle and expanded outward. By 1819, the Erie Canal consisted of seventy-five miles of open waterway. Six years later, the canal in its 363-mile entirety opened with a bang at 10:00 a.m. on October 26, 1825, as a volley of cannon blasts echoed up and then back down its length for three hours all told. (Killed in Weedsport were two men, putting something of a damper on its celebration.) It even featured a consummation of sorts: the wedding of the waters, as on November 4, Governor DeWitt Clinton emptied a caskful of Lake Erie water into the Atlantic. The dimensions of the canal, at first, were four feet in depth and forty feet in width (twenty-eight feet at the canal's bottom); this widened a decade after the canal's inauguration in 1825 to seventy feet and deepened to seven feet. Mules pulled the boats with long ropes at a maximum enforced speed of four miles per hour, which Los Angeles drivers stuck on the 405 might envy.

The impact of the canal went beyond merely the economic. The late nineteenth- and early twentieth-century architect Francis Kimball, looking backward, exulted, "The Erie Canal rubbed Aladdin's lamp. America awoke, catching for the first time the wondrous vision of its own dimensions and power."[69] Without an ounce of assistance from the federal government, a state had undertaken and completed an internal improvement of surpassing import.

Just weeks before his death in 1826, Thomas Jefferson, on receiving commemorative Erie Canal medals, wrote in gratitude, "This great work will immortalize the present authorities of New York; will bless their descendants with wealth and prosperity; and prove to mankind, the superior wisdom of employing the resources of industry in works of improvement rather than of destruction."[70]

Not all was calm water and smoothly sailing barges, however. Ice and snow effectively closed the canal for five months of the year—a disadvantage not shared by the railroads that would, within a few short years, supplant the canal as the transportation bulwark of the New York economy. (With a wink of unintentional irony, the name of the first train to rattle down the tracks in New York was DeWitt Clinton.[71])

Pace Thomas Jefferson, not all outside observers waxed rhapsodic. Nathaniel Hawthorne, writing in 1835 of a journey, confessed that "I was inclined to be poetical about the Grand Canal," having previously regarded DeWitt Clinton as "an enchanter, who had waved his magic wand from the Hudson to Lake Erie, and united them by a watery highway," but he found the real thing a horrible letdown. The canal, wrote Hawthorne, was "an interminable mud-puddle."[72] Yet Hawthorne's journey itself was an unexpected gratuity of sorts: the canal's purpose had been to move produce and freight, not tourists, but in 1825 more than forty thousand people, many of them sightseers, traveled on its waterway.

New York State paid off the construction loans by 1837—coincidentally, the same year as the Panic of 1837, which forced a retrenchment at the state level of ambitious plans for improvement.

The laissez-faire wing of the Jackson–Van Buren Democratic Party in New York, known as the Loco Focos, hated the canal with a white-hot passion and never did reconcile itself to this internal improvement par excellence, fighting its enlargement until the state debt had been paid. They met intermittent success but were unable to stop the enlargement. The state poured another $44.5 million into the rebuilding of the canal in the 1840s, despite Loco Foco cries of special privilege.

As George Rogers Taylor detailed in his standard *The Transportation Revolution, 1815–1860* (1951), the cost of carrying goods per ton-mile from Buffalo to New York City declined from 19.12 cents in 1817, the year ground was broken for the canal, to 1.68 cents between 1830 and 1850.[73] The Erie Canal was an engine of prosperity, though it also altered the economy of Upstate New York in ways not pleasing to everyone, and the rash of copycat canals in such states as Ohio and Indiana were nowhere near as successful.[74]

Canals were scarcer in the South, in part for reasons explicated by historian Ulrich B. Phillips: "The rivers in the South flow mostly in deep valleys or even gorges, which furnish many obstacles to the building of canals along or across their courses, while the very heavy and irregular rainfall and the frequency of freshets and floods, especially after the extensive clearing away of the Piedmont forests, caused great danger of destruction of works, and exerted a deterring influence when canals were considered."[75]

Despite the example set by New York with the Erie, most canals in nineteenth-century America did benefit from federal aid in the form of land grants: 4.5 million acres' worth, to be approximate, a not inconsiderable sum, though it pales before the 130 million acres gifted by the government to the railroads.[76] As John Bell Rae explained in a monograph on federal land grants to canals in the *Journal of Economic History*, these gifts of land came in two waves: the first, in the 1820s and 1830s, were directed to Ohio, Indiana, Illinois, and Wisconsin, and the second, in the 1850s and 1860s, were focused on Michigan and Wisconsin. Prior to these two waves, canal builders were entrepreneurs; while they sometimes had stock purchases by the federal and state governments, they were, in the main, private interests. The canals of the Midwest, by contrast, were state enterprises. Constitutionalists, as well as those whose states were not affected directly, would have raised loud objections to outright federal subsidies for these government-built canals, so the states proposed transfers of land rather than cash instead. Owners and operators of the railroads that would, in time, supplant the canals, learned well this lesson; as Rae writes, "The system by which land was given to the canals was applied, virtually without alteration, to the railroads."[77]

Contrary to myth, it's not true that canal traffic dried up in the face of railroad competition; as George Rogers Taylor notes, tonnage carried on the Erie peaked in 1880.[78] But the building boom was over by 1840, as the financial hardship of the late 1830s inspired statehouse penny-pinching and a reluctance to take on debt. The great retrenchment of the 1840s, which the economist Henry Carter Adams termed "a revulsion of sentiment" against state-sponsored projects, resulted in the transfer of responsibility for the erection and maintenance of infrastructure from governments to individuals and corporations, including the railroads.[79]

Despite the widespread, though by no means universal, approval of the Erie Canal in New York, the resultant political alliances were hazy and sometimes unpredictable. Attitudes toward internal improvements did not always break down along party lines. Many New York Whigs, writes Carol Sheriff in *The Artificial River*, her fine study of the social and cultural effects of the Erie Canal, "opposed federal support for internal improvements; if New York had to pay for its own transportation system, then so, too, should other states."[80] Other, more orthodox Whigs believed devoutly in the potentially salutary effect of subsidy on the public weal. As Glyndon Van Deusen wrote in his monograph on Whig economic thought, "Internal improvements would create a veritable commercial revolution … by facilitating marketing of agricultural and industrial goods in all sections of the country."[81] These would be paid for with revenue from tariffs, which theoretically bolstered domestic industries, or from public land sales, which peopled the continent and created new markets. It was Henry Clay's American System in operation. The harmony, the complementarity, were akin to a superbly made watch. Or so ardent Whigs believed.

Turnpike Nation

Canals were not the only avenues of commerce and travel enjoying a boom in the early nineteenth-century republic. So was the turnpike, and the two were complementary rather than competitive, as turnpikes were typically more direct and shorter routes than canals. You could travel faster on turnpikes: stagecoaches averaged four to six miles per hour, or about double the two to three miles per hour of canal boats, which were slowed by the system of locks. Turnpikes aided personal travel more than they did long-haul freight. Teams of four or six horses pulled freight much less swiftly and efficiently than did the railroads: the average freight train in 1858 traveled 10.69 miles per hour, or about five times faster than horse-drawn wagons or mule-drawn canal boats.[82]

Turnpikes were also less expensive to build than canals. "Excellent stone turnpikes could be constructed at from $5,000 to $10,000 a mile," writes George Rogers Taylor, "whereas most canals required an investment of from about $20,000 to $30,000 a mile," and some, for instance the Chesapeake and Ohio ($60,000 per mile) and the Susquehanna and Tidewater ($80,000 per mile), cost considerably more.[83] Like the canal, the turnpike was not free. Definitionally, a turnpike is a road with a toll or fee assessed for those traveling thereon. The term originally denoted a barrier, typically a long pole placed across a road to block further progress until the traveler had paid a toll. More than ten thousand turnpike miles were smoothed and straightened and surfaced and opened for travel over the first third of the nineteenth century, though this mileage paled before the "free" road mileage under the control of towns and counties.[84] The rough, rutted, bumpy, dusty, muddy—but free—roads were more numerous than the turnpikes.

Almost all turnpikes were private enterprises; efforts to launch public toll roads in Maryland, Rhode Island, and Virginia ran aground in the face of squalling opposition to the tax hikes necessary to publicly finance these ventures.[85] State investment in turnpike stock, however, varied widely; Ohio bought up to 50 percent thereof, and Virginia 40 percent, making turnpikes in those states quasi-public enterprises, but New York, New Jersey, Maryland, and the states of New England "made almost no purchase of turnpike stock."[86] The pikers were on their own.

In the case of Virginia, a state Board of Public Works administered a Fund for Internal Improvement. The state bought up to 40 percent of the capital stock in approved private turnpike companies—a subsidy. The General Turnpike Law of 1817 also prescribed the smallest road dimensions ("sixty feet wide at least, eighteen feet of which shall be well covered with gravel or stone") for the more than 180 turnpikes in the commonwealth.[87] The classic explanation of the utility and justice of tolls was offered by Adam Smith in *The Nature and Causes of the Wealth of Nations*:

> When the carriages which pass over a highway or a bridge, and the lighters which sail on a navigable canal, pay toll in proportion to their weight or tonnage, they pay for the maintenance of those public works exactly in proportion to the wear and tear which they occasion of them. It seems scarce possible to invent a more equitable way of maintaining such works.... When high roads, bridges, canals, &c. are in this manner made and supported by the commerce which is carried on by means of them, they can be made only where that commerce requires them, and consequently where it is proper to make them. Their expense too, their grandeur and magnificence, must be suited to what the commerce can afford to pay.[88]

Even at this early stage, long before the traffic tie-ups and toll plazas of the interstate era, voices of opposition were raised to the very idea of charging travelers to use the roads, even though, as David Levinson, professor of civil engineering, has noted, the concept of tolled passages is as old as the Greek myth of Charon accepting the payment of a coin for ferrying souls across the River Styx.[89] Those who argued for "free" roads—that is, "common roads" without tolls—asserted that one unhappy consequence of turnpikes was "to limit human intercourse to that required for necessary commercial transactions."[90] Harvard geologist Nathaniel Shaler, dean of Harvard's Lawrence Scientific School, wrote, "The farmer who knows he must spend half a dollar for tolls on a visit to the county seat is very apt to abide at home, and so lose the chance of contact with his fellow-men."[91] The fairness issue was dealt with by turnpike and canal evangelist Elkanah Watson, who explained in a 1795 circular that "no tax can operate so fair and so easy, as that of paying a turnpike toll, since every person is taxed in proportion to the benefit he derives from a good road, and all strangers and travellers are made equally tributary to its support—What can be more just?"[92]

Watson found a willing debate partner in a New York state assemblyman who wrote under the nom de plume *Civis*, whom we may assume to be a Jeffersonian Republican. *Civis* scoffed at Watson's assertion of the elemental fairness of turnpikes, seeing them as instruments of "despotism" and "specula-tion." Like certain early Republicans, he assailed corporate charters as licenses of privilege, guarantees of monopoly. Rather than granting such charters, the legislature should open the field to any entrepreneur who wishes to enter. To do otherwise is downright "monarchical."[93] In addition, turnpikes could be granted land via the power of eminent domain, an offense against the most basic property rights and an elevation of commerce over personal liberty.

Though New York is most closely associated with canals in the public memory of early internal improvements, the state was a turnpike hotbed between 1800 and 1830, when more than one-third of all business incorpora-tions (339 of 993) were for turnpikes. Only Pennsylvania, at 46 percent, had a higher share.[94]

In 1792, the Keystone State granted a charter of incorporation to the Philadelphia and Lancaster Turnpike Road Company, builder of the sixty-two-mile-long Philadelphia and Lancaster Turnpike, first of these roads. The state prescribed the route, the width (fifty feet between fences), and the com-position ("bedded with wood, stone, gravel, or any other hard substance, well compacted together") and granted the company the right of eminent do-main.[95] Investors snapped up the $300 shares with a ravenous and, as it turns out, justified optimism. The turnpike was completed in less than three years, at a cost of $465,000, and its thirteen toll-collecting stations were soon doing a land office business.[96] This road was an "immediate success," as travelers were willing to pay the tolls because it offered a superior avenue of conveyance.[97]

Although New York authorized its first turnpike later than any eastern state other than New Jersey, it took to the idea with a fervor. Construction of more than 150 turnpikes occurred in the half-century between 1797 and 1846, with most of them somewhere between fifteen and fifty miles in length. Construction costs averaged about $1,500 per mile.[98] Alas, nearly two-thirds of New York's turnpikes failed.[99]

In their study of New York's experience with turnpikes, Daniel B. Klein and John Majewski note that the turnpike explosion was not detonated by a technological advance or state subsidy, but by an apprehension of its "organi-zational advantages."[100] These included the ability to charge fees; a contrac-tual relationship with workers rather than reliance on road tax days; a wider, deeper pool of potential investors; and the presence of a toll keeper to act as security guard, money handler, and the public face of the company. Tollgates could be erected after the construction of just ten miles of turnpike. When turnpikes met financial distress, they were allowed to establish "half-houses" every five miles, where they charged half the usual rate.[101]

Ideological objections from the libertarian-ish Republicans and later Democrats of New York were few, for the role of the state was limited to issuing the charter of incorporation and setting out rules governing its use, including toll rates. And therein lies the rub—or the rut— that scuttled pikes. For in Klein and Majewski's telling, excessive and often unwise regulation hamstrung New York's turnpike entrepreneurs. From the start, turnpike operators and citizens wrangled over just who should be exempt from tolls. The former's preferred answer was "no one," while the latter's was "me!" Generally, the exemptions included those on their way to or from religious worship, a farm or a mill on a matter of business, a funeral, a blacksmith, a physician or midwife, a polling place, jury duty, or military service, as well as those who lived within a mile of the tollgate.[102] The freebies added up.

Difficulties in enforcement plagued turnpikes, despite a stiff fine (typically ten dollars) for evasion, or what was known as shunpiking. Usually the shunpiker simply detoured around a tollgate—like today's subway fare jumpers, though less obvious and with less leaping ability. The fine for this offense was substantially higher than the standard rates for traveling a New York turnpike, which ranged from twenty-five cents per trip for carriages to four cents for a horse and rider or a horse-drawn sleigh.[103] Fisher Ames, the Massachusetts arch-Federalist who was president of a turnpike company forging a road to and from his native Dedham, lamented that "his company's earnings would be almost 60 percent greater if not for shunpiking."[104]

The widespread failure of turnpikes Klein and Majewski blame on misgovernment by the legislature, which was loath to allow companies to raise rates. Operators grumbled over the excessive exemptions from tolls and could not find effective means of counteracting the shunpikers. If people wanted to beat the tolls, they were going to beat the tolls. Volume on most turnpikes was simply too sparse to meet expenses, let alone supply a healthy return on investment. So investors shied from such risky speculative ventures, and the hullaballoo over the Erie and kindred canals turned their attention waterward. Turnpike abandonment was rife. An 1838 law provided that inactive turnpikes would become public roads. As Gerald Gunderson notes, privately operated turnpikes, responding to market signals, were able to shut down operations much more easily and swiftly than were those that answered to state government shareholders.[105]

Despite the failure of turnpikes in New York, enough interest existed to build more than 150 such roads of greater than ten miles. Klein and Majewski credit this in part to old-fashioned boosterism. The prosperous men of the community wished their communities to prosper as well—for self-interested reasons, of course, but also out of a sense of civic pride. Henry Clay limned this in an 1817 speech to Congress: "I think it very possible that the capitalist who should invest his money in [turnpikes] might not be reimbursed three percent annually upon it; and yet society in various forms, might actually reap fifteen or twenty percent."[106]

Such motivations were less evident in the later experience of California, as Klein and Chi Yin argue in a monograph on the effect of "community enterprise" in the building of toll roads in the Golden State.[107] The gold rush had filled California with men who were, to use the novelist Wallace Stegner's terms, *boomers* rather than *stickers*. They had scrambled to the West Coast to find a fortune, not build a community. They came in search of precious metals, not good citizenship medals. The participatory ethos of New England, the Mid-Atlantic, and the small-town Midwest was foreign to the mining camps and hastily erected boomtowns. As Klein and Yin write, with admirable understatement, "Society in early California was not one where town meetings, door-to-door solicitations, and newspaper campaigns were likely to rally broad support for a road project."[108] One was likelier to encounter a highwayman than a highway booster.

Nonetheless, some 414 toll road charters were granted by the state of California between 1850 and 1902, and 159 such roads were constructed, almost all with exclusively private backing.[109] But the "community esteem" aspect of investment was much less common in California than in New York. The median number of stockholders in a California toll road company was eight, compared to twenty-eight for the mid-nineteenth-century plank road boomlet (which we shall discuss presently) in New York.[110] This concentrated ownership suggests investors with a sharper eye on profit than on community boosting. A considerable number were entrepreneurs who sensed both demand and opportunity. Yet the private toll roads of California were all but vanished by the dawn of the twentieth century.

Klein and Yin cite as the dominant factor in their demise an "ideological and public-policy shift toward centralized government planning." The "Good Roads Movement," they say, virtually erased the choice of private ground transportation. There was no longer a contest between public and private sector but merely "centralized government agency versus decentralized anything."[111]

"The public officials engineering the new system," they conclude, "would scarcely tolerate independently operated highways."[112] As the administrative state grew, turnpikes became outmoded—relics of what progressives regarded as the bad old days of private and semiprivate road policy. The Lancaster Turnpike, last of the Mohicans, had fallen into disrepair and decay by 1880, and the Lancaster Turnpike Road Company dissolved in 1902.

Clay v. Jackson, or The Democrats Take on the American System

Let us leave the state-centered canals and turnpikes, perhaps by way of a good shunpike, and return to federal internal improvements policy in the wake of James Madison's parting gift to the country, his veto of the Bonus Bill. Madison's successor, his fellow Virginian James Monroe, would also wield his veto pen at an apt historical moment, though in the first two years of Monroe's presidency, the eyes of internal improvers were on Congress.

On December 15, 1817, a House committee chaired by Rep. Henry St. George Tucker (R-VA) reported out four resolutions that forced the House to debate first principles when these resolutions came to the floor in March 1818. The committee was stacked with nationalists, so the flavor of its recommendations had never been in doubt. The House considered resolutions "that Congress has power, under the Constitution,"

- "to appropriate money for the construction of post roads, military, and *other roads*, and of canals, and for the improvement of water-courses."[113] This one was approved by a vote of 90–75, with the bulk of nays coming from Virginia, North Carolina, and New England.

- "to construct post roads and military roads; provided that private property not be taken for public use, without just compensation."[114] This was defeated, 84–82.

- "to construct roads and canals necessary for commerce between the States; provided, that private property be not taken for public purposes, without just compensation."[115] This was defeated, 95–71.

- "to construct canals for military purposes; *Provided*, that no private property be taken for any such purpose, without just compensation being made therefor."[116] This was defeated, 83–81.

The cumulative message of the votes was, as Norman K. Risjord notes in *The Old Republicans: Southern Conservatism in the Age of Jefferson*, "confusing."[117] Congress could appropriate money for internal improvements but not authorize those improvements.

The regional breakdown of votes on the second through fourth resolutions was like that of the first resolution. Representatives from the Old Republican redoubts of Virginia and North Carolina teamed with New Englanders in league against the internal improvement faction. The House had sent something of a mixed message, but on three of four roll calls the side of strict construction had prevailed.

Rep. Alexander Smyth, like Henry St. George Tucker a Virginia Republican but one much less disposed to opening the treasury to roadbuilders, spoke for the Old Republicans. "If a general power to establish and make roads had intended to be given ... a special grant of power to establish post roads *only*, would not have been given," argued Rep. Smyth.[118] The adjective *post* severely limited this grant of power. It was incumbent on all faithful friends of liberty to hold fast, to bar the door, for the consolidators were eagerly searching for an "*entering wedge*" that might provide access to the federal treasury. "Experience," lectured Smyth, "has proved that [roads and canals] are most economically made, and best managed, by associations of individuals. So soon as the wants of society shall render such works profitable, individuals will associate, unite their stock, and construct the works."[119] There was no need for Congress to artificially speed this inevitable process along.

Speaker of the House Henry Clay (DR-KY) responded. Clay was formulating his "American System," a cannily named (for who could be against the

American System?) activist, interventionist economic program that combined generous federal support of canals, roads, and waterways with a stiff protective tariff and a national bank. The idea, as Maurice G. Baxter explains in his study *Henry Clay and the American System*, was to "harmoniz[e] all segments of the economy" under the watchful and vigilant guidance of "an intervening national government."[120] In the 1818 debate, Clay accused the strict constructionists of a "water-gruel regimen they would administer to the Constitution."[121] They were starving a people hungry for action! The preservation of the union, said Clay, was the "first and dearest object" of the Constitution, and a program of internal improvements, connecting and binding the disparate states of that union, would facilitate a stronger linkage between them, and a more cohesive union.[122]

Rep. Archibald Austin (R-VA) disagreed with the speaker. Once the pork barrel of internal improvements was thrown open, he predicted, the scramble would create discord and division among the states, as they would "quarrel who shall get the most."[123] There would be, in the phrase of a much later era, donor and donee states. And the stakes were far higher than mere lucre: hard-won American liberties were in the balance. Rep. James Johnson, another Virginia Republican, warned that a Congress in the habit of "an enlargement of the sphere of ... Constitutional and political powers" was setting the stage for a tyrant who will "drive with desolating fury over the rights and liberties of the people of this country."[124]

John Lauritz Larson characterizes the opposition to internal improvements during the Monroe presidency's Era of Good Feelings as issuing from voices "sometimes bitter and narrowly selfish, but always mouthing high principles."[125] Critics of public subsidy of roads and canals are said by Larson to have adhered to "dyspeptic doctrines of Virginia neo-Antifederalists."[126] This is uncharitable. Guiding Reps. Smyth, Austin, and Johnson was something loftier than indigestion or curmudgeonliness. Their Jeffersonian, or Old Republican or Anti-Federalist, fear of consolidation, of a powerful central state run rampant, motivated principled opposition to government subsidy of business, too.

The Virginia Republican in the White House proved to be at least a fitful ally when it came time for him to wield his veto pen. The occasion was a bill extending the Cumberland, or National, Road to the Mississippi River.

Year in and year out, it had received the necessary appropriations, though not without grumbling. Now the grumbling grew louder from such hard-core House constitutionalists as New York's Silas Wood and Pennsylvania's James Buchanan, later to be known as the Bachelor President, who in 1822 was arguing that because Pennsylvania had constructed her own turnpikes, other states ought to do so as well.[127]

As congressional appropriations had risen and fallen over the years with the political tides, sections of the road needed repairs. To forestall its further deterioration, supporters proposed to erect tollgates, the proceeds of which would finance the necessary repairs. Among the most enthusiastic toll-the-Cumberland solons was the colorful Kentucky Democratic senator Richard Mentor Johnson, best known as the putative killer of Tecumseh and lover of Julia Chinn, an enslaved woman who oversaw his domestic affairs.

Congress approved studding the road with tollgates as a form of user fee and sent the bill to President Monroe, who vetoed it on May 4, 1822, with "deep regret," due to his conviction that "Congress do [*sic*] not possess the power under the Constitution to pass such a law."[128] While the federal government could appropriate money for such a road, it simply was not possible, he reasoned, to derive from Article I, Section 8's limited and specific authorization to establish post roads the right to erect a system of turnpike tolls, for this "implies a power to adopt and execute a complete system of internal improvement" under federal control.[129]

Had Benjamin Franklin's canal amendment been approved by the Constitutional Convention thirty-five years earlier, perhaps such an arrangement might have fallen within the ambit of legitimate powers, but that had been defeated 8–3 and left out of the Constitution. Monroe restated his support for an amendment showing clearly the federal government's power to subsidize internal improvements within the states. (Heeding President Monroe's request, Senator James Barbour of Virginia introduced a constitutional amendment giving Congress the power to "pass laws appropriating money for constructing roads and canals, and improving the navigation of water courses."[130] It went nowhere.) Soon thereafter, the president signed a bill giving money for repairs on the Cumberland Road. Appropriations, yes; tolls, no. The distinction seemed Jesuitical. In his final year of office, 1824, Monroe would approve of the General Survey Act, which appropriated monies for a federal survey of roads and canals of national import.

Again, it was the Virginians who rallied to the flag of strict, limited government. Rep. George Tucker, cousin of Henry St. George Tucker, spoke up against the General Survey and for the superiority of private enterprise. The federal government, he argued, had not the local knowledge necessary to undertake a vast system of internal improvements or even a prefatory survey. Had Gallatin gotten his $20 million back in 1808, said Tucker, the capital city would "swarm with hundreds of projectors, with their maps and plans, beautifully illuminated, electioneering for business; and as they would succeed according to their address, and means of conciliating favor, the result would be, that we should have roads without travelers, and canals without navigation, and perhaps without water."[31] It's as if Rep. Tucker had a prevision of the Alaskan Bridge to Nowhere.

The General Survey passed both houses and President Monroe signed it into law. In the Senate, its aye votes came from, among others, Andrew Jackson of Tennessee, who would soon be at the vortex of the argument over the federal role in internal improvements. During the General Survey debate, the redoubtable John Randolph of Virginia, never one for discretion, pointed to an elephant in the room: "If Congress possesses the power to do what is proposed by this bill, they may not only enact a sedition law—for there is precedent—but they may emancipate every slave in the United States."[32]

But if fear of emancipation was an ignoble contributing cause to the anti–internal improvements position of certain Southern politicians, even in some of the most problematic cases there were considerations of high principle as well. (It was also the case, as Southern historian Ulrich B. Phillips noted in a 1905 analysis of transportation in the antebellum South, that the region's population was more scattered, less concentrated, than in the Northeast, and so the demand for better ways of accommodating passenger traffic was far less urgent.[33])

* * *

Perhaps the most vocal and unyielding Southern enemy of federal aid to transportation was Nathaniel Macon, a North Carolina Democratic-Republican of the Jeffersonian stripe who served from 1791 to 1815 in the US House of Representatives and thereafter for another thirteen years in the US Senate. Macon was a strict constructionist, an agrarian, and a habitual caster of nay votes. He disdained to give the federal government an inch for certitude that it would take a mile. Using the example of infrastructure, he told the Senate that "the Government was constantly gaining power by little bits. A wagon road was made under a treaty with an Indian tribe, twenty odd years ago; and now it becomes a great national object, to be kept up by large appropriations. We thus go on by degrees, step by step, until we get almost unlimited power."[134] Senator Macon was referring, of course, to the Cumberland Road, whose fan he was not. He remarked thereof: "I know it is a very pleasant thing to travel over a fine road for nothing, but I should like it better had it cost the Government nothing; but been made by the enterprise of the States."[135]

Nathaniel Macon sounded the alarm over this kind of piecemeal subsidy of roads and canals: "Commence these roads, and there is no telling where it will end; for legislation might be compared to shingling a house—the first row is useless unless you go on, lapping one row over another to the top."[136] Of the 1817 Bonus Bill, Macon said that "this is to be a new plan of legislation for this country. It makes an appropriation of millions for roads and canals, without directing a cent to be expended on any particular road or canal. It is as incorrect as it is new and against the invariable practice of the Government, which has been to make appropriations of money as specific as possible."[137] The Bonus, said Macon, "ought to be employed in the payment of the public debt. In time of peace no exertion ought to be spared to discharge it. It is a safe and good rule to pay debts when you have the means."[138]

Yet though his critics thought him a purblind reactionary, Nathaniel Macon could see the writing on the road. He despaired to Albert Gallatin in 1824, "There are not, I imagine, five members of Congress who entertain the opinions which those did who brought Mr. Jefferson into power, and they are yet mine."[139] Jefferson's secretary of the treasury was an odd choice to receive such a missive, given his enthusiastic advocacy of a wide-ranging program of federally sponsored canals, roads, harbor improvements, and suchlike. Yet Macon and his dwindling band of Old Republicans, foremost among them John Randolph of Virginia, fought vainly to hold back the tide, and they would seek allies where they could.

Like Randolph, Macon admitted to a less noble, in fact ignoble, motivation, or fear. He wrote a pro–American System friend in North Carolina in 1818, "If Congress can make canals they can with propriety emancipate. Be not deceived. I speak soberly in the fear of God and the love of the Constitution. Let not love of improvements or a thirst for glory blind that sober discretion and sound sense with which the Lord has blessed you. Paul was not more anxious or sincere concerning Timothy than I am for you. Your error in this will injure if not destroy our beloved mother, North Carolina, and all the South country."[140] (Macon, though he lived in a modest two-room house, owned seventy slaves, whose labor he did not scruple to appropriate.[141])

But most critics of federal sponsorship of internal improvements based their opposition thereto on more solid, not to mention moral, grounds. Dr. Thomas H. Hall, an eight-term member of Congress from North Carolina and coeval of Macon's, identified himself as a Jacksonian and stalwart foe of what an ally called "those extravagant schemes of Internal Improvement, so inimical to the economy and happiness" of the country.[142] When in 1831 Rep. Hall was attacked by a challenger for failing to support a federal appropriation for an inlet of the Outer Banks, he shot back:

> What in God's name are we coming to in this country, if I am to be blamed for not squandering the people's money upon everything, whether needed or not? Do my fellow citizens really wish me to give away their money to every applicant, for whatever purpose—for the Swash, Nags-Head, and to all persons who may ask for it for any purpose? … Is it possible that my fellow citizens desire to continue the taxes imposed on them by the tariff for such purposes? If so, all I have to say, God help us all…. Let the money be applied to pay the public debt, and then reduce the taxes—this will do more public good, than all the idle expense upon internal improvement, or anything else.[143]

Despite, or perhaps because of, his parsimony, the voters reelected Hall. A nation of beggars, or rivals for government favors, ever on the alert for the main chance, the cheap advantage, was bound to arise unless this cadging, this dunning for dollars, ended.

North Carolina historian Harry L. Watson has described the thoughts of Hall, Macon, and other frugal Tar Heels. The focus was not on the well-rehearsed antebellum Southern defense of states' rights; rather, Watson examined those solons and controversialists of the Old North State who denied that the *state* government ought to subsidize canals, roads, railroads, and improvements (or modifications) to rivers and waterways in aid of navigation. Although the friends of internal improvement won the argument, at least judging from North Carolina's state sponsorship of such by 1860, their opponents offered various spirited objections, among them:

- Internal improvements are a form of class legislation that aids the well-connected at the expense of others. As a *Tarborough Free Press* writer opined, "It is unequal, unjust, oppressive, and radically wrong, that the poor of any county should be compelled to pay for the improvements of such county, to the exclusive benefit of the rich or fine, that reside adjacent to such improvements."[44]

- Internal improvements entailed an increase in taxation, and the money thereby mulcted from citizens could be better spent by those citizens in pursuit of their own interests.

- Internal improvements were a cynical ploy by which opportunistic politicians sought to gain or keep office by rewarding the powerful and those in a position to do them favors.

As Watson noted, opposition to state sponsorship of internal improvements was *not* opposition to *private* sponsorship thereof. The number of nineteenth-century Americans who execrated roads on principle was surpassingly small. The antisubsidy George Howard, editor of the *Tarborough Free Press*, emphasized his support of a privately funded railroad connecting Edgecombe, North Carolina, with outside markets; the transportation needs of his community, he believed, could be met by the private provision of roads, canals, and the like.[145] Federal subsidy to railroads was a nonstarter in the states' rights South, but state sponsorship had its advocates, though "the sentiment of individualism was too strong" for anything like a socialist-tinged movement for state ownership of railroads to develop, even though states eagerly granted corporate charters and purchased stock in the Iron Horse with state money.[146]

An echo of George Howard's libertarian case for infrastructure development resounded in the *American Railroad Journal*, which in 1839 editorialized against "any system of internal improvements under the control of the government."[147] The editor went on to quote from England's *Civil Engineering Journal*, which had asserted that when government acts as "engineer-general" of a railroad, "the rights and interests of all the industrious classes are directly invaded, a monopoly set up, and the spirit of enterprise, of invention, and improvement ceases, and all those vigorous trading impulses which have so eminently contributed to the wealth and to the prosperity of all free and enlightened countries."[148] As Carter Goodrich noted, this was the voice of laissez-faire, of free enterprise, of the night watchman state, and the *American Railroad Journal* would sing these freedom songs throughout the next decade, insisting that "all the canals and railways of this country would have been … better executed by private enterprise … which alone possesses the means, skill, and *integrity* indispensable to success."[149] Free men, given free rein, can conceive, design, build, and run roads, canals, bridges, and railroads. All they need, editorialized the *American Railroad Journal*, "is to be 'let alone.'"[150]

The Improving Mr. Adams

The disputed election of 1824 elevated to the office of the presidency John Quincy Adams, who in his first inaugural address hailed the "magnificence and splendor" of "public works" of the past and called for a concerted federal effort to achieve the same in this new republic. Should this succeed, he predicted, "unborn millions of our posterity who are in future ages to people this continent" would bestow "their most fervent gratitude" on the farsighted advocates of an energetic central government.[151] Adams pursued this path with determination but a measure of political maladroitness, as during his single term of office expenditures on internal improvements were actually *less* than in the first term of his successor and bitter rival, Democrat Andrew Jackson. But he had his triumphs, as when he broke ground for the Chesapeake and Ohio Canal five miles west of Washington, DC on July 4, 1828, in what was known as "the Great National Project."[152] Albert Gallatin, who had proposed two Chesapeake-based canals, was being avenged by this most un-, or even anti-, Jeffersonian president.

George Washington, whose farewell address urged "the progressive improvement of interior communication, by land & water," had envisioned a waterway connecting the Potomac with the Ohio, and so it was fitting that the project got underway during the administration of Adams, the last president in the old Federalist mold.[153] The canal, whose investors included the federal government; the states of Maryland and Virginia; the cities of Washington, Georgetown, and Alexandria; and private interests, was a symbol of man's duty to "subdue the earth," declared Adams,[154] who termed its groundbreaking, bizarrely, "the most fortunate incident" of his life.[155] The president's wife Louisa and his children may have raised an eyebrow at that. And this whole notion of *subduing* the earth may not sit well with the modern-day progressive adulators of John Quincy Adams. In response, the redoubtable Nathaniel Macon sputtered to his Senate colleagues that he "rose with a full heart to say goodbye to an old friend whom he had always loved and admired, the Constitution of the United States," which was being further buried by every shovelful of dirt excavated for the Great National Project.[156]

The John Quincy Adams quadrennium saw four substantial appropriations to private canal companies: $450,000 to the Chesapeake and Delaware Canal Company, $235,000 to the Louisville and Portland Canal Company, $200,000 to the Dismal Swamp Canal Company, and $1 million to the Chesapeake and Ohio Canal Company. In this last instance, the federal government held the "dominant" position among investors, and "state and municipal contributors were to outweig[h] those of private subscribers" by a margin of over $2 million to $607,400.[157] If the injection of substantial federal funds into private infrastructure enterprises heralded the dawning of an age of magnificence and splendor, then Adams was hastening that happy day.

Yet the oft-saturnine Adams left office discouraged. He blamed "the Sable Genius of the South" for serving as an obstacle to his program of internal improvements and a high tariff. "The great effort of my administration was to mature into a permanent and regular system the application of all the superfluous revenues of the Union to internal improvement.... I fell and with me fell, I fear never to rise again, certainly never to rise again in my day, the system of internal improvement by means of national energies."[158] Not exactly, JQA. Eventually, the advocates of an active role for the federal government in the promotion of transportation won a resounding victory with distant ramifications the second President Adams could scarcely have imagined. Indeed, his native Quincy and nearby Boston still bear the scars of not-so-magnificent twentieth-century roadbuilding.

Jackson's Actions

Like John Quincy Adams and his Virginia predecessors, Andrew Jackson of the frontier state of Tennessee valued roads, turnpikes, canals, and other internal improvements as connective tissue of the Union and boons to trade, but, also like Jefferson, Madison, and Monroe (and unlike Adams), he harbored doubts as to the constitutional propriety of federal subsidy thereof. The issue arose when the Congress approved the purchase of 1,500 shares (for $150,000) in the Kentucky-based Maysville, Washington, Paris, and Lexington Turnpike Road Company, which proposed to construct a turnpike linking several cities of the Bluegrass State and, ultimately, connecting with Zanesville, Ohio, to the north and Florence, Alabama, to the south. For the nonce, however, this sixty-plus-mile turnpike was to be entirely situated in Kentucky.

Jackson did not gainsay the value of the road, but he believed that a constitutional amendment must precede any federal appropriation for its construction. The Maysville bill passed the House, 102–86. Senate detractors included Virginia's John Tyler, who in just over a decade would occupy the White House. Tyler gauged this as far more consequential than just another piece of special-interest legislation; should the federal government begin building roads within the states, "all that is dear and should be considered sacred in our institutions is put to hazard."[59] Once the federal government encroached on policies that clearly were within the competency and purview of the states, there would be no stopping the juggernaut. The states would be "mere provinces" of the "imperial monarch" in the District of Columbia.[60]

Elevating principle above policy preference—and spiting his rival Henry Clay of Kentucky in the bargain—President Jackson vetoed the Maysville Road bill on May 27, 1830. As historian Carlton Jackson understatedly observed in his study of Jackson's vetoes of internal improvement bills, "The chances for Jackson's approval of the Maysville project would probably have been better if it had been in any state but Kentucky."[61] Jackson loathed Clay; he believed, with some justice, that the Kentuckian had struck a corrupt bargain to win the presidency for John Quincy Adams over Jackson when the

1824 race had been thrown into the House of Representatives. In exchange for Clay's support in the House, Adams had appointed the Great Compromiser as his secretary of state. Vetoing Maysville hardly made up for Jackson's loss of the presidency six years earlier—but even revenge tasted lukewarm had its satisfactions. You did not cross Andrew Jackson and get away unscathed.

The Maysville Road, said Jackson, was of a "purely local character," unlike the Cumberland, or National Road, which would gain the sobriquet of "The Main Street of America."[162] The Maysville Road's supporters protested that mail from beyond the state's borders was carried over its mileage, making it, they argued, a national road—a post road—but this seemed a stretch.[163] Pronouncing himself "sincerely friendly to the improvement of our country by means of roads and canals," Jackson nevertheless felt himself compelled to veto this legislation, as it lacked constitutional grounding.[164] Moreover, the public debt must be retired before undertaking any ambitious spending program. But Old Hickory had a solution around this problem. As Jackson wrote, "If it be the wish of the people that the construction of roads and canals should be conducted by the Federal Government, it is not only highly expedient, but indispensably necessary, that a previous amendment of the Constitution, delegating the necessary power and defining and restricting its exercise with reference to the sovereignty of the States, should be made. Without it nothing extensively useful can be effected."[165]

Jackson's secretary of state and presidential successor, New York's Martin Van Buren, the Red Fox of Kinderhook, helped in the writing of the Maysville Road veto. Van Buren assured the president that New York was behind him. The Empire State had built the Erie Canal on its own dime; why shouldn't Kentuckians and others do the same? John Randolph toasted Jackson's negative at a dinner in Hampton Roads, Virginia: "The rejection of the Maysville Road Bill—it falls upon the ear like the music of other days."[166] This sentiment was shared widely below the Mason-Dixon Line: as Carlton Jackson notes, while 14 percent of Southern members of Congress had favored the Bonus Bill in 1817, only 1 percent supported the Maysville Road.[167]

Attitudes toward federal sponsorship of infrastructure projects, with certain notable exceptions, would fall along sectional lines, with the West consistently the region most desirous of greater expenditures. New Englanders, by contrast, feared that improving Western roads would encourage out-migration; should the federal government, they asked, subsidize the mo-bility of the population? And Southerners knew that funding of internal improvements was largely by tariffs. As mostly free traders, they worried that a government in need of revenue to fund roads and canals would have incentives to raise tariffs.

Four days after his Maysville veto, President Jackson vetoed the kindred, if smaller in scope, purchase of stock in the Washington Turnpike Road Company for the improvement of a road linking Frederick with Rockville, Maryland. (Stock subscriptions had gained favor as the least politically ob-jectionable means of subsidization.) Later, Jackson would veto another four internal improvement bills, the final one providing federal aid for work eas-ing navigation along the Wabash River. In fact, twenty-two of the fifty-three vetoes exercised by pre-Lincoln presidents involved internal improvements.[168]

Yet if a project was of a national character, Jackson was closer to spend-thrift than scrooge. Before Old Hickory assumed office in March 1829, the Cumberland Road had benefited from federal aid totaling $1,668,000; in the period between Jackson's Maysville Road veto of 1830 and his departure from office in March 1837, $3,728,000 was lavished on it.[169] Jackson's alleged hostil-ity to internal improvements, based on his famous veto, has been exaggerated by historians. Throughout his eight years in office, federal appropriations for internal improvements averaged $1.323 million annually, compared with $702,000 under the rhetorical champion of such improvements, President John Quincy Adams.[170] Moreover, about one-third of the sum total of federal expenditures for internal improvements between 1789 and 1861 were made during Jackson's two terms in office.[171]

Still, strict construction and stinginess with respect to federal appropria-tions would inspirit the largest element of the Democratic Party for decades yet. The next Democratic president after Van Buren, James Knox Polk, who as a Democratic congressman from Tennessee had supported Jackson's veto of the Maysville Road bill, ran on an 1844 platform that denied the federal government the power "to commence or carry on a general system of internal improvements."[172] While platforms are often derided for their flimsiness, Polk actually stood firm on his. He vetoed a $1.378 million harbors and rivers bill on August 3, 1846. Many of its forty-plus projects were of a "local charac-ter," explained Polk, using a Jacksonian locution.[173] The federal government "does not possess [the] power" to make such expenditures, said Polk, calling on the shades of Madison and Jackson for support. Should such projects of a purely local nature become eligible for federal subvention, argued Polk, the floodgates would be opened and all traces of fiscal responsibility would be washed away:

> Should this bill become a law, the principle which it establishes will inevitably lead to large and annually increasing appropriations and drains on the Treasury, for it is not to be doubted that numerous other localities not embraced in its provisions, but quite as much entitled to the favor of the Government as those which are embraced, will demand, through their representatives in Congress, to be placed on an equal footing with them. With such an increase of expenditure must necessarily follow either an increased public debt or increased burdens upon the people by taxation to supply the Treasury with the means of meeting the accumulated demands upon it.[174]

Polk defied Western Democrats with this veto, foreshadowing a much later Southern Democratic president, Jimmy Carter, who nine months into his presidency also angered Western elements of his party by vetoing a $10.1 billion public works bill containing six water projects to which he objected.[175] In the case of the Polk veto, his party was largely with him: only 27 percent of House Democrats had supported this Christmas tree bill, as opposed to 87 percent of Whig representatives.[176] "Polk's aversion to internal improvements had become almost an obsession" by the time of his veto, writes biographer Eugene Irving McCormac.[177] He had defeated Henry Clay, architect of the American System, in the closely contested 1844 presidential election, and he was not about to see Clay's desired reforms enacted with his signature affixed. Though his expansionist policies with respect to the Mexican War may seem to stretch the limits of constitutionalism, Polk insisted on strict economy at home and the old Jefferson-Jackson ideal of equal rights for all, special privileges for none.

The next Democratic president, Franklin Pierce of New Hampshire, the Young Hickory of the Granite State, had voted against every internal improvement bill on the tapis as a member of Congress.[178] Though oft criticized for his performance in office, Pierce had the virtue of consistency when it came to internal improvements. Alas for him, he did *not* have Congress with him. Within a span of forty days in 1856, Franklin Pierce had five vetoes of river- and navigation-related bills overridden.

Furthermore, not every Democratic nominee of the era shared Pierce's constancy. Politicians have ever taken to heart, indeed taken as a virtual credo, Ralph Waldo Emerson's maxim that a foolish consistency is the hobgoblin of little minds, adored by little statesmen and philosophers and divines. As Victor L. Albjerg noted in a seminal 1932 study of antebellum politics, the 1848 Democratic Party platform stated forthrightly that "the Constitution does not confer upon Congress the power to commence and carry on a general system of internal improvement"—and yet the party's presidential nominee, Lewis Cass of Michigan, had, as a US senator, "voted for every internal im- provement bill that had come up."[179] No hobgoblins would trouble the sleep of Lewis Cass!

In the wake of Jacksonian Democrat skepticism regarding Great National Projects of improvement, the action shifted to the states. Over the decade of the 1830s, "state governments borrowed approximately $150 million to finance internal improvement projects," with most of that expended on canals, as Jason Lee writes.[180] As federal enthusiasm for Grand National Projects waned, federal outlays for the first of those projects, the National Road, seemed chronically inadequate. So the states affected—Ohio, Pennsylvania, Maryland, and Virginia—one by one took control of the road, denational- izing it, to the displeasure of nationalists such as Henry Clay, who contended that the road, "being the common property of the whole nation, and under the guardianship of the general government, ought not to be treacherously parted from by it."[181] But it was. Indiana and Illinois assumed ownership of their portions of the road later, in 1848 and 1856, respectively. And in the postbellum era, while the federal government lavishly supported railroads, primarily through grants of land, roadbuilding was returned entirely to the states and local governments—where, the strict constructionists said, it be- longed in the first place.

The purists, those who insisted on private enterprise taking up the internal improvements slack, did not disappear. Congressman Gerrit Smith (Free Soil–NY), the firebrand abolitionist and libertarian champion, denounced government sponsorship of railroads, specifically the Transcontinental Railroad, in an 1854 speech:

> I need not say, that I desire to see a railroad to the Pacific. What American does not desire it? Commerce, travel, the love of country, the love of each part of it, and the deep hope in every true American breast, that we shall ever remain one country;—these, and countless other considerations, all unite in calling for such a useful and pleasant connection—such an iron bond between the Atlantic and the Pacific, the East and the West. Nevertheless, I would not have Government either own, or build the road. Great as is the good to come from the road, it would, nevertheless, be largely overbalanced by the evil of having such a connection of Government with it, as the bill proposes. Indeed, I am free to say, that, much as I desire the road, I had far rather, that it never be built, than built upon the terms of this bill. But the road will be built. Private enterprise is abundantly adequate to the undertaking.[182]

If no private firm or individual desired to initiate such a project, Rep. Smith continued, well, "then it certainly would be a most unprofitable and unwise undertaking for Government."[183] In any event, such subvention of private concerns was in his view an illegitimate act of a federal government that ought to be strictly limited in its functions, lest it swell to tyrannical size.

Planking New York

If Virginia was the epicenter of anti–internal improvement politics, the state of New York was the cradle of creative private and state alternatives to national subsidy. The Empire State was the launching pad for the brief and feverish fad of plank roads, which from the mid-1840s till the mid-1850s were all the rage in the forested Mid-Atlantic and Midwest.

As economist Daniel B. Klein and historian John Majewski explain in *New York History*, plank roads were an import from Russia and Canada. Wooden planks from hemlock and other suitable trees were laid on the earthen roadbed; they "formed a hard flat surface upon which wagons could roll unhindered, with little discomfort to man or beast."[184] The first plank road in America was laid down in Salina, New York, near Syracuse, under the direction of a civil engineer named George Geddes, son of an Erie Canal engineer, who told the townspeople (and readers of *Scientific American*) that plank roads were durable, cheap, and all weather, and would produce sufficient toll revenue to replace the planks when they wore out.

Between 1847 and 1854, write Klein and Majewski, New York State incorporated nearly 350 plank road companies. Nationwide, entrepreneurs laid down more than one thousand plank roads, which were heavily concentrated in New York, Pennsylvania, Ohio, Michigan, and Wisconsin.[185] By 1857, New York, Pennsylvania, New Jersey, and Maryland had seven thousand miles of plank road valued at $10 million. Their cost of construction was approximately $1,500 to $1,800 per mile, compared to $7,500 per mile for the Lancaster Turnpike and $13,000 per mile for the Cumberland Road.[186] (The plank road experiment in the South, centered in Alabama, fizzled.[187] These roads were financed by private investors, though the states established statutory dimensions, maximum tolls, and inspections.)

Consistent with paeans to transportation advances throughout the ages, Matthew Vassar, founder of the college that bears his name and president of the Poughkeepsie and Stormville Plank Road Company, extolled the potential of plank roads, which he called "*people* roads," to "promote social intercourse among neighbors, afford ready dispatch for medical relief in cases of sickness by abridging distance, and remove all occasion for excuse to attend religious worship in bad weather." There would be friendship for the lonely, succor for the sick, balms for the soul, and the cohering of "the social fabric with stronger and more lasting bonds."[188]

Ah, but there was a rub. Boosters estimated the life of a plank road at a minimum of eight years, a maximum of twenty. The New York state legislature pegged the lifespan at a dozen years, with the prospect of extension. Each promoter sought to outdo his predecessors in forecasting a Methuselah-like duration for these wooden highways; a prediction of eternal life for the plank road was undoubtedly in the offing when the indisputable truth became too obvious to ignore. For in practice, they wore out after four years, and became downright dangerous, as "wagon wheels and the slender legs of horses" would slip through the cracks and gaps.[189] The cost of replacement—60 percent of the original cost of construction—was too steep, even with the toll increases permitted by the state legislature. Plank road companies busted in seriatim, one after another. The roads were abandoned or reclaimed by the earth; the planks rotted; the fad was over.

The plank road industry's reliance on private enterprise rather than state subsidy fit perfectly the fiscal conservatism of the 1840s, when states were enacting debt limitations and severely restricting new projects in various ways: for instance, by requiring a legislative supermajority or voter referendum for approval or limiting legislation to single projects so as to prevent Christmas tree bills laden with goodies.

Several states in the antebellum era—Wisconsin (1848), Michigan (1850), Maryland (1851), Minnesota (1858), and Kansas (1859)—actually forbade state public works entirely.[190] In Michigan, a constitutional provision announced that "the State shall not be a party to, or interested in, any work of internal improvement, nor engaged in carrying on such work."[191] This marked a sharp contrast with the mood of a previous generation, as when in 1820 the Missouri state constitution fairly boasted that "internal improvements shall forever be encouraged by the government of this State."[192] Forever was a lot briefer in those days. Even a dyed-in-the-wool Whig like New York governor William Seward, always a friend to energetic government, said in 1840 that "taxation for purposes of internal improvement finds no advocate among the people."[193] The ebb tide had come in. And then the war came.

Political scientist Stephen Minicucci has calculated that between 1790 and 1860, the US government spent \$119.8 million on internal improvements, with almost two-thirds of that (\$77.2 million) in the form of such indirect aid as land grants and revenue from land sales. Of the \$42.6 million in direct aid, a plurality went to navigation (\$14.9 million) and roads (\$10.4 million), with most of that (\$6.8 million) expended upon the National Road, "the single largest federal project of the antebellum era."[194]

The face of the country was changing; its Constitution had showed a certain flexibility, but that was nothing compared with the suppleness it was to display during the next great spasm of internal improvements. The great modern sociologist Robert Nisbet, in *The Sociological Tradition*, wrote that the state-sponsored development of "roads, canals, harbors, and other works of a semi-public nature ... relentlessly leads to a widened scope of governmental administration."[195] This Nisbetian axiom was confirmed along the smoothed surfaces of our next chapter's subject: the Good Roads movement.

2

Good Roads—or Here Come the Wheelmen!

JUST AS ASPHALT and concrete highways didn't directly follow the plank road, wagons and carriages didn't give way immediately to semi-trucks and sedans. First came the two-wheeler. The bicycle boom during the fifteen or so years between the late 1880s and early 1900s is a footnote today. Rubber tires and wheels of equal size made this almost century-old vehicle much easier and safer to ride than the ridiculous-looking high-wheeler bicycles; the innovative design also encouraged a proliferation of female users. The resultant craze saw domestic production skyrocket from 40,000 bicycles in 1890, on the cusp of the wave, to 1.2 million in 1896, or thirty times more. Observers estimated that in the *fin de siècle*, 2.5 million Americans rode bikes in a nation with "250 bicycle factories, 24 tire makers, and 600 concerns dealing in bicycle sundries."[1] Owners tended to be urban residents of the middle and upper classes. The contraptions were not inexpensive at first: the average price of a new bicycle was between $100 and $150 in 1893 and $80 in 1897 before plummeting to a far more affordable $3 to $15 in 1902.[2] But the craze never took root on the farm, where pedalers were viewed even more askance than peddlers.

The first warning sign of trouble came with the formation of that perennial ill omen: the creation of a lobby. Or, more charitably, an association of individuals united by mutual interest: in this case, bicycling. The League of American Wheelmen (LAW) was born in May 1880 at Newport, Rhode Island, the tony resort community, so it was not exactly an assemblage of horny-handed sons of toil. Bicycle men, writers, manufacturers—gentlemen all—sired the LAW, whose constitution pledged to "promote the general interests of cycling; to ascertain, defend and protect the rights of wheelmen; [and] to facilitate tour-ing."[3] The LAW welcomed "any amateur white wheelman of good character."[4] Its membership consisted largely of "clerks, bookkeepers, businessmen, and professionals."[5] Three-quarters of the LAW's members hailed from Illinois, Massachusetts, New Jersey, New York, Ohio, and Pennsylvania. The average bicyclist was far likelier to be a clubbable gent from Boston, even a Cabot or Lodge, than a Mississippi dirt farmer. As Gary Allan Tobin noted in the *Journal of Popular Culture,* "Massachusetts had more than twice the number of League members in its clubs than were enrolled from the twenty-six states of the Plains, Rocky Mountains, South, and Southwest combined."[6] They rode on Beacon Street; not so much in Dodge City.

Besides its promotion of vigorous physical activity and the joys of bicy-cling, which were facilitated by its publication of maps and guides and erec-tion of road signs, the LAW backed legislation expanding the rights of cyclists, such as securing their access to parks and roads. The LAW achieved its first notable legislative victory in 1887, when New York governor David B. Hill signed the "Liberty Bill," which was a major step toward the establishment of "the right of the bicycle to use any road that is open to the horse-drawn ve-hicle."[7] Other states followed New York's lead, as the LAW, backed financially by bicycle manufacturer Albert A. Pope, pursued the right of wheelmen and wheelwomen to the roads.

But the condition of those roads cried out for melioration, at least in the hearing of the cyclists. In 1888, the League, which had chapters in many states and cities, took on a new project: a major campaign for good roads to be coordinated by its National Committee for Highway Improvement, which published books and pamphlets about road paving and related matters. In 1889, the National Committee for Highway Improvement produced model legislative language to create state highway commissions and impose general taxes to pay for road improvements, but it found no takers. As an agrarian organization in Michigan scoffed, "The farmers must bear the expense while bicyclists and pleasure-riding citizens will reap the larger benefits."[8] So, the LAW retrenched. "We must concentrate first on education, then agitation, and finally legislation," said its president.[9]

A Roads Improvement Bureau was born, its mission the diffusion of propaganda supporting the cause. *Good Roads*, the League's magazine, had by 1895 a circulation of seventy-five thousand. League membership topped one hundred thousand. And the good news was propagated far and wide: between 1889 and 1900, the LAW distributed more than five million pamphlets.[10] Yet good roads enthusiasts found, as one historian lamented, "that educating the farmers, who were steeped in individualistic traditions, to the multiple benefits of good roads was frequently a futile undertaking."[11] (The phraseology suggests the problem with so much of the historiography of the subject: it accepts, unexamined, the progressive assumptions. Is preferring that decision making be kept local rather than transferred to state capitals, and the reluctance to subsidize through taxes the hobbies of others, in this case cyclists and automobile tourists, really a form of ignorance out of which farmers must be "educated"?)

Still, a sizable majority of farmers remained obdurate. What were the bicyclists to do? First you try to coerce 'em. And if you can't coerce 'em, seduce 'em. There were alternatives to this two-pronged strategy. For instance, Franklin Smith sought to instruct readers of *Popular Science Monthly* in the practical applicability of the laissez-faire philosophy of Herbert Spencer using the example of a campaign to "provide side paths along the country roads for bicycling" in Rochester, New York.[12] Smith related that in early 1896, the New York state legislature passed a bill that would have imposed a tax of one dollar on bicycles within Monroe County, Rochester's location, for the purpose of building such paths. The proposal was an outgrowth of an arrangement in nearby Niagara County under which all bicyclists were taxed in order to fund bike path construction throughout the county.

Smith denounced this idea as "indiscriminate," for the tax would fall on bicyclists both within and without Rochester, and on those who would and would not cycle along the paths. The bill called for an appointed five-person commission to select the paths and contractors and for the county treasurer to seize and sell at auction the bicycle of anyone who failed to pay the tax.[13] Smith flailed this legislation as "an amazing exhibition of selfishness, and of indifference to the rights of others" by those "impatient with the delay involved in voluntary enterprise."[14] Its advocates, he said, unthinkingly endorsed "the perfect propriety of coercing the bicyclists that did not care to contribute."[15] They were little better than thieves.

As an alternative to mulcting the unwilling, Smith proposed the radical idea that "those good people that want something done for their own benefit … pay for it themselves."[16] Why, he wondered, did those good people have such desiccated imaginations; were they incapable of sympathizing with the "poor owners of bicycles that had been forced to practice the most rigid economy to buy them—the shop girls, the mechanics and laborers, the servant girls and messenger boys"?[17] These others were what a kindred American soul of Herbert Spencer's, the sociologist William Graham Sumner, called *the forgotten men*. They paid the price of the schemes cooked up by the activists and the lawmakers and the busybodies.

Rochester's mayor and common council rejected the action of the state legislature, sparing the city's bicyclists the levy. But what happened next was Franklin Smith's object lesson in social reform, Herbert Spencer style. Voluntary associations dedicated to the construction of bike paths sprang up in Monroe County. Contributions poured in—and not only from hobbyists. "People that never rode a wheel gave," wrote Smith. "Nor were contributions confined to money; they included cinders, ashes, and gravel for the paths and team work from farmers." Paths were built for bicyclists, and fellowship followed, as they worked together in a common and voluntary cause. And, not incidentally, Smith found a sidestepping of "politics and politicians."[18]

Enacted elsewhere, bike taxation laws like that of New York were fought just as bitterly. An 1899 Oregon law permitting counties to tax wheelmen "funded the creation of nearly fifty-nine miles of six-foot-wide gravel path" throughout Portland, but a legal challenge by a Portland rider who objected to the $1.25 tax was upheld by the state supreme court.[19] Likewise, a similar law was struck down in the state of Washington.

In retrospect, for certain historians, a what-might-have-been quality to this era continues. James Longhurst, writing in the *Journal of Policy History*, says that we too often underestimate the bicycling era by reducing it to a charming, quaintly romantic outburst. Rather, he says, it provided, for a few short but tantalizing years, "an alternative vision of American transportation," as towns and cities were linked by dedicated bike paths—called side paths, with surfaces of gravel or cinder—financed by public and private sources, with a user-fee component. The bicycle, says Longhurst, seemed, if only briefly, "the future of technology," and the conveyance of choice for personal transportation.[20]

The moment vanished. There were isolated success stories, as in Minneapolis, where privately raised monies financed six miles of bike paths that were laid down by municipal employees.[21] But voluntary contributions proved insufficient to develop the extensive network of side paths envisioned by those who dreamed of a two-wheeled future in which bicycle paths connected New York City and Buffalo, Chicago and Minneapolis—indeed, all the larger cities of the United States. Politically, the movement never lost its upper-crust tincture, so that munificent subsidy thereof reeked of pandering to a special interest. It just seemed elite, twee, haughty.

If cycling's earliest political agenda had a libertarian aspect in seeking to deregulate the field of operations, it soon sought to enlist governments at various levels in the promotion of cycling, whether via the relatively unobjectionable emplacement of road signs or, much more controversially, increased financial support (state and federal) and more centralized control of road-building and maintenance through the creation of state road departments. This situation led to what one historian calls "recreational imperialism," as urban cyclists—tourists, essentially—made bold to dictate road policies to the natives: farmers and rural people who lived along, rather than merely recreated along, those roads.[22] A little dust or dirt was acceptable to the urban tourist as he pedaled away under the country sky, birdsong and distant dog barking filling his ears, but what some of those farm folk called "roads" seemed more like crags or quicksand to the Boston gentlemen and ladies out for a leisurely jaunt. Smooth roads for pedaling without a constant fear of collision with jags and bumps was their desideratum.

At first, the cyclists and their mouthpieces alternately mocked and castigated the farmers, setting up "a direct conflict between cosmopolitan and rural visions of what roads might be."[23] It was all very well for affluent bicycle tourists to issue their peremptory demands for better roads in the hinterlands, but those who actually lived in those hinterlands were, after all, the ones on whom the responsibility for maintaining these paths fell. This was their home. It was not a playground, or the setting of a vast infrastructure program or an experiment in uplift. Pouring salt in the wound, the cyclists "picknicked [*sic*] in [the farmers'] fields, helped themselves to fruit and flowers on private property, and wrote about farmers in patronizing dialect stories," writes Christopher Wells.[24] Their bicycles sometimes scared the horses; their extravagant plans for improving the roads scared the residents.

As Wells writes, "For well-heeled urbanites to invade their territory, insult their roads, and decry their public spiritedness struck rural Americans as the height of hypocrisy, especially since agricultural regions footed the bill for the upkeep and maintenance of rural roads."[25] The agrarian populist Farmers' Alliance, at its 1892 national convention, declared itself "unalterably opposed to, and would condemn any method proposing the bonding of state, county, or district for road building."[26] The farmer was not going to be debt saddled to aid the leisure activities of urban bicyclists and citified dandies. This was stated even more plainly by the Michigan Grange, which vowed hostility to legislation under which "the farmers must bear the expense, while bicyclists and pleasure-riding citizens will reap the larger benefits."[27] There was a class-based aspect to these sallies. They depicted the noble husbandman, the horny-handed son of toil, exploited by shrewd and decadent urbanites. Or as an Iowa farmer put the complaint in the vulgate at an 1893 convention, "We don't want any eastern bicycle fellers or one-hoss lawyers with patent leather boots, to tell us how to fix the roads we use."[28]

The propaganda machine of the LAW switched gears. Faintly derisive or sneering remarks directed at the humble yeoman were out; just as in the musical *Oklahoma* it was resolved that the farmer and the cowman should be friends, so was this amity now the goal for the farmer and the wheelman. As Christopher Wells phrases it, the challenge became "convincing farmers to view roads with different eyes, more modern eyes."[29] The arrival of a more modern technology helped. Bicyclists may have thought they were setting the pace, but they would be passed by and pushed off the track by a mode of transport many had at first viewed as an ally. One was Colonel Albert Augustus Pope, a New England bicycle manufacturer and inveterate promoter, a major sugar daddy of the LAW, whose later efforts at motor vehicle production would meet with desultory success and then plunge him into bankruptcy. Pope was hardly a disinterested participant in the debate over improving roads. As he told a convention of carriage makers in 1889, "Good roads mean for you and me better business."³⁰ So, he called for federal subsidy of roads, which he assumed would help the manufacturers of bicycles and carriages—the automobile had yet to come barreling over the hill. As late as 1903, Pope was remarking that "representatives of automobiling have been content to take a secondary place in the agitation" for good roads.³¹

Pope had pushed a petition drive, which in 1892 obtained close to 150,000 signatures, favoring the creation of a federal department of roads. A decade later he viewed motorists as essential allies, though their reputation was problematic. Like the cyclist, the owner of an early automobile created suspicion of upper crust–dom. Albert Augustus Pope, though, was both candor personified and dissembler. In an essay in *Munsey's Magazine*, Colonel Pope (notice how the honorific dignifies, or is meant to dignify, the product) was blunt to the point of being impolitic. He sympathized with the automotorist who, having bought a vehicle, "has nowhere to use it" and must "choose between bad roads and worse." Eschewing even the pretense of populism, Pope asked plaintively, "Why should so many of our foremost automobilists go to Europe every year to enjoy the pleasure of a tour?"³² Ought not the government ride to their rescue?

Pope conceded that the politics of the issue were complicated. Many Americans believed that autos were "a rich man's toy, or the horse's natural enemy." They would, he was certain, fight tooth, nail, and hobnail against subsidizing auto tourism. In fact, Pope said that he had known instances in which the endorsement of a good roads measure by an automobile club had spelled its death. This "prejudice," he shook his head, was something "which only time and education can overcome."³³ So the proper strategy was dishonesty. Or, rather, deception. "Automobile enthusiasts for good roads," he argued, "should hide their identity under a bushel." This is not to say that they should remain silent or inactive, merely that their true motive had to be disguised. "As ordinary citizens, their influence will be incalculable, for every automobilist is necessarily a man of some means and importance."³⁴ They should act in an individual capacity as men of stature rather than in their collective capacity as wealthy motorists seeking government assistance for their hobby.

These auxiliaries quickly assumed the lead position. As hard as they ped-aled, the cyclists were soon outpaced by automotorists. Wheelmen were ab-sorbed into a broader Good Roads movement in which automotive interests displaced them. As if to rub their faces into the macadam, the side paths on which they rode were often incorporated into the widened automobile-servicing roads. Until the resurgence of bike path enthusiasm in the late twentieth century, cyclists were forced to share the road with mechanical behemoths whose dominance was emphasized by a multisensory mélange of horn-honking, exhaust-spewing bravado.

Though the Ford Motor Company would later claim that the Model T "started the movement for good roads," this credit more properly belongs to the bicyclists of America.[35] The wheelmen had been the most articulate and influential promoters of good roads into the twentieth century, but then they gave way, for good, to the motorists, with whom they overlapped to a degree. (See Carlton Reid's *Roads Were Not Built for Cars* for an engagingly feisty defense of the early bicyclists of the Good Roads movement.)

* * *

Mockery of the poor state of rural roads was a staple of late nineteenth-cen-tury journalism, especially in progressive quarters. The crude, ill-maintained, barely passable path tended by indolent rustics was almost a stock character, along with the farmer's daughter, the traveling salesman, and the a-yup/nope laconic New Englander. And in the cities, the manure and urine deposited by horses was enough to overwhelm the senses of even possessors of the strongest olfactory organs. Improvers had a field day (which stretched out for decades) depicting the quicksand-like conditions in the sticks. "The dirt roads of America are heavy drinkers," editorialized *Good Roads Magazine* (1892) in the closest it ever came to humor: "They lead a staggering and uncertain course from town to town; smear themselves with thick mire; and for four months in the year are unfit for the company of respectable people."[36] It is worth noting that the editor of *Good Roads*, I. B. Potter, was a New York City civil engineer who did not, to understate matters, traverse daily the mudholes of the outlands.

Maintenance of rural roads was the chore of every able-bodied male of the community. Working off the "road tax" usually occupied a day or two or three of labor. As with conscription into the Union Army during the Civil War, one could buy his way out by paying an assessment, but the greater portion of the citizenry chose to take part in what were also social occasions. This cash road tax typically varied between $1 and $5 annually. There were fines for noncompliance, though instances of such appear rare. The work started when the rhythm of the community allowed it—that is to say, when the demands of farm life and labor were least pressing.

For instance, the New York statute read: "Every person owning or occupying land in the town in which he or she resides, and every male inhabitant above the age of twenty-one years residing in the town where the assessment is made, shall be assessed to work on public highways in such town."[37] As during the Civil War, Union men of means could purchase substitutes, who would take their place on the road gang in exchange for (usually) monetary considerations. Those people levied could also send horses, wagons, plows, or other useful instruments in partial payment of this tax. To progressives' consternation, men working off their road tax obligation often found time to converse, joke, sometimes drink, and otherwise engage in fellowship, rather than labor cheerlessly for the dictated eight hours of work per day for a few days per year of roadwork.

Township jurisdictions were too large for this intensely local work. Elected highway commissioners divided the towns into districts, which in turn elected overseers to supervise the work. Crews labored over the roads on which they were themselves dependent. This work was done not for the sake of attracting tourists, or easing the long-distance travels of strangers, but for the community itself. The road district, as historian Hal S. Barron writes, "embodied the principles of home rule and self-reliant independence that epitomized rural republican ideology."[38]

The neighborhood road crews worked with pickaxe and shovel, hoe and rake, ox and horse, and mule and plough. To some, this savored of democracy, of small-scale neighborliness, as the men of a village came together in common cause to keep and improve the roads that connected them with each other and to the broader world. But to progressives, such a grassroots system was "ignorant and inefficient," as Nathaniel Shaler sniffed in *Scribner's*.

The learned Shaler described these "road-making picnic[s]" with withering contempt:

> Arriving on the ground long after the usual time of beginning work, the road-makers proceeded to discuss the general question of road-making and other matters of public concern, until slow-acting conscience convinces them that they should be about their task. They then with much deliberation take the mud out of the road-side ditches, if, indeed, the way is ditched at all, and plaster the same on the centre of the road. A plough is brought into requisition, which destroys the best part of the road, that which is partly grassed and bush-grown, and the soft mass is heaped up in the central parts of the way. The sloughs or cradle-holes are filled with this material, or perhaps a little brush may be cut and heaped in, making a very frail support for the wheels. An hour or two is consumed at noon-day by lunch and a further discussion of public affairs. A little work is done in the afternoon, and at the end of the day the road-making is abandoned until the next year.[39]

A devastating picture, and faintly amusing as well, though one may wonder just how acquainted the Harvard professor and dean Shaler was with rural road tax days. One doubts very much that his hands ever grew calluses from wielding a shovel on road day.

Working out the road tax was adjudged "medieval" by progressive journalists and partisans, though it might just as well have been seen as small-scale democracy, or participatory democracy, in action.[40] Elected highway commissioners and overseers supervised the maintenance of roads in this decentralized and democratic system, which good roads advocates insisted was archaic and inefficient and badly in need of direction from a central authority, preferably located in the state capital or, in their fondest wishes, the national capital. Wage and convict labor on regular schedules they judged superior to farmers working out the road tax with their neighbors during convenient periods.

To good roads advocates, "sitting on the fence smoking clay pipes and swapping stale stories has long been synonymous with 'working out the road tax.'"[41] They seemed oblivious to, if not contemptuous of, the worries of rural tribunes that centralizing the administration of roadwork would drain the lifeblood from the local body politic. They found the phraseology of these rural critics of centralization, studded with words such as *tyranny* and *despotism*, absurdly overblown. Dire warnings that good roads reforms spelled the end of self-government and marked the ominous transferal of responsibilities from the human scale to the mass scale were belittled as the paranoid ravings of unlettered bumpkins.

The basic reforms demanded by the Good Roads movement seemed so arrantly obvious that they could scarcely conceive of legitimate grounds for opposition. Administration, they believed, should be shifted from districts to townships, and then further to the county or state level, except in the case of primitive roads in the most forlorn precincts; and the antiquated road tax and roadwork days should go the way of plank roads, to be replaced by general taxation. It frustrated the captains of road improvement no end that agrarian loudmouths would not concede the incontrovertibility of their case. "The farmers' fear of increased taxation stands seriously in the way of thorough road improvement," complained a Pennsylvania observer in 1890.[42] Many small farmers who bartered and grew primarily for home consumption operated within a cash-scarce economy; an annual levy would be a genuine hardship, whereas a few days working off the road tax were an opportunity for fellowship as well as making a contribution to the public weal. Cash poor but time rich, they also suspected advocates of good roads, especially engineers, of coveting not only tax dollars but tax-supported government positions as well.

Good roads, as Charles L. Dearing pointed out in his standard history of American highway policy, "did not arouse deep emotions or create bitter antagonisms," unlike slavery or prohibition, though it was not quite the slam dunk ("An improved highway system was a common good about which there could be no quarrel") claimed by Dearing.[43] (Why is it that some are so quick to assert that there can be *no quarrel* over certain political issues that have no particular moral or ethical issues involved? Was the centralization of power inherent in the demands of the Good Roads movement really beyond debate?) In any event, the movement was centripetal in both philosophy and practice. As early as 1870, wrote Dearing, "the academic writers on American highways realized that some centralized control was essential to the development of a system of modern highways built in accordance with the most progressive engineering ideas."[44]

Among the side benefits of a national system of roads, as the vice president of a Massachusetts paving company instructed readers of the decidedly pick-and-shovel-shy *Annals of the American Academy of Political Science*, would be the concomitant standardization of methods of road construction. A road made in Montana would be of the same material as a road made in Boston; regional variations or idiosyncrasies would be ground out by the regularization of roadbuilding practices.[45]

This was prescient. The National Road was the first American road macadamized, or surfaced with layers of stone, and this method prevailed on the finer-quality American roads into the early twentieth century. (The construction technique called *macadamizing* was an import from Scotland. An engineer named Thomas Telford, "the Colossus of Roads," surfaced roads with a gravel–crushed stone mixture, a method refined by the Scottish businessman John Loudon McAdam, who lent his name to the process, with the addition of a supernumerary *A*, and thus achieved transportation immortality.) Tar, asphalt, and brick were popular surfaces as the automobile age revved up, with asphalt eventually becoming the paving material of choice, so that almost 95 percent of America's two million miles plus of paved roads are today covered with asphalt.[46]

Instead of a burdensome source of taxation and a vexatious avenue for annoying cyclists or those newfangled automobiles, improved roads became a gift from on high to the farmer. They offered greater possibilities for social interaction with neighbors and promised packed church pews, gleaming and sophisticated consolidated schools, and children content at home, with young people enjoying more options thanks to these easily navigated roads. Their choice was framed for them: "Farmers could pay a cash tax to the government to finance road improvements, or they could pay a de facto 'mud tax'—in the form of higher transportation expenses—by moving their produce over the poor roads that already existed."[47] The third choice—the status quo of working off the road tax, or road labor days—was subtly omitted from the list.

Coxey's Army Goes Marching On

The Army of the Commonweal of Christ, best known as Coxey's Army, one of those mass marches of the age before protest was choreographed for television or ginned up by social media, began in Massillon, Ohio, on Easter Sunday, March 25, 1894, in the midst of a depression in which one-fifth of the nation's workforce was unemployed. The army, a picturesque group led by Jacob S. Coxey, a prosperous if eccentric businessman, began a trek to Washington to demand relief in the form of a good roads program. This brainchild of Coxey's blended two of his primary policy interests: a federal commitment to improving roads and a significant increase in the money supply.

Coxey proposed to kill the two malevolent birds of bad roads and depression with one giant stone: a "massive project of building and repairing roads around the nation."[48] This would give work to the unemployed, paid for by state- and county-issued bonds backed by $500 million in US government–printed paper money.[49] A job, paying $1.50 a day, would be available to anyone who wanted one. To pressure Congress into passing his scheme, Coxey envisioned and then led a march of the unemployed on Washington. The army was said to have simply been responding to an advertised need by the federal government. The US commissioner of agriculture had lamented in 1888 that "the common roads of the United States have been neglected and are inferior to those of any other civilized country in the world."[50] Why not raise an army to defeat this scourge?

Coxey was no down-and-outer. He owned a silica sand quarry in Massillon, bred (and bet on) racehorses, and was prominent in the inflationist Greenback Party. He'd also founded the Good Roads Association of the United States and published a newsletter in which he beat his favorite drums. The *Washington Post*, no friend to populist eruptions, headlined a story about Coxey "Candidate for an Asylum: The Crazy Idea of a Wealthy Resident of Massillon, Ohio."[51] He was no crazier than any other perfervid political enthusiast, though the fact that he named a son Legal Tender Coxey is no testament to his sanity. (Little Legal Tender, alas, died at age seven of scarlet fever.) Coxey's sidekick, a colorful labor radical and Buffalo Bill dress-alike from California named Carl Browne, explained that he was the Cerebellum of Christ and Coxey was Christ's Cerebrum; combine them, as the army had, and Congress would have no choice but to accept the demands of the Army of the Commonweal of Christ. Adding to the mystery, another leader of the army, a patent medicine quack named A. P. B. Bozarro, went by the appellation "The Great Unknown."

Carl Browne predicted that an army of one hundred thousand would descend on Washington to demand enactment of the good roads program. Perhaps one hundred marchers set out from Massillon, behind colors carried by Jasper Johnson, a black man from West Virginia, and his bulldog Bunker Hill.[52] The ragtag band that eventually showed up in the nation's capital, fortified by marchers joining from different towns and cities across the fruited plain, numbered perhaps four to five hundred.

The rights to assemble, petition, and speak were, it seems, nullities in Washington, DC. On May Day 1894, mounted police stopped Coxey, who hoped to address the marchers from the steps of the Capitol. When Carl Browne, dressed in fringed buckskin, declared, "I am an American citizen. I stand on my constitutional rights," he was beaten and arrested.[53] And for good measure the cops cuffed another entertainingly named member of the army, Christopher Columbus Jones. The charges were carrying banners on Capitol grounds and trampling the grass. Each miscreant got twenty days in jail. Over the next several weeks, ragtag bands of the unemployed would continue to march on the District of Columbia, unwanted by the authorities, unheard by the powers that be. Coxey's Army became a punchline, ridiculed by the press, briefly woven into popular culture by the phrase "enough food to feed Coxey's Army"—meaning that one has prepared far more comestibles than the meager turnout could ever eat. "Coxey's Army" became "a synonym for a tattered aggregation of disreputables."[54] As for Jacob Coxey, he lived to a Methuselahian age (ninety-seven), running for office frequently on various tickets (People's Party, Republican, Independent, Farmer-Labor, Union, and Democrat, among others) and marketing Coxe-e-Lax, a laxative.

Bills introduced by Senator William Peffer, a Kansas Populist, incorporated Coxey's ideas, but they went nowhere. Peffer's Good Roads Bill authorized the secretary of the treasury to "have engraved and printed ... five hundred millions of dollars of Treasury notes ... in denominations of one, two, five, and ten dollars, and to be placed in a fund to be known as the 'general county-road fund system of the United States.'"[55] The secretary of war was authorized to "take charge of the construction of the said general county-road system of the United States," paying laborers not less than $1.50 per eight-hour day.[56] For all the ridicule poor Coxey and his bedraggled followers endured, the Good Roads Bill was not entirely alien to the internal improvements tradition. During both the Great Depression and the late twentieth-century age of *Crumbling Infrastructure*, Coxey's plan to put the unemployed to work on the nation's roads would have been downright mainstream.

Good Roads—or Else!

General Roy Stone was the hard driver of the Good Roads movement. Stone, a civil engineer who went from Union College to the Union Army, performed heroically at the Battle of Gettysburg and enjoyed a postwar career that involved him in a series of infrastructure projects. With the encouragement of officials from the LAW, Stone in 1892 drafted legislation that would have created a National Highway Commission to act as a clearinghouse for information on the latest advances in roadbuilding and also plant the seeds for a national academy of road and bridgebuilding: a kind of pacific West Point for civil engineers.

The first national good roads convention met in Chicago in October 1892, coeval with the Columbian Exposition. It endorsed General Stone's bill and called for good roads organizations "planted, if possible, in all the School Districts of the country," a sign of the intertwined nature of good roads and school consolidation.[57] Riding the momentum, the second national convention was three months later, in Washington, DC.

General Stone's bill found sponsors in the US Senate and House of Representatives; he and the Wheelmen lobbied vigorously for its enactment, supported by an avalanche of letters and telegrams from LAW members. To those who questioned whether or not federal oversight or subsidy of roadbuilding was a legitimate and constitutional activity of the US government, Stone replied that this was but a "simple, harmless bill," at once a progressive advance but also utterly unobjectionable.[58] The United States had "the worst roads in the civilized world."[59] What kind of blinkered mossback could object to the mere dispensing of information? The states and counties were not capable of efficient road construction or maintenance; only the national government, which rose above petty and provincial concerns and saw farther, longer, deeper, could supervise the necessarily mammoth project of getting America up to speed.

Congress dropped the national school part of Stone's proposal but otherwise moved it along, albeit with a name change. The only person to testify before the House Agriculture Committee in opposition to the proposal was an official of the National Grange (which in 1907 would do a volte-face by endorsing good roads, specifically aid to farm-to-market roads). That is not to say that it met no hard questioning. When Rep. C. B. Kilgore (D-TX) asked, "Is not the purpose of that proposition to open a way to Federal supervision over dirt roads?," Rep. William Hatch (D-MO) assured him, "It is not; and there is not a member on the Committee who would entertain that proposition for a moment."[60]

The fib having been told, the measure was sold. Tucked into an appropriations act, it passed both houses of Congress, and lame-duck president Benjamin Harrison signed it into law in March 1893. Its road-relevant language read: "To enable the Secretary of Agriculture to make inquiries in regard to the systems of road management throughout the United States, to make investigations in regard to the best method of road-making, to prepare publications on this subject suitable for distribution, and to enable him to assist the agricultural colleges and experiment stations in disseminating information on this subject, ten thousand dollars."[61] The fact that this office was tucked into the Department of Agriculture says much about the politics of the matter—and which interest group the good roads enthusiasts were trying to court.

General Stone was the first chieftain of what was at first titled the Office of Road Inquiry (ORI). His superior, Department of Agriculture secretary Sterling Morton, a fiscal conservative whose conception of the proper sphere of the federal government did not overlap with that of Stone, instructed the general: "The Department is to furnish information, not to direct and formulate any system of organization, however efficient or desirable it may be. Any such effort on its part, would soon make it subject to hostile criticism."[62] Barred from making or directing the making of roads, the ORI was instead a clearinghouse, a disseminator of information, a publisher of bulletins, a laboratory tester of materials, a spreader of the gospel of good roads: a propagandist, in many ways, on behalf of enhanced government efforts to build roads.

As Earl Swift, author of *The Big Roads: The Untold Story of the Engineers, Visionaries, and Trailblazers Who Created the American Superhighways* (2011) writes, Stone's appointment was a flagrant case of "a lobbyist pushing for government action that he winds up leading."[63] It is a story that political economists know all too well, having told it for decades now: a government agency is created, and the business or sector that the agency is charged with regulating or overseeing captures its machinery and deploys it for the purpose of the aggrandizement of the business or sector. It is rare, though, for the chief promoter of the agency to have the keys to its bureaucratic kingdom. While the office's $10,000 annual budget was reduced to $8,000 because of the deep recession beginning in 1893, that was a mere speed bump in the road.

The ORI and the LAW quickly developed a symbiotic relationship. The ORI allowed the League to send out material supporting ORI initiatives using the government frank—that is, without cost, or, rather, at cost to those who paid the taxes. The LAW sometimes paid for the printing of ORI publications; it also paid expenses for ORI officials when they traveled to good roads meetings. Whether logrolling or back-scratching, the lobby and the government agency worked in concert to bolster their concerted power and influence. It is an old story, whether on two wheels or four.

An 1898 ORI circular titled *Must the Farmer Pay for Good Roads?*—the answer was no, at least not if the federal government picked up the tab—was sent to more than three hundred thousand farmers on a mailing list provided by the LAW, whose chairman of its Highways Improvement Committee, Otto Dorner, was its author.[64]

The ORI and its successors would publish technical bulletins and circulars about tires, brick paving, maintenance of country roads, new construction, and suchlike, as well as, in a more blatantly promotional move, the proceedings of good roads conventions—whose speakers, you may be assured, represented only one side of the issue. The propagandists were at the helm, and it was full throttle. General Stone was a frequent speaker at these conclaves, as well as before state legislatures. He assured attendees at one such gathering that the lack of good roads was the "last great stain upon our civilization."[65] (Jim Crow, anyone?). He threw out various estimates of the cost that subpar roads imposed on the US economy: $300 million annually, $600 million annually … the sky, it seems, was the limit.[66] This "bad-road tax" dwarfed the piddly sum Congress had appropriated for the ORI—why, an investment of twenty times as much would pay for itself!

Good roads men enjoyed topping each other in their estimates of how much bad roads cost the American farmer and consumer. J. A. Holmes of North Carolina threw out a figure of $10 million for his state; his counterparts in Maryland bid $3 million. To call these calculations back-of-the-envelope would be flattering them.[67]

General Stone stressed the need to counteract the "negative or hostile attitude of the rural population towards all effective legislation" regarding good roads.[68] Good roads propagandists insisted that the farmer would gain in increased trade and efficiency far more than he would pay in taxes. The putative "mud tax," or the alleged cost of nonimproved roads, which was calculated offhandedly by estimating the tonnage of farm products and the length they were hauled to market and throwing up a guess as to how much more rapidly they could be moved from farm to market over better roads, became a standard factoid. So, too, it was claimed, would the value of farmland rise, and social life be enriched, and church attendance would boom, and neighbors would see more of each other, and children would attend school with greater frequency.

President Theodore Roosevelt's Country Life Commission affirmed the salutary effects of better roads: "Highways that are usable at all times of the year are now imperative not only for the marketing of produce but for the elevation of the social and intellectual status of the open country."[69] Progressive uplift was in the air; the presumed vacuity of the social and intellectual life of the farm family was a target for urban uplifters, and if in the process the measures undertaken benefited urban dwellers, the well-off, and those ideologically committed to the expansion of governmental powers, well, these were said to be mere collateral benefits.

Moreover, road improvements hiked real estate values. As prominent geologist Albert Perry Brigham explained, "If a farm neighbourhood is reached by a good road, a heavy tax is lifted from each bushel of produce, and the region itself becomes a desirable place to live, and prospective buyers are as willing to pay for these benefits as for rich soils, heavy timber, good fences, and unfailing springs of water."[70] Good roads, by facilitating movement away from the farm, would actually encourage in-migration as well as stability of population, as young people would have incentive to stay at home in these newly thriving rural shires—or so argued the highwaymen. Church attendance, too, would rise. One rhapsodist theorized that roads bring people together, and "with a more intense mingling probably comes a higher degree of thought and culture."[71] Thank God this optimist never lived to see a Burt Reynolds *Smokey and the Bandit* movie.

Albert Perry Brigham, perhaps spinning fanciful daydreams conjured from his boyhood in Perry, New York, rhapsodized, "If the farmer and his wife, or particularly his sons and daughters, can finish their toilsome day and easily visit their neighbours three miles away in the evening, or enjoy the opportunities of the town, they will think better of rural life, and cease to rob the farm of its more intelligent and more ambitious men and women."[72] Who knows, perhaps Albert Perry Brigham himself might have stayed in Perry if only its rustic roads were not so rutted, so muddy, so dusty, so ice hardened, so impassable. (In fact, the rural population continued, unabated, its steady decline.) Brigham, once cranked up, could not stop. "The duties of citizenship will be better performed," he predicted, "and no longer will a rainy election day prevent a reasonably full expression of the political convictions of the rural voter. And he will be far more sure to have convictions which are worth recording in a ballot, for with good roads will come, in the end, the daily paper, the telephone, the habit of alert thinking, and prompt and forcible action."[73] Put another way, impassable roads would no longer be an impregnable barrier to propaganda, to yellow journalism, to scandal sheets, to the roorback and the guttersnipery of those who would persuade the isolated farmer to vote for Prohibition, for candidates favoring war or sedition laws or free stuff or whatever the charlatans and mountebanks of the day had promised, or threatened.

The trump card, played so consistently in American history, was that good roads were on the *right side of history*. They were progressive, favored by all forward-thinking and educated people. As the redoubtable Albert Perry Brigham concluded his exhortation to members of the American Geographical Society, "If America be the most progressive nation in the world, her citizens will not much longer endure medieval discomforts when they go out to mingle with their fellows and market the fruits of their fields."[74] Always, the fallback was the language of progressivism, of keeping up with the global

Joneses, of inevitability. Get out of the way, rube, because the road is coming, ready or not.

Farmers in New York fought the wheelmen and their taxing schemes on behalf of "the democratic ideal of community self-government," and, not incidentally, low taxes, writes Michael Fein.[75] In response, their venerable system of road maintenance was mocked as "the old plan of loafing out a road tax under the direction of incompetent pathmasters" by the likes of Albert Perry Brigham, who before becoming a noted geologist had grown up in rural New York, among these loafers and incompetents.[76] How scornful men can be when they rise above their raising.

* * *

President McKinley's secretary of agriculture, "Tama Jim" Wilson, gave General Stone a much longer leash than had the parsimonious and cautiously constitutionalist Cleveland administration, and he took advantage of it. Authorized to "prepare didactic reports and statements upon the subjects of road making and road management suitable for publication and distribution as bulletins of this Department," the general was not loath to wax didactic.[77] He took to didacticism like a vulture to roadkill, telling a Buffalo convention of schoolteachers to "preach Good Roads" in the classroom.[78] (General Stone took several months out from his road evangelism in 1898 to participate in the occupation of Puerto Rico during the Spanish-American War. Alas for him, the rainy season undermined his ambitious roadbuilding plans on the island, while his lobbying campaign for promotion to major general was foiled by President McKinley. Stone resigned his position at ORI in late 1898, replaced by Martin Dodge, though he stayed a staunch advocate of good roads.)

In 1899, the ORI became the Office of Public Road Inquiries, or OPRI, and ramped up its object-lesson road program, supervised by Asbury Park, New Jersey's General E. G. Harrison. Under this program, the boss sent out a team of builders by rail to construct road segments of from one-half to one and one-half miles in towns thought in need of enlightenment. When the segment was finished, the people of the surrounding area were invited to inspect it and listen to a lecture by General Harrison elucidating the marvels they were seeing. The road show, which would build over four hundred object-lesson roads, chugged along from stop to stop, bringing its traveling mercies to cowtowns and midsized burgs and even larger cities. The hope was that in each town, this edifying lesson would beget a local chapter of the Good Roads Association.

The railroad companies eagerly cooperated in this program, though they would have reason to rue this cooperation later. Though its president grumbled that it was "a large amount to throw in the mud," the Illinois Central Railway, for instance, spent $50,000 at the turn of the century to assist in setting up road conventions and object lessons all the way from Chicago to New Orleans.[79] After all, good roads would facilitate the movement of farm produce to the railroads. The idea that improved roads themselves were fully equipped to serve as means of conveyance seemed fanciful, or at least far off.

The public relations offensive of the ORI and OPRI would be the envy of any Hollywood publicist. By 1912, as the contemporary historians of the Federal Highway Administration (FHWA) note, its "27 lecturers were giving 1,139 lectures," while its in-house publicists were giving copy to over 2,500 newspapers reaching ten million Americans.[80] The practical and even moral case for good roads—or, more accurately, for state and national subsidization of road construction and improvements—was ubiquitous in the national press, as "between 1910 and 1915, it is safe to say that no national issue received greater coverage in the country and city newspapers."[81]

* * *

Liberation from government service can liberate the tongue. Though General Roy Stone had never been coy about his warm feelings toward federal involvement in roadbuilding, in retirement he exulted to the National Good Roads Convention in St. Louis that "good roads are coming whether by easy ways or hard. Federal aid is in the air; our young statesmen are eager to promote it, and our oldest no longer have the cold shivers when it is mentioned. It has reached the very top"[82] (by which he meant President Theodore Roosevelt, who addressed that same April 1903 convention on the subject of "Good Roads as an Element in National Greatness"). Given that the United States was now "the mightiest republic that the world has ever seen," the president orated, its citizens "have a right to demand that such a nation build good roads."[83] The National Good Roads Association whose convention the president addressed was, in essence, a partner—and not necessarily a junior partner, or helpmeet—to the OPRI.

Martin Dodge, General Stone's successor, made explicit the link between the internal improvements movement of the early republic and the Good Roads movement in a 1900 piece in the *League of American Wheelmen Magazine*. Titled "Ideas of Clay and Calhoun: A Return to Them Is Now Imperative," Dodge referenced the bicycle, the automobile, and the suburban streetcar and their need for "rapid and permanent improvement" of the highways on which they ride. Just as the federal government appropriates money for the improvement of rivers and harbors, Dodge argued—if *argued* is not giving too much credit to his peremptory assertion—that "no one can deny the justice" of a claim for federal support of these overland methods of transportation. "National Platforms of both the great political parties" should incorporate a demand for federal support, concluded the OPRI director.[84] So much for refraining from politicking!

Yet Dodge was careful in his 1901 OPRI report to insist that his nascent bureaucracy was in no way a passkey to the federal treasury for the Good Roads movement. He called it a "misconception which appears to exist in the minds of some to the effect that increased appropriations for this work may lead to National aid."[85] Perish the thought! And when the OPRI's budget trebled to $30,000 in 1903, that augured nothing more than that the federal government was, as ever, avid and eager to increase the sum of human knowledge without augmenting its power one whit. And one fruit of that knowledge: the revelation in 1904 of an America dappled by 2,151,570 miles of rural public roads and 1,598 miles of toll roads with stone surfaces. Total public expenditures on these roads in 1904 were $79.77 million, only $2.6 million of which came from the states.[86]

The Dawning of a New Age

No sooner had Coxey's Army met defeat than inventors in Europe and America were by trial and error groping their way toward a gasoline-powered automobile. In 1895, a Rochester, New York, patent attorney and tinkerer named George Selden obtained a US patent for an "improved road engine." Numerous other Americans were at work in the same field, most of them outpacing lawyer Selden, who would lose a landmark patent infringement case against Henry Ford.[87] The Duryea brothers of Springfield, Massachusetts, sold the first American-made gasoline automobile in 1896, and as the nineteenth century came to a close, speculation grew about the potential of these self-propelled vehicles to replace the horse. (That same year saw the founding of the first automobile club, the American Motor League.)

In 1899, thirty American manufacturers turned out 2,500 automobiles.[88] The turn of the century, an occasion for taking stock and making predictions, found Americans anticipating that the automobile would soon graduate from curiosity to everyday means of conveyance. The press acted in virtual unanimity as a cheerleader for this latest fad. Promoters and enthusiasts began undertaking lengthy trips, including multiweek, cross-country jaunts, to show the potential of the automobile, though the mud and dust and ice of the primitive roads posed formidable challenges to the intrepid traveler.

The automobile would prove a revolutionary development in human history. It greatly facilitated movement of both persons and goods, generated opportunities for trade and employment that were previously unimaginable, and gave people a far wider range of choices in where to live and work. But these extraordinary benefits were not without cost—costs measured not only in dollars and cents, but also in lives lost and lives displaced. In his study of the American adoption of the automobile, James J. Flink, professor of comparative culture at the University of California, Irvine, wrote that "since its introduction in the United States in 1895, the motor vehicle has been the most significant force shaping the development of modern American civilization."[89] Just a partial list of its consequences, its achievements, and its costs include the assembly line, great advances in getting goods to market, population dislocations, environmental effects, increased mobility, the birth and growth of mammoth associated industries (including oil and gas), suburbanization, the consolidation of rural schools, the destruction of city neighborhoods by interstate construction, altered courtship patterns and leisure activities, NASCAR and stock car culture, inspiration behind numerous films and pop music songs, accidental deaths numbering now in the millions—the list could be extended indefinitely.

The livery stable and the horseshoer rapidly disappeared from cities, though not, of course, from the countryside. (In 1908, the farm horse population was almost twenty million, while there were 198,000 registered motor vehicles.[90]) The animal and the machine seemed to many inimical; there wasn't enough room in this town, or at least on this avenue, for the both of them. One populist congressman, Rep. William "Alfalfa Bill" Murray of Oklahoma, proposed separate paths for horses and autos, so that never the twain would meet.[91]

Flink notes that "horse breeders, livery stable owners, and horse-drawn vehicle drivers' associations are the only groups for which a clear case of vehement opposition to the motor vehicle can be clearly established."[92] They protested the dangers posed by the speed of these horseless carriages and called for banning them from the public roads. Occasionally, of course, these early automobiles were seen as symbols of wealth and conspicuous consumption, but the employment provided by the burgeoning industry quelled class resentments. Yet many farmers and rural people objected to automobile tourism as disruptive to good farming and husbandry practices, though few went so far as the farmers near Rochester, Minnesota, who "plowed up roads, making them unsuited to automobile travel but still passable by horse and carriage."[93] For the most part, rural hostility to the automobile was limited to advocacy of speed limits and their enforcement and resistance to progressive good roads proposals.

In response, automobile owners pointed to the usual language regulating the speed of horse-drawn conveyances—"reasonable and proper"—and suggested that the same standard govern motor vehicles.[94] Given the far greater potential for speed of motorized vehicles, this suggestion was a nonstarter, and so statutory limits were imposed, perhaps most notably in New York, which in 1901 set a generous limit of twenty miles per hour on motor vehicles traveling within its boundaries. Speed limits in most states of the early automobile age ranged from twenty to thirty miles per hour, though there were states that posted no limits.

Certain intellectuals, too, looked with disfavor on these motorized four-wheelers. A British MP of Independent Liberal affiliation with the evocative name of Cathcart Watson called cars "slaughtering, stinking engines of iniq-uity," which outdoes even the automobile-hating Russell Kirk, the American conservative man of letters, who dubbed them "mechanical Jacobins."[95] With perhaps only five to eight thousand automobiles scattered throughout the entire country, the industry was a bit player in the Good Roads movement of 1900, though within the decade that would change. There was no shortage of roads in preautomobile America: in 1904, total road mileage within the United States exceeded 2.15 million. But just 7 percent of those miles "had been improved with gravel, shell, oil, or some other substance."[96] And in eleven states, less than 1 percent of the roads were improved. Road conditions were best in New England and the Mid-Atlantic states, and worst in the South and the rural Midwest. In 1904, the Office of Public Roads (OPR) reported surfacing of just over 7 percent of American roads, typically with gravel. By 1909 that figure was 8.66 percent, a meager advance.[97]

A 1908 article in *Scientific American* titled "The Political Economy of Good Roads" claimed that while "the superb roads" of Europe enabled its farm produce to be hauled for just "12 cents a ton a mile," the "frightful conditions of almost all American roads" made the comparable figure in the United States fully twenty-five cents a ton a mile.[98] Given that, according to *Scientific American*, the average trip to market for American farm products was 9.4 miles, the savings to the American farmer if his roads were in the allegedly superb condition of European roads would be $1.23 a ton a mile.[99] The good roads partisans were making pocketbook, or bank account, appeals.

The Post Office Delivers

The Post Office Department was another agency of the federal government that encouraged good roads, in this case, through the development of rural free delivery (RFD) to homes. No longer would farm folk have to travel into town to the post office to retrieve their mail; the US government would bring it straight to their door. This innovation was greeted by many country people as a great benefit, but it came with a catch: the post office would only deliver along rural routes with passable, or passably improved, roads. Boulder-strewn paths, mountains of snow, brown pools of mud: all that *neither rain, nor snow, nor heat, nor gloom of night* bravado did not apply to delivery in the hinterlands. (And to this day, the US Postal Service will tell you that this creed is *not* its official motto.[100])

The locals made pledges of improvement, and the post office held them to their pledges. As Wayne E. Fuller writes in his history of RFD, postal inspectors surveyed the roads twice yearly, and if they found them subpar, they ordered repairs. Starting in 1906, the OPR also got in on the action; on request from the post office, OPR engineers inspected questionable roads and issued directions to local authorities for their melioration. "Nothing else brought the sense of urgency to the Good Roads movement that rural delivery did," says Fuller, and that urgency was nudged along by the Post Office Department and the OPR, which the OPRI had been retitled in 1905.[101] (It would undergo more name changes than a grifting con man: in 1915 the office would receive an appellative upgrade to the Bureau of Public Roads; in 1939 it would become the Public Roads Administration, reverting to the Bureau of Public Roads a decade later; and in 1967 it was subsumed under the Federal Highway Administration [FHWA].)

The constitutional authority to provide post roads was the most effective entering wedge the good roads people had found, and they exploited it for all it was worth. As an observer wrote with great satisfaction in 1904, "In some cases it has been necessary to threaten discontinuance of the delivery service unless the roads were improved, and results have been forthcoming. Thus public policy and private interest conspire to the great end."[102] Some might call this blackmail. But the spread of RFD virtually transformed every rural road into a post road, thus bringing it within the ambit of constitutional legitimacy.

Erstwhile champions of states' rights found wiggle room to change their views. Colonel J. M. Faulkner of Alabama, a Confederate veteran, told a good roads conference that while he was still "a strict constructionist of the Constitution of the United States," he recognized that "good roads and good mail delivery go hand in hand." Given that the American people "are entitled to both," he cheerfully stretched that strict constructionism just far enough to take in federal aid to rural roads.[103]

On the front lines, the rural mail carrier reported on impassable or poorly maintained roads, and local road commissioners were usually quick to respond to any complaints, lest the mail was interrupted. (Early RFD was nonmotorized, of course; the horse was the means of locomotion, although the post office began experimenting with motor vehicles to collect mail from street boxes as early as 1896.) Because a carrier's pay was likely withheld if he did not complete his route, the carrier was avid for the removal of any obstacles to doing so. Rain, snow, sleet, the dead of night: there wasn't much a letter carrier could do to alter these; they simply endured. But muddy or dusty or rutted roads: a simple threat to abort delivery could lead directly to speedy efforts at remediation.

To drive home the reality of who was boss and who was supplicant, the post office required officials in towns whose approval for RFD was borderline or touch and go to sign this pledge reeking of subservience and deference: "I have been informed that you are about to recommend the establishment of rural free delivery mails in my section, but that you hesitate to do so on account of the bad roads. I assure you that I will do all that I can to improve the roads over which you recommend the establishment of rural free delivery."[104] All that was missing was a tug on the forelock and a beseeching *pretty please*? Notably, the Southern states were pressured to improve their infrastructure if they wanted the postman to knock once, not to mention twice. In 1900, the post office turned down a large majority of petitions for RFD received from Mississippi (92 percent) and North Carolina (87.5 percent).[105]

Within a dozen years of the inauguration of RFD, the US Post Office Department estimated that rural roads had been improved to the tune of more than $70 million.[106] The carrot and stick were working in perfect harmony. By 1908, "46,369 RFD routes served about 4,125,000 families along 975,000 miles of road."[107] Everyone likes getting the mail; rural politicians took notice. And as OPR director Logan Waller Page noted, RFD was an efficacious way of ensuring that "correct methods of road building and road maintenance will be introduced into practically every section of the United States."[108] Thus would a kingdom be built. RFD and the bicycle formed a potent and mostly forgotten one–two combination in the fight to win national support of better roads.

* * *

No sooner had the fledgling automobile industry hatched than it produced that most predictable, often lamented, chancre on the body politic: an automobile industry lobby. Though consisting of various parts, a common interest united it: increased government spending on industry infrastructure. In time, the lobby comprised, among other components, the American Automobile Association, the Portland Cement Association, the American Road Builders Association, the National Brick Paving Manufacturers Association, the Rubber Association of the United States, and the various regional associations of highway officials and engineers, whose powerful national voice was the American Association of State Highway Officials, or AASHO, a tricky pronunciation. (Today it styles itself the American Association of State Highway and Transportation Officials, or AASHTO.)

The American Automobile Association, or AAA, founded in 1902, asserted its position as the voice of the motorist. Today we think of the AAA as the organization that peddles insurance, offers maps and jumps, and, most importantly, dispatches a tow truck when your car breaks down. But the AAA was present at the creation of the lobby. The AAA's president, W. E. Scarritt, offered a predictive toast at a 1904 Waldorf-Astoria dinner featuring Rep. Walter Preston Brownlow, Senator Asbury Churchwell Latimer, Martin Dodge, Colonel Pope, and others. Scarritt said that his organization "stands for three things—good roads, good law, and good behavior. The automobile is the last word of engineering skill. Yesterday it was the plaything of a few, today it is a servant of the many, tomorrow it will be the necessity of humanity."[109]

If the early clashes in the good roads crusade pitted farmers versus bicyclists, then tourists, and then car owners, the AAA was the bumptious spokesman for the last named. The question, as Rep. John Marshall Robison (R-KY) asked, was "Do we want to create a 'tourist' system of roads or strengthen and build up our present 'farm-to-market' system? Do we want to destroy the 'producers-to-consumers' system and install a 'joy-rider' system?" The AAA and the city interests "want to take care of the joy riders of America. They nowhere seem concerned about the farmers getting their products to market or the millions of consumers in these cities having the benefit of these products,"[110] huffed the congressman. Nor were they much concerned with matters of federalism. The AAA and the National Automobile Chamber of Commerce went as far as to support *federal* registration of all motor vehicles.[111]

Washington's Concern?

Coincident with the advent of the automobile were the first serious efforts at federal sponsorship of roads—though these roads were still traversed by four-legged beasts and four-wheeled wagons or carriages rather than motorized vehicles. In 1902, Rep. Peter Otey (D-VA) proposed a federal appropriation of $100 million to create a Good Roads Fund to aid the states with roadbuilding. This was a case of defining the outer limits of debate, as the measure had no real chance of passage.[112] In a sense, this was the coming-out party for those who sought an extensive federal role in the field. General Roy Stone told the 1903 National Good Roads Convention that while in 1892 "we dared not whisper, 'National aid to road building' save in secret; now we can shout it on all the highways and byways."[113] Finally, the truth could be told; they need not dissemble anymore. Well, not dissemble much, anyway.

Achieving a higher public profile were bills introduced early in 1904 by Rep. Walter Preston Brownlow (R-TN) and Senator Asbury Churchwell Latimer (D-SC), which in combination marked the first tentative steps toward federal involvement in road construction. Senator Latimer, representing a state that had jealously guarded its rights as it conceived of them in the century previous—though it had also produced John C. Calhoun, author of the Bonus Bill—proposed the expenditure of $24 million, divided equally over three years, doled out to the states proportionate to their population for the purpose of aiding in the improvement or construction of public roads. Later, these would become matching grants, as the states had to put up equivalent amounts to receive the bounty. An appointed Bureau of Public Highways would administer the monies, planted within the Department of Agriculture.

Senator Latimer insisted on the justness of federal aid. The US mail, the US military, and all manner of interstate commerce used the roads. What more justification did he need? The "mud tax" was bogging down the entire country, not just its rural backwaters.[114] Senator Latimer's bill would winch America out of the mire. Rep. Brownlow could point to the equivocal remarks of President Theodore Roosevelt, fellow Republican, who had declared, "We sympathize with and approve of the policy of building good roads" in his annual message of December 7, 1903, though the president forbore mentioning federal aid.[115]

The *Washington Post* derided the Brownlow-Latimer legislation as "stupendous paternalism"—how times change!—to which Rep. Brownlow retorted, "Paternalism is a club with which public men try to kill off measures to which they are opposed."[16] Well, yes, though it is hardly an empty word, devoid of meaning. It denotes a government that has usurped functions properly belonging to individual, family, or community, as, in the case of the last named, roadbuilding once was. The Senate Committee on Agriculture and Forestry approved the Brownlow-Latimer bill, but it stalled in Congress. It would be resurrected in various and multiple forms over the next dozen years, but not until 1916 would the Congress enact a program of federal aid to highways.

By now the constitutional objections were nugatory, at least as far as the federal legislature and courts were concerned. In *Wilson v. Shaw* (1907), a case regarding the Panama Canal, Supreme Court justice David J. Brewer located "the power of Congress to construct interstate highways" within the federal government's right to regulate interstate commerce. And as the indefatigable FHWA historian Richard F. Weingroff notes, in 1915 the Joint Committee on Federal Aid in the Construction of Post Roads casually disposed of the once-weighty question of the constitutionality thereof in three airy paragraphs:

> The constitutionality of the appropriations [for the National Road] was supported chiefly upon some one or all of the following express Federal powers: To establish post roads, to regulate commerce, to declare war, to provide for the common defense, to promote the general welfare.
>
> Among those of legal training a technical discussion of the constitutionality of national highway appropriations would no doubt be interesting, but we believe the time has long since passed when controversy over this question could be deemed appropriate. Even a cursory review of the ever-expanding activities of this Government, covering the purchase of Louisiana and Alaska, the improvement of harbors and interior rivers, appropriations for educational work, construction of reclamation projects, purchase of private lands for the formation of public forest reserves for protection of watersheds, demonstrates that a discussion of the constitutional question is purely academic.

Federal aid to good roads will accomplish several of the objects indicated by the framers of the Constitution—establish post roads, regulate commerce, provide for the common defense, and promote the general welfare. Above all, it will promote the general welfare.[117]

And those alleged ancillary benefits were a powerful selling point. As Senator John H. Bankhead (D-AL), who had pushed unsuccessfully for a $500,000 appropriation to improve rural post roads, said in 1909, "Good roads will make farm life attractive; they will bring the isolated dweller closer to his neighbor, and I feel confident they will check the movement of our rural population to the great cities."[118] Perhaps they lessened the isolation of the farm dweller, but Bankhead's other prediction was well wide of the mark. The rural population of the United States has been in constant decline since, from 60.4 percent of the total US population in 1900 to 48.8 percent in 1920, 43.5 percent in 1940, 30.1 percent in 1960, and, as the interstate was completed and the Good Roads movement can be said to have been rendered irrelevant, 26.3 percent in 1980.[119]

Cradle of the DMV

As was the case a century earlier with canals, those states and localities that had built and kept a network of passable roads looked askance at those with poorer roads who came crying to Washington for funding.

New Jersey, in 1891, was the first state to aid localities in building and keeping roads: it contributed one-third of the cost of such work done by its counties. In exchange for this aid, localities ceded a measure of authority over their roads to the state government. The trade-off was local control for cash. It was a trade that, in time, localities within every other state would make. Massachusetts followed suit two years later and upped the ante, paying up to three-quarters of the cost for road projects. (All three of the original members of the Bay State's highway department were also members of the LAW.[120]) As with other such reforms, eastern states (Connecticut, Maryland, New York, Vermont) were first on board the bandwagon, with California (1895) a western outlier. Most likely, the Golden State legislature had a faint presentiment that the automobile was going to be big doings down the road. The last of the old forty-eight states to offer aid in the matter of roadbuilding were Indiana and South Carolina, which tagged along in 1917.[121]

In 1904, property and poll taxes represented the largest component (67.5 percent) of the revenues raised for roadwork, followed distantly by road taxes and labor (24.8 percent), state and local bond issues (4.4 percent), and state aid (3.3 percent). *Federal aid* was not even a line item on the balance sheet. A decade later, state aid had risen to 10.2 percent of the revenue stream, with the North Atlantic states the most generous, or spendthrift, at 26.6 percent, and the states of the South Atlantic and South Central regions the most frugal at 3.8 and 1.7 percent, respectively. By 1921, regional variations had lessened, if not disappeared: the national average of state aid as a percentage of the revenue source of roadwork was 48.7, with regional figures of 56.9 for the South Atlantic, 54.6 for the North Atlantic, 53.4 for the West, 46.5 for the North Central, and 34.1 for the South Central.[122]

* * *

In 1901, New York, then as now not averse to firing up the paperwork machine, was the first state to institute compulsory motor vehicle registration. After a two-year hiccup, New York's neighbors Connecticut, Massachusetts, New Jersey, and Pennsylvania joined the club in 1903, as did Minnesota and Missouri. By 1905, twenty-three states required registration, and the last of the holdouts, Louisiana, had fallen in line by 1914.[123] American motor vehicle registration mushroomed from 78,000 in 1905 to 458,500 just five years later.[124]

Automobile owners contested these laws early on, arguing, for instance, that since horse-drawn carriages did not require compulsory registration nor should automobiles. States ignored this argument. Registration was not, at first, a money grab by state legislatures. The fees "were barely sufficient to cover the cost of administering the regulatory measures," noted James W. Martin in his account of the early history of automobile registration.[125] Typically, these fees promised "perennial registration": pay once and your vehicle never needs registering again. (Revenue-seeking state officials would soon correct that mistake! All states required annual registration by 1921, with Minnesota the last to fall in line.) Mostly, these were also flat fees that made no distinction between cars and trucks, or among horsepower levels, gross weight, or tire size. Such gradations were introduced in 1906 in New Jersey, Ohio, and Vermont, which charged more steeply for higher-horsepower vehicles.[126] In subsequent years, most states charged varying rates for pleasure cars, commercial cars, trucks, motorcycles, taxis, and other forms of motorized transportation, although, consistent with the principles of federalism, there was no uniformity in these levies. States, as Justice Brandeis said, were the laboratories of democracy. In early years, horsepower was the most common basis of registration fees (nineteen states used this standard of measurement in 1924), with weight (thirteen) and a combination of horsepower and weight (eight) next in line. The other states based this fee on such standards as selling price and cubic inch displacement, or, in certain cases, they kept a flat-rate charge.[127]

The rationale for these fees, or taxes, was that motorists required governmental services *qua* motorists: roads and road maintenance, signs, and other aids to the regulation of traffic, and law enforcement. Across the ocean, Herbert Asquith, the chancellor of the exchequer of Great Britain, endorsed such a levy on automobiles, though with a haughty twist, saying that it would be an "almost ideal tax, because it is a tax on a luxury which is apt to degenerate into a nuisance."[128] The chancellor, also known as the First Earl of Oxford and Asquith, was vilified by classical liberals for his fondness for taxes and imposts, though in this case there seems to have been a supercilious disdain of motorized vehicles at work, too. His successor as chancellor, Lloyd George, secured taxes on automobiles (based on horsepower) and gasoline, proceeds of which were shipped to local governments by a central Road Board.[129] The Road Fund made a fat and tempting target for a succession of chancellors of the exchequer, among them Winston Churchill and Neville Chamberlain, who raided it for purposes other than road maintenance or construction. As a result, writes James A. Dunn Jr., "spending on highways in Britain stagnated" during the middle years of the twentieth century, and congestion worsened considerably.[130]

Back in the States, by 1912, the number of registered motor vehicles approached one million (944,000), though these numbers are unreliable, for only gradually did states end the practice of "perennial registration," so that unused or discarded vehicles were still counted in their inflated numbers.[131]

The earliest owners of automobiles were higher-income men, most prominently physicians, who used the vehicles in their practices, but ownership soon became widespread, among not only the urban middle class but also the more prosperous farmers. Ownership lagged in the South, which was cash poorer than the rest of the country; in 1910, the eight states with the lowest ratio of auto registration to population were, in descending order, Oklahoma, West Virginia, Arkansas, Florida, Alabama, Mississippi, Tennessee, and Kentucky.[132] Nonetheless, the motor vehicle had embedded itself in American life and the American landscape.

Down on the Farm

Rural people often distrusted the good roads gang, suspicioning a scheme to increase their tax burden and erode their self-government. There was, in Pennsylvania, a Farmers' Anti-Automobile Association; a Farmers' Anti-Automobile League, founded in Evanston, Illinois, proposed at its 1909 convention in Montana that its members "give up Sunday to chasing automobiles, shooting, and shouting at them."[133] In New York, one farmer complained, "If you abolish the road system, you add a large percentage, I think about twenty-five, to the already too heavy cash tax the farmer must pay. Now the farmer can pay his road tax in labor of self, teams, tools, and hired men, and when his crops are not suffering for work." Centralization of authority, he continued, "will increase the horde of engineers, superintendents, contractors, & c. After a little while, dishonest, lazy, incompetent inefficient men would do your road work even worse than is now complained of. We hard working, discouraged, overtaxed farmers want improvements but not revolution."[134]

His was not a lone voice in New York, which had a long history of spirited resistance to centripetal forces. A New York pathmaster warned that these good roads reforms represented "one of the greatest centralizing tendencies of the age." He pled, "Let not the State enter the business of road-making.... The problem will be solved in the good old democratic way by each district working out its own highway tax."[135] Nor did all these cries of protest arise from the sticks. An urban critic of the Good Roads movement from New York's Queens County said, "It is always easier to advocate the expenditure of other people's money than it is to put our hands into our own pockets."[136]

Even with tentative steps toward state funding of roads, foes feared the "entering wedge" of a profligate and tyrannous system. The *New York Times* mocked these libertarian recusants for a "ridiculous display of ignorance."[137] The elite press haughtily dismissed rural concerns. When a pair of reforms went down to defeat in New York in 1896 and 1897, the *New York Times* blamed the "whole soggy mass of rural conservatism."[138] Objections to taxation and centralization—the pith of the American Revolutionary cause in 1776—were now pooh-poohed as the perversions of reactionary yokels.

After meeting ferocious rural resistance to the abolition of the local road tax, among other reforms, New York legislators decided to buy off the country folk. Disbursals from the state legislature were proving too mingy for the most fervent good roads advocates, so in 1905 they presented New Yorkers with a proposal that the state finance highway work with a $50 million bond issue. It passed with 76 percent of the statewide popular vote, losing in just three of New York's rural counties. Though automobile owners lobbied hard for the bill, their efforts were marginal, with only 8,625 autos registered in New York in 1905. Rather, as Michael R. Fein writes, "fiscal conservatism" was "decidedly rejected" in a harbinger of the Empire State's early twentieth-century embrace of progressivism, aided by a cannily inserted provision that distributed the $50 million equally among counties, regardless of need or population.[139] In time, farmers around the nation would make their peace with the good roads lobby, depriving it of an effective counterweight and giving the highwaymen an open road.

* * *

The steady march of good roads cut its swath early through Iowa, which in 1904 ranked third among states in total road mileage (Texas and Missouri were first and second), though fewer than 1,700 of its 102,448 miles of road were surfaced. Based on this fact, those who sought improvement termed it a stuck-in-the-mud state.[140] Blame for this situation was of course laid on Iowa's localized system of road construction and maintenance. Able-bodied men of twenty-one to forty-five years of age spent two days per year working off their road tax, though in certain cases it was possible to substitute the payment of cash. Men labored on the roads within three miles of their home in what amounted to a communal workday. As Rodney O. Davis noted in his study of Iowa and the Good Roads movement, this "tradition of self-government at county, township, and lower levels was deeply rooted and jealously guarded."[141]

But as any farmer will tell you, with the application of enough force, that which is rooted can be uprooted. The agitation for good roads—whose advocates certainly won the issue-framing battle, as the implication was that their opponents favored bad roads—began in urban areas, in Iowa as elsewhere. The first Good Roads convention held in the state (in Iowa City) called for abolishing township road districts and transferring control to a single commissioner. Centralization was the answer. In 1902, this demand was enacted into law.

Certain farmers, sensing an ill shifting of winds, protested. Their ancient—by Iowan standards—system of localized road care was under threat, and down the road they could envision further concentration of power in ever more remote centers. But the most influential statewide journals of agriculture welcomed this shift as betokening an era of enlightenment and improved farm-to-market roads, not to mention the consolidation of rural schools, which was endowed by progressives with talismanic powers to ward off rustic ignorance.

A farmer from Bloomfield, Iowa, while professing himself a friend to farm-to-market roads, complained in a letter to the Iowa farm journal *The Homestead* that "the greatest howl [for good roads] is coming from a class who would hardly know a plow from a self-binder; they are the automobile and bicycle factories and improved road tool builders." These were not, he said, members of the "overall brigade," but rather city men urging state action that would enrich themselves and their industries.[142] Another Iowa farmer, writing in *The Homestead* in 1903, made an eloquent case based on an earlier American political philosophy: "The tendency and drift of public sentiment and all legislation is toward centralization and consolidation, when it ought to be in the other direction, to distribute power and divide honors, and make the individual more responsible, instead of the township, the county, or the mass of people."[143] But his eloquence was not persuasive. The next year, the state legislature created an Iowa State Highway Commission, affiliated with

Iowa State University; the measure passed both houses easily, drawing but four dissenting votes.

The profusion of local highway offices was either a sign of healthy grassroots democracy or an example of democracy gone wild, depending on one's stance toward localism and decentralism. In Illinois, for instance, in 1912, there were 1,600 units of local governance, with three road commissioners for each, making a total of 4,800 officials drawing salaries from the road tax.[144] Progressives urged the abolition of what they regarded as an archaic system and its replacement by a professionalized bureaucracy centered in Springfield. In 1913, a sweeping reform bill created the office of state highway engineer, a three-member appointed state highway commission, and appointed county superintendents of highways. As David R. Wrone writes in his account of the Good Roads movement in Illinois, "In essence, responsibility for the roads was taken away from the townships and placed under the counties, with the consultation and assistance of the state."[145]

Though much subsequent scholarship has denied an ideological basis for the Good Roads movement, the often-fierce opposition suggests that not everyone saw it as a bland, unobjectionable, omni-partisan issue. Jason Lee notes that between 1906 and 1924, thirty of the sixty-nine statewide ballot measures calling for road improvements were defeated, some by margins of as high as 4–1.[146] The proposals called for such measures as special taxes, bond measures, the establishment of state commissions, the use of convict labor, and gasoline taxes, among others. Farmers and rural people often made up the bulk of the opposition; organizations such as the state Grange were often in the forefront of the naysayers.

In his doctoral dissertation on the economic aspects of the Good Roads movement, Lee found that "the presence of farmers led to a significant reduction in the amount of local road expenditure."[147] In states such as New York and Illinois, the baleful hand of city political machines was sometimes suspected of manipulating campaigns to boost state highway spending. Machine politicos had a talent for seizing and then doling out dollars to friends and those in a position to do them favors. Assessing county-level data from non-Southern regions during the first two decades of the twentieth century, Lee found that "increasing the share of the county population who are employed as farmers by one percentage point decreases the amount of road expenditure per mile by 1.7 percent." He discovered a "strong negative relationship" between farmers and the support for public expenditures on good roads.[148]

Rural states lagged in rates of automobile ownership: in 1910, the states with the highest ratios of population to registered motor vehicles were Oklahoma (2,437–1), West Virginia (1,388), Arkansas (1,369), and Alabama (1,201); those jurisdictions with the lowest ratios were the District of Columbia (52.4), California (53.9), and Rhode Island (91.8). Yet by 1930, these chasms had narrowed considerably. Oklahoma now had 4.3 persons to each registered motor vehicle and West Virginia had 6.4, while the District of Columbia was at 3.1 and California 2.8.[149] If, in these earliest days of the Great Depression, there was not yet a chicken in every pot, there was nearly a car in every garage.

Build Roads, Centralize Schools—and Hear the Clanking of the Chains

The consolidation of rural schools, a project of late nineteenth- and early twentieth-century progressive educators and mid-twentieth-century Cold Warriors, was advertised as a beneficial byproduct of the Good Roads movement. Better roads, it was claimed, would enable students to travel farther distances, so small rural schools could be shuttered, and administration could be transferred to professional educators using all the latest techniques of scientific management. As was the case with other progressive enthusiasms of the early twentieth century, school consolidation was based in the belief that bigger was better, and that trained professionals were the most efficient and effective supervisors of civic life.

Like good roads, school consolidation was, from first to last, a project bearing the stamp of the Progressive movement, with its faith in credentialed and (allegedly) dispassionate experts. Senator William H. Thompson (D-KS) said in 1916 that "the success of the consolidated schools depends almost entirely upon the condition of the public roads."[150] If automobiles or the new form of mass transportation known as buses could not traverse roads due to the combination of poor weather and poor road maintenance, then they could not convey pupils to school.

Geologist and good-roads promoter Albert Perry Brigham rejoiced in the "improvement in education that must result from good roads. It means regular attendance of thousands of youth, and it also is the indispensable preliminary to the consolidation of rural schools."[151] This was more in the nature of a threat than a promise, as education researchers would learn much later, for consolidation was at best a mixed bag, bringing in its wake long bus rides, larger classes, increased costs to taxpayers, enhanced feelings of atomization and disconnectedness among students, and, in many instances, no compensating improvements in test scores. In any event, Jason Lee found that improvement to roads could "explain 10 percent of the observed change in the fraction of rural schools consolidated in the Midwest" between 1906 and 1916, as well as a significant percentage of the increase in average number of school days attended per pupil.[152]

This latter feature was a bugbear of progressive consolidators. They pointed to the shorter school years in rural areas, where children were expected by their families to help in planting or bringing in the crops. For instance, in 1905 urban schools in the north central section of the United States were open for business on an average of 193 days annually, while the comparable figure for rural schools in the north central region was 147 days.[153] Left unexamined was the assumption that more school days were an unequivocal benefit for the children; critics of public education and the "un-schoolers" of later eras might argue that playing an essential role in a family business like a small farm is as enriching an experience as sitting in a classroom.

As one 1930s study of school consolidation put it, "So closely related are consolidation and transportation that the success of the transportation system largely determines the success of the consolidation project."[154] Improved roads made it possible to close local schools and draw in students from a much wider area, typically by busing. Rural states and the rural regions of more urban states were the targets here: partially as a result of the spread of good roads, the number of schools nationwide plummeted by more than 100,000 in the middle portion of the twentieth century, from 217,000 in 1920 to 83,000 in the late 1980s.[155] Not coincidentally, the number of school buses in operation rose from 26,685 in 1925 to 93,306 in 1940.[156]

Average school size increased from 87 students in 1930 to 440 students in 1970.[157] These developments were applauded across the board—except by disgruntled rural parents—until the 1960s and '70s, when education researchers overturned many of the assumptions of the progressive and Cold Warrior advocates of consolidation. It turned out that smaller schools, without long bus rides, offered social and developmental advantages to their pupils, and that they held their own academically with larger schools. But by this time, of course, tens of thousands of small districts were wiped out, and the path to relocalizing education seemed steep.

One eye-opening study confuting the education establishment's assertion of the unalloyed benefits of consolidation was conducted by Christopher R. Berry of the University of Chicago and Martin R. West of Brown University, who related their findings in the *Journal of Law, Economics, & Organization*. Using data from the US Census for white men born between 1920 and 1949, they discovered that "students from states with smaller schools obtained higher returns to education and completed more years of schooling," while "students from states with larger schools earned significantly lower wages later in life."[158] They concluded that "any gains from consolidation were outweighed by the harmful effects of larger schools."[159]

The findings of Berry and West, and other scholars who have reached similar conclusions, do not pinpoint just why these smaller schools lead to better outcomes for students, though speculation usually centers on the greater sense of belonging and community and parental involvement. The Good Roads movement, whatever its intentions and undeniable accomplishments, killed off scores of thousands of these schools.

The Sound of the Men ...

The dirty little secret of the Good Roads movement is that a considerable amount of the work on Southern roads was performed by mostly African American prisoners working on chain gangs—an arrangement conceptualized and executed not by stereotypical redneck tobacky-chawin' redneck sheriffs out of *Cool Hand Luke* but by progressives who regarded the road gangs as "an example of penal humanitarianism, state-sponsored economic modernization and efficiency, and racial moderation," as historian Alex Lichtenstein writes.[160]

General Roy Stone of the ORI had been an advocate of convict labor; Sterling Morton, the Cleveland administration's secretary of agriculture, was not, and instructed him not to proselytize therefor. But the practice spread. Progressives in North Carolina, for instance, reviled the venerable community workday on local roads, calling it "about as well suited to the purpose as were the old militia musters to the development of actual soldiers."[161] Ninety of the Tar Heel State's one hundred counties retained this model as of 1904, a source of embarrassment to the North Carolina Good Roads Association, whose members crusaded for convict labor to replace the labor of free men. Georgia was even more retrograde; 129 of its 137 counties relied still on local men pitching in on road days. Why should free men be conscripted to work the roads, asked advocates of convict labor, when prisoners were available?

North Carolina state geologist and good roads advocate Joseph A. Holmes urged his comrades to action, saying, "The use of convict labor has been the beginning and the basis of the modern road building in the southern states."[162] Men of progressive inclinations heeded the call. In Georgia, where felony convicts (91 percent of whom were black) had previously worked in coal mines and sawmills, brickyards, and turpentine farms, they were marched out to the roads in 1908. Admittedly, chain gang laborers inhaled fresh air and exercised muscles that in idleness might have turned to flab, but as Lichtenstein points out, corporal punishment, beatings, verminous food, and woefully inadequate medical treatment were also part of the package.[163] Yet Georgia governor Hoke Smith, a Southern progressive, boasted to the state's general assembly, "As a result of placing the convicts upon the public roads an enthusiasm has been aroused throughout the entire state for good roads."[164] (The classic 1932 pulp memoir *I Am a Fugitive from a Georgia Chain Gang!*, made into a classic movie with Paul Muni, was to be another result.)

Governor Smith had the numbers to back him up. The percentage of surfaced roads in Georgia rose from 7.27 in 1909 to as much as 25 in 1914. "By the end of 1915," writes Lichtenstein, "Georgia had 13,000 miles of surfaced roads, more than any other southern state, and the fifth largest number of miles of surfaced rural roads in the United States."[165] Left behind in this road-surfacing jag were the eleven counties without chain gang labor, which the state geologist of Georgia pitied for "hav[ing] no improved roads."[166] As a saying common at the time in Georgia went, "Bad men make good roads."[167]

But the roadmakers weren't usually *that* bad: typically, murderers, rapists, and arsonists were not permitted to venture beyond the bounds of the prison. The belief was that sight of the convicts in their distinctive prison garb, toiling under the hot noonday sun, would deter onlookers, especially young men, from following that same path. Sam Cooke sang a song about men working so hard all day long on the chain gang, frowning and moaning their lives away: it was not a life choice to emulate.

The Feds Come to the Aid

The two major political parties had ignored good roads in their 1904 platforms, but by the next presidential election, the issue had forced itself onto the national agenda. In 1908, the Democrats, with Nebraska populist William Jennings Bryan at the ticket's head for the third time in a dozen years, devoted a single-sentence plank to the issue: "We favor Federal aid to State and local authorities in the construction and maintenance of post roads."[168] The Republicans, having nominated the more conservative William Howard Taft, were more periphrastic and less emphatic: "We recognize the social and economical advantages of good country roads, maintained more and more largely at public expense, and less and less at the expense of the abutting owner. In this work we commend the growing practice of State aid, and we approve the efforts of the National Agricultural Department by experiments and otherwise to make clear to the public the best methods of road construction."[169]

Four years later, a Woodrow Wilson–led Democracy repeated its 1908 plank, substituting the word "national" for "federal," while the Taft Republicans ignored the issue.[170] The Progressive Party, or the Bull Moose, which nominated ex-president Theodore Roosevelt to return to office, outbid both established parties and adopted a good roads platform plank that read: "We recognize the vital importance of good roads and we pledge our party to foster their extension in every proper way, and we favor the early construction of National highways. We also favor the extension of the rural free delivery service."[171]

In 1912, the politicians who write those platforms were forced to deal with the issue at a level of specificity rather than the usual abstraction. A front-burner bill of that year sponsored by Rep. Dorsey Shackleford (D-MO) had leveraged federal roadbuilding aid on the popular foundation of RFD. Shackleford proposed that the US government pay a fee of either $25, $20, or $15 per mile to the states for the use by the post office of rural roads. The fee depended on macadamized, gravel, or dirt roads. Those not meeting standards set by the secretary of agriculture were not eligible for aid—or, rather, rent.[172] Indirectly, under this bill, the feds would encourage surface improvements for the nation's roads.

Rep. Shackleford explained, "These roads will enable our farmers to get their products to market more promptly and cheaply, thus giving to the consumer his food fresher and at lower cost. These roads will give to our rural communities better schools and churches. These roads will give our farmers more opportunities for the benefits and joys of social intercourse."[173] They were, it seems, such an unalloyed good that only a churl or congenital misanthrope could oppose them—or are you against fresher foods and better roads?

Shackleford's deft handling of the constitutional issue—tying federal aid directly to postal roads—swept away the opposition of many rural representatives, and his bill passed the House by a vote of 240–86. Opponents counterattacked; surprisingly, those opponents were not so much archconstitutionalists or fiscal conservatives as they were automobile interests, who scorned the "Knights of the dirt roads" and lobbied for federal aid to highways, not hicks.[174] Shackleford was proposing to spend money on roads that started "nowhere and ended nowhere."[175] The Automobile Association of America, eventually to become a prepotent lobby for federal aid to the highway industry, urged senators to oppose the Shackleford bill, lest its example set the pattern for rural-oriented highway aid rather than subsidy of a sophisticated nationwide network.

The Senate rejected the bill, which had in any case faced a probable veto by President William Howard Taft, who had told his assistant, "I do not believe in involving the Federal treasury in a weight of obligation to build roads that the States ought to build."[176] His successor would think, and act, differently. For President Wilson signed into law the Federal Aid Road Act of 1916, which was a distant cousin of legislation introduced by Rep. Shackleford, but a very close approximation of a bill largely drawn up by the AASHO. The AASHO-written bill, which became the 1916 act, authorized the federal government to distribute to the states $75 million over five years for the purpose of aiding road projects on a 50–50 split. Authorizations under the act were in the sum of $5 million for fiscal year 1917, $10 million for FY 1918, $15 million for FY 1919, $20 million for FY 1920, and $25 million for FY 1921, with an additional $10 million dedicated to the construction of roads and trails in or adjacent to national forests. Only states with highway agencies were eligible for the monies, which were apportioned by formulae that considered population, area, and rural delivery mileage. States had to apply to the secretary of agriculture for aid to specific projects. To forestall the development of government-subsidized turnpikes, roads constructed under the act could not charge tolls.

Restricting these expenditures to rural post roads, a cursory gesture to appease constitutionalists, was too confining; a 1920 amendment to a post office appropriation bill redefined "rural post road" as "any public road a major portion of which is now used, or can be used, or forms a connecting link not to exceed ten miles in length of any road or roads now or hereafter used for the transportation of the United States mails."[77] As FHWA historian Richard F. Weingroff noted, "This definition retained the 'post road' concept from the Constitution, but essentially made every road, including the long-distance roads, eligible for Federal-aid funding."[78] The alteration did not go unnoticed. Senator Charles S. Thomas, a Colorado Democrat, scoffed that the change "commits the United States to the improvement of every cattle trail, every cow path, and every right of way in the United States."[79] Just so. This definition, said Senator James Wadsworth (R-NY), was so capacious as to include "any and every road in the United States."[80] And so the fiction that federal aid to nonfederal roads fell within the enumerated powers of the Constitution as written and ratified was gently laid to rest as a quaint irrelevancy in the new age.

An interstate system of roads was of tertiary importance. President Wilson's Secretary of Agriculture David Houston said, "I suppose everybody will agree that the railroad is the national road for the vast majority of people."[81] Long-distance personal travel via the roads seemed as distant as the quarrels of the Austro-Hungarian Empire.

As Charles L. Dearing writes, other objections to federal aid in the period leading up to 1916 included arguments "that there was no money in the Treasury; that the nation should concentrate on national defense plans; that the measure was pork-barrel and analogous to river and harbor bills; that federal administration of the fund would prove impracticable; that federal aid for local road improvements would discourage state-aid programs; and that it was unconstitutional."[182] That last point, though no less cogent than it had been a century earlier, had lost most of its forensic power.

Representatives from northeastern states, where roadbuilding had progressed furthest, sometimes looked with disfavor on federal involvement, as it would serve to transfer funds to other sections—to which solons from the other sections replied that it was their turn. Weren't large sums spent on programs of disproportionate benefit to residents of these favored regions? "The South has been for years paying great pension bills where the people of other sections of the country have had their feet in the long trough drinking all the slop," said Rep. Percy Quin (D-MS) during the 1916 debate.[183] (Rep. Quin was adverting to an ever-widening circle of Union veterans of the War Between the States who received pensions thanks to the vigorous lobbying of the Grand Army of the Republic. Confederate veterans were ineligible for federal pensions, though there were some, mostly disabled or indigent, who received parsimonious stipends from their own states.[184])

There was another aspect to this matter of sectional fairness. New York accounted for fully one-third of state highway spending in 1916. Why, its members of Congress asked, should the state be forced to subsidize road-building in sister states that had mostly neglected this task? Moreover, the 1916 law barred work on urban streets with federal-aid funds. So only two of New York's thirty US representatives voted for the 1916 act.[185] Among the sharpest critics of federal aid to state roads was Rep. Thomas Dunne (R-NY), a Rochester-area Republican who happened to be chairman of the House Committee on Roads. His skepticism of infrastructure spending led Rep. James B. Aswell to complain, "He has voted against road building every time, although he is on the Roads Committee. He did not preside at the meeting of that committee when this bill was reported. He has been bitterly opposed to road building."[186]

Rep. Aswell's lament captures perfectly the unexamined assumption of those who sup, and ladle, at the public trough; namely, the job of a committee on roads, or education, or defense, or science, is to funnel tax monies into roads, education, defense, or science. Representatives are, in this view, middlemen, facilitators, agents of those special interests whose focus is within the bailiwick of the committees. To dissent, to question or try to disrupt the steady flow of tax dollars, is to be a mere naysayer, an obstructionist, or a Dr. No—a doctor who is seldom in the house, at least the House of Representatives.

Henceforth good roads enjoyed smooth sailing, or at least calm and peaceful driving, within both major parties. The Wilson Democrats of 1916 were positively effusive: "The happiness, comfort, and prosperity of rural life, and the development of the city, are alike conserved by the construction of public highways. We, therefore, favor national aid in the construction of post roads and roads for like purposes."[187] The Republicans, with eastern establishment fixture Charles Evans Hughes at the top of the ticket, put forth a more general and far-reaching statement: "The entire transportation system of the country has become essentially national. We, therefore, favor such action by legislation, or, if necessary, through an amendment to the Constitution of the United States, as will result in placing it under complete Federal control."[188] This was with an eye to railroad regulation, obviously, but its rubric, *transportation*, undeniably included highways.

Four years later, the Warren Harding–led Republicans announced, in a public roads and highways plank, "We favor liberal appropriations in cooperation with the States for the construction of highways, which will bring about a reduction in transportation costs, better marketing of farm products, improvement in rural postal delivery, as well as meet the needs of military defense."[189] The Democrats, this time nominating Ohio's James Cox, praised the Wilson-signed 1916 federal act and looked forward to its further implementation:

> Improved roads are of vital importance not only to commerce and industry but also to agriculture and rural life. The Federal Road Act of 1916, enacted by a Democratic Congress, represented the first systematic effort of the government to insure the building of an adequate system of roads in this country. The act, as amended, has resulted in placing the movement for improved highways on a progressive and substantial basis in every State in the Union and in bringing under actual construction more than 13,000 miles of roads suited to the traffic needs of the communities in which they are located.[190]

From this point on it was all boilerplate.

The Army Runs on Roads

Although European governments (France, Germany, and England) early on "realized the military potential of the motor vehicle" engaging in various experiments and exercises to assess its usefulness, the United States, with its less militarist heritage, hesitated.[191] Within the US military were serious doubters as to the usefulness in wartime of automobiles and trucks. Major J. B. Mott, after inspecting German and French maneuvers in 1900, opined that while the vehicles had "come to stay," the superiority of European road conditions to those stateside meant that "auto-traction cars" would be far more effective in the service of continental armies than in those of the United States.[192]

Though military automobiles render "enormous service ... to the armies of Europe, where the highways are level and well built, and the distances comparatively small, I do not believe they would be of sufficient value on the rough American roads, and over enormous tracts of country as in the United States," wrote Major Mott. "Our needs differ considerably from those of the European countries. The latter must always prepare for possible war on their own soil, and their conditions favor the use of auto cars, while the possibility of hostilities within the United States are remote, and their utility is highly problematical."[193] Mott's analysis suited an America that refrained from military involvement beyond its borders, but in the new century his remarks would seem anachronistic. Major Mott did not realize that within less than a score of years, the US Army would be fighting a land war on the European continent, and that it would be a massive presence in Europe over the last three-fifths of the twentieth century. Trucks, tanks, and auto-traction cars would come in very handy.

And half a century later, military necessity was offered as a primary reason for the building of roads for motor vehicles in what became the largest public works project in American history. Nevertheless, the idea of dual civilian/military highway systems never got traction in the United States. As early as 1819, Secretary of War John C. Calhoun reported:

A judicious system of roads and canals, constructed for the convenience of commerce, and the transportation of the mail only, without any preference as to military operations, is itself, among the most efficient means for 'the more complete defense of the United States.' Without adverting to the fact, that the roads and canals, which such a system would require, are, with few exceptions, precisely those which would be required for the operations of war; such a system, by consolidating our Union, increasing our wealth and fiscal capacity, would add greatly to our resources in war.[194]

In the fervor surrounding the First World War, Senator George E. Chamberlain (D-OR) introduced legislation "to provide for taking over, improvement, relocation, construction, and maintenance of a system of National highways and State highways, designed to facilitate the movement of troops, equipment, munitions, and supplies" in service of the national defense of the United States.[195] This was going too far, even for the most foaming war hawks. There would be no parallel lines on the map, one for the army and one for civilians. But the link between infrastructure and defense was growing ever firmer.

In 1921, the War Department made explicit its noninterest in a dedicated system of defense highways when it adopted a series of principles governing its relations to highways, the first of which read, "Roads which must be constructed for commerce and national development will, in general, be identical with those required for military purposes."[196] So while military necessity might be adduced as a primary reason for construction, the Department of War (or, later, Defense) neither designed nor helped to build those roads.

Yet the war and its aftermath proved a gold strike for the nascent road lobby. A 1919 post office appropriations bill authorized the secretary of war to transfer to the secretary of agriculture "all available war materials, equipment, and supplies not needed for the purpose of the War Department but suitable for use in the improvement of highways."[197] Material, equipment, and supplies, as the secretary of war elucidated in a subsequent letter, included everything from steam shovels to locomotive cranes to hand tools, and from twenty-ton Holt caterpillar tractors to transits to mundane office supplies. Plows and trailers, steam pumps and air drills, engineers' levels, and road graders: the list of transferred material was deep and varied.[198]

A supplemental act of Congress the following year specified that the secretary of war was to transfer "certain surplus motor-propelled vehicles and motor equipment and road-making material" to the federal government for use by the states.[199] Over five thousand trucks and autos were quickly delivered to the forty-eight states by April 1, 1920, and soon the number would exceed twenty thousand. No entity in the world owned more motor trucks than the US government, and in an act approximating federalism, it was going to share the surplusage with the states. These heavy trucks, in turn, would cause considerable damage to roads, whose repair would then be the responsibility of subnational levels of government.

Down the Road with Ike

Several months after the armistice, the US War Department undertook what may be understood, depending on one's vantage point, as a historic experiment, a nuts-and-bolts test of national infrastructure capacity, or a headline-hogging stunt with its Transcontinental Motor Train, a 3,239-mile convoy from Washington, DC to San Francisco. Fortuitously, but with long-range ramifications, Lieutenant Colonel Dwight David Eisenhower, twenty-eight years of age, volunteered to serve as one of the motor train's two tank officers. (The other was his great friend and prankster Sereno Brett.) The Transcontinental Motor Train was a sight to behold. It stretched for two miles and consisted of about three hundred men and eighty-one vehicles: forty-six trucks, eleven passenger cars, nine motorcycles, five ambulances, a tractor, several trailers, and a monstrous-looking, winch-armed contraption called the Militor, whose job it was to rescue vehicles stuck in the mud or the mire.[200]

The War Department's goals were several: to test the durability of military vehicles, to determine the usefulness of the country's rudimentary highway system as a component of the national defense, and, secondarily, to encourage young men to join an army that was shrinking rapidly due to the end of hostilities in Europe. This trip, sedulously covered by the press, was for all involved a memorable adventure. Yet the chief officer of the Motor Transport Corps suggested another motive: "To demonstrate the practicability of long distance motor commercial transportation and the consequent necessity for the expenditure of governmental appropriations to provide necessary highways."[201] In other words, the caravan would serve as a high-profile, taxpayer-funded advertisement for greater taxpayer expenditures on good roads. An army film crew traveled with the convoy to record its adventures for the moviegoing public.

In retrospect, Dwight Eisenhower captured the primary purpose of the coast-to-coast truck convoy: "The trip would dramatize the need for better main highways."[202] The Transcontinental Motor Train was seen off on July 7, 1919, at the Ellipse in Washington, DC, by a delegation including Secretary of War Newton Baker, Harvey Firestone of tire fame (not Harvey Fierstein of *Torch Song Trilogy* fame), Frank Seiberling of Goodyear Tires, and various senators and congressmen and military brass. Eisenhower puckishly recalled of the dignitaries, "Each had something to say about the role of these road pioneers; not all of them were brief. My luck was running; we missed the ceremony."[203]

The first day, the train made good time: over six miles an hour. Brick or concrete paved certain roads, but most surfaces were dirt, stone, and gravel, or dust and mud. The pace was sub–Indianapolis Speedway. There were broken fan belts, broken magnetos, broken accelerator springs. A film of the motor trip would show a montage of men and vehicles fording creeks, getting stuck in and then winched out of the mud, with truck tires plunging through the wooden planks of old bridges, accidents aplenty, and bridges without adequate clearance, all giving the maintenance crew steady work. Trucks, trailers, cars, and motorcycles coursed over fine brick pavement in Pennsylvania, the ruts and slop of Nebraska, the desert sands and High Sierras of Nevada, and for a stretch in Wyoming they followed an abandoned railroad bed. Parades and brass bands, Rotarians and fireworks, long-winded orators and disabled Civil War veterans, and distinguished citizens of burgs, hamlets, and backwaters met the convoy. Machine guns saluted them with a round of fire in Clinton, Iowa; in Kimball, Nebraska, and other towns along the way, the soldiers danced with the local girls, appropriately supervised. When prairie winds whipped the dust and obscured the visibility of drivers, the caravan sometimes stretched out for as long as five miles. The motor train averaged about five miles per hour for the trip, which, as Henry Petroski notes, was "not much faster than a brisk walk."[204]

Upon their arrival in San Francisco on September 6, sixty-two days after they had set out, the city greeted the boys as conquering heroes as they paraded through the streets. The motor train's influence on Eisenhower, though seminal, can be overrated; while "the old convoy had started me thinking about good, two-lane highways," Ike recalled in his retirement, it took the experience of the Second World War and "the autobahns of modern Germany" to teach him "the wisdom of broader ribbons across the land."[205]

Taxing Gas

Licensing fees came nowhere close to meeting the expenses associated with the proliferation of automobiles. These expenses only grew greater with the pounding taken by the roads on which heavy trucks and other military vehicles traveled. So, in the year after the armistice, 1919, a trio of western states—Colorado, New Mexico, and Oregon—took the lead in implementing a gasoline tax. Great Britain had adopted such in 1910, and Congress debated a two-cent-per-gallon tax in 1914 and 1915, but it fell well short of passage.

Oregon was the first out of the gate. The state government required dealers to pay a one-cent-per-gallon tax to a state fund each month. The preamble to the Oregon law established that this was a user tax intended to pay for maintenance and construction of highways on which gasoline-powered vehicles traveled.[206] Colorado and New Mexico, acting independently rather than in concert, imposed one- and two-cent-per-gallon taxes, respectively, within the next six weeks.

Surprisingly, as John Chynoweth Burnham noted in the *Mississippi Valley Historical Review*, these three measures received scant publicity or legislative opposition. Not even the petroleum industry offered much in the way of dissent. The president of Standard Oil of California, where a tax was later adopted, explained that a penny-per-gallon levy just seemed too puny to bother with.[207] He was either naive or a model of nearsightedness to believe that once enacted, the tax would remain at one penny. From small things, as the saying goes, big things one day come. (Standard would change its corporate tune by 1926.)

Après Colorado and New Mexico, the deluge. Pushed primarily by newly empowered state highway officials, the gasoline tax caught fire. Over the next four years, thirty-one states enacted this levy. The last state to do so was New York. (The state would soon get over its tax-phobia.)

In many of the states, the tax was approved unanimously by legislatures, leading an incredulous Tennessee collector of revenue to ask, "Who ever heard, before, of a popular tax?"[208] The oil industry held any objections in check, as long as the tax was modest, believing that the resultant construction and maintenance of roads would spur greater demand for its product. Even the AAA did not line up in opposition to a measure that increased the cost of the fuel that its members used. The tax was barely felt, it said, given the contemporaneous decline in gasoline prices due to refined refining techniques and the Great Depression.

Reliance on gasoline taxes and registration fees for highway construction and maintenance increased; they constituted 18.5 percent of all such expenditures in 1921 and rose to over half (55.8 percent) in 1930, with a corresponding reduction in reliance on property taxes and general revenues.[209] By the 1920s, politicians eyed the gasoline tax as a more fecund source of revenue than registration fees. As Harry A. Barth of the University of Oklahoma noted in his 1924 study of the taxation of passenger automobiles, the popularity of this imposition was "based on the eternal verity that if one pays a tax in driblets, one really pays no tax at all."[210] It's death, or at least beggary, by a thousand nicks and cuts. And besides, Barth believed, it embodied a certain rough justice, for gasoline consumption is correlated, though very imperfectly, with usage of the roads. However, it failed his test of progressivity as it made no distinction between different grades of gasoline and the price of the automobile itself, and because rural roads received disproportionate government aid, it could be seen as a transfer of wealth from city to rural motorists.[211]

The Era of Good Feelings about an impost on gasoline could not last. In 1929, the American Petroleum Institute's board of directors resolved "that we do not oppose the levying of a gasoline tax where all the revenue derived therefrom is used solely for highway construction and maintenance purposes; but we oppose the fixing of a rate per gallon tax beyond reasonable bounds, or where the rate the consumer must pay is out of equitable proportion to the price of the gasoline."[212] But for all the talk in later years about the all-powerful oil industry, it was helpless before the juggernaut of the gas tax. The average rate in the forty-eight states rose from 3.04 cents per gallon in 1928 to 5.44 in 1938. "Gasoline is cheap—only the tax is high," protested the oil industry, to no avail.

Further inflaming the industry's pique was the practice, which spread during the Depression, of diverting a part of the proceeds from the gasoline tax to social welfare or education programs. The percentage of diverted gas tax funds rose from 2 in the late 1920s to 9 in 1932 and a high of 19 in 1936, setting in motion a chain reaction of state constitutional amendments and similar strictures, supported by the industry as well as the AAA, forbidding diversion.[213] (Minnesota was the first state to enact such limits, in 1920; by 1942, fourteen states had done so.) Even Congress got into the act, threatening by the Hayden-Cartwright Act of 1934 to penalize states that diverted gas tax funds. (Only two states were punished, but the others got the message.[214])

Selling the States

A 1918 Illinois referendum proposed a $60 million bond issue, financed by automobile licensing fees, to construct 4,800 miles of roads throughout the Land of Lincoln. The Illinois Highway Improvement Association, whose vice president, a powerhouse in the Illinois Bankers Association, had written the ballot measure, wheeled into action, distributing an astonishing six million "maps, folders, posters, and pamphlets."[215] The referendum was approved by a four-to-one margin, though the 4,800 miles of roads required a second bond issue for completion. As usual, advocates had underestimated the cost of the project. (Ironically, only two of Illinois's 102 counties rejected the good roads bond, rural Hamilton and DeWitt, each of which was named for a notable proponent of internal improvements: Alexander Hamilton and DeWitt Clinton.)

In the case of the Sunflower State, as Mary Rowland explained in "Kansas and the Highways, 1917–1930," local control of road building and maintenance was forfeited to "professional engineers who used regulatory means to ensure control."[216] Local liberties were being forfeited, warned advocates of decentralized governance, and once gone, they would never come back. The state, as would the federal government in due time, was tempting the people and their local elected officials with the lure of money—and too late did those who snapped at the bait learn the eternal truth that he who takes the king's shilling becomes the king's man.

The federal government sparked this centripetalizing chain of events in 1916, when it made states eligible for federal road aid if they jumped through a series of hoops, including the creation of a state highway commission. Though in retrospect this was clearly the "opening wedge" of significant federal involvement, at the time state representatives hoped (against all experience) that the attached strings would be few and flexible.[217] As Mary Rowland details, this condition was seen as a mere formality by many Kansans, who planned to take the money yet still run their own affairs. Counties would remain the locus of power, as Kansas would "take the best of the old, localism, and blend it with the best of the new, federal money."[218] What could possibly go wrong?

So, in 1917 the state legislature created a three-person Kansas Highway Commission, which would pass along federal monies to the counties. Ah, but there was a rub (isn't there always a rub?): the federal act placed responsibility for construction with the states, not subdivisions thereof. So, Kansans, and their elected representatives, were presented with a choice: cede power from the counties to the state and receive federal funds or retain the old decentralized model and forsake federal funds.

The first order of business for the good roads lobby in Kansas was to overcome a state constitutional stricture against internal improvements. Its tactic was an amendment, submitted to the public for a vote in 1920, whose relevant language read: "The state shall never be a party in carrying on any works of internal improvements except to aid in the construction of roads and highways and the reimbursement for the cost of permanent improvements of roads and highways."[219] In other words, the state shall never engage in internal improvements except when it engages in internal improvements. Governor Henry J. Allen pushed for the amendment, backed by a powerful phalanx including B. F. Goodrich Rubber Co., Sinclair Refining, the state's Chamber of Commerce, the Kansas Bankers Association, and others who had a direct interest in the expenditure of government funds in this matter.

Opponents, who included the Grange and the Farmers' Union, agrarian Democrats, and limited-government proponents, saw this as being about much more than merely surfacing roads. Critical principles were at stake. The rhetoric, never understated, skirted hyperbole but rang with portent. Reno County commissioner Rodney A. Elward fumed that the envisioned regime "gives the state engineer autocratic power over localities, and I shall resist the enforcement of the law, just as my father resisted the enforcement of the Dred Scott decision though he got into jail for it…. [T]he integrity of local self-government is of infinitely more importance than improved highways."[220] Farmer V. C. Bryson warned that "Kansas is fast coming under the domination of Centralization of Power that is going to prove as destructive to her citizens as [the Bolsheviks]."[221] After a furious campaign, voters approved the amendment by a tally of 284,689–193,347.

Several years of fitful and desultory progress in road construction followed, until in 1925 the US Department of Agriculture threatened to cut off federal monies to Kansas unless the state boosted its spending and further centralized administration of its highway program. Gun to its head, Kansas acquiesced by a series of steps, the capstone being statewide approval by a margin of greater than 3–1 of constitutional amendments expanding the state's power to "adopt, construct, reconstruct, and maintain a state system of highways" and giving the state the power to levy taxes on motor vehicles and motor fuels.[222] The Grange and the Farmers' Union once again supplied the backbone of the opposition, but they were vastly outspent by the Kansas Association of Chambers of Commerce and other business groups.

The voices of localism were weakening, as was the potency of the old populists, who had been suspicious of centralized power. State Senator Smith L. Jackson of Garnett might thunder that rejecting federal aid would do little harm to Kansas but be a "terrible blow to the Cement Trust, Brick Combine, Road Machinery people and … there might be a few engineers inconvenienced,"[223] but his brand of feisty do-it-yourself populism was waning. Kansans and their legislators had "wanted federal money," concludes Mary Rowland, "and would accept whatever state centralization was necessary to insure the funds."[224]

Christopher W. Wells argues in "The Changing Nature of Country Roads" that the Good Roads movement worked a subtle alteration in the way rural people conceived of roads: they morphed from "natural phenomena," shaped in part by weather, which were best tended to by members of organic communities, to "technological" artifacts that required supervision and subsidy by ever more remote levels of government. Swept away, as a result, were "older, longstanding rural ideas and traditions," from communal roadwork day to local decision making.[225]

Hal S. Barron, examining the decline of localism in road administration in the postbellum North, posits that the traditional rural defense of local self-government was under an onslaught by both the hometown booster class and outside urban interests, among them engineers, hobbyists, and bureaucrats. The forces of modernity and centralization advanced steadily, vanquishing what these forces believed to be archaic republican notions, and, as a result, power flowed upward, to ever more distant and unresponsive levels. Battered, local self-government then enervated and was mostly destroyed.

It was "the battle between local priorities and cosmopolitan goals over roads that helped to shape the modern state," writes Barron.[226] All the while, those defending local priorities against this evolving modern state were depicted by partisans of the latter as, at best, ignorant of their own interests. Whenever voters rejected bond issues, for instance, their collective "nay" did not stand for frugality but an outburst of barely explicable resistance to the inevitable. A Raleigh newspaper editorialized of anti–internal improvement North Carolina voters: "The people were not always the best judges of their own interest."[227] If they refuse to defer to their betters, well, then their betters need to take matters into their own hands.

Even a modern publication of the FHWA paints the Good Roads movement as an essentially altruistic endeavor by urban and civic leaders who fretted over the damage done to rural America by bad roads, and who generously uplifted their country cousins with the liberal application of state and federal funds and centralized administration.[228] (This view is contested by some contemporary scholars. Christopher Wells, in his thoughtful study of shifting attitudes toward country roads, concludes, "So many rural Americans rallied to the good-roads standard ... that the urban origins of the good-roads agenda are commonly downplayed or are overlooked entirely."[229])

In the final tally, good roads progressives won a smashing political victory, getting everything they wanted. For they demanded, and eventually achieved, three major reforms. Charles L. Dearing of the Brookings Institution itemized this trio in his Public Roads Administration–supported history of American highway policy up until 1941:

1. "Money taxes gradually replaced the statute labor system."[230] General taxes came to subsidize road construction and maintenance, which were now overseen by professional engineers and performed by employees of the state and local government.

2. "The taxing and administrative unit was steadily expanded in size."[231] The township and road district were supplanted by larger units, up to and including the state government and its highway department. This came with a price: in exchange for state aid, citizens and local governments ceded power to the central authorities. As Michael R. Fein notes, local officials in New York made "devil's bargains ... to sacrifice time-honored powers in order to secure the quick distribution of state resources to cash-poor localities."[232] Those powers, once relinquished, would never return.

3. Initiation of federal aid, which rose from $63.6 million in 1921 to $1.17 billion in 1939, of which over 80 percent was part of New Deal relief efforts. Over that same period, state expenditures for highway purposes rose from $280 million to $780 million.[233]

Racing Down the Lincoln

The first transcontinental automobile journey was made by Horatio Nelson, a Vermont doctor and son-in-law to a wealthy patent medicine manufacturer, who in 1903 won a $50 bet that he could travel across country in one of those newfangled vehicles. A tyro behind the wheel, Dr. Jackson enlisted a mechanic named Sewall K. Crocker to serve as his wingman extraordinaire. They left the Bay Area on May 23, 1903, and drove a northerly route, avoiding the desert, which had foiled earlier such attempts. Accompanied by a goggle-wearing bulldog named Bud, a mascot right out of central casting, they arrived in New York City sixty-three days and countless auto repairs later. Jackson never collected on his bet, but his Winton automobile, christened *The Vermont*, did make it into the Smithsonian.

If there was a transcontinental railroad, reasoned automotorists, why not a transcontinental highway that might enable less adventurous souls than Dr. Nelson, mechanic Crocker, and bulldog Bud to traverse this great land? As early as 1895, General Stone of the ORI envisioned what he called the Great

American Road. He told an audience in Tennessee: "A great national highway might be constructed, called perhaps 'The Great Road of America,' which should first join together the States along the Atlantic seaboard; then strike across the country on a central line, say from Washington to San Francisco, joining there another line which connects the States of the Pacific Coast; this road to be built, not by the general government alone, but by the States, under such arrangements as they may make within their own borders, and by the government through the territories and its own lands and reservations."[234]

He was not the only such dreamer. In 1913, Carl Fisher, a Hoosier bicycle repairman and racer and stunt driver—he once rode a bike across a tightrope strung twelve stories high between two buildings in downtown Indianapolis while wearing a padded suit and supported by ropes: he was crazy but he wasn't stupid—conceived his own idea of a transcontinental highway.[235] Fisher was a character and then some. He was the proprietor of Indy's biggest bicycle store and its first auto dealership. Known colloquially as "Crazy Carl," he once "flew across Indianapolis in a car suspended from a huge balloon."[236] More entrepreneurially, he was the builder/impresario of the brick-paved Indianapolis Speedway.

But Carl Fisher's biggest dream was of a "Coast-to-Coast Rock Highway" stretching across America. It would span from Times Square in New York City to Lincoln Park in San Francisco and would be subsidized not by himself—there were limits to his craziness—but by Henry Ford and other titans of the emerging automobile industry who would pool their funds ("one-third of 1 percent of their gross revenue") until they had collected $10 million.[237] That, thought Fisher, ought to be enough, though he really had no idea. He did know that government was an unreliable partner, for as he groused, "The highways of America are built chiefly of politics, whereas the proper material is crushed rock or concrete."[238] (Concrete was the paving material of choice by the 1920s; though it was the most expensive form of surfacing, it was durable and low maintenance and had an "excellent record" of withstanding truck travel.[239])

Henry Ford declined the honor of paying for Carl Fisher's road, preferring that taxpayers bear the cost. "I believe in spending money to educate the public to the necessity of building good roads, and let everybody contribute their share in proper taxes," harrumphed Ford.[240] He would manufacture the cars—he envisioned the Model T as a car for rural Americans and their subpar roads—but Uncle Sam and his forty-eight junior partners in the states would have to supply the paths. (The Model T drove better on poor roads than on smoother roads designed for higher speeds. As roads improved, the Model A replaced the Model T.[241]) Other titans of the new industry, among them Frank Seiberling of Goodyear Tire & Rubber, Roy Chapin of the Hudson Motor Car Company, and Henry Bourne Joy, owner of the Packard Motor Car Company, responded more enthusiastically than had Henry Ford. Within a month, automobile interests had pledged $1 million to Fisher's highway.

Fisher's original moniker—the Coast-to-Coast Rock Highway—lacked panache, to put it mildly. So, he latched onto Henry Joy's suggestion that they dub it the Lincoln Highway, for no one ever made any headway arguing against honoring the sixteenth president of the United States. Thus was born, in 1913, the Lincoln Highway Association, whose pledges now totaled $4 million toward a road that Fisher realized would cost a lot more that $10 million and take up to twenty years to construct. But Carl Fisher, the entrepreneurial genius who paved the Indy Speedway with bricks and (more or less) invented Miami Beach, was a man undaunted.

A fierce tussle ensued over the route, naturally, as boosters and governors and chambers of commerce clamored for the Lincoln Highway to run through their town, their county, their state. This was free, if contentious, publicity, and the Lincoln Highway Association was nothing if not media savvy. Stories and hopeful predictions of the transcontinental route were featured prominently in newspapers and magazines, and the association, whose leaders were all too aware of the condition of roads, especially those west of the East Coast, "offered free cement to any community willing to find the labor to pour it."[242]

The "preparedness" campaign of President Woodrow Wilson prior to US entry into the First World War served as a boost for the fledgling industry as well as the envisioned Lincoln Highway. Colonel R. P. Davidson, who in 1915 had led a small unit of military cadets on a journey from Wisconsin to San Francisco as a kind of proto–motor train, saw the road as a vital link in the national defense. "As a military necessity," he said, "the Lincoln Highway should be constructed so that the heaviest artillery could be rushed from one coast to the other with the rapidity and efficiency which German roads have allowed in Teuton maneuvers."[243] Joy, the Packard chieftain, was among the most bellicose jingoes in the run-up to war, denouncing those who preferred to sit the carnage out as "bloodless, gutless pacifists" and urging the United States to take on not only Germany but Mexico as well.[244] As Peter Davies notes in his history of the Lincoln Highway, the war came, and Packard supplied over fifteen thousand trucks to the US Army.[245]

Henry Joy and Carl Fisher never did raise the $10 million they needed, and while sections of the highway were constructed of concrete, which was billed as a quantum leap ahead of dirt, other segments remained in various stages of completion and repair. Much of the Lincoln Highway was incorporated into the federal-aid system under the Federal Highway Act of 1921, but in 1925 the numeration of federal highways by the Bureau of Public Roads effectively dispelled the romance of the Lincoln Highway, whose transcontinental continuity had been broken into US routes 1, 30, 40, 50, 530 ... none of them having quite the ring of *Lincoln*. The fabled Lincoln Highway lost much of its luster when it lost its name. Soulless bureaucrats be damned! Packard's Henry Joy mourned that "the government, so far as has been within its power, has obliterated the Lincoln Highway from the memory of man."[246] (This triumph of the killjoy engineers also did in such named big roads as the Dixie Highway, the Meridian Highway, and the Jefferson Highway.)

The last activity of the Lincoln Highway Association was the 1928 placing of small roadside markers reading "This highway dedicated to Abraham Lincoln" at intervals of a mile or so across the nation.[247] The Lincoln Highway did serve as an object lesson in the practicability of long-distance roads, or what skeptics called "peacock alleys" down which the rich would tool their fancy automobiles.[248] A national highway system came to seem less dreamy and impractical; perhaps, with the infusion of significant sums of federal monies, it could be achieved. (Even with Lincoln's name stripped from the highway, the route kept its purchase on imaginations. L. B. Miller, manager of an x-ray company and "King of the Lincoln Highway," set the pace for cross-country travel when in 1927 he and a partner traveled from San Francisco to New York City—their layover in Gotham lasted all of one minute—and then back to San Francisco again in just 167 hours and 59 minutes, or one minute less than one week.[249])

* * *

The aforementioned Federal Highway Act of 1921 required the states to designate up to 7 percent of their highway mileage as "primary" roads that would be eligible for federal aid, though these nominations were subject to approval by the secretary of agriculture. The federal nose was getting increasingly under the macadam. Funds dispensed under this act had to be used for these roads, which were mostly expanded and surfaced iterations of the paths and traces and stump-and-rut roads of yesteryear. The 1921 act also envisioned "an adequate and connected system of highways, interstate in character," though the assumption was their development had to be the responsibility of the states.[250]

The Roaring '20s featured a roaring automobile industry. Americans bought 1.6 million motorized vehicles in 1921 alone. In 1922, more than ten thousand federal-aid highway miles were constructed, and as Earl Swift details, the nascent roadbuilding industry prospered: "More than 200 American companies made cement, 127 made paving brick, and 42, asphalt; another 380 provided crushed stone, and 340 shipped sand and gravel."[251]

The automobile also helped killed off the trolley car, which in the 1920s had been the primary form of urban mass transit. These cars, which ran on electric traction, had been ubiquitous in small, midsized, and large cities in the early twentieth century. Nostalgics recall them with misty water-colored memories, as they do street-corner newsboys and raucous speakeasies, and sometimes blame the automobile companies for nefariously snuffing them, though in fact they were done in by a combination of high accident rates, low (usually a nickel) fares, rampant corruption, the sloth and sloppiness bred of monopoly status, escalating labor costs, and failure to properly maintain their rolling stock.[252] Moreover, trolleys were taxed at "substantially higher" rates than were other public utilities, as urban historian Stanley Mallach has written.[253] Cities increasingly burdened them with demands (free transport for public employees and children, street maintenance beyond care for tracks and trolley cars) that proved to be great disadvantages.

Although a new generation of managers improved conditions in the 1920s, buses supplanted trolleys, as they "required no obstructive and ugly poles, wires, and tracks, and they could be loaded at the curb rather than in so-called safety zones in the middle of streets."[254] Buses were flexible, inexpensive, and fast, especially when moving on a dedicated lane or road. (Transportation economists have long understood the advantages of the humble bus. Edward Glaeser, professor of economics at Harvard, jokes that "forty years of transportation economics at Harvard can be boiled down to four words: 'Bus Good, Train Bad.'"[255])

But even the convenience of the bus could not compete with the sense of freedom so many found in the automobile. It multiplied their choices in life: of job, of home, of recreation. And as those choices multiplied, and the suburbs expanded, population increased in far-flung places that trolleys, or buses, could not profitably serve. Add in the escalating government expenditures to help the motorists and motor car companies, especially in the form of highways, and the writing was on the trolley car station wall.

Ike's Autobahn:
The National System of Interstate and
Defense Highways

THE GREAT DEPRESSION put the brakes on the more gran-
diose dreams of the highway lobby, though the nation's roads did not suffer
from neglect in the doling out of New Deal relief funds. The Works Progress Administration, the New Deal's capacious public employment program,
which put everyone from novelists to camp counselors to work on the federal
dime, expended about three-quarters of its $11 billion on public works proj-
ects. Similarly, the Public Works Administration (PWA), whose focus was
primarily on the construction of durable public works rather than providing
make-work jobs to the unemployed, subsidized the erection of public schools
and hospitals, sewers and water systems, but the single largest component of
its portfolio was streets and highways, which accounted for one-third of PWA
projects and 15.7 percent, or about $1.3 billion, of funds expended.[1]

All told, between 1934 and 1937 New Deal programs expended $2.8 bil-
lion on roadwork, though in 1938 President Franklin D. Roosevelt, opining
that these programs "do not provide as much work as other methods of taking care of the unemployed," requested and received a reduction in federal
highway spending.[2] The federal government in this era also discovered the
revenue-boosting potential inherent in the burgeoning automotive sector.
The Revenue Act of 1932 included a penny-a-gallon gas tax; however, it was
dedicated to deficit reduction, not transportation-related projects. This was
no mere lagniappe added to the treasury; the $124.9 million raised by the
gasoline tax equaled 7 percent of total internal revenue during FY 1933.[3]

The gas tax was advertised as an emergency measure, a response to the dire
economic straits in which the country found itself, but like most emergency

measures increasing the scope of government, it soon became a permanent feature. As is so often the case, war embedded this impost ever more deeply into the federal tax code. In response to the Second World War, the gas tax was raised to 1.5 cents per gallon, and then to 2 cents per gallon during the Korean War.

Despite the diversion of the penny-a-gallon gas tax, and President Roosevelt's reservations about the usefulness of government-subsidized roadwork, Jason Scott Smith, in *Building New Deal Liberalism: The Political Economy of Public Works, 1933–1936*, declared that "the program that most explicitly drew upon the legacy of New Deal public works at home was the national highway system."[4] He concluded his study with the assertion that "New Deal public works and the highway programs and defense contracts that succeeded them forged an expression of New Deal liberalism in mortar, concrete, and steel."[5]

In February 1938, President Roosevelt sketched out for Thomas H. Mac-Donald, the Iowa-bred civil engineer heading the Bureau of Public Roads, an envisaged national highway system based on six lines, three horizontal and three vertical, stretching from the Atlantic to the Pacific and from Canada to Mexico and the southern shores. FDR assumed that tolls would support these, though as to specifics he was hazy. But MacDonald had his marching orders. In 1939, he and his lieutenant Herbert Fairbank produced *Toll Roads and Free Roads*, an ambitious delineation of a system of what they called "interregional" highways spanning the country. Financing by tolls was not workable, they claimed, because projected traffic on many of the routes would not come close to covering the cost of construction and maintenance except in the Washington-Boston corridor. Instead of FDR's fanciful sextet of gridlike roads, MacDonald and Fairbank proposed an untolled network of highways, 26,700 miles in total, linking the nation's largest cities. This would be a "system of direct interregional highways designed to facilitate the long and expeditious movements that may be necessary in the national defense, and similarly wide-ranging travel of motorists in their own vehicles."[6]

Two years later, President Roosevelt asked MacDonald to elaborate on this outline. The result was *Interregional Highways* (1944), a blueprint for a thirty-nine-thousand-mile interstate system linking the nation's major cities, though it left the exact nature of intracity expressways to later planners. (MacDonald was a caricature of the "just the facts, ma'am, all right angles" engineer. This erstwhile chief engineer of Iowa quadrupled his salary to $6,000 annually when in 1919 he moved to Washington to head the Bureau of Public Roads. He was a grim, humorless, and supremely talented martinet whose wife called him "Mr. MacDonald" and who would not permit employees to share an elevator ride with him, though he made an exception for his secretary.[7] These were no later-in-life affectations; as a boy, MacDonald ordered his younger brothers and sister to call him "sir."[8] MacDonald explored new frontiers in uptightness: he even wore a coat and tie while riding horseback.[9] Thomas H. MacDonald was dismissed by Secretary of Commerce Sinclair Weeks in early 1953, thirty-four years after he had become the chief of the American road. On receiving the news, the widower reportedly told his secretary—the one whom he had permitted to share his elevator all these years—"I've just been fired, so we might as well get married."[10] The romantic devil!)

Weaponizing Highways

The Second World War put a stop to most highway construction. A virtual moratorium thereon was in place until hostilities ceased. Yet the war, though it diverted federal spending away from domestic transportation during fighting, was an inevitable boon to highways. Transportation officials played up the national defense aspects of their bailiwick, conjuring the ghosts of Rome and its military road system, and pointing with a finely calibrated mixture of threat and admiration to the German Autobahn, which permitted the German army to transport men and equipment at average speeds of fifty miles per hour and up, as compared to other roads, where the pace of travel did not even reach twenty-five.

The clouds of war carried the seeds of opportunity. A. W. Brandt, superintendent of public works for New York State, scored the Roosevelt administration in 1940 for failing to recognize "the fact that our highway systems are not adequate to properly protect us against the blitzkrieg method warfare"[11]—this, of course, even before the United States had joined the war, and when the prospect of a German air assault on the American mainland was so remote a possibility as to be almost unthinkable. But Brandt was confident that FDR would soon come to his senses, and that Congress would authorize the necessary billions of dollars to bolster the national defense by subsidizing the construction of new and better highways.

Sure, Brandt admitted, such a program would require "the expenditure of huge sums" for equipment and sundries "that may never be used," but not to worry. This "highway system will not rust out and become obsolete or useless because foreign powers fail to attack us. It will be used from the day it is completed just as all peace-time highways are used, and will more than pay for itself over the years in savings to the commerce of our country in addition to the added recreational use that will be afforded our people."[12]

So, the prospect of war, whether realistic or not, whether realized or not, would produce political cover for the construction of new and better roads. In November 1941, the linkage of national defense and public highways was explicit when under the Defense Highway Act, the federal government offered $10 million in matching funds to the states for postwar road planning. Yet the states needed to understand that their rights were distinctly secondary to those of the national government in time of war. In 1940, as the war clouds gathered, Mr. MacDonald rejected the entirety of the state of Oklahoma's $5 million federal-aid highway program because "it was scattered throughout the State with little regard to strategic needs."[13] After Pearl Harbor, national defense needs were the overriding criteria in all disbursements of federal highway assistance.

In April 1941, President Roosevelt appointed a seven-man Interregional Highway Committee to plan a postwar national road network. The committee was skeptic-less, a congeries of "planners, state road engineers, and old-fashioned political appointees," as Mark H. Rose and Raymond A. Mohl wrote, and included New Deal brain truster Rexford Guy Tugwell, perhaps the most centralizing and least democratic figure ever to have the ear of a US president.[14] The challenges conceded by the committee were merely technocratic and political; constitutional and aesthetic complications were not even an afterthought.

The committee was, however, prescient on at least one score. On September 9, 1941, committee member Bibb Graves, former governor of Alabama (and a member of the University of Alabama's first intercollegiate football team), "suggested earmarking federal automotive taxes for highway purposes," foreshadowing the Highway Trust Fund of the next decade.[15] The committee recommended the creation of a national network of interregional highways, as Thomas MacDonald had called them, but these were retitled "interstate highways" in the Federal-Aid Highway Act of 1944. The interregional highways would total thirty-nine thousand miles, of which more than half (twenty-one thousand) would be rural two-lane highways. Most already existed; the surfaces and specs simply needed updating. Alas, although this National System of Interstate Highways had a new name, there was no new funding to go with it. The routes composing this system would be jointly selected by the federal and state governments and would connect 90 percent of all American cities with populations above fifty thousand as well as forty-two state capitals, but it was not to exceed forty thousand miles. Financing thereof would be on a 50–50 federal-state split, which was not generous enough for the states to act, especially given the war-created backlog of repair and maintenance work on existing highways. A primary purpose, according to the 1944 act, was "to serve the national defense."[16]

The 1944 act subdivided the federal-aid system three ways, into primary, secondary, and extension roads. Though eligible for federal aid, these were not federal roads; such did not exist, nor do they exist today, except in the extremely limited cases of roads on federal lands. But the blueprint, or blueprints, for the interstate had been created, while the man whose name would eventually be attached to the system, Dwight D. Eisenhower, was half a world away, serving as the supreme Allied commander in Europe.

The war took its toll on the roads. Rather than by rail, trucks shipped the majority of defense materiel overland during World War II within the United States, thereby punishing roads that were not built to bear the weight of military vehicles. But that only fed the need for more funding. General Philip Fleming, administrator of the Federal Works Agency, the catchall bureaucracy created in 1939 to house the various public works departments of the national government, told a congressional hearing in 1948 that highways had been vital to the success of the US military: "There were wings and fuselages and turrets and engines moving over our highways to Kansas and Texas and being assembled there in finished airplanes. There were mechanical parts moved up into New Hampshire which became bomb sights. So our highways really were a part of our national effort. Without them I do not know where we would have been in our war effort."[17]

Return of the Turnpike

As an added bonus, or so it was claimed, urban highway construction would result in the "elimination of slums and blighted areas," as a publication of the American Concrete Institute—never known for its particular solicitude for the urban poor—predicted in 1943.[18] Property in such areas was cheaper to acquire and easier to condemn, and you didn't face the kind of hyperarticulate opposition that one might encounter if trying to blast a superhighway through, say, Greenwich, Connecticut, or Concord, Massachusetts.

Thomas H. MacDonald laid out the case for urban expressways in a 1947 number of *The American City*. Like a canny old pro, he stacks the deck at the outset. The cities of the nation, he says, are faced with a question: "Shall we build highways which will enable traffic to move into and through the city quickly and safely, or shall we try to get along with things as they are?"[19] Well, if you put it *that* way ... MacDonald raises strawmen, which he knocks down in rapid succession, but the first of these is, as would be revealed in the long run, made of sterner stuff than straw. Objections have arisen, writes MacDonald, on the grounds that the envisioned expressways "necessitat[e] razing a large number of dwellings at a time when the city is in the throes of an acute housing shortage."[20] Yet, as MacDonald correctly notes, the supposed shortage can be alleviated simply by building more housing, at public expense if need be. But the more fundamental matter—that of the extensive use of eminent domain and the bulldozer to wipe out homes to make room for highways—he manages less adroitly.

As was typical when professional engineers addressed lay audiences, Mac-Donald assures readers that "anyone who is familiar with expressway design" will understand that this objection is baseless: "Admittedly," he writes, "an expressway through a densely populated area does involve razing numerous buildings, including many dwellings. In most instances, routes selected for expressways, as they approach the center of the city, pass through 'blighted' sections where property values are low, and most of the buildings are of the type that should be torn down in any case, to rid the city of its slums."[21] This attitude was an ominous foretaste of the cavalier treatment center cities were going to get from the highwaymen. Mass demolition of homes was advertised as an act of benevolence, of concern for the poor, of humanitarianism. And the definition of *blighted* was stretched so thoroughly that by the 1970s, it included solid working-class neighborhoods, white, black, or mixed, as well as areas of unquestionable poverty.

By 1949, Los Angeles—center of opposition to a 1910 California state highway bond issue—was the model car-centered urban culture. Its average of 2.9 persons per automobile dwarfed the persons per car ratio of Chicago (5.1) and New York City (8.7).[22] It was also, in the 1930s, the birthplace of the freeway—that is, a controlled-access, high-speed highway—which took hold as the Golden State experienced a wartime and postwar boom. The coiner of the term *freeway*, Edward M. Bassett, a New York City attorney and ex-congressman who is known as the "Father of American Zoning," explained in 1930 that a freeway does not necessarily mean that the road is without tolls, but it does provide "freedom from grade intersections and from private entrance ways, stores, and factories." Specifically, a freeway "will have no sidewalks and will be free from pedestrians. In general, it will allow a free flow of vehicular traffic."[23] Vehicles enter and exit the road at specified points, usually spaced at least one and often several miles apart. (When the National System of Interstate and Defense Highways was officially born in 1956, it incorporated about 8,600 existing freeway miles.[24])

Yet the word *freeway* implies, if not dictates, the absence of fees. And so, across the nation, *"Who pays?"* was the question of the hour. The specter of Senator Russell Long's immortal doggerel—*Don't tax you / Don't tax me / Tax that fellow behind the tree*—hovered over the incipient debate. Speaking for the American Trucking Association, director of research William A. Bresnahan bemoaned in 1952 that his industry was becoming "the whipping boy for those who are seeking an easy, or selfish or punitive answer to the question" of who should pay for the highways.[25]

In 1947, truckers had been a major component of an unsuccessful nation-wide petition campaign to convince Congress to repeal federal gasoline taxes, claiming this was "special class taxation," because "the burden is determined by the distance the taxpayer must drive to or from his farm or his place of employment."[26] These taxes discriminated against commuters in addition to truckers. Mr. Bresnahan of the American Trucking Association posited that three general groups benefited from highways. His ordering was instructive. First up were property owners, who gained from their access to the streets, avenues, and boulevards. Of course, this was a double-edged sword, as the highwaymen also had the power to seize property via eminent domain or drive property values down by their arbitrary or invidious placement of roads. An expressway running through one's backyard was not exactly a stimulant to property values, nor was a fast food and truck stop–clotted interchange just down the street.

The second group to gain from highways, according to the spokesman for the American Trucking Association, was the public. The roads gave them better access to fire and police protection, commercial establishments, and the like, not to mention the fact, so often pounded home during the Cold War, that new and improved roads were allegedly critical to the national defense. The third, and last named, beneficiaries were those who owned motor vehicles, trucks (though not explicitly mentioned) among them. This group had been hard-pressed, even mistreated, asserted Bresnahan, who noted that while taxes on motor vehicles accounted for 34 percent of total road expenditures in 1925, they had swollen to an unconscionable 103 percent in 1950.[27] Vehicle owners were being singled out and punished. It was time to offload the burden from them and onto property owners and non–property owners. Surely boosting the property tax and general taxes was a fairer method of raising the necessary funds than putting the onus on motorists and truckers. Few outside the industry bought the argument. Truckers were now, in Senator Long's ditty, the fellow behind the tree.

At the state level, the issuance of bonds became popular to finance road-building. While in 1945 state and local governments raised $47 million for roads by issuing bonds, five years later the total exceeded $600 million.[28] Raising highway construction monies via bonds required less mucking about in the daily political mire; it wasn't as laborious a task as working through the appropriations process. Thus, it held greater appeal for the engineers, who liked to imagine themselves outside of, or above, politics.

The pride of the American road engineers in the pre-Interstate Era was the 160-mile Pennsylvania Turnpike, which opened in October 1940 after a breakneck construction pace of just twenty months. Federally subsidized by the PWA ($25 million) and the Reconstruction Finance Corporation ($35 million), this tolled highway was considered a model of engineering elegance and, as a political selling point, a means of alleviating severe unemployment in the Keystone State. Its success set off a round of toll road building, and cars were soon barreling down turnpikes opened in Maine (1947), New Hampshire (1948), and New Jersey (1952). Built between 1949 and 1960 and incorporated into the interstate system, the New York State Thruway was a 570-mile toll road trapezoid-without-a-bottom connecting southwestern New York State and Buffalo with New York City.[29]

Though they would be loath to admit the fact, New York's solons were inspired by the example of their neighbor to the south to undertake their own transstate toll road, the New York State Thruway, which linked not only New York City with Albany and Albany with Buffalo, but also the state of New York with Massachusetts, Connecticut, New Jersey, Pennsylvania, and Ontario. By the time Thruway planning got underway in the early 1940s, writes Michael R. Fein, the "decline of local prerogative, a process begun in the 1890s, was all but complete."[30] The superhighway would go where the engineers wanted it to go, local protests and property rights be damned. The plaints and howls of farmers whose land had been seized was mere background static. Deference to "remote authority" was all the rage; the pathmasters of the 1880s would not have recognized this regime.[31]

In the immediate postwar period, New York Governor Thomas E. Dewey proposed a massive expansion of state highway spending: he would out-Roosevelt the party of Roosevelt. Governor Dewey boasted that "the Republican party has picked up the banner of liberal and progressive government from the faltering hands of the Democratic party."[32] The number of state highway engineers rocketed from five hundred to about two thousand in 1946, the year ground was broken for the Thruway. Yet Governor Dewey's version of the Erie Canal was not without opposition. Urban Democrats called it a "luxury boulevard," preferring that the money be spent on their constituents rather than cross-state motorists.[33] The less rosy the economic picture appeared, the more favorable Dewey grew to make the Thruway a toll road, which offended those who believed that free travel over highways was a kind of natural birthright.

Construction moved at a pace that makes rush-hour traffic in Manhattan seem like the Indy 500. In 1950, four years after groundbreaking, just thirteen miles of the Thruway were completed. The New York State Thruway Authority, the governmental agency in charge of the roadway, which had "removed from direct public oversight" this longest toll superhighway in the nation,[34] came under attack for its arrogance and constant chest-beating publicity mongering. Governor Dewey, sensing that things were going off track, was reduced to citing the dubious rationale of military necessity for his prized roadway. The Korean War was heating up. "I do not mean to be an alarmist," said Dewey, alarmingly, "but it is the business of the government to be prepared, as many people are now realizing. If anyone ever does drop a bomb on New York City, you won't hear any more arguments about whether New York City needs the Thruway."[35] You know a politico's pet project is in trouble when he goes nuclear. (Dewey's warning was buttressed by that of James Forrestal, Truman's secretary of defense, who wrote in 1949 that "modern warfare" could "require movement of much of [a city's] population and industry," and in that movement a national system of highways would be of vital import.[36])

The Thruway bypassed central cities, so while it did not wreak the same architectural destruction as the interstate did, it drew commercial traffic away from downtown businesses and to new fringe developments. The superhighway ran parallel to the old main drags of central New York State, routes 5 and 20, and merchants feared—correctly, it turned out—that traffic, and therefore business, would be diverted from these channels. The Thruway bisected other towns, such as Fultonville, and local civic life withered as a result. Homes and businesses were condemned, seized, and razed via eminent domain, sometimes accompanied by heartbreaking acts of defiance by the owners.

In 1955, New York citizens—the motorists for whom the Thruway Authority insisted it spoke—got to have their say about the superhighway. A $750 million bond issue was placed on the ballot, despite the now ex-governor Dewey's past assurances that state indebtedness was not necessary to build and support the state's highways. To the surprise of New York's transportation establishment, the bond issue went down, winning barely 40 percent of the vote. This proved to be a mere blip, however, as the road crew came back the next year with a more modest bond issue that won approval. New Yorkers would, for years, chafe at the perceived unfairness of the Thruway. They had paid for their cross-state superhighway, and they paid tolls every time they used it in order to support its upkeep, and yet they were also paying federal gas taxes that would be used to build and maintain free highways in their sister states. It was the Erie Canal all over again!

The Thruway served, as Michael Fein wrote in *Paving the Way* (2008), his insightful study of roadbuilding in New York, as the culmination of a process by which road "construction was no longer the organic product of local desires but the work of large, centralized, bureaucratic agencies."[37] The late nineteenth-century local democratic model in which town highway commissioners and pathmasters, in consultation with the community, coordinated the location and construction of roads in almost twenty thousand local road districts had given way, in successive waves, to a less democratic, less localized, and finally almost wholly centralized system in which decision-making power was transferred to the state highway commission, the state department of public works, and ultimately a congeries of federal and state agencies, including the FHWA, in which the voices of citizens were so much white noise, and power rested with unelected government officials and engineers.

Ike's Pyramid

The Interstate Highway System (IHS), said the aptly named Earl Swift in his *The Big Roads: The Untold Story of the Engineers, Visionaries, and Trailblazers Who Created the American Superhighways* (2011), is "the greatest public works project in history, dwarfing Egypt's pyramids, the Panama Canal, and China's Great Wall."[38] Swift was not alone in playing the hyperbole game; William G. Wing, writing in *Audubon*, said that the interstate bested not only the Great Wall, the pyramids, and the Panama Canal, but also Noah's Ark and the Tower of Babel to boot.[39] With less magniloquence but no less trenchancy, Rose and Mohl have declared that "few public policy initiatives have had as dramatic and lasting an impact on modern America as the decision to build the Interstate Highway System."[40]

Candidate Eisenhower had said during the 1952 campaign that "a network of modern roads is as necessary to defense as it is to our national economy and personal safety."[41] This turned out to be more than just another election-year platitude. As president, Eisenhower, who had an old-fashioned, green-eye-shade Republican's aversion to debt, instructed his aides in April 1954 to come up with a "dramatic plan to get 50 billion dollars' worth of self-liquidating highways under construction."[42] So while the scale was to be grand, this vast enterprise was to pay for itself, presumably through tolls or fees, though the method of financing was open to negotiation. President Eisenhower went into this with his eyes wide open; this was not a modestly conceived and strictly limited initiative that got away from its progenitor. He admitted to being influenced by the "superlative system of German Autobahnen" he had seen during the Second World War, and he was set on the realization of what he proudly called "the biggest peacetime construction project of any description ever undertaken by the United States or any other country."[43]

The public rollout of what would become the National System of Interstate and Defense Highways occurred on July 12, 1954, at a meeting of the National Governors' Conference in Lake George, New York. President Eisenhower was to have delivered the address, but his sister-in-law had just died, so Vice President Richard M. Nixon pinch-hit. He went for the long ball. After the typically stiff Nixonian prologue, with jokes so feeble they couldn't even provoke a mild chuckle from a TV sitcom laugh track, the vice president put bat to ball, proposing a ten-year, $50 billion highway program. Such an ambitious project would be essential to national defense, explained Nixon, who related the story of Second Lieutenant Dwight D. Eisenhower's cross-country trek of 1919. The all-weather road mileage in the nation then totaled around 300,000 miles, he said, as opposed to 1.8 million miles thirty-five years later. Similarly, the number of cars and trucks in the country had risen from 7.6 million to more than 56 million.[44] But infrastructure had not kept pace, and the American people had paid a heavy price in four ways.

First and most obvious were the casualties, which rivaled those of a mid-level war. Close to forty thousand Americans died on the highways every year, and well over one million were injured. (Left unexplored was whether the fault lay as much, if not more, with bad drivers and poorly designed automobiles than with bad roads.) Second, the lost hours that were whiled away in traffic jams and congested roads: a perennial complaint that in our day has only worsened and sparked calls for private tolls roads as an alleviator. Third, civil suits were jamming up the courts—a justification so weak that it had to be discarded, never seen again. Fourth, and sexiest—if any line of argument borrowed from Thomas E. Dewey can be thought sexy—were "the appalling inadequacies to meet the demands of catastrophe or defense, should an atomic war come."[45]

To meet and overcome these obstacles to safety and prosperity, the vice president, speaking for the president, laid down a quartet of guiding principles for his highway plan. First, that it comprehend the entirety of the realm: "Transcontinental travel—intercity communication—access highways—and farm-to-market movement—metropolitan area congestion—bottlenecks—and parking."[46] Second, that each individual project be "self-liquidating," whether through the collection of tolls or a hike in the gasoline tax or via federal aid in cases of national import. Third, that it be based in the harmonious and cooperative interaction of federal, state, and local governments, with the prerogatives of the latter two not swallowed up by the first. (Not adduced were previous examples of the federal government taking over the financing of an activity but leaving its administration and supervision to the localities.) Fourth, that it undertake in earnest the planning and construction of the long-discussed but never-consummated interstate highway system, which was to be funded by the federal government in cooperation with the states and consist of both new and modernized highways.[47]

The governors were by no means unanimous in their enthusiasm for Vice President Nixon's call for an increased federal role in roadbuilding. Certain governors, like Pennsylvania Republican John Fine, son of a coal miner, were demanding the elimination of the federal gasoline tax, with the states inheriting that taxing power. But the die was cast. A Republican president had proposed a vast public works project of Rooseveltian scope: the sheen of bipartisanship was on it. Within the administration, however, the drawing of battle lines began. As noted, Thomas MacDonald was out at the Bureau of Public Roads. MacDonald had already passed the federal government's mandatory retirement age of seventy, but exceptions could be, and were, made for fixtures such as the joylessly competent Iowan. Incoming administrators cast jaundiced eyes at bureaucrats who create their own fiefdoms, and new commerce secretary Sinclair Weeks summarily canned MacDonald, replacing him with Francis V. du Pont of the Delaware royal family. Du Pont was president of that family's chemical company and a respected grandee of Delaware GOP politics. He kept MacDonald's staff, relaxed regimentation in the office, and became immensely popular with employees of the Bureau of Public Roads. His policy preference was for the federal government to finance the entirety of the interstate. Sinclair Weeks's undersecretary of commerce for transportation, Robert B. Murray Jr., preferred that the states finance the system via the imposition of tolls.

But the pertinacious bulldog of tolling the interstate was General John S. Bragdon, who, like Eisenhower, had been a member of the West Point class of 1915. General Bragdon served as an adviser on public works planning to the Council of Economic Advisers and as special assistant to the president for Public Works Planning. Philosophically, he was a centralizing nationalist, who believed the federal government should play the dominant role in constructing the toll-financed interstate. Sure, this ran in the face of four decades of federal highway policy since the 1916 act, but the era of the free ride was over.

The whole project would be overseen by a National Highway Authority in Bragdon's vision and would brook minimal interference from those annoying state and local highway departments. In fact, state highway departments would be roadkill under the Bragdon plan. This was politically impossible and contrary to American tradition, yet Bragdon offered trenchant if unheeded advice as well. He fought hard for tolls, being a pay-as-you-go man. And he urged the exclusion from the plan of inner-city expressways, whose cost of as much as $16 million per mile vastly exceeded the average $1-million-per-mile cost of intercity expressways. The differential was due to "land acquisition costs, the relocation of utilities, a larger number of interchanges, and more complex engineering and design problems."[48] The interstate, General Bragdon believed, ought to be built up to the edge of the city, at which point a series of outer loops would permit long-distance travelers to bypass the denser urban area. The design and funding of inner-city roads would be the responsibility of the cities and states. Bragdon was right on the matter of the cost of intraurban expressways, which typically exceeded the construction cost of nonurban expressways by a factor of ten or more.

Eisenhower, whose bureaucratic savvy has by now become an axiom of political science, appointed a pair of committees to study the matter and report back to him: the President's Advisory Committee on a National Highway Program and an Interagency Committee, the latter supplying its findings and recommendations to the former. The Interagency Committee, helmed by Francis du Pont of the Bureau of Public Roads, consisted of representatives from cabinet departments (Commerce, Defense, and Treasury) as well as the Budget Bureau and the Council of Economic Advisers.

The President's Advisory Committee on a National Highway Program, born September 7, 1954, was better known as the Clay Committee, not for its malleability, but for its leader, General Lucius DuBignon Clay, a trusted friend and military comrade of the president's. Clay appointed four men to his committee; they were notably unskeptical of the case for a massive outlay of government funds for road construction. The quartet consisted of Stephen Bechtel of the famed engineering firm; William Roberts of Allis-Chalmers, the Milwaukee-based manufacturer of industrial and agricultural heavy equipment; S. Sloan Colt of Bankers' Trust; and David Beck, head of the International Brotherhood of Teamsters. From truckers to bankers to engineers to manufacturers to military men, the Clay Committee had covered the bases. (Clay wisely rejected suggestions that he add the autocratic New York builder-destroyer Robert Moses to the committee.) Frank Turner, a Texas highway engineer and former MacDonald aide, did most of the grunt work, leg work, and head work for the Clay Committee.

General Clay later explained:

> Steve Bechtel had more experience in the construction field than anyone in America. He wasn't involved in road building, but had a comprehensive knowledge of the construction industry. Bill Roberts built construction equipment; he knew what the problems were there. Mr. Colt was experienced in finance. We had to determine how we wanted to finance this, and so his experience was invaluable. And Dave Beck of the Teamsters certainly had an interest in highways, and he gave us labor representation.[49]

General Clay had little interest in the doings of the rival, or complementary, Interagency Committee; his group was the cynosure of action, the generator of ideas. The Clay Committee conducted its first public hearing on October 7, 1954, in the Executive Office Building in Washington. First principles, he made clear, were not up for debate: "The question really is not whether or not we need highway improvements. It is, rather, how we may get them quickly, economically, and how they may be financed sensibly and within reason."[50]

Representatives of the AAA and the American Petroleum Institute told the Clay Committee that for any big highway program, general revenues rather than gasoline taxes must finance it. Representatives of the rubber industry shared this position as well. Advocates of fishing from the general revenue pond emphasized the national defense angle—if roads kept us all safe from a communist attack, shouldn't all share the burden of paying for them?—but they found virtually no support outside their special-interest warren.

Committee consultations with federal officials and governors followed the public hearings, and in January 1955 General Clay presented his committee's recommendations to the president, who was, it seems, nonplussed by Clay's eschewing of tolls and a pay-as-you-go method of finance.

The president sent the Clay Committee's report to Congress on February 22, 1955. It laid out a $101 billion expenditure by all levels of government over ten years, of which $31.2 billion would be spent by the federal government: $25 billion for the interstate, $5.25 billion for federal-aid primary and secondary roads, $750,000 for federal-aid urban roads, and $225,000 for federal forest highways. The remaining $69.8 billion would be spent by the states and smaller governmental subdivisions. (Under the then-current arrangement, around $47 billion, or less than half that envisioned by the Clay Committee, would have been spent on federal-aid roads by federal, state, and local governments.)

Clay's centerpiece was a $27 billion IHS, with the federal government supplying $25 billion and the states responsible for the other $2 billion in fulfillment of a 90–10 federal-state split. Financing of the noninterstate federal primary, secondary, urban, and rural highways was a 50–50 split between the federal and state governments. The objective of completing the interstate by 1964 was asserted confidently. (In fact, the last link opened in Colorado in 1992. And as for that $27 billion cost estimate? It was revised upward two years later to $41 billion, then to $76 billion in 1972 and $89 billion in 1975, and finally came in at $128.9 billion.[51])

Most unusually, the plan adopted from the Clay Commission and forwarded to Congress by the president called for the creation of a Federal Highway Corporation, which would issue up to $21 billion in bonds to underwrite the building of the interstate system. These bonds would have a maximum maturity schedule of thirty years and be paid off by revenue generated by federal taxes on gasoline and lubricating oil. They would not, however, have federal government guarantees nor be part of the national debt. The purchase of unguaranteed bonds might seem risky, but General Clay thought that this was a gossamer-thin obstacle, because of course the federal government would assume what amounted to its moral, if not legal, responsibility. There was also a question of the legality of what appeared a permanent appropriation from the tax on gasoline; could one Congress bind future Congresses to this obligation?

In his accompanying letter to Congress, President Eisenhower's endorsement of the financing mechanism was tepid, to say the least: "I am inclined to the view that it is sounder to finance this program by special bond issues, to be paid off by the above-mentioned revenues which will be collected during the useful life of the roads and pledged to this purpose, rather than by an increase in general revenue obligations."[52] *Inclined to the view* is not exactly a hearty and resolute endorsement.

The letter was more muscular in stacking up reasons for increased federal support of the "gigantic enterprise" that was the nation's highway system. There was the annual death toll on the roads of greater than thirty-six thousand and the annual injury tally of upward of one million Americans. (Highway fatalities had crept upward with the spread of the automobile, doubling from their total of almost twenty thousand in 1924.[53]) There was the cost due to substandard roads, congestion, and other consequences of physical deterioration of the roads, which, to pick a number out of the air, the White House pegged at more than $5 billion annually.[54] And of course there was national defense. The *E*-word—evacuation—featured prominently in prointerstate argumentation. The Clay Committee had gravely prophesied that "large-scale evacuation of the cities would be needed in the event of A-bomb or H-bomb attack."[55]

Eisenhower, unlike civilian political allies and rivals such as Richard Nixon, John F. Kennedy, and Lyndon B. Johnson, was reluctant to fall back on minatory military rationales for his domestic programs. He would, on leaving office, warn his countrymen against what he memorably termed the military-industrial complex, as well as a scientific priesthood that was arrogating unto itself decision-making powers that properly belonged elsewhere. But the president, in his letter to Congress introducing his Clay-derived program, did include a paragraph on its national defense implications: "In case of an atomic attack on our key cities, the road net must permit quick evacuation of target areas, mobilization of defense forces and maintenance of every essential economic function. But the present system in critical areas would be the breeder of a deadly congestion within hours of attack."[56]

The administration put forward the claim that, in case of atomic war, "at least seventy million people" could flee to safety via the projected interstate system. As historian Tom Lewis has noted, "the Interstate Highway System was an organic part of the very military-industrial complex" against which President Eisenhower warned in his famous farewell address.[58]

The immediate response was less than euphoric. Raymond Moley, erstwhile bulwark of FDR's brain trust who was now a conservative Republican writing for *Newsweek*, called it "a soldier's dream, in this case the large but not economy-size dream of a general of the Corps of Engineers." The financing mechanism came in for especial mockery and condemnation. Moley termed it "a stooge" agency that amounted to "downright fraud."[59] The *Wall Street Journal* condemned its "hocus-pocus bookkeeping," and the Scripps-Howard chain editorialized that this was a "gold-brick scheme" that "would hike the Federal debt without acknowledging it."[60]

Congress Has Its Say

The eighty-fourth Congress convened in January 1955 with a very slight Democratic edge in the Senate (48–47, with one independent, Wayne Morse of Oregon, who would presently affiliate with the Democrats) and a larger Democratic advantage (232–203) in the House of Representatives. Yet a vast expansion of the federal highway program was not a partisan issue. Dissenters were exceedingly rare. *Congressional Digest*, which devoted a special issue to the subject, declared that "it is a foregone conclusion that a bigger highway program will be initiated sometime during the life of the present Congress."[61]

The devils were in the details, but those devils were not nearly potent enough to derail the juggernaut.

On February 11, 1955, Senator Albert Gore (D-TN), chairman of the Senate Subcommittee on Public Roads, offered an alternative to the Eisenhower-Clay plan, S. 1048. (Gore, too, had seen the Autobahn while serving in Europe during the Second World War, and he was aware of its military usefulness.) Senator Gore's bill would fund interstate construction on a 2–1 federal-state basis, with the federal part paid for by congressional appropriations. Gore also called for a doubling of the yearly authorizations over a five-year period.

Senator Gore, sensing that the financing mechanism was the weakness of the administration's proposal, zeroed in on it. Of the bond interest, estimated at over $11 billion, he said, "That money should be spent on roads."[62] The liberal Democrat Gore had positioned himself as the fiscally responsible pay-as-you-go man. Another liberal stalwart, Senator Richard L. Neuberger (D-OR), echoed Gore when he charged the Republicans with wishing to saddle Americans and their children with an interest burden of $11.5 billion. Neuberger, too, hastily affirmed the absolute imperative of building highways, bridges, and even viaducts, and quickly, but his preferred method of financing was to increase the federal gasoline tax by a penny a gallon, supplemented by appropriations from general revenues.[63]

Senator Edward Martin (R-PA) dutifully introduced the administration's bill as S. 1160 on February 22, 1955, or eleven days after Senator Gore dropped his plan in the hopper, and the day after Gore's subcommittee hearings kicked off with the senator offering the disingenuously sanctimonious observation that "heretofore the federal-aid highway bills have never been regarded as political. I surely hope that they never will be so regarded."[64] Oh, please! In fact, the Gore and Eisenhower plans marked a fork in the road of US highway policy: the former continued down a well-driven path, albeit at a higher rate of speed, while the latter elevated the policy to an entirely different plane, both in terms of its scope and its method of financing.

There were, however, recusants who did not fall in line, at least at first. Giving off faint echoes of the old agrarian position, the American Farm Bureau Federation expressed distrust of a centralized highway program. It spoke for "maintaining strong, independent, and responsible state and local governments," a condition that the Farm Bureau feared would be undermined by an administration proposal that would reduce state governments to "little more than administrative agencies for the federal government."[65] States' rights was the organization's watchword; and in this spirit the Farm Bureau called for the repeal of the federal gasoline tax with the assumption that this impost would then be levied by state governments.[66] (Significantly, as John J. Martin Jr., legislative counsel of the AAA, noted at the time, many of the major players in the debate who had previously advocated repealing the federal gasoline tax and returning such power to the states now kept a studied silence on the question, as the political landscape had changed enough to make it "highly unrealistic to ask for repeal of this tax."[67]) The Farm Bureau and the Farmers' Union also criticized Eisenhower and Clay for ignoring the rural farm-to-market roads that had lured husbandmen into the good roads camps half a century earlier.

Inverting the usual lay of the ideological land, Secretary of Commerce Sinclair Weeks testified before the Senate Public Works Committee that the Eisenhower administration opposed Senator Gore's plan because "it emphasizes State and local needs far more than the national needs."[68] So much for Republican constitutionalism! Admittedly, party platforms are not worth the paper they used to be printed on, but the 1952 GOP platform had indicted the Democrats for "weaken[ing] local self-government which is the cornerstone of the freedom of men."[69] The desirability of superordinating federal to state and local control, it seems, depends on which party holds the reins in Washington.

Even within the executive branch there was dissent. Arthur Burns, chairman of the Council of Economic Advisers, agreed with General Bragdon on the matter of tolls, as did Secretary of the Treasury George Humphrey. The treasury secretary, though something of the house penny-pincher in the Eisenhower administration, was avid for this brand of spending. "America lives on wheels," he said, "and we have to provide the highways to keep America living on wheels and keep the kind and form of life we want."[70] The lives-on-wheels trope was virtually an automobile industry slogan, though to live in perpetual motion would induce a paralyzing vertigo. To live, one must occasionally stop moving. Dizziness is the enemy of clarity, of lucidity, of calm. Given that the American Dream so often celebrated by encomiastic politicians was centered on the ownership of a home—an antidote to living on wheels—one wonders just which "kind and form of life" Humphrey was eulogizing.

Toll roads, despite their underdog status in the debate, were not exactly an anachronism like monocles or sidecars. As the 1950s came to an end, more than four thousand miles of tolled road ran through forty states.[71] But truckers and motorist organizations would serve as the bulwark of any antitoll alliance, and in tandem they were formidable.

Meanwhile, Joseph Campbell, whom Eisenhower had recently appointed comptroller-general of the United States (which is to say the director of the General Accounting Office), told the Senate Public Works Committee on March 28, 1955, that the "proposed method of financing is objectionable" since the monies borrowed would not be counted against the debt obligations of the United States.[72] And yet these would be "moral and equitable obligations of the United States" because they had been issued by the Federal Highway Corporation, a creation of that government. The accounting flim-flammery involved offended Campbell, an accountant. He recommended instead that congressional appropriations fund the federal highway program plainly and honestly.[73]

The bond-issuing Federal Highway Corporation had an even more powerful foe in Senator Harry Byrd (D-VA), chairman of the Senate Finance Committee. A Virginia state senator in the 1910s, Byrd had been a good roads man but, to him, good roads had to be paved according to sound fiscal and accounting principles. At age twenty-one, the to-the-manor-born Byrd had been president of the ninety-two-mile Shenandoah Valley Turnpike Company, said to be the best road in the Old Dominion. (The state bought the turnpike in 1918 and tolls were removed.[74])

Senator Byrd stayed a pay-as-you-go man. He preferred that any new roads were funded by gasoline taxes or automobile fees levied at the state, not national, level. A fiscal hawk with strong talons, he tore at the Eisenhower-Clay funding mechanism. "It is a violent assumption," he said on January 18, 1955, choosing an unusual adjective, to predict that at maturity the thirty-year bonds envisioned by Clay's group would be paid off. He cast a wary glance at the 90–10 federal-state split with respect to interstate expenditures and called the financing mechanism "unique … and thoroughly unsound."[75]

The idea that a federal corporation, "without either assets or income, would borrow $20 billion from the public," guaranteed by the treasury but not included in the record of debts or obligations of the US government, astonished Byrd. He harrumphed that these "procedures violate financing principles, defy budgetary control, and evade Federal debt law."[76] And that wasn't his only beef. Given that "power follows the purse," Senator Byrd cautioned the states against accepting these subsidies and thereby subordinating their transportation policies to that of the federal government.[77] The states, he believed, would come to bitterly regret such a cession.

Lest anyone accuse him of being a mere obstructionist, Senator Byrd proposed an alternative. Federal aid to primary, secondary, and urban roads would continue the long-standing matching basis. The federal gasoline tax, then two cents per gallon, would be repealed, with the assumption (but not the requirement) that the states would reimpose it at a similar level.[78] (The then-average of state motor fuel taxes in the forty-eight states plus the District of Columbia was 5.46 cents per gallon.[79]) Under Byrd's plan, the federal contribution to state roadbuilding, repair, and maintenance would be financed by retaining the tax on lubricating oil and instituting a new half-cent-per-gallon tax on gasoline.

Senator Byrd expanded on this alternative vision before his Senate Finance Committee on March 18, 1955. Byrd's seat was unusually safe; in his most recent race he'd been reelected with 73 percent of the vote, as the Republicans didn't even bother fielding a candidate. Nevertheless, he was careful to assure listeners as well as the folks back home that he understood "the need for very substantial sums for road improvement."[80] But in conjuring up a "dummy corporation" out of thin air, and authorizing it to borrow $21 billion despite its lack of assets or income, Congress would be creating a terrible precedent for similar outrages against the public fisc and common sense.[81]

On top of the fraud involved, the measure would "take the longest step yet toward concentrating power in the Federal Government," warned Senator Byrd, by scrapping the matching-funds formula and making Washington, DC the dispenser and de facto overseer of roads, heretofore a task within the purview of the states.[82] "In these days when we are continuously piling up debt to be paid by our children and grandchildren," said Senator Byrd, "the least we can do is to keep the books honest and make full disclosure of the obligations we are incurring. There probably never was a corporation—public or private—with assets so small and liabilities so large as proposed in Senate bill 1160."[83] The president's plan, concluded Senator Byrd, was "pure pork barrel."[84] And it would have the pernicious effect of causing an ominous imbalance in the relationship between the federal government and the states. The Federal Highway Corporation betokened both federal overreach and federal spenthriftness: it would receive no quarter from the chairman of the Senate Finance Committee.

Fellow skeptics of the Federal Highway Corporation within the administration sang the Byrd song. Secretary of the Treasury Humphrey, who had been an advocate of tolls during the in-house debate over the package, told the Senate Public Works Committee on March 22, 1955, that he would "not object" to financing the program via a hike in the federal gasoline tax.[85] As President Eisenhower noted in his postpresidential memoir *Mandate for Change*, he, too, preferred "a system of self-financing toll highways" to the Clay Committee's bond-financing scheme.[86] He had, against his better judgment, backed the wrong financing horse in 1955.

Looking back, the postpresidential Eisenhower saw the creation of the IHS as exigent. "Ours was a nation on the move," he wrote. "Much of our merchandise moved by truck. We took to the roads for recreation. And we needed roads for defense."[87] But would undertaking the grandest public works project in the history of the world merely accommodate those trends, or would it accelerate and encourage them?

Though Eisenhower would leave the nation with an impassioned and prescient warning against the "military-industrial complex" in his extraordinary farewell address, and though he exhibited a gruff seen-it-all skepticism when it came to matters like the space race, *Sputnik* panic, and the alleged "missile gap," he insisted that a federally subsidized network of highways was essential to the national defense. "Our roads ought to be avenues of escape for persons living in big cities threatened by aerial attack or natural disaster," he wrote in *Mandate for Change*, "but I knew that if such a crisis ever occurred, our obsolescent highways, too small for the flood of traffic of an entire city's people going one way, would turn into traps of death and destruction."[88] (Perhaps he had been jolted by a viewing of Ray Milland's flee-to-the-hills nuclear nightmare film *Panic in Year Zero!*, which had been released the year before he wrote this?)

This was no after-the-fact rationalization. At the time, the president adduced national defense as a significant reason for the IHS, saying, "Large-scale evacuation of cities would be needed in the event of A-bomb or H-bomb attack. The Federal Civil Defense Administrator has said the withdrawal task is the biggest problem ever faced in the world. It has been determined as a matter of Federal policy that at least seventy million people would have to be evacuated from target areas in case of threatened or actual enemy attack.... The rapid improvement of the complete forty-thousand-mile interstate system, including the necessary urban connections thereto, is therefore vital as a civil-defense measure."[89]

Relief of congestion—the garden-variety kind, not the chaotic scenes found in *Panic in Year Zero!*—was also a selling point, at least for those who drove in the populous metropoles. A creative official of the AAA deployed a medical metaphor, saying that if the highways were America's "major arteries of commerce," then the nation was suffering from "arterial occlusion." Not bad; but this was the dawn of the Space Age, and he unwisely shifted images from the human body to the celestial realm, writing, in one of those contextless assertions typical of the era, that if the nation's sixty-one million motor vehicles were "joined bumper to bumper," they would "reach from here to the moon."[90] There was no congestion in the vacuum of space, though the race to the moon was soon to join the nascent IHS as the two great, or at least expensive, public works projects of the American Century. (Dwight Eisenhower, though a space skeptic, had contributed to the strange status of the moon as a measurement standard in *Mandate for Change*, wherein he wrote of the interstates that "the amount of concrete poured to form these roadways would build eighty Hoover Dams or six sidewalks to the moon. To build them, bulldozers and shovels would move enough dirt and rock to bury all of Connecticut two feet deep."[91] Not that anyone would want to do that.)

Curiously, national defense seemed an afterthought during congressional testimony in 1955. Attorney General Herbert Brownell raised the specter of an "atomic attack" and peremptorily asserted that the necessity of an IHS "cannot be really a matter of dispute" because of the demands of national defense, but as these hearings were not televised or widely reported, there was little need to exaggerate the national defense aspect of a public works overhaul.[92]

Drive, He Said

On April 29, 1955, Senator Gore's subcommittee reported out his bill by a vote of 6–3. Two weeks later, on May 12, the full Senate Public Works Committee rejected by a vote of 9–4 the administration bill, S. 1160—the builders rejecting the Clay, you might say—and substituted by a vote of 8–5 the Gore bill.[93] Democrats, after two decades of being castigated by Republicans for fiscal irresponsibility, surely enjoyed tut-tutting in the committee's report that the administration's proposed financing of the interstate was "not conducive to sound fiscal management."[94] The committee's bill provided for a 90–10 federal-state split of interstate costs. One thing that seemingly all sides could agree on was that states would be getting a dollar's worth of roadwork for just a dime—meaning there would be no fiscal incentive for them to exercise anything resembling parsimony.

As a means of attracting organized labor's support, Senator Gore had included in his bill a provision requiring work done thereunder to be in accordance with the Davis-Bacon Act, the 1931 law mandating that workers be paid prevailing wage, which in practice meant the union wage. Prior to this, Davis-Bacon was interpreted as applying only to contracts with the federal government, but henceforth highway contracts to which the states and federal government were parties would be covered as well. Labor leaders argued that if the feds were footing 90 percent of the bill for work on the interstate, the federal wage law ought to supersede state laws. Despite opposition from the Eisenhower administration, contractors, and the US Chamber of Commerce, Davis-Bacon was solidly attached to the interstate legislation. Approval of the Gore bill was by voice vote in the full Senate on May 25, 1955, after the administration's bill went down by a vote of 60–31.

But avenues of House passage were studded with roadblocks. Indeed, no companion bill to the Gore proposal found sponsors in the peoples' chamber. After several weeks of springtime hearings by the House Public Works Committee, George H. Fallon (D-MD)—the *H*, Congress-watchers joked, stood for "Highways," of which Fallon was an unabashed booster—took up a bill that hiked federal gasoline taxes (to three cents per gallon) and diesel fuel taxes (to six cents a gallon) and vastly increased taxes on large truck tires from five to fifty cents per pound.

The truckers hyperventilated, then went into action. Boosting taxes by a factor of ten was an obvious nonstarter. In fact, it was a finisher. Moreover, the trucking industry objected to paying taxes for what it regarded as an overly urban-oriented system. John J. Martin Jr., a knowledgeable, if not exactly disinterested, observer, laid the failure of this particular piece of legislation to the "tremendous pressure brought by the trucking, oil, rubber, and allied interests."[95] They flooded members of the House with over one hundred thousand letters and telegrams as the issue came to a head in July, and enlisted the Teamsters and two thousand lobbyists to further ramp up the pressure.

After rejecting an administration-friendly proposal by a vote of 19–14, the House Public Works Committee reported out a revised Fallon bill with lower taxes on truck tires. But the turned-up heat did not relent. By the overwhelming margin of 292–123, the full House rejected Fallon's bill. George Hyde "Highway" Fallon, Maryland's prince of pork, failed even to carry a majority of his fellow Democrats. (Democrats voted against Fallon by 128–94, while Republicans opposed his offering by 164–29.[96]) House Democratic leaders pinned the blame on the men behind the eighteen-wheelers. Truckers, said House majority whip Carl Albert (D-OK), "are the ones that would get the most commercial benefit from the program.... Yet they are the ones who killed the bill."[97] (He was not wrong: the interstate unquestionably profited the trucking industry. Today, trucks move over 70 percent of freight tonnage in the United States.[98]) House majority leader John McCormack (D-MA) sighed, "Everyone wants a highway program but no one wants to pay for it. I have a sneaky idea that the truckers of the country played an important part in what happened."[99]

Arthur Burns urged Eisenhower to consider "calling a special session" of Congress so that a compromise highway bill might be hammered out, but the president demurred.[100] The six sidewalks to the moon, not to mention the Nutmeg State buried under two feet of rock, would have to wait until 1956. A year later, "the key to success," as Rose and Mohl put it, "was providing something for everyone without imposing high taxes on truckers."[101] The highway lobby, smarting from its defeat, shifted into high gear, and the foes of the 1955 bill were either pacified by gentler treatment in 1956 or had, on reflection, come to see that a massive public works roadbuilding project would redound to the benefit of those who manufacture or produce rubber and tires and petroleum and those who drive and sell trucks.

From its infancy, the highway lobby had whined about an "inadequacy of funds" and "grossly inadequate budget."[102] Yet in 1956 all the elements of this lobby—the contractors and builders of roads and suppliers of material, the gasoline and trucking and automobile industries, the asphalt and stone and cement industries, the trade associations in automobile-related industries, the AASHO and all those other public employees who would benefit from an accelerated and enlarged program of highway construction and maintenance—were, for the moment anyway, propitiated.

President Eisenhower did not sell the interstate as a catalyst for economic growth, but other of its partisans (who were evidently unaware of the concept of opportunity costs) assured the public that the program would create 440,000 new jobs.[103]

To drive home the something-for-everyone point, in 1956 the Bureau of Public Roads distributed to every member of Congress a yellow-covered, one-hundred-page document titled *General Location of National System of Interstate Highways Including All Additional Routes at Urban Areas.* The Yellow Book, as it was known, contained maps depicting a United States crisscrossed by interstate highways—highways that would benefit (or so it was assumed, for what highway had ever done any harm?) cities as well. As Tom Lewis writes in *Divided Highways* (1997), his history of the interstate, "only one representative whose city appeared in the Yellow Book voted against the 1956 highway bill. He failed to be reelected to the 85th Congress."[104]

The Federal-Aid Highway Act of 1956 and the Highway Revenue Act—the bills authorizing interstate construction and paying for it, respectively—moved on separate if parallel tracks toward an easy passage. On April 27, 1956, the House approved H.R. 10660, which authorized expenditures for highway programs including the National System of Interstate and Defense Highways and set up a Highway Trust Fund, by a vote of 388–19. The Senate passed H.R. 10660, with amendments, by voice vote on May 29, though when the conference committee report came before both chambers, the House approved it by voice vote but the Senate, in passing it on June 26, 1956, found its unanimity broken. The vote therein was 89–1, with Russell Long (D-LA) the lone dissenter. Senator Long explained, "It is my judgment that the highway users are already paying more than enough taxes for all the roads which the federal government expects to assist in building and for all the roads authorized by the proposed legislation…. I should be glad to vote for a highway bill (that did not) shift the burden to the highway users, in order to afford tax relief for persons who are better able to pay."[105] The president signed the bill on June 29, 1956, from a hospital bed at Walter Reed Army Medical Center, where he had undergone surgery for ileitis.

The central and historic feature of the Federal-Aid Highway Act of 1956 was its creation of the National System of Interstate and Defense Highways; that *defense* was added as a kind of Cold War talisman to ensure easy passage, just as, two years later, the first major investment—or intrusion, depending on one's point of view—of the federal government into higher education was denominated the National Defense Education Act of 1958.

National defense had become, if not the last refuge of scoundrels, the first refuge of congressional bill-titlers. The *D*-word added gravitas to even a frivolous measure, let alone something as basic as infrastructure. Defense bulked up the education bill, too, just in case anyone thought its purpose too eggheady. And it gave the interstate a seriousness of purpose for those who might be inclined to think it just another pork barrel measure, albeit one on a nationwide scale.

To reassure the states of a continued flow of cash, the act authorized the expenditure of $24.825 billion over thirteen years, which was thought sufficient or nearly so to complete construction of the Interstate System, whose envisaged length was boosted from forty thousand to forty-one thousand miles. Though the interstate constituted just over 1 percent of the total road mileage in the United States, it was projected to "carry approximately 30 percent of all traffic."[106] The act provided for a 50–50 federal-state split in the financing of federal-aid roads, which were placed in three tiers: primary (which received 45 percent of the total), secondary (30 percent), and urban (25 percent). The three-year authorization for fiscal years 1957–59 for these federal-aid roads totaled $1.85 billion.

The parallel Highway Revenue Act of 1956 created the Highway Trust Fund, which was to serve as the exchequer of federal highway expenditures. A series of taxes fed the fund, notably a bump in the federal gasoline tax from two to three cents per gallon. (In defiance of every known law relative to the growth of government, the act called for halving the gas tax to 1.5 cents per gallon in 1972, sixteen years hence. Instead, the reduction date was pushed back in later Federal Highway Acts. The gas tax was hiked to four cents per gallon in 1959, the level at which it remained until 1982.) Other revenue streams for the Highway Trust Fund included eight cents per pound on tire rubber, nine cents per pound on tube rubber, and 10 percent of the manufacturer's sale price on new truck, bus, and trailer sales. Congress had, in effect, ceded control over highway spending until 1972.

The idea of a dedicated Highway Trust Fund raised eyebrows. Why, it was asked, should gasoline taxes be directed solely toward roadwork, when federal taxes on alcohol, for instance, were not funneled to alcohol treatment centers or the enforcement of drunk-driving laws? But this carping did not dent the near unanimity of Congress. The oil industry, which had criticized the gasoline tax beginning in the late 1920s, did not oppose the creation of the gas tax–dependent Highway Trust Fund in 1956. Even the penurious Virginia Senator Byrd made peace with the Highway Trust Fund.

The 1956 act also proscribed tolls on interstates, though it made an exception for existing toll roads. Thus, the Connecticut, Massachusetts, Ohio, and Pennsylvania Turnpikes, the Indiana Toll Road, and the New York State Thruway were grandfathered into the system, though all new interstate roads or segments had to be toll free. This struck residents and politicos of those states, among them Daniel Patrick Moynihan, an early interstate critic who would in 1976 be elected to the US Senate as a Democrat from New York, as tremendously unfair. Why should New Yorkers pay for what others got for free? (Or "free"?)

The Federal-Aid Highway Act of 1956 also banned restaurants and service stations on interstates, which spurred the clustering of truck stops, fast-food joints, and gas stations just off the interchanges. This was a gold strike for some businesses and a disadvantage for others, and it did residential property values in the immediate vicinity no favors.[107] Few potential homebuyers list *easy access to truck stops* as a criterion in their search.

The Morning After

In the immediate aftermath of passage, no one, it seemed, whispered a word of opposition to the general principle behind the new law; their cavils were reserved for details, especially over the always-contested matter of who gets stuck with the bill. As Gary T. Schwartz notes, the Eisenhower-era liberals, chanting the slogan "Better Schools, Better Hospitals, Better Roads," were all for the 1956 act, and while a Byrdian conservative here or there suggested that roadbuilding was a state, and not a federal, function, their voices were drowned out by the clamor of Chamber of Commerce Republicans and champions of anything associated with national defense. The press, whether daily or ideological, was virtually unanimous in its cheerleading for the interstates. The *New Republic*, longtime tribune of establishment liberalism, ran a single bland four-paragraph article on the interstate issue in the critical 1954–1956 period.[108]

As Daniel Patrick Moynihan later wrote, "Conservatives think of roads as good for business. Liberals think of them as part of the litany of public investment they so love."[109] And besides, federal highway spending creates an enormous pot of money that will be spent on high-profile projects that offer picturesque photo opportunities. From the vantage point of 1970, Moynihan posited that the interstate "was a program which the twenty-first century will almost certainly judge to have had more influence on the shape and development of American cities, the distribution of population within metropolitan areas and across the nation as a whole, the location of industry and various kinds of employment opportunities (and, through all these, immense influence on race relations and the welfare of black Americans) than any initiative of the middle third of the twentieth century."[110]

But the contours of these eventual consequences were visible at first only to the most discerning. Fiscal conservatives fretted over escalating costs—by 1958, the estimated price of completing the interstate had been revised upward to $37.6 billion—but some conventional liberals honed in on what, in retrospect, seems the trivial matter of billboards.

The supplemental Federal-Aid Highway Act of 1958 added restrictions on outdoor advertising. The Department of Commerce regulated billboards within 660 feet of the right-of-way. Part of Lady Bird Johnson's efforts at improving the aesthetics of superhighways during her husband's presidency, culminating in the Highway Beautification Act of 1965, would expand greatly on this, though to the more radical critics of the interstate the billboards that so irritated the First Lady were an afterthought, a footnote, to the more general destruction wreaked by the system. (Lady Bird was not the first to take offense at the clutter and vulgarity of the American roadside. In 1927, Mrs. John D. Rockefeller Jr. launched a campaign to improve the aesthetic quality of refreshment stands, which, after a tour by highway of historic sites, she had found most deplorable. She enlisted the aid of Alon Bement, director of the New York City Art Center, who sniffed that these "ulcerous little huts" and "the so-called 'hot dog' industry" were blights on the landscape. Surely the proprietors of these nasty little establishments would take the advice of their social betters and spruce up! Astonishingly, at least to Bement and Mrs. Rockefeller, they did not. For as the Portland *Oregonian* said, it was almost inconceivable that "the members of the Art Center, who are raising all this cultural hob, ever ate 'hot dogs.'"[111])

New legal and logistical issues cropped up. The limited-access concept puzzled many of those who had been used to entering and exiting highways at frequent crossroads; on the interstate, entrance and exit ramps were typically found miles apart. While the new road might be literally in one's backyard, access thereto might require a drive of ten or even twenty miles. Due to complications in negotiating rights of access by residents and businesses along the US routes that were to serve as the skeleton of the interstate, more than half of the system's roads were constructed on new alignments, which actually shortened the system as originally conceived by more than one thousand miles.[112]

The interstate also was something of a killjoy, or a damper on the romanticism of the open American road. Consider the iconic Route 66, the 2,200-mile transmission belt of Okies and those Midlanders seeking paradise, or at least jobs, in the Golden State. It was the romantic road of blazing neon motel signs, biscuit-and-gravy truck stop diners, of hit pop songs and the lure of whatever was over the next rise. Much of US 66 had been laid out parallel to railroad tracks and in the grooves of old wagon trails.[113] Unspooling from Chicago to Los Angeles, it was "the mother road, the road of flight," as John Steinbeck wrote in *The Grapes of Wrath*. Route 66 was the stuff of myth in a way that US 90, for instance, never could be. Nat King Cole recorded Bobby

Troup's song "(Get Your Kicks on) Route 66" in 1946 and raced up the charts. (Troup called Route 66 "possibly the worst road I've ever taken in my life," but it sure was good to him.[114]) The road also lent itself to an offbeat early 1960s TV series.

Along its roadside bloomed various travel-catering businesses, including restaurants and gas stations, motels, and tourist camps. But when the Eisenhowerian superhighways supplanted Route 66 and its kindred US routes as the road of choice for westward travelers, business dried up. "When the interstate came, traffic just stopped, like that," one merchant told Peter B. Dedek, author of *Hip to the Trip: A Cultural History of Route 66.*[115] Much of US 66 was realigned or widened; in other areas, the interstate ran parallel to the old road, rendering it supernumerary. The interstate system incorporated parts of Route 66; some stretches were simply abandoned, and weeds eventually grew up between the concrete cracks. Other segments became little-used local roads. Similarly, the old Cumberland Road, or National Road, aka US Route 40, was shoved aside by Interstate 70.[116] The FHWA officially retired the US 66 designation in 1985, but the lure of nostalgia (and tourist dollars) has brought stretches of the road back to life today. Still, the Federal-Aid Highway Act of 1956 effectively eighty-sixed Route 66 as a vital force in American cultural and economic life. But when one romance dies, another often is born. For there was the fact, repeated in hushed tones of awe by the interstate's most fervent fans, that one could now drive from coast to coast without ever stopping at a traffic light. *Stop* was not part of the lexicon of this greatest public work!

Expressways enabled the automobile commuting culture and fed the sense of freedom that an automobile and an open (or at least not overly clogged) road brings. They encouraged growth and development in areas and sections favored by their presence, while discouraging such in areas not so favored. They contributed to the suburbanization of America, an argument for which Nathaniel Baum-Snow supplied empirical evidence in a 2007 paper in the *Quarterly Journal of Economics*. While the population in US metropolitan areas grew by 72 percent between 1950 and 1990, the population of central cities declined by 17 percent over that same period. There are, of course, numerous contributing factors to that decline, but Baum-Snow, in subjecting the spatial distribution of the population to the predictions of land use theory, estimated that had the interstate system not been built, the aggregate population of the affected central cities would have grown by 8 percent rather than decline by 17 percent over the four-decade period.[117]

The interstates contributed in a mercilessly direct way to urban depopulation as well. Federally subsidized expressways devastated the core of certain cities and displaced up to one million people unlucky enough to live in their path. "By the 1960s," write Rose and Mohl, "federal highway construction was demolishing 37,000 urban housing units each year."[118] Only after the interstate had largely been constructed did the human scatterings become eligible for relocation assistance. It was too little, too late.

Although raising the specter of mass displacement did not happen during the 1955–56 debate, warning signs soon appeared. Bertram D. Tallamy, superintendent of public works in New York State, and the man who oversaw the construction of the tolled New York State Thruway (though Governor Thomas E. Dewey's name graces the road), was Eisenhower's choice as the nation's first federal highway administrator. (Massachusetts governor John Volpe served briefly as interim administrator before Tallamy could leave Albany to take the job.) Tallamy was a mentee of Robert Moses, which augured poorly for relations between the roadbuilders and those who found their persons or their property in their path—for Robert Moses was the king of wrack and ruin.[119] Moses, longtime head of the New York State park system, park commissioner of New York City, secretary of state under Governor Al Smith, and holder of upward of a dozen unelected positions, wielded almost incomprehensible power over the placement of infrastructure, parks, and people in New York State between the 1920s and the 1960s.

Robert Moses was a man who gave imperiousness a bad name, a man who reached for eminent domain with as little thought as others reach for a tissue. When mere citizens objected to having their homes confiscated and razed by government to make room for highways, Moses sneered, "When you operate in an overbuilt metropolis, you have to hack your way with a meat axe. I'm just going to keep right on building. You do the best you can to stop it."[120] All told, his infrastructural exertions evicted close to half a million people, as Robert Caro estimated in his devastating biography *The Power Broker*.[121] Moses operated in the hazy civic netherworld of public authorities and modern bureaucracy. He ran for office once, in 1934, as the Republican candidate for governor of New York. Democrat Herbert H. Lehman trounced him, 2,201,729–1,393,638. The people had spoken: the bastards! Democracy was too messy for Robert Moses. He scorned "old-line politicians" as feeble-minded enemies of progress, of innovation. Their concerns were petty: a new sidewalk here, a minor adjustment in the tax rate, or a little graft on the side. Moses thought bigger thoughts. He dripped arrogance the way a man in the tropics might drip sweat. He told readers of the *Atlantic* in 1946, when he was riding high, demolishing homes and upending cities, especially in the greater New York area, with multilane highways, that he'd been battling "the greater part of twenty years" against "reactionaries, mossbacks, rural-minded legislators, sharpshooters for taxpayers' organizations, and legalistic comma-chasers."[122] It was simply inconceivable to Moses that anyone, anywhere, could oppose one of his highways unless they were mentally or morally flawed. The gnats who annoyed him chased commas—but Robert Moses had the power of erasure.

Though he may have haughtily regarded the highway lobby as graspers and vulgarians, Moses shared their dream of a network of superhighways crisscrossing greater New York. Moses's plan to pockmark Manhattan with three elevated expressways was eventually defeated. The successful fight to stop construction of the ten-lane elevated Lower Manhattan Expressway and save 2,200 families, 800 businesses, and over 400 buildings from dispossession and/or demolition resulted in the virtual canonization of its leader, the brilliant explicator of urban life Jane Jacobs.[123] Moses planned to ram a four-lane highway through historic Washington Square in Greenwich Village, long a cultural landmark and center of bohemian life. Social critic Lewis Mumford called the proposal "nothing less than civic vandalism." Resistance was limited, at first, to those who lived in the immediate area, but it became a *cause célèbre* in New York, partly due to the spirited leadership of Jane Jacobs and partly, no doubt, because people like associating themselves with hip causes. Most of those who fought the good and ultimately successful fight to save Washington Square considered themselves card-carrying progressives, and yet their labors, as Mumford pointed out, led to the defeat of one of the most assertively progressive of all causes: infrastructure modernization.[124]

Nevertheless, in the late 1950s the spirit of Moses was abroad in the land. Eminent domain and the destruction of neighborhoods were a win-win situation, in the jargon of a later era. The homes and apartments of some

Greenwich Village residents may have been saved, but at the same time eight thousand people were being displaced from the Bay Ridge section of Brooklyn and twice that many were uprooted in Staten Island to make way for the Verrazano-Narrows Bridge connecting those two boroughs. This mass removal of people also bore the fingerprints of Robert Moses—that is, overcoming the opposition not only of the people of Bay Ridge, but also of the borough president of Brooklyn. As Lewis Mumford asked, "What is Brooklyn to the highway engineer—except a place to go through quickly, at whatever necessary sacrifice of peace and amenity by its inhabitants?"[125]

Robert Moses had foreseen potential opposition to the interstate system, which is why he advocated swiftness: build the roads before those most directly affected ever knew what hit 'em. He told the Clay Committee in 1954 that inner-city segments would be "the hardest to locate, the most difficult to clear, the most expensive to acquire and build, and the most controversial from the point of view of selfish and shortsighted opposition."[126] To regard those whose homes were to be seized and demolished by government via eminent domain as "selfish and shortsighted" says more about Mr. Moses than it does about those thus threatened.

At the dawn of the Interstate Era, demolition was seen as a positive good. Milwaukee City Attorney Walter Mattison boasted to a meeting of the American Bar Association that his city intended to route federally funded expressways through areas of what he considered blight, since this would kill two birds with one stone: it would demolish the slums *and* save on right-of-way "purchase" costs.[127] Complaints in Milwaukee and elsewhere were expected to be minimal. Most people favor the idea of highways and their provision of easier access to places they want to go. They just don't want them routed through the middle of their house or down the center of their neighborhood. But on this crucial political matter, the highwaymen gravely miscalculated.

Curiously, the interstate's eponym shared the concerns of those who objected to the destructive policies of the Mattisons and the Moses's. The impact of the interstate on cities didn't hit President Eisenhower until he was stuck in traffic in the Washington metro area in 1959. Puzzled by this—Why was there interstate construction in the city? Weren't these superhighways intended to further inter-, rather than intra-, city traffic?—the president consulted General Bragdon. The general, likely still smarting from his defeat over tolling the interstates, shared the president's dismay.

Eisenhower denied any intention to demolish neighborhoods, seize homes and businesses, and otherwise raze cities. General Bragdon, in a memorandum written after a meeting with the president in November 1959, wrote that "the president confirmed the fact that his idea had always been that the transcontinental network for interstate and intercity travel and the Defense significances are paramount and that routing within cities is primarily the responsibility of the cities. The president was forceful on this point."[128] To settle the matter, Eisenhower met with both Bragdon and FHWA administrator Bertram Tallamy in April 1960. The former made his case against urban interstates at length; the latter, understanding brevity to be the soul of wit, and the president's preferred mode of presentation, produced for Eisenhower the Yellow Book, which had been delivered to the desk of every member of the House and Senate during the debate over the interstate legislation, and which clearly delineated the urban routes of the proposed system.

The question settled, the president accepted Tallamy's point, however reluctantly, and the federal government did not call off its incipient war on the cities. Eisenhower, according to notes of the meeting, "went on to say that the matter of running Interstate routes through the congested parts of the cities was entirely against his original concept and wishes; that he never anticipated that the program would turn out this way." He lamented that in the matter of city-slicing freeways, "his hands were virtually tied."[128]

Worth emphasizing, however, is that the cities, or more accurately their political leadership, were not passive victims of the interstate but eager participants. When word of General Bragdon's desire to scrap inner-city expressways was leaked, mayors and urban activists "deluged President Eisenhower with letters of protest."[130] Federal monies were up for grabs, and municipal officials were not going to be elbowed out of the scrum over concerns as trifling as parsimony and the displacement of the poor.

4

We're Not Going to Take It Anymore: Americans Revolt against the Freeway

FOR A DECADE, the 1950s, which in retrospect many have viewed as staid and conservative, risk averse, and steady-as-she-goes, there was astonishingly little dissent against a gargantuan federal project that promised, up-front, to change America in vital, perhaps irrevocable, ways: to cover it with vast networks of highways; to accelerate it, to speed it toward some greater destiny; to bring its cities into closer contact than ever before; to achieve a revolution in commercial transportation; to finally fulfill John C. Calhoun's dream of binding the nation together with a perfect system of roads ... perhaps even of conquering space. Why, when this futuristic-sounding system was completed, it would be possible for a driver—presumably one who had laid in a sufficient quantity of NoDoz or amphetamines—to traverse the nation, coast to coast, in forty-eight hours. Producers, consumers, truckers, gas station attendants: who wouldn't love the interstate? This was the ultimate win-win-win-win situation.

Since congressional opposition was sparse, if not nonexistent, with the disputes centering on *how* to pay for the program rather than *why* the program should even exist, the recusants were a small and scattered band of writers, poets, intellectuals, contrarians, and libertarians. Academics of the day showed little interest in the nascent interstate. UCLA law professor and former US Department of Transportation official Gary T. Schwartz, writing in 1976, remarked on the "surprising fact that the scholarly literature on the program is glaringly thin."[1]

Perspective was the missing element among those who constituted the consensus. They were too close to it all. From across the ocean came a note of query from Geoffrey Crowther of the *Economist*. After seeing the United States on a twelve-thousand-mile automobile journey, the bemused Crowther told the Committee for Economic Development in New York City: "I find myself puzzled by the statements—that are taken for granted in this country now—that your highways are obsolete. I think I can claim to know as much about them now as anybody in this room and I say it is not so. Your highway system is magnificent. It is overburdened in the immediate vicinity of the large cities; but get away from the large cities and your highways are empty. I wonder if the matter has been investigated as thoroughly as it should be."[2]

It was too late, of course; the time for such investigation of first principles—of the *need* or lack thereof for rapid construction of the interstate system—was in 1954, 1955, and 1956, when the only fractious discussion centered on the best method of raising revenue. Grady Clay, urban affairs editor of the *Louisville Courier-Journal*, who bore the surname of the great Kentucky advocate of internal improvements, was, perhaps ironically, among the very first vocal critics of the interstate, which he predicted in 1957 would be a "monstrous dragon let loose upon the American landscape."[3] His remonstrance, delivered to a notably cool reception from the American Planning and Civic Association, was echoed by a city planner from Cleveland, James Lister, who conceded that the highway planners "may solve the traffic problem—but if they cut our cities and urban counties to shreds and tatters in the process, then we will be worse off than we were before."[4] The interstate, they feared, would be a force for homogenization, standardization, dreariness: one place would end up looking much the same as the other, all local and regional particularities leveled by the remorselessness of The Road.

It was already happening. Bostonians of the 1950s were outraged by the neighborhood destruction and concrete blight of the three-and-a-half-mile, $110 million John F. Fitzgerald Expressway, known by its clinical name of the Central Artery, which was built over the course of the decade and finished in its final year. Mere streets and shops cowered in its enormous wake; it seemed designed to drive home the point to the plebs that they do not matter, and that the automobile outranks mere people. Its chief lesson, explained Richard A. Miller in 1959 in the *Architectural Forum*, was that "urban expressway planning is far too important to leave solely in the hands of highway engineers and politicians."[5] Alan Altshuler, who would serve as the Massachusetts secretary of transportation in the early 1970s, drew another lesson. The Central Artery, said Altshuler, was "a highway juggernaut driven by the lure of 90 percent federal dollars that had nothing to do with the welfare of Greater Boston."[6]

Lewis Mumford leveled the first powerful broadside against the new IHS in the April 1958 number of the *Architectural Record*. Mumford began his seminal essay "The Highway and the City" in prophetic voice:

> When the American people, through their Congress, voted last year for a twenty-six-billion-dollar highway program, the most charitable thing to assume about this action is that they hadn't the faintest notion of what they were doing. Within the next fifteen years they will doubtless find out; but by that time it will be too late to correct all the damage to our cities and our countryside, to say nothing of the efficient organization of industry and transportation, that this ill-conceived and absurdly unbalanced program will have wrought.[7]

Putting aside Mumford's naiveté—did the learned man really think that Congress expressed then (or now, or ever) the people's will?—he was prescient in foreseeing the cost of this sacrifice to the "religion of the motor car."[8] For these roads would not simply be useful connectors linking one metropolis to the next; they would have to penetrate the city's membrane, leaving in their wake "a tomb of concrete roads and ramps covering the dead corpse of a city."[9] This would be an act of governmental intervention in the social, economic, and cultural life of American cities on a scale without precedent. Its ramifications would spread throughout the body politic, and the physical United States, for generations. He dismissed the national defense rationale as a "specious guise" inserted for cheap political gain. "Perhaps," wrote Mumford, "our age will be known to the future historian as the age of the bulldozer and the exterminator."[10]

Less apocalyptic, but equally if not more so mantic, was Daniel Patrick Moynihan's "New Roads and Urban Chaos," which appeared in the *Reporter*'s April 14, 1960 edition. Moynihan, then a Syracuse University professor, was later a picturesque intellectual within the Kennedy, Johnson, and Nixon administrations, and finally a four-term Democratic US senator from New York. He moved, or rather strode, between the worlds of academe and gritty politics, or theory and practice, and with Professor William Nash of Harvard and other dons of MIT and Harvard would organize a successful petition drive in the late 1960s to save 4,600 residents of Cambridge, Massachusetts, from being displaced by a freeway connecting downtown Boston with its suburbs to the north. (In language that would today be viewed as suspiciously reactionary, Brandeis sociologist Gordon Fellman asked during the Cambridge dispute, "Why shouldn't the maintenance of stable neighborhoods be of higher value than the whims of the driver?"[11])

Moynihan and others believed that the forty-one-thousand-mile length of the IHS was excessive. Too many roads were built. As Jerry L. Mashaw argued in an early 1970s paper applying public choice analysis to highway construction, the introduction of a market mechanism that substituted a measure of efficiency rather than the vague "need" likely would sharply reduce the number and mileage of new highway projects.[12] This is true of privately built toll roads, which will not attract sufficient capital without the promise of a return on investment from users of the highway. But when the federal and state governments are making these decisions, heedless—to an extent—of the demand for particular roads, and heavily buffeted by pressure from politicians and the highway lobby, the bias lies on the side of overbuilding.

Ironically—or not, the senator would argue—Moynihan as US senator became closely identified with the major post–Robert Moses highway project in New York City: Westway, a proposed $2.3 billion, four-mile stretch of underground highway on Manhattan's West Side. Senator Moynihan was Westway's chief sponsor as it wended its way, unsuccessfully, through the political, bureaucratic, and regulatory thickets. He insisted that he had not changed his mind since his seminal 1960 broadside "New Roads and Urban Chaos." In fact, he repeated his denunciation of the interstate system's crimes against urban America—"they were throwing up a Chinese wall across Wilmington, they were driving educational institutions out of downtown Louisville, they were plowing through the center of Reno"—while defending this post-chaos roadway.[13] But Moynihan argued that we had drawn the wrong lesson from these disasters in urban planning. Rather than learn from our mistakes and figure out a way to build roads right, "we responded by learning to stop it."[14]

The country had lost confidence, he mourned in a *New York Times* requiem for Westway, which was officially killed in 1985 when New York governor Mario Cuomo and New York City mayor Ed Koch traded in $1.7 billion in federal money targeted to Westway in exchange for funds for mass transit and highway improvements in the city. We had entered a prolonged period of "stasis." Wasn't Westway a gift to real estate developers? asked the *Times*. Of course, but "the most extraordinary real estate development in the history of the United States has been the Interstate Highway program," replied Moynihan, citing "the fortunes made by where the interchanges were."[15] The whole history of government-funded internal improvements is filled with examples of private interests profiting by guessing right, or by having access to inside information. This was an unavoidable byproduct, Moynihan seemed to suggest, and well worth it given the majestic creations of which well-financed engineers are capable.[16]

The Dawning of Dissent

As it dawned on observers that the IHS was no typical brick-and-mortar, or concrete-and-asphalt, infrastructure project but a gargantuan, nation-changing enterprise, other voices of disapprobation chimed in. With the Eisenhower administration winding down, the *Wall Street Journal* editorialized that the interstate was "a vast program thrown together, imperfectly conceived and grossly mismanaged, and in due course becoming a veritable playground for extravagance, waste, and corruption."[17] There were plenty of stories that played as variations on the old pork barrel theme: for instance, the three interchanges built in desert Nevada for $383,000 that were projected to serve a grand total of eighty-nine vehicles each day—among them, cars driving to and fro "a house of ill repute."[18]

Critics alleged that even slipshod planning had compromised the ostensible military utility of the interstates. The secretary of commerce, in consultation with state highway officials, required a minimum clearance of fourteen feet for interstate bridges. Two and a half years and two thousand bridges and underpasses later, the Department of Defense revealed that it needed seventeen-foot clearance for certain of its vehicles and weapons. What to do? An agreed compromise of sixteen feet is what; it's not so easy to add three feet of concrete and steel. This compromise meant a little less bridge modification (only $730 million in 1960 dollars) and clear passage for most, though not all, military vehicles.[19]

Reader's Digest warned in 1960 that "haste, waste, mismanagement, and outright graft are making a multibillion-dollar rathole out of the Federal Highway Program." The *Digest*'s Karl Detzer called it a "nightmare of recklessness, extravagance, special privilege, bureaucratic stupidity, and sometimes outright thievery."[20] Yet his language, so redolent of the Old Right, of complaints about flushing money down ratholes and government bungling, served a point of view seldom encountered on the Old Right. For Detzer argued that the main problem with the federal highway program was that it was *insufficiently centralized*! The states had too much say-so, which, he claimed, was a recipe for waste. Uncle Sam was footing the bill, wrote Detzer, but the states were in charge. Roads were duplicated, as new interstates paralleled existing highways. Unnecessary roads were being built due to pressure from local chamber of commerce–types and politicians, who were in the back pockets of local real estate, cement, asphalt, and steel manufacturers.[21] This would not be happening, Detzer implied, if Uncle Sam were doling out the dough.

This state of affairs should have come as no surprise: decades earlier, Senator Alben Barkley (D-KY), majority leader and later Harry Truman's vice president, had said in opposing what would become the Hatch Act (restricting the political actions of public employees) that "we all know that there is not a state in the Union in which the political organization which is in control of the state does not prostitute for its own political purposes the employment of men and women on the highway, and within the offices constructing and conducting the highway."[22] Infrastructure had long been a political football, or rather a breakaway run to the pork barrel, in many states and localities.

The pork barrel has always attracted grafters, chiselers, and outright crooks, and the press occasionally featured tales of corruption from the highwaymen. Payoffs were made to gain contracts—though the real scandal, as usual, was what was legal: contributions by contractors to politicians of both parties who were able to steer lucrative business their way. Inside information and tipoffs allowed the favored few to make a killing in land speculation by buying and/or selling near interstate exchanges. (Officials of the Carpenters' Union cashed a cool $78,000 when they bought and sold land near Gary, Indiana, through which, they learned, a highway was to traverse.[23])

But extravagance, waste, and corruption were par for the course in federal spending programs; the threat posed by the interstate went beyond such routine and venial flaws. It had the potential to change the nation itself: its landscape, its cities, its neighborhoods. The interstate would alter traffic patterns, leaving certain businesses to die of commercial inanition while bringing customers and prosperity to others. It had always been so. As a Georgia business owner said as early as 1926, "The place of trade is where the automobiles go....A central location is no longer a good one."[24]

And there was the secondary, or even tertiary, matter of what some would call highway robbery. Because almost three-quarters (72 percent) of the interstate's forty-one thousand miles would be laid out on new right-of-way, new territory, governments would take, as Tom Lewis writes, "more land by eminent domain than had been taken in the entire history of road building in the United States."[25] Much of the remaining 28 percent of interstate mileage would require the widening of roads and attendant land acquisitions. (Interstate rights-of-way were, on average, ten times wider than those of the older highways.) The scope of this land transfer, or theft, as critics would call it, was massive. The interstate would necessitate the acquisition, whether by force or the payment by the state of what it chose to call fair market value, of 730,000 parcels of land.[26] Though the feds were paying 90 percent of the bills, responsibility for acquiring this land devolved upon state highway departments.[27]

Engineers laid out the pathways, but appraisers set the putatively fair market price for which those unfortunate enough to live in those paths would be paid for the homes that the wrecking balls and bulldozers would soon raze to dust and stone and debris. As *Time* noted in 1958, the key was to find the "pacesetter" of the threatened neighborhood.[28] Get him to sign, and the others, or most of the others, will fall in line. Those who don't will live, for a brief time, in a nearly abandoned neighborhood before they inevitably lose their home once the authorities pursue legal condemnation.

Time magazine, celebrator of the American Century, while not critical of the interstate, did note as early as 1958 that this great benefaction to mankind came with a cost. Hundreds of thousands of Americans, *Time* explained, "are having their lives abruptly changed—but not always with the touch of a fairy godmother."[29] For instance, after the Tri-State Tollway cut its swath through Hazel Crest, Illinois, students who formerly had walked four blocks to their school now rode the bus, circuitously, for two and a half miles because the new tollway blocked their walkway. (Hazel Crest, despite a population of fourteen thousand, no longer has its own high school. Consolidation and roadbuilding put an end to local secondary education.)

Expressways rend and rive cities, dividing neighbors from erstwhile neighbors, worshippers from churches, customers from favorite shops. Their lives and livelihoods are disrupted and in the most tragic cases uprooted. *Time* quoted one Seattle art dealer whose home and art gallery were to be demolished by the Everett-Seattle-Tacoma Freeway: "I'm a great believer in progress. But what a pity progress has to cost so much."[30] So successful had the publicists and prophets of internal improvements been that a woman whose home and business were being seized by the state felt it necessary to preface her disappointment with a pro forma statement in favor of progress, and by implication the internal improvement in question!

Conservatives woke, gradually, to the price tag attached to this public works spectacular. That price was measured not only in dollars but in the obliteration of history, of architecture, of community. Though *National Review*, flagship of the post–World War II American Right, was largely quiet on the matter of highways, its attention instead absorbed by matters overseas, its house traditionalist, Russell Kirk, used his column to condemn the Bureau of Public Roads for "knocking down living communities of great historical and architectural interest," instancing the Federal period Southwark neighborhood of Philadelphia and the threatened destruction of the Vieux Carré in New Orleans.[31] If Lyndon Johnson means what he says about beautifying the nation's highways, said Kirk, he will "restrain [his] minions" in the federal transportation bureaucracy.[32]

Liberals wondered if the IHS was the best possible use of public resources. Senator Eugene McCarthy (D-MN) predicted that the end result of the program was that Americans would "be able to drive eighty miles an hour along superhighways from one polluted stream to another, from one urban slum to another, from one rundown college campus to another."[33] Or as that exemplary American Tory George Kennan wrote in *Around the Cragged Hill* (1993), "Wherever [the automobile] advances, neighborliness and the sense of community are impaired."[34] Sameness replaced local character; chains supplanted Mom and Pops. By 1971, Holiday Inn had placed 545 of its hotels just off interstate exchanges.[35]

Senator William Proxmire (D-WI), the iconoclastic friend of the taxpayer and scourge of pork (except when it came to Wisconsin's agricultural programs), criticized the ban on interstate tolls. He said,

> Much could be done to reduce rush-hour congestion on our highways and to encourage increased use of public transportation if rush-hour drivers were made to pay the full cost of their road use. Technically there are feasible ways of accomplishing this: through parking charges, license fees, tolls, and metered charges. Yet, little use has been made of these devices in the United States.
>
> One reason may be that the prohibition in federal law against tolls of any kind on federally aided highways restricts the freedom of city governments to choose the types of road user charges best suited to local conditions. I submit that our federal laws should encourage national pricing of road use, not interfere with it.[36]

Senator Proxmire was three or four decades ahead of his time. Likely more—for that time has not yet come.

Heyday—and Twilight—of the Engineers

In the postwar era, the baton of social progress was passed from social welfare activists, settlement house directors, and faith-based organizations to trained managers, scientists, and engineers. Or at least that was what the latter cohort demanded. Robert Moses, writing in 1946, loftily praised the likes of Jane Addams and Jacob Riis for "awaken[ing] the sleeping conscience of a generation too busy making money and enjoying it to give thought to their less fortunate fellow men." (Oh, the moral hauteur!) Moses thanked them for their labors in the vineyards of social uplift but lamented that it was "doubly hard to prove to them that their work is done, that the task is now one of engineering and management, and that they must turn the job over to administrators."[37]

Begone, sob sisters of yore! Hard, cold, calculating men of science were now the do-gooders. The old order passeth away; the new technocratic order was here. And it included, not as a bug but as a feature, the razing of entire neighborhoods, the seizure of homes and businesses by eminent domain on a scale never before seen in the United States, and the displacement of upward of a million Americans, usually men and women of modest means, whose only sin was happening to reside on land coveted by Robert Moses and his fellow roadbuilders. (Not every homeowner went peacefully. In one famous 1964 case, Romaine Tenney, a Vermont farmer, set fire to his property and committed suicide as the state prepared to knock down his home to make way for I-91. The economist Bruce L. Benson makes the case that the "holdout problem" that the condemners use to justify eminent domain would be much less formidable if private entities were responsible for assembling the land and building the roads.[38])

A 1957 symposium in *Better Roads* magazine asked state highway engineers, "How much information about proposed highway routes should be given out before the location of a route is definitely determined?" While certain respondents were the very model of transparency, others preferred to treat mere citizens like so many mushrooms, keeping them in the dark. For instance:

—Daniel K. Kelly of Mississippi: "I would run several lines, and when I had decided which one I was going to use, I would prepare the condemnation papers very secretly. Then I would drop them in the file all at once so that no one would have any advance notice."[39]

—W. W. Seltzer of Pennsylvania: "When surveys are being made for studies of future highway locations, we have many inquiries from individuals and organizations. It is our policy, however, not to give out any information before the highway alignment has been definitely established and the property has been condemned. In Pennsylvania, condemnation is effected by the governor's approval of the right-of-way plan. Before the date of approval, we give out just as little information as possible."[40]

In the teeth of such arrogance, blowback was inevitable.

The engineers and technocrats owned the first dozen years of the interstate's public image. This "golden age," as historians Mark H. Rose and Raymond A. Mohl wrote in *Interstate: Highway Politics and Policy since 1939* (2012), offered engineers "growing prestige, rising salaries, and the sense of accomplishment that came with completing massive projects."[41] But by the late 1960s a generation of revisionists seized the initiative. Just as with Vietnam, the interstate had been sold under false pretenses. The road that was to bind the nation, to connect its cities with gleaming state-of-the-art highways, to fulfill the promises of generations of infrastructure advocates, was despoiling the environment, wracking cities, displacing enormous masses of people, trashing property rights, and symbolizing Washington's lofty disdain for its subjects. The engineers and builders were no longer heroic men blazing paths for civilization in hostile wildernesses; rather, in the new show they were cast as villains, "with their indifference to people and their compensating, overweening respect for the straight line and wide swath."[42] They wanted, finally, to "lattice the face of the earth with concrete"—and stick anyone who buys a gallon of gasoline with the bill.[43]

Critics appeared, almost overnight, and piled on the bemused engineers. Their handiwork, it was alleged, was destroying the habitat of game fish, straightening out meandering streams and denuding them of their charm, robbing birds of their nesting areas, bordering highways with invasive plant species, altering drainage systems, and otherwise making government-subsidized war on the natural world.[44] The engineers dismissed them as "petunia planters, bird watchers, and do-gooders," but those castigating the highwaymen for despoiling the natural world included even the hunters and fishermen of the venerable outdoorsmen publication *Field & Stream*.[45]

Massachusetts Institute of Technology professor of chemical engineering John T. Howard voiced the then-prevailing suspicion of his brotherhood when he said, "It does not belittle them to say that, just as war is too important to leave to the generals, so highways are too important to leave to the highway engineers."[46] The "small vociferous minority" of "so-called artistic and creative people" who constituted the tiny segment of antihighway fanatics, in the words of the president of the AASHO in 1967, had within two or three years swelled to include a large vociferous band of housewives and taxpayer advocates.[47]

Even the AAA, twelve million members strong represented by 235 clubs throughout North America, that middle-class bulwark of the highway lobby, was, suddenly, painted in lurid hues. A writer in the *Washingtonian* described the AAA as dedicated to "building more and more freeways to be coagulated with more and more gasoline-burning cars that will then demand more and more freeways, ad infinitum."[48] Little did the author know that the age of freeway building was about to end, and many members of the AAA, though desirous of hotel discounts, battery jumps, and cut-rate towing when their cars conked out, were ambivalent about the paving of America at taxpayer, and especially taxpaying motorist, expense.

One of the most vehement of the revisionists was Ben Kelley, who had been from 1967 to 1969 the first director of the FHWA's Office of Public Affairs. (The FHWA, successor to the various iterations of the Bureau of Public Roads, was born on October 15, 1966.) In *The Pavers and the Paved* (1971), Kelley offered an insiders' account of what he saw as an out-of-control federal program. He was, as Tom Lewis writes, considered a renegade by the Road Gang, a Benedict Arnold turncoat "perfidiously using inside information to aid the opponents of progress."[49] When Kelley unloaded on the highwaymen in an appearance on NBC's *Today Show*, the Highway Users Federation for Safety and Mobility, a Washington, DC–based front group of the highway lobby, fired back. Kelley was, said Donald W. Maness, a federation official, getting "a hell of a lot of people—especially nincompoop housewives ... all hot and bothered about the pollution, misuse of *their* taxes—blah, blah, blah."[50]

Oops! The Maness memo was meant for federation eyes only, but it leaked. to the embarrassment of a highway lobby that was in the middle of a public relations counteroffensive. This campaign was nothing if not unsubtle. To parry the trope that the industry and its political allies sought to pave paradise, as well as any other spot that lacked asphalt or concrete, the highway lobby asserted that "it would take until the year 26972 to completely pave over this nation."[51] Well, okay. That is the contextless factoid that stops conversation without shedding any light on the matter at hand. The federation, when not denouncing nincompoop housewives and ordinary citizens who objected to the waste of their tax dollars, sent a small army of representatives and speechmakers around the country, giving public addresses about the undeniable advantages of the automobile—without it we would be riding horses, and those going on foot would be avoiding "mountains and seas of horse excrement"—as well as, less incontrovertibly, "the myth of the highway lobby." (The real highway lobby, argued the agents of—well, the highway lobby—was anyone who benefits from highways, which is another way of saying "the entire American public.")[52]

The highway lobby's counterattack gave new meaning to the phrase *tin ear*. A February 1970 press release from the federal Department of Transportation tried to turn the destruction of a Wilmington, Delaware, neighborhood by roadbuilders into an uplifting tale of urban rejuvenation: "The budding basketball star of tomorrow could be a kid who learned how to dribble, pass, and shoot because an Interstate highway came through the neighborhood. And this same youth, who whiled away hours of his life wondering what to do next, can now cavort on a basketball court laid out under a structurally modern viaduct."[53] Yikes—talk about an expensive and destructive way to build a basketball court! The *Milwaukee Journal*, taking note of this stumble-bum campaign by the Bureau of Public Roads, editorialized that "the number of playgrounds built below freeways doesn't begin to make up for the open land and even parks now occupied by freeways" or the pain of the people "displaced by freeways."[54]

Nor did it alleviate the human cost of government run riot. Psychologist Marvin G. Cline cautioned the highwaymen "to distinguish between slum-blighted areas, and low-cost areas."[55] When Boston's West End was urbanly renewed, wrote Cline, many residents exhibited "the clinical syndrome of grief. A depression similar to the experiences one has at the loss of a loved one seems to have persisted in some cases over a period of years."[56] As highway critic A. Q. Mowbray lamented, "The library shelves are full of reports on the *economic* impact of highway building; reports on the *human* impact are all but nonexistent."[57]

What with discontent flaring over the Vietnam War, the national defense rationale for the IHS fell into disuse. The decade had begun with President Kennedy emphasizing the *defense* part of the National System of Interstate and Defense Highways. Kennedy, explaining his support for the federal gasoline tax, said that the system was "essential to a National defense that will always depend, regardless of new weapon developments, on quick motor transportation of men and materiel from one site to another."[58] Given that by the late 1960s the supernumerary addition of the *D*-word seemed to many to be an attempt to make "opposition to [the interstate] seem somehow unpatriotic," as Daniel Hapgood noted in the *Washington Monthly*, the national defense justification faded as time went by.[59]

But safety of a different kind made a powerful talking point. The uniform design of the interstate's 55,500 bridges and 16,000-plus exits and entrances may have contributed to aesthetic monotony, but it also enhanced driver safety. The price of declining fatalities was a certain sterility or dullness, and most drivers were content with the tradeoff. John Steinbeck, in *Travels with Charley in Search of America* (1962), might complain that "when we get these thruways across the whole country, as we will and must, it will be possible to drive from New York to California without seeing a single thing."[60] But in nonurban areas, speed and convenience were powerful assets for the roadbuilders.

The Empire Gets Struck Back

Coincident with the surge in antiwar activism of the mid-1960s was a rebellion against the highwaymen. Before the decade was out, fights over highways had raged or were raging in Atlantic City, Baltimore, Boston, Charleston (West Virginia), Charlotte, Chicago, Cleveland, Columbus, Detroit, Indianapolis, Memphis, Milwaukee, Nashville, Newark, New Orleans, New York City, Philadelphia, Pittsburgh, San Francisco, St. Louis, and Washington, DC, among others. Homer Bigart in the *New York Times* was moved to simile in a 1967 account of urban resistance to a program that had, he wrote, "sent great rivers of concrete creeping like lava through residential neighborhoods and commercial areas, dislocating families, schools, churches and businesses."[61]

Not that the cities were innocent victims in all this. Their mayors had lobbied fiercely for the interstates to penetrate their boundaries; Mayor Albert Cobo of Detroit was moved to rhapsody, pronouncing the urban freeway "a thing of beauty."[62] Over the period 1947–1969, about ninety-eight thousand homes were razed for highways alone in California.[63] All part of the price of progress, according to the engineers, though the vehemence of the displaced and the bad press inherent in photos of elderly widows weeping as wrecking balls knocked down their homes had shaken their certitude.

And so the revolt against the freeway began, fittingly, in car-crazed California, specifically in San Francisco, which rejected the eight-lane

Embarcadero Freeway, a "double-decked concrete monster," and forfeited $280 million in highway funds for two projects.[64] The price of these freeways was the city's soul, and that price was too high. For years, until its demolition in 1991, the partially built and never finished Embarcadero stood as a hideous reminder of what might have been. But the City by the Bay's resistance encompassed more than just the Embarcadero. The San Francisco rebellion began in 1959, when the city's board of supervisors rescinded its approval of seven freeways. Seven years and several revisions later, the supervisors rejected two new designs, one for a Panhandle Freeway that would uproot hundreds of citizens and the other for a Golden Gate Freeway, aka the Embarcadero, slicing through Fisherman's Wharf and separating the city from the bay.

Despite San Francisco's reputation as a haven for Beats and poets and avant-garde characters, its antifreeway revolt was decidedly middle class. Neighborhood organizations of people fearful of losing their homes and their communities to the highwaymen gathered petition signatures and packed public meetings. With churches and parishes threatened, they were aided by priests and Catholic laypeople. Folk singers and ecology activists joined in, while on the other side, construction unions lobbied hard and in their self-interest. Unlike in other cities, notes regional historian William Issel, San Francisco's freeway battle had no racial or ethnic aspect; the coalition was broad based, and there was no sense that the white establishment was targeting minority neighborhoods.

Critically, a localist provision in California law enabled the San Franciscans to fight the Embarcadero on more even terms than were available to other freeway rebels. State law held that "no street or road could be closed until approved by local government authorities," which proved to be a most valuable monkey wrench in the rebels' toolkit.[65] Governor Edmund G. "Pat" Brown, a conventional New Deal Democrat, was furious, especially when his hometown *San Francisco Chronicle* mocked him as a construction-mad dictator for whom expensive and destructive public works were the alpha and omega of governance. "Let 'em eat cement," commanded a fat, berobed, and pompously regal Governor Brown in one typical *Chronicle* cartoon.[66]

The "cement octopus" against which the protest singer Malvina Reynolds (best known for her hit "Little Boxes") warbled was, for the most part, kept at bay.[67] "There's a cement octopus sits in Sacramento, I think," begins the

Reynolds tune; "Red tape to eat, gasoline taxes to drink / And it grows by day and it grows by night / And it rolls over everything in sight." That octopus looked an awful lot like Governor Brown, whose son, Jerry, rose to prominence in the mid-1970s as one of a new breed of post–New Deal Democratic governors who spoke of limits and frugality and were viewed warily, at best, by labor unions and advocates of public works.

San Francisco aside, the freeway rebels often took heavy losses before they could claim any victories. In Camden, New Jersey, I-95 displaced 1,289 families.[68] In Cleveland, nineteen thousand men, women, and children were moved to make way for roads. In Milwaukee, the North-South Expressway displaced six hundred families over sixteen blocks in a section that was 70 percent African American. This was not a slum; though housing values were below average for the city, most housing was either single-family homes or duplexes rather than low-income high-rises. Rates of homeownership were higher than was typical in urban cores. As the aptly surnamed Patricia A. House wrote in her study of Milwaukee families displaced by the North-South Expressway, the road destroyed "a relatively stable Negro neighborhood."[69]

In Miami, a "massive interchange" consuming almost thirty square blocks of the cultural heart of the city's African American district was frankly intended, according to one city planner, as a "complete slum clearance effectively removing every Negro family from the present city limits." Opposition was feeble; ten thousand people were displaced, and the Overtown neighborhood was practically eviscerated.[70]

In Tennessee, the North Nashville project was a three-mile segment of Interstate 40 that lay waste to a historically black neighborhood. Conceived in the late 1950s, the North Nashville project was given a cursory and sleepy public hearing in 1957, and then a decade later folks woke up to the fact that the rights-of-way had been assembled. So, 100 square blocks were "walled off" from the rest of Nashville, and 234 African American–owned businesses, 650 houses, 27 apartment buildings, and certain churches were leveled. One local businessman, Flem B. Otey III, thirty-one-year-old proprietor of Otey's Quality Grocery in North Nashville, told a reporter that the highwaymen were waging an assault on the wellspring of American prosperity: free enterprise. "No race or group has ever gotten out of the ghetto except by the entrepreneurial route," said Otey, an African American. "But now they're closing that route off."[71]

By 1967, an I-40 Steering Committee was fighting back, losing several rounds in the bureaucracy and the courts, as it was too late to steer the bulldozer away from the community. Desperate pleas to Secretary of Transportation Alan Boyd were not met unsympathetically, but as FHWA administrator Lowell Bridwell explained, "An overwhelming factor was that the right-of-way had been purchased and cleared so that the disruption in the sense of moving people out was over and done with."[72] The cows had the left the barn, and the barn had been burned down. Although district judge Frank Gray Jr. sympathized with the citizens opposed to the I-40 onslaught, he was unable to find evidence of racial bias in the choice of a route. The US Court of Appeals agreed, the US Supreme Court refused to review the case, and I-40, with some slight modifications, cut its punishing swathe, to the approval of the mayor, governor, and Nashville Area Chamber of Commerce.

In New Orleans, the highwaymen proposed an eight-lane elevated expressway towering over the French Quarter and dividing it from the Mississippi River. The first draft of this assault on historic New Orleans, which John W. Lawrence, dean of the Tulane School of Architecture, called "an act of barbarism," had been sketched by pencil in 1946 by the decidedly non–New Orleanian Robert Moses.[73] To New South boosters, eager to ape the ways of eastern sophisticates, anything Robert Moses and the superstar builders of Gotham touched was golden.

Though this segment had not been included in the Yellow Book of 1956, the chorus of establishment voices from all corners of New Orleans would have succeeded in making the Riverfront Expressway part of the interstate system had not a determined opposition risen up. Supporters of the expressway included House majority whip Hale Boggs (D-LA), the New Orleans City Planning Commission, the local Chamber of Commerce, the state Department of Highways, and others. Like other southern cities of the era, New Orleans had a business class that was embarrassed by the bad light the region had been cast during the civil rights era. It sought a progressive image, and modern highways were part of that. So was pro football: the fact that the NFL awarded a franchise (the New Orleans Saints) to the city in 1966 was adduced as a reason for leveling part of the French Quarter—even though the Saints would play just seven regular-season games during the 365-day year.

The Vieux Carré fought 'em off, although I-10 claimed a section of the black "Treme" neighborhood. For the rest of the city, the Saints, but not Moses, went marching in.[74] Elevated highways, à la that envisioned for New Orleans by Robert Moses, had once been in vogue but were now universally reviled. These putative cures for congestion turned out to be eyesores and daggers through the heart of neighborhoods in cities from Columbus to Montgomery, and Miami to Baltimore.

Baltimore was yet another American city on the hit list of the indefatigable Moses, who in 1944 proposed an east-west inner-city expressway that would throw nineteen thousand people out of their homes, a development that Moses hailed, because "the more of them that are wiped out the healthier Baltimore will be in the long run." Moses attributed opposition to razing homes and businesses to "people who don't believe in automobiles, live in the past, and honestly believe they have no debt to the future."[75] This was rich, given that Moses, unlike virtually all of those people he was criticizing, never even learned how to drive and did not own a car.

The Chesapeake Bay would prove more difficult for Moses to part than the Red Sea. Baltimoreans rebelled, among them the brilliant and caustic Sage of Baltimore, H. L. Mencken, who called the Moses scheme a "completely idiotic undertaking."[76] Priced as high as $50 million, the plan drew dust as well as scorn. Later attempts in the interstate era to scarify Baltimore met limited success; similar to the case in San Francisco, local officials had the power to block "state highway plans within the city boundaries" and did so, backed by such neighborhood activist groups as the Relocation Action Movement (RAM), Southeast Council Against the Road (SCAR), and Movement Against Destruction (MAD), all strong acronyms that spanned the city's constituent groups from middle-class black to working-class white to upper-middle-class civic leaders.[77] Baltimore would fall on the hard times common to many midsized cities of the Northeast—but it retained most of its bones, which made possible such signs of renaissance as the Inner Harbor.

Anti-interstate rebels won increasingly scattered victories. In Morristown, New Jersey, citizens upset over a proposed six-lane highway that would have split the town wore tricornered hats and colonial white shirts and carried muskets while protesting in front of the picturesque setting of George Washington's Revolutionary War headquarters. Infused with the spirit of '76, they stopped the worst of the damage.[78]

Affluent residents of the Cleveland, Ohio, suburb of Shaker Heights successfully prevented the proposed eight-lane I-290 from riding roughshod through their community, bisecting a park and bulldozing homes.[79]

The people of Kansas City rose up to block construction of the South Midtown Freeway, which since 1951 the Missouri State Highway Department had envisioned as an eight- to ten-lane north-south expressway cutting through city neighborhoods and displacing thousands of residents. The highway had the support of the city's establishment: the Kansas City Chamber of Commerce, the Building Trades Council, and Kansas City's two daily newspapers enthusiastically greeted the prospect of what they feted as a job-creating gift from the federal government. The opposition was concentrated among African Americans, who enlisted the legal assistance of the NAACP in stopping what they scornfully regarded as a white highway that sliced through black blocks without having exits or entrances in those neighborhoods. It didn't hurt, politically, to have the Polish American Catholic Democrats Club of Kansas City in their corner.[80]

The protests flared in the early and mid-1970s. One resident lamented at a public hearing of the state highway department that "planners don't have people in mind when they plan these things. They don't care about our schools that are uprooted. They don't care about the psychological impact on our children."[81] A lawsuit, filed in 1973 and litigated for a dozen years, resulted in a scaled-back project, a four-lane parkway that nevertheless is today an "accident-heavy" roadway due to the intersections added to the plan in response to citizen complaints about lack of local access.[82]

The nation's capital saw its city government, which in subsequent years would be held up as a model of inefficiency, stand up to an imperious Congress that desired faster transport from suburbs into city and back again for its members. In Washington, DC, the chairman of "Niggers, Incorporated," formed to oppose the highwaymen, urged his neighbors to "take up arms to defend their neighborhoods" against the government pavers.[83] "No more white highways through black bedrooms," rang the battle cry. They found an improbable ally in Secretary of Transportation Alan Boyd, who said, "We're going to have to find a better way to build freeways than by disrupting those without political clout."[84]

Posters damning a "White Man's Road ... thru Black Man's Home!" plastered the city.[85] One leader of the District's anti-freeway forces, Reverend Channing E. Phillips, scoffed at the hackneyed jobs argument offered by the white politicians: "We are told, for example, that the freeways will make it easier for inner-city residents to get to employment opportunities in the sub-urbs, because freeways are two-way avenues. Who's kidding who? Freeways do not employ anybody except quite temporarily. If the jobs are not there, no one goes there. And if the employment skills do not exist, a man can drive forever."[86]

Three dissenters to the House Public Works Committee's high-handed attempt to stuff the Three Sisters Bridge and North Central Freeway down the throats of Washington, Maryland, and Virginia residents—Reps. Max Mc-Carthy (D-NY), Fred Schwengel (R-IA), and Jerome R. Waldie (D-CA)—decried the committee's commitment to the pork barrel and its arrogant edict. "The District's highway program," declared the dissenters, "has become a Frankenstein monster which devours far too great a proportion of the District's limited land and financial resources."[87]

Despite the blackmail of Rep. William Natcher (D-KY), chairman of the House District of Columbia Appropriations Subcommittee, who withheld funding for the city's subway system, and defying the prohighway *Washington Post* and *Washington Star*, the capital city's two major newspapers, the District's city council held firm: the Three Sisters Bridge collapsed politically before ever being built. The DC fight brought together, in the words of the *Saturday Evening Post*, an unusual coalition of "Georgetown matrons" and "militant low-income Negroes."[88]

Rep. Natcher and company aside, eventually, these grassroots uprisings found friends in high places. Senator Joseph S. Clark (D-PA) took to the floor of the self-proclaimed world's greatest deliberative body in April 1966 and unburdened himself of a scathing critique of the interstate: "It is time that Congress took a look at the highway program, because it is presently being operated by barbarians, and we ought to have some civilized understanding of just what we do to spots of historic interest and great beauty by the build-ing of eight-lane highways through the middle of our cities."[89] Who matters more: the people who drive through a place or those who live there? Who should decide where the roads go? Who should pay for them? If homeowners resist, what ought the government to do: accede to their wishes or knock down their homes?

The Old Guard had its answers, and it circled the wagons. Rep. John C. Kluczynski (D-IL), a loyal congressional foot soldier of Chicago mayor Richard Daley's machine and chairman of the Subcommittee on Roads of the House Public Works Committee, after acknowledging the small business-people and homeowners whose land had been taken for interstate construction in Chicago and New York City, chirped, "Well, we are not against progress. I am for better roads. We need more of them.... We want more roads."[90] As for those who questioned this greatest public works project in the history of mankind, Rep. Kluczynski called them "people with big mouths running around the country making loud noises and doing all they can to distort the truth."[91]

Not that the highwaymen had no heart. In the mid-1960s, when the majority (100 of 175) of little Glenfield, Pennsylvania's houses were to be demolished to create an I-65 interchange, a state highway administrator told residents, "The state feels bad about seeing you move, but there's no use crying that you don't want to. You have to move. Glenfield will be one big interchange."[92] To which councilman Wendell M. Jordan Sr. replied in a letter, "Beware the treading feet of the giant in the name of progress! Move out of the way or be crushed! This is one of the most cold-blooded acts ever performed by a large governing body against a defenseless child of its own making."[93] Or as a Michigan highway official sputtered when citizens of the Detroit suburb of Pleasant Ridge, Michigan, objected to losing property to I-696, "Pleasant Ridge has a history of opposition. They ought to raze it, pave it, and turn it into a parking lot."[94]

The old saw about the exception proving the rule has never been stated with quite such force as by Elmer Timby, president of the American Road Builders Association, who in the midst of the freeway fights of the late 1960s told the Senate Public Works Committee that "the loudly declared instances of desecration of portions of cities, of disregard for homeowners, and similar derogatory statements with respect to recent urban highways are merely examples of less than perfect exceptions which prove the general adequacy of the program."[95]

And other than that, Mrs. Lincoln, how did you like the show?

The Bureaucracy Buckles

The bureaucratic shuffle that placed the Bureau of Public Roads, formerly resident in the Department of Commerce, under the FHWA within the new Department of Transportation (created in 1966, beginning operations in April 1967) led to a "softening of the narrowly technocratic engineering mentality that had dominated the Bureau of Public Roads," write Rose and Mohl.[96] President Johnson's secretary of transportation, Alan S. Boyd, a Florida attorney, and Nixon appointee John Volpe shut down controversial projects, reined in the concrete-at-any-cost crowd, and at least lent an ear to those who were being thrown out of their homes by the highwaymen.

More than half (twenty-four thousand) of the interstate mileage was in place by the time Secretary Boyd took office. He set the change of tone in a series of speeches and remarks in which he said, among other things, that expressways should be "an integral part of the community, not a cement barrier or concrete river which threatens to inundate an urban area," and "the so-called freeway revolts around the country have been a good thing."[97]

In an interview more than three decades after leaving office, Boyd looked back on the Bureau of Public Roads engineers with a mixture of admiration and frustration: "I have never dealt with finer professional and more honorable and honest people. Their view of life was that God's greatest gift to America was concrete. They really believed that paving America was the greatest thing that could be done for America."[98] Boyd described an epiphany at a meeting with Baltimore residents who were threatened with uprooting:

> One of these men told me his life story, in effect. He said that as a kid he had gone to school, he had gotten through high school, he got a job as a stevedore. He went into the army as a volunteer in World War II. He came out and went back to stevedoring, bought a little house, raised two children, put them through college, and always paid his mortgage, even if he didn't have enough money to put food on the table. Then along comes the highway system, and says, "For the greater good, we're going to take your house. We're going to pay you"—I think

he said—"$28,000." He said, "There is no way I can buy a house like the one I have for $28,000, and I haven't got any money other than that, other than what you give me." He said, "White folks—that ain't fair." That made an impact. I'll tell you. It really made an impact on me.[99]

Nixon's Secretary of Transportation John Volpe, a former construction contractor and governor of Massachusetts, thought to be a pave-it-all-over guy and therefore an ally, surprised the highway lobby. Secretary Volpe, who as governor had called for a doubling of the interstate's mileage, told a Kansas City audience in January 1970, as completed interstate mileage neared thirty thousand, that "you *could* very well develop the greatest network of freeways and interchanges in the world; you *could* pour concrete from one end of the metropolitan area to the other; you *could* condemn property, demolish neighborhoods, wipe out business blocks, and build parking lots on every corner—but you would face the very real and very dangerous possibility that you might not have much of a city left in which to do business."[100] Volpe saved, among other urban neighborhoods, the French Quarter of New Orleans. He had the full support of the administration, notably John Ehrlichman, assistant to the president for domestic affairs.[101]

Among Volpe's lieutenants was Francis C. Turner, federal highway administrator, who was solidly in the pro–road warrior camp and decidedly *not* a critic of concrete. In the midst of the late '60s and early '70s freeway revolt, Turner downplayed the "carpings of a few dedicated critics" who were "blinded by their desire to discredit" this most magnificent achievement of the federal governnment.[102] Enmeshed within a bureaucratic culture that had long derided the handful of dissenters from its project as caviling eggheads and dreamy nature lovers, Turner was unable to see that this time, the opponents were fighting to defend their homes and neighborhoods from what they saw as the destructive and impersonal juggernaut of Big Government. He was speaking the language of Robert Moses in an age that had come to revile the master builder.

President Nixon, in this as in such other matters as revenue sharing and poverty programs, was something of a decentralist. He sought to transfer responsibility for constructing highways to more local, whether state or metropolitan, governments. Nixon was buttressed by his urban affairs adviser, Daniel Patrick Moynihan. A writer from the ghetto in Newark, New Jersey, wrote to Moynihan:

> "Dear Sir we are writing you all for help and justice here in New Jersey. We are asking you all to go forward and help us…. We need peace and justice here in Newark and all over New Jersey. They are tearing down our homes and building up medical collages and motor clubs and parking lots and we need decent private homes to live in. They are tearing down our best schools and churches to build a highway.[103]

The Newarkian had chosen the right target for his or her letter; no one in national politics (with the possible exceptions of Senators Harry Byrd, Eugene McCarthy, and William Proxmire) had been as trenchant a critic of rampant highway building as Moynihan. But limited tools were at his disposal.

Only in 1962 did federal law acknowledge those displaced by highways, and all the Federal Highway Act of that year did was require that states provide information—not aid, or even moving expenses—to the uprooted. (In 1962, only eight states paid moving expenses for those it was kicking out of their houses or apartments.)

As the wife of a Providence, Rhode Island, jewelry and polishing company owner mourned after their business was eaten up by the highwaymen, "We lost everything—it was a terrible thing—I can't understand how the city of Providence would permit it. The whole idea of forcing anyone out of a tax-paying business is like communism to me. The whole thing is un-American."[104] Responding to such *cri de coeur*, the Federal-Aid Highway Act of 1968 forbade the secretary of transportation from approving any project that displaced a person, business, or farm operation unless those displaced were given "fair and reasonable relocation and other payments" to move to "decent, safe, and sanitary dwellings" in "areas not generally less desirable" than those from which the person or business was being removed.[105] A 1970 act extended this limited assistance to victims of other federally funded projects as well.

In that same year, the Federal Highway Act of 1970 took a halfway step toward the diversion of gasoline taxes away from automobile-related purposes. States were allowed to spend a small part of their Highway Trust Fund bounty for bus lanes and waiting areas and the like. After years of trying, this was like hitting on the password that opens the safe doors, at least a crack. The Highway Trust Fund was "the fountainhead from which flows the money to build the new roads," in former FHWA public affairs director Ben Kelley's phrasing.[106] Others termed it "a guaranteed annual wage for the highway industry," the gift that keeps on giving, since it absolves Congress of the responsibility for passing revenue bills to fund the federal-aid system.[107] It promised, or seemed to promise, subsidy in perpetuity.

The highway lobby's stronghold, once breached, gave way inch by inch. The Federal-Aid Highway Act of 1973 diverted $1 billion from the Highway Trust Fund in 1975 and 1976 for buses and rail transit. It also allowed municipalities to trade in Trust Fund monies that had been marked for canceled freeways and receive an equivalent amount for mass transit, though not from the Highway Trust Fund. Funneling these funds to private bus and rail systems was not allowed, thus discouraging the revivification of private rail in America. (Nearly all rail freight, by contrast, is owned privately.)

The long-fought-for goal of the public transit interests—busting the Highway Trust Fund and permitting subways and rail cars and buses to share in the bounty—had been achieved. (Parenthetically, the father of mass transit diversion from the Highway Trust Fund was New Jersey Democratic senator Harrison Williams, who had proposed an urban mass transit trust fund financed from taxes on motor fuels. The transit lobby is reluctant to claim him as progenitor and paladin, however, for the notoriously corrupt Senator Williams resigned from the Senate in 1982 after it was revealed that he had accepted bribes as part of the FBI's Abscam investigation. Even his name was removed from the Harrison Williams Metropark train station in Iselin, New Jersey. Decline doesn't get starker than that.)

President Gerald Ford proposed in 1975 what was, in the context of the usual incrementalism surrounding the issue, a radical reform. Under Ford's plan, half of the four-cent-per-gallon federal gasoline tax would be kept by the US Treasury; of the remaining two cents, one cent each would go to the Highway Trust Fund and the states. Ford explained that the Trust Fund was "a classic example of a federal program that has expanded over the years into areas of state and local responsibility, distorting the priorities of those governments."[108] It was time to return power to where it belonged. The interstate was nearing completion: in 1975, 37,125 miles of a projected 42,000-mile system were in use.[109]

But a weak and accidental president was no match for the highway lobby, which, as James A. Dunn Jr. noted in his work on comparative transportation policy, was now joined by the mass transit lobby, which, having sunk its teeth into the copious blubber of the Highway Trust Fund, was not about to relinquish its grip. Ford's proposal stalled.

5

Crumbling Infrastructure or
Focus-Group Buzzwords?

THE CLUMSY, TONGUE-CLOTTING word *infrastructure*, which had usually been deployed in a military sense as "the installations that form the basis for any operation or system," had fallen into desuetude until the dawn of the Reagan Age, when it came to be a virtual synonym for public works and internal improvements, especially those related to highways and bridges.[1]

Although infrastructure has seldom been discussed outside the context of an activist government for these last four decades, in fact the federal government owns very little of what it is called upon to subsidize. According to the FHWA, state and local governments own 96.3 percent of America's more than 4.1 million miles of road and 98.3 percent of its more than 607,000 bridges. (Close to three-quarters—73 percent in each case—of the public road mileage and bridges are in rural areas.)[2]

Defining infrastructure more broadly, so as to include airports, schools, harbors, factories, trains, and suchlike, we can say that the federal government owns just 3 percent of the nation's infrastructure, and just 13 percent of those infrastructure assets are owned by *any* level of government. And as Chris Edwards of the Cato Institute points out, of the approximately $3.5 trillion US capital investment in nondefense infrastructure, fully 86 percent is made by the private sector, with 8 percent by state and local governments and just 6 percent by the federal government.[3] This is why Ronald Utt, for instance, insists that the alleged crisis in infrastructure is really a crisis of "monopoly socialism," since the elements most often cited as being in disrepair are government owned or government financed. Private infrastructure—residential housing, farms, office buildings, hotels, shopping centers—is experiencing no such crisis.[4]

But when the *I*-word burst on the scene in 1981, such qualifications were the last thing a compliant media wished to report. For the sky was falling, and the Chicken Littles were the heroes of the day. The urtext in the crumbling infrastructure corpus was *America in Ruins: The Decaying Infrastructure* by Pat Choate, then a senior policy analyst at TRW, and Susan Walter, then manager for state government issues at General Electric.[5] First published in 1981 by the Council of State Planning Agencies, a National Governors Association affiliate, and reissued two years later by Duke University Press, *America in Ruins* was latched onto by Democrats and labor supporters as just the right antidote to what they regarded as penny-pinching Reaganism. Published during Ronald Reagan's first term, when Democrats were searching for programmatic responses to both Reagan's free-market rhetoric and the recession in the industrial Northeast, *America in Ruins* garnered significant coverage in the *New York Times* as well as cover stories in *Time* and *Newsweek*. Our roads and bridges and water and sewer systems were said to be crumbling—the cover of the paperback of *America in Ruins* depicted Roman ruins, implying the same fate awaited the American Empire unless massive infusions of federal dollars revitalized this moribund network.

Pat Choate, who would ride his coauthorship to fame as the philosopher-king of Crumbling Infrastructure and as Ross Perot's vice presidential candidate in 1996, was a Texas-born *policy entrepreneur*, to use the curious locution of his dazzled DC admirers. The term was defined for *New York Times Magazine* contributor Randall Rothenberg by William A. Galston of the Roosevelt Center for American Policy Studies: "A policy entrepreneur is analogous to the entrepreneur in the private sector. He is the person who creates the venture, who invents the concept of the product and then goes out and markets it."[6] The analogy breaks down on the critical matter of funding: the entrepreneur must raise funds in the private market, while the policy entrepreneur is pursuing taxpayer monies via political means. Choate understood that packaging would be critical to the success of his various policy ventures. As he later explained, "Words are codes. I think it's really important to have the right name for something."[7] Thus *crumbling* became the adjective du jour for *infrastructure*.

The thesis of the Choate-Walter book is that "the United States is seriously underinvesting in public infrastructure."[8] The word choice is critical here; as economist Edward M. Gramlich wrote in a 1994 survey of literature on the subject, "Political liberals and liberal politicians saw a way to rescue government spending and projects from the assaults of Reaganism, and even a way to avoid otherwise necessary budget cuts—just call the spending infrastructure investment."[9] Who, after all, could be against investment? Improvident, pennywise but pound-foolish myopes, that's who! The sort who would throw the baby out with the bathwater, cut off their noses to spite their faces, and otherwise engage in shortsighted self-defeating actions warned against by any number of hoary apothegms. The fallacy Choate and Walter looked to demolish was that "public works expenditures must be drastically curtailed in the face of current economic conditions." Within the book's first fifty words, the authors tell us that America's public works are "wearing out," "obsolescent," and "deteriorated."[10] The consequences of this decrepitude are declining productivity and economic malaise.

The authors recommend a national inventory of needed public works, which would serve as the basis of a capital budget. Highways, bridges, water systems, harbors, subways, rail beds, dams, even jails: the authors compile an extensive catalogue of repairs and new construction that would daunt even the most spendthrift legislator. Given that *public works*, the term Choate and Walter seem to prefer, is synonymous to many with pork barrel—a phrase they term "too glib"— they sternly declare that any program must "minimize corruption and waste"—which is, of course, easier said than done.[11] They acknowledge that user fees and privatization may in some cases be appropriate strategies for addressing the problem, but the centerpiece of their reform suggestions is a national public works capital budget, the enactment and execution of which would enhance "economic renewal" and the rebuilding of America.[12]

America in Ruins was a desperately needed booster shot for advocates of generous spending on internal improvements. The *New York Times* ran a lengthy story on its 1981 release, surely a first for a publication of the Council of State Planning Agencies, not theretofore known as a hot press. The *Times* story was entirely credulous and may as well have been prepared by the Choate-Walter publicity department. Noting that public works spending at all levels of government had declined since the near-completion of the IHS, it repeated the book's talking points without quoting any skeptics or critics of greatly increased expenditures.[13]

The House Democratic Caucus adopted the issue with gusto in 1982, as a recession was setting in, and the party was in search of concrete proposals to win back the defecting Reagan Democrats. *Newsweek*, a magazine with a Democratic liberal bias, in a major story on "The Decaying of America" quoted Choate complaining that "we've been squandering a major part of our national wealth" by ignoring what *Newsweek*, in breathless prose, depicted as a nation in collapse.[14] In fact, the *Newsweek* story led with a science-fiction scenario in which New York City's water system gives way, leading to a horrifying (and outlandish) concatenation of events including a citywide blackout, stopped elevators in Gotham's skyscrapers, stalled and darkened subways, fires raging, sewers backed up, and the Queensboro Bridge toppling into the East River, carrying thousands of panicked New Yorkers into a watery grave. Whew! Surely no price is too big to pay to avoid *that* nightmare. (Not that New York City's water system couldn't use more than just TLC. A study by the Center for an Urban Future found that the "average age of New York City's 6,400 miles of sewage mains is approximately 84 years.... Its 6,800 miles of water mains are approximately 69 years old, and its 6,300 miles of gas mains are 56 years old." The average age of bridges in Manhattan and the Bronx is seventy-two years, and the average age of all 1,445 bridges in the five boroughs is sixty-three years.[15])

Newsweek goes on to paint the national *mise en scène* in the most lurid colors. Roads, bridges, rails, and waterworks are not only crumbling and deteriorating, they are actually on the verge of collapse—and the Reagan administration, depicted as Scrooge-like meanies, actually wants to reduce spending on these woefully underfunded systems. Those who resist a free spending orgy are "penny-wise and pothole foolish," in the stilted soundbite of one man advertised as a Massachusetts policy expert. (Fourteen years later, this sage was sentenced to thirty-three months in prison and fined $1 million for "taking secret payments from Merrill Lynch & Co. while serving as a government financial adviser."[16] Oops—those policy experts are full of surprises.) These dire warnings did not, of course, come to pass. Nor did the sharp spending reductions against which the quoted policy experts warned. And to be fair, one skeptic, E. S. Savas, assistant secretary for housing and urban development in the Reagan administration, is quoted as saying that "the fact that there are potholes all over America doesn't mean that it's time for the Federal government to pay for filling them."[17]

What *Newsweek* does not consider is just why, if infrastructure spending is (allegedly) so popular with voters, there is so much deferred maintenance. The answer recalls Frédéric Bastiat's distinction between the seen and the unseen. Maintenance—the filling of potholes, most prosaically—is not sexy, to say the least. Often it is virtually invisible. No politician ever called a press conference to boast that he had secured funding to fix a low shoulder on a state highway. It is far sexier, and more politically rewarding, to associate oneself with a visible new project; for press releases, headlines, and photo ops duly follow. The result is an inefficient, even dangerous, misallocation of resources, with essential upkeep neglected while unnecessary and expensive projects are constructed.

The economist William F. Shughart II has written about this with a keen understanding of the Hurricane Katrina disaster that hit New Orleans in 2005. For years, as Shughart discusses, basic and routine maintenance of the levees that were supposed to protect New Orleans from floodwaters were neglected by federal, state, and local governments, while the region's politicized levee boards had been building yacht basins and bikepaths. As Shughart explains, "The failure to shore up the city's defenses ... originated in a democratic process that provides a larger political payoff to new public works and real estate development initiatives than to maintaining existing infrastructure."[18] More generally, he concludes, "Because publicly financed infrastructure deteriorates slowly and often invisibly, politicians and bureaucrats have little to lose by deferring repairs and neglecting routine maintenance."[19]

Newsweek puts forth a number of policy options, ranging from a national capital budget—which, it is implied, would magically take public works spending out of politics, presumably relocating it in the land of unicorns and fairies—to higher user fees to a revived Reconstruction Finance Corporation, which would loan $25 billion to hard-pressed cities to fund their internal improvements. Eventually, the 1982–83 recession ended and the sky-is-falling hysteria dissipated, but even the mobile pieces of infrastructure are politically fixed and are with us always.

Infrastructure, Eternally

George Will has joked that the American Society of Civil Engineers (ASCE) may as well program its computers to insert the adjective *crumbling* before any use of the noun *infrastructure*.[20] The venerable ASCE cannot merely be dismissed as another grungy and greedy hands-out special interest. Founded in 1852, it claims 152,000-plus members in government, industry, academia, and private practice. These are the men and women who conceive, design, construct, and run the roads, bridges, waterworks, airports, parks, ports, and schools—and more. Theirs is an honorable and necessary profession, but they have, to put it mildly, a strong self-interest in boosting expenditures on these projects to a maximal level.

ASCE began issuing its *Infrastructure Report Card* in 1998 and made it quadrennial beginning in 2001. If the nation's infrastructure were a student, it would cower in fearful anticipation of a tongue-lashing or a whupping every four years, as it racks up Cs and Ds as predictably as a slow pupil in a fast class. It's deteriorating, it's crumbling, it's frankly a mess. (In 1988, a decade before ASCE began issuing its report cards, a federally sponsored National Council on Public Works put out *Fragile Foundations: A Report on America's Public Works*. This government-generated council gave the nation's infrastructure a middling grade of C. So, either the pupil has gotten much worse over the last thirty years or the grader is much tougher or—dare we say it—biased?)

To read the ASCE *Infrastructure Report Card* is a ticket to a gallery of horrors. But first, just to assure readers that this is not a naked exercise in self-aggrandizement, Norma Jean Mattie, ASCE president, tells us up-front in the most recent (2017) 110-page opus of disaster that "failing to act to re-build America's infrastructure costs every American family $3,400 a year."[21] So, by ponying up an extra dime or so per gallon of gasoline and maybe a couple of hundred bucks on the old 1040 one can save one's family $3,400 a year? Well, not quite. Just as in the 2013 report, the 2017 ASCE report card awards America's infrastructure a grade of D+. That + is a nice touch—like a dim-witted student being rewarded because he brought the teacher an apple, or whatever the modern equivalent of that stereotypical gift might be. Then again, D is the highest grade ASCE has given out since its first report in 1998.

The nation's rail infrastructure scored highest in 2017 with a B, with bridges, ports, and solid waste notching a C+. The other dozen categories come off as absolute dullards, scoring D+ (energy, hazardous waste, parks and recreation, schools, wastewater) and D (aviation, dams, drinking water, inland waterways, levees, roads)—and in the basement, transit (D–).[22]

Before we learn just how large an infusion of taxpayer money is needed to bring these grades up to a respectable level, we are once again told that these deplorable conditions are costing American families $3,400 a year, or about $9 per day. The cost of meeting infrastructure needs by 2025 is claimed to be greater than *$2 trillion*, which might sound like a lot, but "global competitiveness" demands that we close this "infrastructure investment gap"[23]—shades of the nonexistent "missile gap" that was such an issue in the Cold War presidential election of 1960! A majority of the $2.06 trillion gap between needs and funding—$1.1 trillion—is for surface transportation. Failure to act means that we are facing a catastrophe, at least judging from the numbers produced by the economic sorcerers at ASCE. If Washington does not act by 2025, they warn us, this inaction will cause $3.9 trillion in losses to US GDP, $7 trillion in lost business sales, and 2.5 million lost American jobs.[24] So as you can see, it will actually cost much more *not to act* than to spend the $2 trillion. Case closed. The US share of GDP devoted to infrastructure must rise from its current 2.5 percent to 3.5 percent by 2025, declares ASCE.[25] China, after all, devotes 9 percent of its GDP to infrastructure, and what better economic model to follow than that exemplar of freedom and widespread prosperity?[26]

For each category in the ASCE report, a factoid, or soundbite, leads off. We learn, for example, that 15,498 dams are "high-hazard potential," and 3,571 power outages are reported each year, and 49 percent of sea vessels "experience delays across the inland waterway system" (it's tough to make that one sound terribly threatening), and Americans generate 258 million tons of municipal solid waste annually.[27]

Bridges fare (somewhat) better than roads in the ASCE study. In 2017, bridges notched their second consecutive C+, and they have never fallen below

C-. ASCE noted that almost 40 percent of the 614,387 bridges in the United States are at least fifty years old and that the average age of an American bridge is forty-three years, which tells us nothing about their sturdiness or structural integrity. About 9 percent—56,007—were judged structurally deficient in 2016, and across those bridges traveled 188 million vehicles per day.[28] What the report does not tell us is that the fatality rate for the 188 million trips was zero, and that the percentage of structurally deficient bridges in the United States had been 24.1 percent in 1990. Moreover, the FHWA emphasizes that "the classification of a bridge as structurally deficient does not mean that it is likely to collapse or that it is unsafe."[29]

The five states with the highest percentage of structurally deficient bridges in 2016, the year cited by ASCE's latest scare survey, were Rhode Island (24.9); Iowa (20.5—surely not the bridges of Madison County!); Pennsylvania (19.8); South Dakota (19.6); and West Virginia (17.3—country roads, take me home, just not over one of those creaking bridges). The quintet with the lowest percentage of structurally deficient bridges consisted of Nevada (1.6); Texas (1.7); Florida (2.1); Arizona (2.6); and Utah (3.1).[30]

Substandard bridges have lower load limits, and this undoubtedly exacts an economic cost, as they force "companies to use smaller vehicles to transport goods or take roundabout routes, thereby increasing the time and cost associated with maintaining supply chains."[31] On the flip side, the trucking industry pushes for higher maximum allowable vehicle weights on roads and bridges, which sometimes exceed the limits recommended by the engineers. The result, of course, is a more rapid deterioration in road and bridge quality.

ASCE's recommendations to bring the grade of American bridges up from its mediocre C+ to stratospheric heights (which for ASCE is a B) lead with, first and foremost and always, "increased funding from all levels of government." That tune seems to play on continuous loop. Next, declares ASCE, the tax on motor fuels must increase and henceforth be tied to inflation, which would obviate the need for legislative approval of later tax increases. For as we know, voters can be churlish about such increases—best to take them off the table and simply make them automatic. Of course, this measure, like the more general increase in funding, applies to highways as well. While ASCE dare not use the *T*-word—tolls—it does suggest that mileage-based user fees need further study and evaluation in pilot programs.[32]

In its breathless section about the wretched state of American roads, where potholes and congestion are alleged to be costing us eons in time (6.9 billion hours squandered in traffic) and oceans of fuel (3.1 billion gallons wasted) every year, ASCE delivers one of the great contextless facts in infrastructural history: that is, that US roads carried people and goods more than three trillion miles in 2016—"or more than three hundred round trips between Earth and Pluto."[33] Wow! Pluto was downgraded from planet to dwarf planet in 2006, a decade earlier, but its name packs more punch than Neptune, the most distant of the planets as defined by the International Astronomical Union.

Will it be expensive to repair this trans-Plutonian highway? Sure. But it pays for itself! ASCE, referencing the FHWA, asserts that "each dollar spent on road, highway, and bridge improvements returns $5.20 in the form of lower vehicle maintenance costs, decreased delays, reduced fuel consumption, improved safety, lower road and bridge maintenance costs, and reduced emissions as a result of improved traffic flow."[34] So really, the sky—or Pluto—is the limit as far as government expenditures go, since spending on highways and bridges is like a magic machine into which government inserts a dollar bill and out pops a fiver. As with bridges, increased taxes and possibly user fees are proposed as revenue sources. But ASCE insists that time is of the essence: the grade for roads was a C+ in ASCE's 1998 report card and has floated between D– and D+ ever since.

Venturing a bit too far down the road, ASCE has even come out for an extension of the IHS. This had seemed to be a long-settled matter. Finished in 1992, the interstate may have cost over $125 billion and took thirty-five years, or about $100 billion and twenty-plus years longer than predicted. But nothing is over till Uncle Sam says it is over; the federal government did not officially declare the IHS, swelled through various redefinitions to 46,726 miles, completed until 1996.

Ah, but ASCE, the vanguard of the modern internal improvements lobby, informs us that not only are there seventy urban areas with populations exceeding fifty thousand that are without an interstate link, but there is also *no direct interstate connection between Las Vegas and Phoenix.*[35] What is this, the Third World?! Sure, the job will "take money, of course, and lots of it," admits ASCE, but Deputy Executive Director Lawrence H. Roth believes that "infrastructure is really a social issue just like education, Medicare, and Medicaid," and therefore ought to be insulated from political pressures to hold the line on spending.[36] To question the construction of a Las Vegas–Phoenix interstate link is akin to gainsaying the value of public education. As Adam J. White cracked in the *New Atlantis*, "Asking civil engineers whether America needs to invest in infrastructure is like asking a barber whether you need a haircut."[37]

Contra ASCE, five analysts from the Rand Institute declared, with the brio of the little boy who shouted that the emperor had no clothes, that "not everything is broken." That was the title of their 111-page 2017 report on US transportation and water infrastructure. The authorial quintet refused to buy into the shopworn narrative of crumbling bridges and roads disintegrating before our very eyes. A maintenance backlog exists, they conceded, but "the data do not support a picture of precipitous decline in total national spending or in the condition of the assets." The reality, they said, is "far more nuanced and challenging."[38] As they noted, total government infrastructure spending, translated into current dollars, has remained fairly constant since 1956, the *annus mirabilis* of US internal improvements. Highway spending declined between 1964 and 1980, as the interstate neared completion and substantial maintenance work was not yet needed, but it flattened out thereafter, as aging or obsolete roads needed repair or modernization. Water, rail, and mass transit spending has been either flat or increasing since 1980.[39]

For a funny thing has happened over the course of this Era of Crumbling Infrastructure: if ever the infrastructure *were* crumbling, it is doing less crumbling today than before. Indisputably, incontrovertibly, our highways and roads and bridges are in better shape today than at the dawn of the Reagan administration, when the adjective *crumbling* become joined at the hip to the noun *infrastructure*. Data from state highway departments and the US Department of Transportation reveal that the condition of highway infrastructure at the state level has improved significantly over the past three decades. For instance, the percentage of rural interstates rated "poor" by the FHWA dropped sharply from 6.6 in 1989 to 1.85 in 2015, the last time these assessments were made, while the percentage of "poor" urban interstates declined over that same period from 6.6 to 5.02. The states with the worst-conditioned rural interstate mileage were, from the bottom, Alaska, Colorado, Washington, Wisconsin, and New York. Those with the poorest-conditioned urban interstate mileage were, also from the bottom up, California, New Jersey,

New York, Louisiana, and Hawaii, which in sum accounted for about half of the nation's poor-condition interstate mileage.[40]

There is, believe it or not, an International Roughness Index, or IRI, which has nothing to do with football or more sordid activities but rather measures a road's health using a truck-pulled, wheel-mounted laser to calculate an automobile's suspension movement over a road. Average IRIs have improved greatly since state highway departments began reporting them to the FHWA in 1989.[41] Only about 3 percent of rural roads have roughness indices below the good or acceptable threshold, though the figure is closer to 20 percent for urban highways. California again sits at the bottom of the class, with only about 15 percent of its urban roads achieving a good score.[42]

Duke University civil engineering professor Henry Petroski, in his engaging book *The Road Taken: The History and Future of America's Infrastructure* (2016), provides a rebuttal to the crumbling bridges hysteria, writing that "bridge failures are simply not very common. One major failure every thirty years is certainly no indictment" of engineers and builders.[43]

According to the National Bridge Inventory, the percentage of the nation's six-hundred-thousand-plus bridges rated either structurally deficient or functionally obsolescent fell from 37.8 in 1989 to 21.65 in 2015. Rhode Island, at 52 percent, led the deficiency pack, while Arizona, at 9.01 percent, was last, though in this case, as in the Bible, the last shall be first.[44] Most importantly, the fatality rate has declined from 2.16 fatalities per one hundred million vehicle miles driven in 1989 to 1.13 in 2015. Massachusetts had the lowest rate and South Carolina the highest.[45] Curiously, however, after years of decline, traffic fatalities surged upward in 2015–2016, likely due to distracted driving by cell phone and smartphone users. This anomalous blip seems to be correcting: motor vehicle crashes claimed 37,133 lives in 2017, or 1.16 fatalities per one hundred million vehicle miles traveled, but both numbers were down from the previous two years, and well under the historic highs of just under fifty-five thousand in the early 1970s.[46]

The Reason Foundation, compiling data in eleven categories including the above mentioned as well as traffic congestion, capital and administrative costs per mile, and total highway expenditures per mile, among other measurements, adjudged North Dakota the state with the best highway system, as it ranked third in urban interstate pavement condition, fourth in rural interstate pavement condition, fourth in urbanized traffic congestion, and third in maintenance disbursements per mile. At the other end of the scale was New Jersey, which suffered from the worst urban congestion and the highest per-mile cost—incredibly, it was almost double that of the state with the second-highest per-mile cost, Florida. We may assume that the Garden State also had the most corpses buried in cement and under or within other public works, though Reason did not offer those numbers. Rounding out the top ten states in the Reason Foundation survey of overall performance and cost-effectiveness were Kansas, South Dakota, Nebraska, South Carolina, Montana, Idaho, Wyoming, Missouri, and Utah. South Carolina is the outlier in that group; otherwise the states of the Plains and Rocky Mountains dominate.[47]

Everyone references ASCE in advocating for greater infrastructure spending. The organized labor–affiliated Economic Policy Institute cites ASCE "experts" in its recommendations for vast increases in such expenditures—er, investments.[48] The liberal establishmentarians of the Center on Budget and Policy Priorities base their case for state intervention to reverse "crumbling" roads and bridges on the dunce-hat grade given out to American infrastructure in the ASCE report card.[49] When former Indianapolis Republican Mayor Stephen Goldsmith of the Ash Center for Democratic Governance and Innovation of Harvard's Kennedy School sought to make the case for greater private investment in maintaining the nation's water resources infrastructure, he produced the dreaded ASCE report card.[50]

To be fair, there are legitimate concerns about the state of America's infrastructure. Just as not every bridge is crumbling, nor is every claim of obsolescence or deterioration of the nation's public plant hyperbolic. Commutes, especially in and around our largest cities, are aggravating and costly. The electric grid in the United States experiences more frequent blackouts than in the past, and in fact blackouts are more common in the United States than in the rest of the developed world. One University of Minnesota researcher calculates that the average electrical customer in the northeastern United States loses power for 214 minutes annually, as opposed to four minutes per year for the average customer in Japan.[51]

Moreover, the seemingly inevitable spread of self-driving automobiles will require a sharpening and refinement of the highways: lane stripings and markings must be clear, and snow removal requires technological advancement so as not to interfere with the driverless automobile's sensors.[52] But these are superable problems and rank low on the sexiness scale. They don't have the wow factor of a good old-fashioned tragedy.

Wasting Catastrophes

Among the catastrophic events adduced by the crumbling infrastructure crowd was the collapse of the I-35 bridge in Minneapolis in 2007. A deck truss failed in this eight-lane, 1,907-foot bridge spanning the Mississippi River, sending 111 vehicles into the water. Thirteen people died, and 145 were injured. The tragedy was exploited by those who favored spending more money on infrastructure, though the National Transportation Safety Board (NTSB) found that it was caused by a design error in the bridge's gusset plates, exacerbated by the weight of construction vehicles deployed that day on the vulnerable section of the bridge.[53] Even more frequent inspections by federal or state overseers, concluded the NTSB, would not have detected this design error. The fact that this piece of infrastructure crumbled, leading to a horrific result, had nothing to do with inadequate spending by the federal government.

But in obedience to former Clinton administration senior adviser, Obama chief of staff, and Chicago mayor Rahm Emanuel's dictum that "you never want a serious crisis to go to waste," *Civil Engineering*, the magazine of ASCE, published a breathless—or as breathless as an engineer can be—special report on the "infrastructure crisis," highlighted by the Minneapolis bridge collapse, which it blamed not on design error, but rather "years of neglect, underfunding, and a lack of leadership and vision."[54] The *New York Times* responded to the Minneapolis tragedy with gross scaremongering, claiming that "the nation's physical foundations seem to be crumbling beneath us."[55] Former Harvard president and secretary of the treasury in the Clinton administration Lawrence Summers gravely intoned that "profound questions about America's future are raised by collapsing bridges,"[56] though unhelpfully, he did not list any of the questions, and one doubts that he had in mind the existential bridge collapse questions that novelist-playwright Thornton Wilder raised in his Pulitzer Prize–winning *The Bridge of San Luis Rey* (1927). Rather bumptiously, *Civil Engineering* even slipped a bit of special pleading into its coverage of the Minneapolis collapse. It complained that state departments of transportation rely "heavily on visual inspections carried out by technicians rather than by licensed professional engineers."[57] Just a trade association doing its job? Perhaps. Though the self-interest here is embarrassingly transparent.

Similarly, the highway lobby sought to exploit the May 23, 2013, collapse of a bridge on I-5S near Mount Vernon in Washington State. In this instance, a truck tractor hauling a flatbed semitrailer, and escorted by a Dodge pickup truck, struck the bridge when the driver traveled in a lane with inadequate overhead clearance. The truck tractor made it across the bridge, but shortly thereafter one span of the twelve-span bridge fell into the Skagit River, carrying two passenger vehicles into the water. No one was seriously injured. The NTSB concluded that the accident was caused primarily by driver error, to which cell phone use contributed.[58] As Randal O'Toole wrote in *US News & World Report*, "The bridge was more than fifty years old, but it would have fallen if that truck had tried to cross it the day it opened."[59] Yet because the bridge had been rated "functionally obsolete" by the FHWA, its collapse immediately elevated it to a high-profile position in the gallery of infrastructure horrors. The forever-crumbling crowd gasped that up to 10 percent of the nation's more than six hundred thousand bridges met this definition. Yet functional obsolescence, as the Washington State Department of Transportation explained, can mean that a bridge has substandard lane widths, overly narrow shoulders, or insufficient vertical clearance for large trucks.[60] It does not imply decrepitude.

Stimulating Lies

The jobs argument is still the most politically compelling case for infrastructure spending. Although much of the public is justly suspicious of government jobs programs, which call to mind such politically driven programs as the Comprehensive Employment and Training Act (CETA) of the 1970s, which in the public mind was a mixture of make-work boondoggling and cushy jobs for the sons and daughters of the connected, road and bridge spending conjures up images of salt-of-the-earth, blue-collar workers with jackhammers and pickaxes and cement trucks creating and manicuring the highways and bridges over which we drive. Certainly, the populist associations of brick and mortar and asphalt with employment helped propel Donald Trump to victory in 2016. Brookings Institution analysts estimate that fourteen million Americans, or about 11 percent of the workforce, are employed in infrastructure-related fields, doing good honest work like driving trucks, piloting planes, reading meters, and laying down asphalt.[61] The president's Council of Economic Advisers estimated in 2014 that more than two-thirds (68 percent) of near-term infrastructure jobs were in the construction field, as opposed to 10 percent in manufacturing and 6 percent in retail.[62] These are, for the most part, the trades subsidized by infrastructure spending.

Yet grandiose claims for big infrastructure programs can wither on further examination. Despite the salesmanship of its authors, only $48.1 billion, or 4 percent, of the Obama administration's $814 billion stimulus package, the American Recovery and Reinvestment Act of 2009, went toward highway projects.[63] Still, $48.1 billion is real money. But Andrew Garin of Harvard found that four years after its enactment, the act's highway spending had had *zero* effect on county-level road construction employment.[64] As to the stimulus effect of public works spending, there is no scholarly consensus. Economist Clifford Winston of the Brookings Institution writes that "transportation policy is so inefficient that infrastructure spending fails to generate the large promised benefits."[65] Unlike in the private sector, government is under no pressure to earn a return on investment. Four RAND Corporation analysts concluded after a survey of relevant literature on the subject that "studies differ on, or ignore, whether the benefits stemming from infrastructure outweigh the costs of building it," but a consensus seems to have formed around the proposition that "private capital investment tends to have larger effects on economic outcomes than public capital investment or highway investment, although public investment can serve as a complement to private investment."[66]

Estimates of the impact of infrastructure spending vary wildly and often according to the predilections of the analyst. Trump advisers Wilbur Ross and Peter Navarro claim that an additional $200 billion in infrastructure spending boosts the GDP by more than 1 percent.[67] *Moody's Analytics* estimates that each $1 spent on infrastructure "generates $1.44 in demand."[68] A trio of economists from Northwestern claim that every dollar spent by the government "stimulates another $2.77 in private-sector economic activity," while across town in the Windy City, University of Chicago economists Andrew Mountford and Harald Uhrig have found that each dollar "in government purchases displaces $3.88 in private-sector economic activity."[69] This points to the matter, seldom acknowledged by the stimulus crowd, of alternative uses of those expended funds, whether within the private sector or in different government projects. In the timeless observation of Frédéric Bastiat, "The State opens a road, builds a palace, straightens a street, cuts a canal; and so gives work to certain workmen—this is what is seen: but it deprives certain other workmen of work, and this is what is not seen."[70]

Economist Alicia Munnell, examining state-level data for the years 1970–86, estimated that an increase of 1 percent in public capital expenditures produced an increase of 0.15 of 1 percent in state output: a significant benefit. Munnell's study was often cited. But when Robert Krol of California State University, Northridge, ran Munnell's numbers controlling for differences in state production functions, he found no evidence "to support the notion that higher levels of public capital increase economic activity."[71]

The lack of scholarly backing for the stimulative effect of government expenditures has not, of course, dampened the enthusiasm for such among those for whom such projects are an ideological or self-interested mission. Writing in the *Oxford Review of Economic Policy*, Atif Ansar, Bent Flyvbjerg, Alexander Budzier, and Daniel Lunn, all of Oxford University, analyzed the impact of China's extraordinary infrastructure spending on the economic growth of that nation. Their study focused on ninety-five road and rail projects built between 1984 and 2008. The researchers concluded that "contrary to the conventional wisdom, infrastructure investments do not typically lead to economic growth."[72] China, they found, had overinvested in underperforming projects, and this profligacy, coupled with poor management, had actually retarded China's economic growth and set the table for a potential "infrastructure-led national financial and economic crisis."[73]

Flyvbjerg, the Danish scholar, is a major figure in the political economy of infrastructure. He has exposed the uneconomical nature of so-called megaprojects such as high-speed rail, the Olympics, particle accelerators, and other showy and hyperexpensive endeavors always launched with great fanfare and the preening presence of credit-taking politicians. Ninety percent of these white elephants had cost overruns, and their overruns often exceed 50 percent, according to Flyvbjerg.[74] It's not only grifters who boost construction costs. The Davis-Bacon Act, which requires the payment of the local prevailing wage on all federally funded projects whose cost exceeds $2,000, is also an inflation machine. As mentioned in Chapter 4, the Davis-Bacon Act, enacted in 1931, applied to federal highways via the 1956 highway act. In a report of April 27, 1979, the US General Accounting Office recommended the repeal of Davis-Bacon, which it termed unnecessary, inflationary, and based on inaccurate wage rates.[75] In the face of furious lobbying by construction unions, Davis-Bacon survived, though it was modified at the margins. Later research has revealed that Davis-Bacon drives up construction costs on federally funded projects by at least 10 percent or by as much as 25 percent. The Congressional Budget Office estimates that a repeal of Davis-Bacon could result in savings to the federal highway program of $700 million annually.[76]

About half of the states also have prevailing wage laws, mini-Davis-Bacons, which also drive up the cost of public works. A study by Mike Clark of the state of Kentucky's Legislative Research Commission found that the Bluegrass State's prevailing wage law, enacted in 1940, was responsible in 1999–2000 for a gap of $3.68 per hour between prevailing wage projects (weighted mean of $19.78 per hour) and nonprevailing wage projects ($16.10 per hour).[77] (Kentucky's legislature repealed its state prevailing wage law in 2017.)

Another fiscally conservative proposal whose chances of enactment are somewhere between nil and negative infinitude is the repeal of the Buy America provisions that require the iron and steel used in highway construction and repair to have been made in the United States. President Biden is likelier to take a Fox cohosting gig with Tucker Carlson than he is to entertain any repeal or even modification of this requirement.[78]

At the very least, as economist Robert Krol writes in a paper for the Mercatus Center, future infrastructure projects should be subject to more rigorous cost-benefit calculations than in the past. For one thing, says Krol, outside parties with no direct ties to the project in question must be part of a peer-review process. Secondly, their (often impossibly rosy) traffic flow estimates must also be compared with those of similar projects to flag the more hyperbolic claims. And thirdly, cost-benefit estimates should be reckoned with varying assumptions, plugging in a range of figures for such variables as interest and inflation rates.[79] One would assume that these commonsense reforms had been adopted decades ago, but such assumptions do not hold when the contending parties have as their primary desideratum the prying open of the pork barrel.

About cost overruns, Willie Brown, former speaker of the California Assembly, and former mayor of San Francisco, offered a startlingly frank take on political salesmanship and the need to shade, or at least conceal, the truth. Speaking about the enormous $300 million cost overrun on San Francisco's intermodal Salesforce (née Transbay) Transit Center, Brown explained, "We always knew the initial estimate was way under the real cost. Just like we never had a real cost for the Central Subway or the Bay Bridge or any other massive construction project. So get off it. In the world of civic projects, the first budget is really a down payment. If people knew the real cost from the start, nothing would ever be approved. The idea is to get going. Start digging a hole and make it so big, there's no alternative to coming up with the money to fill it in."[80]

Brown's rakish honesty is refreshing, at least to those who are not stuck with the bill for these big holes. But while he may be unusually direct, his experience is hardly unique. Martin Wachs, then a professor of urban planning at UCLA and, of equal pertinence, a member of the Ethics Committee of the American Institute of Certified Planners, raised more than a few eyebrows in 1989 with an essay for the *APA Journal* about planners who lie with numbers. Wachs did not discount the difficulty a planner encounters as he or she walks the tightrope between being a scientist, or expert, whose role is revelation of the truth, and being an advocate, whose job is to use the data to make the best case possible for his or her client. Wachs confessed that he had been conflicted in just this manner during his own years as a consultant, and his interest in the ethics of planning had led him to compile case studies of this very subject. He instanced the example of a transportation consultant working for a county board of supervisors who estimated that a new light rail transit route under consideration would carry about two thousand passengers per day. Not good enough, the chairman of the board informed her. The county would not receive a federal grant unless demand reached twelve thousand passengers daily. Whether she chose career advancement or honesty we don't know.

In Wachs's own case, he recalled telling a client that he could not with any degree of accuracy predict the daily usage of a facility because there were no comparable facilities in the region, and no real data on which to base a forecast. "If you won't forecast, I'll get another consultant," said the client, who did just that. You get what you pay for in the forecasting business, and if one consultant won't forecast to please, there are others who will. Unfortunately, the best advocates are often those most skilled at dissembling, or at applying the patina of disinterested scholarship to raw political gamesmanship. Writes Wachs:

> The most effective planner is sometimes the one who can cloak advocacy in the guise of scientific or technical rationality. Rather than stating that we favor a particular highway project or renewal program for ideological reasons or because our clients stand to gain more from that project than from alternatives, we adjust data and assumptions until we can say that *the data* clearly show that the preferred option is best. Our recommendation is not merely personal judgment or preference, we claim, but the result of a neutral process of analysis.[81]

Bent Flyvbjerg teamed with two other Danes, Mette Skamris Holm and Soren Buhl, to conduct a major study of cost estimations in public works projects. Published in the *Journal of the American Planning Association* in 2002, the study's sample included 258 transportation infrastructure projects in Europe (181), North America (61), and other areas (16) whose combined cost was $90 billion (US). This was the largest study of its kind. Bearing the blunt and non-euphemistic title "Underestimating Costs in Public Works Projects: Error or Lie?," the article answers the titular question with the latter choice. With "overwhelming" statistical significance, the authors found that "the cost estimates used to decide whether [important infrastructure] projects should be built are highly and systematically misleading."[82]

The average cost escalation for all 258 projects was 27.6 percent, with rail (44.7 percent) experiencing the highest gap between projected cost and actual cost and roads (20.4 percent) the lowest. Underestimating cost happened in about 90 percent of all projects. The extent of underestimation seems to have been fairly constant over the last seven decades, suggesting that those who promote large-scale public works have learned nothing about more accurate estimation—or, rather, they have learned all too well the lessons of their pre-decessors: namely, that deception pays. If the ubiquitous overestimates were simply a matter of appraiser optimism, the gap between predicted and actual cost would have closed over the decades, as actors refined their calculations. But it did not.[83]

Why the large underestimation of the true costs of infrastructure projects? The Danish authors have four explanations: technical, economic, psychologi-cal, and political. They find that simple error cannot explain the deviation, and the best explanation is "strategic misrepresentation," or, to put it plainly, "lying."[84] "Lying pays off, or at least economic agents believe it does," write the Danish researchers. They cite Martin Wachs, and they second, with volu-minous evidence, his belief of promoter dishonesty. In their attempts to win public and political support for their projects, the partisans of large public works projects deceive: "The cost estimates used in public debates, media cov-erage, and decision making for transportation infrastructure development are highly, systematically, and significantly deceptive."[85] Bent Flyvbjerg and his colleagues conclude that when the topic at hand is whether or not a particu-lar infrastructure project should be undertaken, "legislators, administrators, investors, media representatives, and members of the public who value honest numbers should not trust cost estimates and cost-benefit analyses produced by project promoters and their analysts."[86]

Yet the promise, however illusory, of jobs created by infrastructure spend-ing is still an essential talking point, especially for politicians with sizable blue-collar constituencies. For instance, when in October 2011 Michigan governor Rick Snyder, a Republican venture capitalist, issued a message bear-ing the ominous title "Reinventing Michigan's Infrastructure: Better Roads Drive Better Jobs," he hauled out all the euphemisms. Government spending was *investment*, and nothing was quite so harmful as a "lack of investment."[87] Doing nothing—which is to say not undertaking substantial taxpayer-sub-sidized public works projects—was unacceptable. (A Democratic governor might have escalated this to *unconscionable*.)

By down-is-up and white-is-black and open-is-closed reasoning, *investing* in infrastructure "saves money."[88] Governor Snyder foreclosed one method of raising funds for this increased investment: that of toll roads and pay-as-you-go user fees, which he treated as exotic, quite possibly dangerous (at least to his reelection) proposals akin to radically experimental medicines that could kill a patient upon ingestion. Rather than assess tolls on drivers who use the roads that are rebuilt or modernized, Governor Snyder went to the old familiar well. Bemoaning the fact that Michigan had not raised its 19 cents per gallon state gasoline tax since 1997—ancient history!—he called for a shift to a uniform percentage tax on gasoline at the wholesale level that would raise an equivalent sum of money without the pesky requirement of the legislative approval that would be needed to boost gasoline taxes at the pump.

The governor did not get the tax collection shift he desired, but he did get a healthy hike in investable funds when in 2017 the Michigan gasoline tax rose from 19 to 26.3 cents per gallon, and the diesel fuel tax zoomed from 15 to 26.3 cents per gallon. Even better, from the point of view of politicians who dread voting to raise taxes, beginning in 2022 these taxes are indexed to inflation. Vehicle registration fees also rose by 20 percent in 2017. As New Year's revelers rang in the New Year, Michigan jumped overnight from eighteenth to sixth in state gasoline tax levels, trailing only Pennsylvania, Washington, Hawaii, New York, and New Jersey. Within four years of the tax hikes, Michigan was projected to be spending an additional $1.2 billion yearly on roads and bridges.[89] Whether this investment produces the benefits promised is a question for which Bent Flyvbjerg and colleagues could offer an educated guess.

Who Gets What?

Federal highway funds have been disbursed under varying formulae, taking into account a state's population, miles of road (or "lane miles," which advantages urban areas, since roads therein tend to be four, six, or eight lanes, as opposed to the two-lane highways in rural America), and miles of unfinished interstate. Sometimes legislators dispense with the pretense that there is a rational basis for this spending and just dole it out to whoever sits on the right committees.

Earmarking, or the practice of Congress specifically directing transportation funding to individual projects rather than permitting the relevant state and local officials to make those determinations, teemed like mushrooms after a downpour during the late twentieth and early twenty-first centuries. Often written into the conference committee report, these instructions to spend Amount X on Project Y were no mere recommendations; they were legally binding. Earmarking was exceedingly rare in the dim mists of the past—like, say, during the Reagan administration. A US House of Representatives point of order in 1913 effectively barred legislation directing funds to specific highway projects, though as the century wound down the point of order became blunted. There were but ten earmarked items in the 1982 highway bill representing less than $1 billion; that rose to 152 earmarks in the Surface Transportation and Uniform Relocation Assistance Act of 1987, which drew a veto from President Reagan, who cracked, "I haven't seen this much lard since I handed out blue ribbons at the Iowa State Fair."[90] Congress, notoriously pork hungry, overrode the veto. Highway bill earmarks rose to 538 in 1991 before Congress packed 1,850 earmarks into the futuristically named Transportation Equity Act for the 21st Century, or TEA-21, of 1998, and then a whopping 5,671 earmarks in the Safe, Accountable, Flexible, Efficient Transportation Equity Act: A Legacy for Users (SAFETEA-LU) of 2005.[91]

Earmarks offer politicians the opportunity for good publicity with little downside. For while voters may dislike taxation and spending in the abstract, few will be irritated by a newspaper photo of their local congressman, noggin covered by a yellow construction hardhat, surveying the repair work being done on a local bridge or pothole-rutted road. As a transportation analyst told scholar Gian-Claudia Sciara, "There's no such thing as a Republican or Democratic pothole. Everybody's got needs for infrastructure improvements."[92]

But certain needs are needier than others. The inspector general of the US Department of Transportation reported in 2007 that *99 percent*—7,724 of 7,760—of highway, mass transit, and aviation earmarked projects "either were not subject to the agencies' review and selection process or bypassed the states' normal planning and programming processes."[93] Perhaps the most famous earmark was the "Bridge to Nowhere," a $398 million hunk of pork linking Alaska's Gravina Island, population fifty, to the mainland, and "saving island residents the trouble of a seven-minute ferry ride."[94] Slipped into an FY 2006 omnibus spending bill by a pair of powerful Republican legislators from the Last Frontier, Senator Ted Stevens and Rep. Don Young, this boondoggle proved to be a bridge *way* too far, or at least too implausible, and it was dropped from the legislation under the merciless ridicule of the press and non-Alaskan politicians. In part due to the mocking publicity afforded the Bridge to Nowhere and other egregious acts of pork barrelism, in 2011 Congress limited earmarking—indeed, seemed to proscribe the practice—although "soft earmarking," or designating a project a priority without attaching a dollar value thereto, endures. In any event, the overwhelming majority (92 percent) of highway spending through the end of FY 2020 is apportioned by statutory formula under the Fixing America's Surface Transportation (FAST) Act of 2015, which is up from the previous figure of 84 percent.[95]

Federal highway (and, since 1973, mass transit, light rail, bus, and bicycle lane) spending is reauthorized by Congress every several years, as urban and rural interests, and solons from donor and donee states, square off over who gets the choicest seats around the pork barrel. Of course, it is not advertised in such squalid terms; rather, senators and representatives bandy about such words as *equity* and *sustainability*. This is not to say that such concerns are improper or misplaced; the highway program has a lot to answer for, especially to those whose homes and businesses and neighborhoods were destroyed in the roadbuilding orgy of the late 1950s and 1960s.

But the formulae to disburse transportation funds are not necessarily products of cool, dispassionate reasoning. In their study of the geographic distribution of federal highway aid between 1974 and 2008, Pengyu Zhu and Jeffrey R. Brown found that the key determinants of whether a state is a donor (which means it contributes more to the Highway Trust Fund than it receives) or a donee (it receives more than it contributes) is its degree of nonurbanness and its representation on the four relevant congressional committees.

There are winners and losers in this redistribution of funds, and while political liberals are believed to consider the redistribution of wealth more favorably than do conservatives, no such distinction exists with respect to highway funding. Rather, if you hail from a donee state, then the formulae are fine and dandy, and if you hail from a donor state, you cry out for reform. Abstract notions of justice have nothing to do with it. For instance, the most vocal senatorial liberal of the 1980s and 1990s, Senator Howard Metzenbaum (D-OH), took to the floor in 1991 to say that the:

debate [is] about numbers. It has to do with the fact that a number of States have been shortchanged over a period of years, and there may very well have been a reason for that to have occurred, because some of the Western States did not have as much tax revenue, had longer highways, so that kind of arrangement was made … [but today] the basic issue has to do with the fairness and equity of some States getting 85 cents on the dollar and some States getting $2 and $3 and $7 on the dollar paid in.[96]

Whether or not Ohio has a higher per capita income than some donee states was of no account. From each according to his means, to each according to his needs, may be a venerable socialist slogan, but no one takes this as an operating principle when Washington is doling out transportation monies to the states.

Texas has fared especially poorly: a study of the first fifty years of the Highway Trust Fund found that the Lone Star State had the lowest return (eighty-eight cents back for every dollar contributed) of any state. A total of fourteen states had been shortchanged in the sense of receiving less in federal highway aid than their residents had paid in taxes, though there was no obvious geographic profile to this group, which besides Texas included California, Florida, Georgia, Indiana, Michigan, Missouri, New Jersey, North Carolina, Ohio, Oklahoma, South Carolina, Tennessee, and Wisconsin. (The South and Midwest are slightly overrepresented, and the Northeast and Upper Rocky Mountain states are slightly underrepresented.) The states with the highest rate of return—those receiving more than twice their contributions over the Trust Fund's first half century—skewed rural: Alaska, Hawaii, Montana, North Dakota, South Dakota, and Vermont, as well as Rhode Island and the rural-phobic District of Columbia. Alaska's receipt-to-contribution ratio was a devilish 6.66.[97]

This kind of redistribution from the Michigans to the Montanas led to the emplacement of a floor guaranteeing that a state receives back from the federal government a minimum percentage of the federal highway taxes paid by its motorists. This floor was set at 85 percent by the Surface Transportation Assistance Act (STAA) of 1982; 90 percent by the Intermodal Surface Transportation Efficiency Act (ISTEA) of 1991; 90.5 percent in 1998 by TEA-21, the Transportation Equity Act for the 21st Century; and then at 92 percent by the even more ridiculously acronymed SAFETEA-LU (Safe, Accountable, Flexible, Efficient Transportation Equity Act: A Legacy for Users), the adjective-clotted and subtitled law enacted in 2005. The rallying cry of the donor states was voiced by Senator Trent Lott (R-MS), who was, aptly, a yell leader as a student at Ole Miss: "Mississippi is getting tired of dirt roads; we want some asphalt!"[98]

As Zhu and Brown point out, however, the increasing use of general fund revenues may conceal the redistributive effects of highway spending and make up for shortfalls in the Highway Trust Fund. (The fund virtually vanished in 2014 until Congress revived it with an infusion of $11 billion.) In addition, these funding floors have loopholes that excluded certain expenditures, including, in particular cases, earmarks.[99]

More fundamentally, the push toward equity raises a question that strikes to the very root of the highway program: If monies are to be apportioned roughly on the basis of how much a state's motorists have paid into the Highway Trust Fund, then why not eliminate the middleman and devolve the collection and disbursement of gasoline and related taxes to the states?

Why the disparities in the first place? Typical explanations have included differences between states in such categories as demand for and mileage of highways; wealth and the ability to pay for highways; the disproportionate influence of rural states in the Senate; and the operations of the congressional pork barrel. Zhu and Brown examined four hypotheses explaining the redistribution of highway funds: differences in need; differences in economic health and wealth; rural bias; and political representation on relevant congressional committees. Using data spanning the years 1974–2008, the researchers found that the two hypotheses most frequently used to justify the redistribution of highway funds—that they meet the varying needs of states and they assist poorer states—were "not good explanations." The other two hypotheses—that they are skewed toward rural states and states with representation on the committees that oversee the highway program (the House Committee on Transportation and Infrastructure, the Senate Environment and Public Works Committee, and the House and Senate Appropriations Committees)—received stronger support. Rewarding states due to advantageously placed members of Congress and their degree of rurality, say the authors, are not "compelling policy reasons for the continued existence of geographic redistribution."[100] If the federal highway program exists merely to send back to the states what the residents thereof have paid in taxes, then what justification is there for not turning the program over to the fifty states?

On a parallel track, Brian Knight, an economist at Brown University, examined transportation-related votes in the US House of Representatives during the debate over the 1998 TEA-21 bill and found that lawmakers were more likely to vote for measures that increased spending within their districts. This casts doubt on the naive assumption, which enjoyed its heyday in mid-twentieth-century political science, that "the federal government acts as a benevolent social planner, maximizing national welfare." Rather, the government appears to consist "of agents facing incentives to serve local, rather than national, interests."[101] The very fact that the fiercest struggles over highway policy have to do with the divvying up of the spoils suggests the nonpolitical—or, perhaps, the *entirely* political—nature of the issue. No grand overarching philosophies are debated; ideas, principles, and ideologies are all safely off to the side. The only thing that matters is getting more for your constituents.

In a 1997 paper, political scientist Patrick J. Sellers examined the power of pork, which is often assumed but rarely evaluated empirically. Sellers hypothesized that in congressional races, fiscal liberals would do better in districts to which pork flowed—or, rather, was shipped (the image of pork flowing being decidedly unappetizing)—while fiscal conservatives would perform better in pork-starved districts. The key, he posited, was consistency: in high-pork districts, a fiscal liberal would benefit electorally from federal allocations more than does a fiscal conservative, while the opposite is the case in low-pork districts. Parsing data from the Federal Assistance Awards Data System as well as ratings from the National Taxpayers' Union, Professor Sellers confirmed his thesis. Loud and proud spendthrifts find it easier to claim credit for that new bridge than do green-eyeshade budget hawks.[102]

The diversion of Highway Trust Fund monies to mass transit, which now consumes about 15 percent of Trust Fund revenues, undermines the plaint of urban representatives that the highway program favors their country cousins. As analyst Emily Goff points out, six cities—Boston, Chicago, New York, Philadelphia, San Francisco, and Washington, DC—generate most transit ridership, with New York City alone the locale of four of every ten transit riders. Due to the Trust Fund diversion, writes Goff, "a Montana cattle rancher ...

pays gas taxes to subsidize a Manhattan stockbroker's subway commute."[103] This is inevitable when government parcels out subsidies: there are winners and losers, and the former have no shortage of credible-sounding defenses for their good fortune.

Senator Mike Lee, the Utah Republican with a decentralist bent, has sponsored, in multiple sessions, the Transportation Empowerment Act, or S. 3190 in the 115th Congress. Its primary provision would reduce, over five years, the federal gasoline tax from 18.4 cents per gallon to 3.7 cents per gallon. The much-reduced federal gas tax revenue, subsequently block-granted to the states, would force states to raise their own gasoline taxes to levels sensitive to local needs and conditions. "Under this new system," said Lee, "Americans would no longer have to send significant gas-tax revenue to Washington, where politicians, bureaucrats, and lobbyists take their cut before sending it back with strings attached."[104]

> By cutting out the federal middleman," Lee explained, "we can protect these funds from greedy politicians and special interests.... And we can lessen the influence of distant bureaucrats in Washington who waste the money on inefficient and nonhighway projects.... All 50 states would be empowered to meet their diverse transportation needs. Some communities could build more roads, while others could repair old ones. Some might build highways, others light rail. All would be free to experiment with innovative green technologies, and could find new ways to finance their projects.[105]

There is some boilerplate in the rhetoric, to be sure, but Senator Lee harkens back to a Jeffersonian, or Harry Byrdian, or perhaps we should just say small-*f* federalist, preference for local decision making with respect to infrastructure projects and local financing thereof. Previous post–Interstate Highway Act of 1956 manifestations of this philosophy—for instance, President Ford's failed attempt to reduce the federal gas tax—have failed to gain traction, and Senator Lee's effort awaits the emergence of a corresponding decentralist tendency within the Democratic Party. (A vision of a return to small-*f* federalist principles was limned by the 1990s Milwaukee Democratic Mayor John Norquist, a champion of the New Urbanism who decried "tin-cup urbanism" and called for the revitalization of cities through a devolution of power from the federal government to the localities.[106] Norquist was also an incisive critic of the way blunderbuss roadbuilding had sucked the life from cities. "If Paul had been facing a grade-separated highway on the road to Damascus," he said, "maybe he wouldn't have seen the light."[107])

Tear It Down!

The Highway Trust Fund's reputation as an ATM for the road lobby was battered by charges of inadequacy, as it stumbled into and through middle age, belittled as too scant, too exiguous to meet the challenges of the modern age. Mass transiteers raided it; critics even succeeded in razing certain of its more dubious "monuments."

First, the raiders. Senator Daniel Patrick Moynihan, by then a grizzled veteran of infrastructure politics, concluded in 1991: "We've poured enough concrete."[108] In that year Moynihan help to shepherd through Congress the Intermodal Surface Transportation Efficiency Act (ISTEA) of 1991, the first big post-interstate measure in the field. ISTEA blurred the lines between expenditures for highways and mass transit, allowing local metropolitan planning organizations to decide the proper balance within each area between transit and highway spending. In this way, decision making was localized to a greater extent than had been envisioned in 1956, when all power, or so it seemed, lay within the state highway departments.[109] By 1991, butter was in, guns were out. ISTEA's legislative language asserted that "the construction of the Interstate Highway System ... greatly enhanced economic growth in the United States," but, unlike the 1956 acts, it made no mention of its alleged fortifying of the national defense.[110]

Hailed as revolutionary, not least for ISTEA's use of the ugly buzzword *intermodal*, which most nonwonks find esoteric, the free-market transportation analyst Randal O'Toole mocked ISTEA as the "Urban Immobility and Pork-Barrel Act" for directing monies to light rail, which is notoriously inefficient.[111] (Bus good, train bad, as the axiom goes.) Mass transit, despite the ballyhoo of 1991, still accounts for just 1.5 percent of all miles traveled in the United States.[112] In fact, the percentage of Highway Trust Fund monies diverted to mass transit exceeds the percentage of Americans who use mass transit—a percentage that has shrunk since 1980.[113] Americans show no signs of trading in their cars for mass transit. The FHWA reports that the average American driver lays down 13,476 miles per year, or about eighty times more miles than the average American travels annually by public transit.[114] As Joel Garreau says, while the automobile "goes where you want to go when you want to go, trains ... require you to go where someone else wants you to go when someone else wants you to go."[115]

But even in a car-crazed culture, sometimes enough is enough. So widespread has been the retrospective revulsion against the damage done by the 1960s-era interstates that a teardown movement has notched significant victories. In certain cases, the highways are simply worn out, and traffic patterns have altered in the years since they were built to make them obsolete. But in other cases, vengeance is mine, saith scarred cities, sometimes aided by Mother Nature. In the case of San Francisco's hated Embarcadero, the 1989 Loma Prieta earthquake finished the job. A street-level boulevard has been its welcome replacement. New Haven, Connecticut, demolished the much-loathed Oak Street Connector. Portland, Oregon, opened its Willamette River waterfront by razing Harbor Drive. Behind the leadership of New Urbanist mayor John Norquist, Milwaukee demolished the prohibitively expensive and "lightly used" Park East Freeway.[116] Hopeful New Urbanists have targeted aging and strangulating elevated expressways in Buffalo, Syracuse, and other cities for possible demolition. The joint forces of the highway lobby, federal dollars, and the state and federal departments of transportation no longer seem quite so unbeatable.

Not every teardown is met, however, with ringing endorsements. In Boston, replacing the much-derided Central Artery, the elevated highway and civic eyesore tinted in ghostly green, was a parodically wasteful underground network known informally as the Big Dig. The Central Artery, as Nicole Gelinas of the Manhattan Institute explained, was a physical and psychological scar on Boston that "barred pedestrians from the water ... overwhelmed low-rise streets, a historic outdoor fruit and vegetable market, and even the historic Faneuil Hall with traffic noise and shadow. It erased swaths of the working-class Italian North End, displacing 573 businesses—mostly small shops and trading firms—and hundreds of families."[117] On top of that it was ugly and soon made obsolete by volumes of traffic beyond its capacity to handle. Shutting down the artery and shunting its traffic beneath the city met with widespread approval at first. No homes would be destroyed, the unions would be happy, and hey, the feds would pay 90 percent, since Governor Dukakis and Speaker O'Neill argued successfully that because the Central Artery predated the interstate system and had been incorporated thereinto, the Big Dig should be eligible for 90–10 interstate financing.

But politics are a vicissitudinary thing. Tip O'Neill could not remain speaker forever. Other states grumbled over what they saw as special treatment for the Bay State. In 1987, President Reagan's veto of an interstate highway authorization bill containing critical money for the Big Dig was overridden by a single vote—that of North Carolina Democratic Senator Terry Sanford, who had voted against the bill at first because it contained insufficient pork for the Tar Heel State, but who ignominiously switched his vote and greenlighted the Big Dig as part of a logrolling deal to save tobacco subsidies.[118]

As stories of Big Dig wastefulness spread, the feds stopped paying 90 percent; in fact, they capped their contribution. Massachusetts was on its own. Over the three decades from drawing board to its completion in 2005, the Big Dig became, as Noah Bierman writes in the *Boston Globe*, "political shorthand for bloat and delay, with shoddiness thrown in for good measure."[119]

Championed by such gold-medal, bringers-home-of-bacon as House Speaker O'Neill, the project cost $14.8 billion, rather more than the 1982 estimate of $2.6 billion. But as Nicole Gelinas notes, the Big Dig was a clear upgrade over the Central Artery, as travel times through Boston have been sharply reduced and the North End, reconnected with the rest of Boston, has seen a dramatic revitalization. Nevertheless, the Big Dig's notoriety was such that its example helped to kill a plan to replace an elevated highway in Seattle with a tunnel. City planners and New Urbanists who dreamed of razing elevated highways in Louisville and elsewhere and rerouting traffic underground ran into the irrefutable fact that the Big Dig, a similar project, had been "obscenely expensive" and "the ultimate pork barrel project," in the words of one frustrated Louisville reformer.[120] A bankrupting cure can be barely better than the disease.

Eternal Life Ain't What It Used to Be: The Highway Trust Fund as Sexagenarian

The Highway Trust Fund, its impregnability breached by transit, its more monstrous concrete creations under assault, no longer seemed enough to achieve its goals. As highway-spending advocates do not tire of reminding us, the last hike of the federal gasoline tax was in 1993, more than a quarter of a century ago, and its real value has since fallen by 39 percent. While the federal gas tax has remained constant for an unusually long time, it rose by more than 400 percent (from 4 cents to 18.4 cents) between 1982 and 1994. (The gas tax was hiked to 4 cents per gallon in 1959, a level at which it remained until more than doubling, to 9 cents per gallon, under the Surface Transportation Assistance Act of 1982. The special Mass Transit Account received 1 cent of this nickel-a-gallon hike.) The Omnibus Reconciliation Act of 1990 boosted the tax by another nickel, to 14 cents per gallon, with half of the increase (2.5 cents per gallon) streaming into the Highway Trust Fund (one-fifth of that, or 0.5 cents per gallon, went to the Mass Transit Account) and the other half (2.5 cents per gallon) disappearing into the general revenue pool. This was less of a break with tradition than it seemed: the original federal gasoline tax in 1931 had been put mostly toward lowering the deficit.

In 1993, Congress hiked the federal gas tax by another 4.3 cents per gallon, later adjusting it slightly upward and ending the diversion to general revenues so that the total tax as the twentieth century ended was 18.4 cents per gallon, where it still stands today. Deficit reduction is no longer a target of the tax, though the part given to mass transit has increased to 2.68 cents per gallon. The current federal excise tax on diesel fuel is 24.4 cents per gallon. As this book went to press, state gasoline taxes and fees ranged from a whopping 57.6 cents per gallon in Pennsylvania and 49.4 cents in Washington State to a low of 8.95 cents per gallon in Alaska.[121] The Golden State, as usual, stands out. California's state gasoline tax jumped by 12 cents per gallon in November 2017, to 39.8 cents, and by another 7.5 cents in July 2019. Combined with the 18.4 cents per gallon federal tax, California motorists are taxed at a rate of 65.7 cents for each gallon of gasoline they pump. Adding insult to injury, California "taxes the tax," mulcting another 7.25 to 9.75 percent of the total tax-fattened purchase price via the state sales tax.[122]

Even this, to the more conventionally minded members of the Fourth Estate, is too little. ASCE's quadrennial report is a hook on which sententious newspaper editorialists hang their periodic pleas for higher gasoline taxes. For instance, the *New York Times*, whose editorial writers are less likely to own an automobile than those of any other daily newspaper in the country, given the comparatively low rate of automobile ownership in Manhattan and Brooklyn, has called on "Congress to overcome its longstanding terror of offending the nation's motorists and raise the tax on gasoline and diesel fuel."[123] Referencing the dolorous assertions of ASCE, the oracles of the *Times* call for a 15 cent per gallon hike in the gas tax, which as they note "would add just $3 to the cost of a 20-gallon fill-up": chickenfeed to a *New York Times* editorialist, especially one who does not own a Ford Focus or old Chevy Impala—though perhaps he owns a Prius as he commutes to his Westchester County home.[124] But this is a real burden on working people, and in particular those who have to travel great distances to reach their jobs. Just as it is easy to call on other men to die in wars that you will not have to fight, so is it devilishly simple to demand the imposition of taxes on others—especially others of a lower socioeconomic class—that one will not himself have to pay.

The expanded use of electric vehicles and others that do not rely on petroleum products has removed an increasing number of relatively affluent motorists from coverage by the gas tax, and boosts in fuel efficiency have reduced the tax bill for many others. The rise of alternative-fuel vehicles is starting to make a travesty of the user-fee rationale for the gas tax. In the 1950s, when the Highway Trust Fund was born, variations in average miles per gallon were not large for most automobiles. The chasm between gas guzzlers and Priuses, old junkers and Teslas, had not yet opened. President Gerald Ford, whose very surname and home state of Michigan bespoke *Automobile*, helped to widen this gap.

CAFE (Corporate Average Fuel Economy) standards, introduced in the Energy Policy Conservation Act of 1975 as a response to the gas station queues and semipanic of the oil crisis of the mid-1970s, mandated an average miles per gallon for the cars and light trucks of each manufacturer in a given model year. For passenger cars, this rose from 18.0 in 1978 to 30.2 (24.1 for light trucks) in 2011, when a series of modifications set varying standards depending on the "footprint" of the vehicle. The CAFE standards may have led to greater fuel efficiency—though it is also possible that increases in fuel efficiency encourage more driving, which actually *increases* emissions—but on one point there is little debate: they have helped to shrink the Highway Trust Fund. Hybrids, electric cars, and other alternatives to gasoline-powered vehicles loom ominously over the Highway Trust Fund's future. The more they populate the road, the thinner the trust fund becomes. As always, reform has unintended consequences.

Vehicles not powered by gasoline are, in a literal sense, "free riders" on the highway. They pay no gasoline tax and in fact lap up subsidies in the form of tax credits. They are fast making the Highway Trust Fund obsolete, or at least patently unfair. Given that owners of alternative-fuel vehicles skew toward higher levels of income and formal education, the gasoline tax has taken on a regressive cast. (More than 75 percent of Tesla buyers earn over $100,000 annually.[125]) Very few of the working poor own hybrid or electric vehicles; the older-model, down-market cars they tend to drive get lousier mileage than later models and more upscale autos, so they are buying more gasoline per mile traveled than are those who make considerably larger incomes.

Moreover, the incentives embedded in the tax are often "perverse," as economist Clifford Winston, a tolling advocate, notes, since, for instance, trucks are taxed at a higher rate the more axles they have, even though additional axles provide better weight distribution and thereby cause less harm to the roads.[126] A mileage-based user fee would capture the miles traveled by electric vehicles and thus make the method of highway revenue-raising less regressive, but any attempt to shift the burden of taxation from Group A to Group B will call down the furies from Group B, which in this case is a demographic cohort with higher income, education level, and political engagement than Group A—which is to say it would be a tough row to hoe.

At this writing, seventeen states have imposed fees on electric vehicles, and others are debating them. The big environmental lobbies are on the defensive, and as any football coach knows, the best defense is a good offense. So the Sierra Club, for instance, deplores these "unfairly punitive" fees and accuses the tax-shifters of "punishing people and families who are seeking to reduce their carbon footprint and drive some of the most efficient and fun cars out there. States must act to care for our roads, highways, bridges, and their maintenance, but not on the backs of families who choose to drive electric vehicles."[127] Ignoring the fairness issue, and never once letting the *R*-word—regressive—pass their lips or emerge from their word processors, the Sierrans risibly seek to frame this as a battle between good old Middle-American families and ... Big Oil!

And not only the nefarious ne'er-do-wells of Big Oil, who have lost a bit of their bogeyman vibe since the oil-shortage days of the 1970s, but also the Kochs!, those all-purpose villains in the world of the upper-middle-class Left, who are said by their enemies to be anti–electric car. The evidence? The American Legislative Exchange Council, a conservative association of state-level free-market advocates, funded in part by the Kochs, has come out against government subsidies for electric vehicles. "When oil tycoons consider a rise in EV drivers to be a threat to their wallets, you know EVs are taking off," declared the Sierra Club website.[128] The establishment environmental movement has long been chastised for its resolutely upper-crust membership and outlook, but this really is too much: to oppose subsidies to the wealthiest slice of the car-buying public is to be the cat's-paw, the stooge, the unwitting tool of Big Oil and the Koch empire! So, what is to be done? Bringing the federal gasoline tax up to a level sufficient to cover Highway Trust Fund payments would require a hike of about thirty cents per gallon, which makes it a political nonstarter nonpareil, with its most passionate supporters limited to urban members of Congress whose districts contain relatively few automobile owners. Relying solely on this revenue source would require a one-third reduction in federal highway funding and a two-thirds reduction in federal transit funding.[129] And while poll respondents consistently support higher funding for road and bridge repair, they just as consistently oppose raising the federal gasoline tax or imposing tolls to pay for it.

Today, as never before, transportation policymakers are casting about for alternatives to the Highway Trust Fund as it now exists. One way is simply to scrap the Highway Trust Fund and parcel out transportation funding from general revenues. That would certainly put an end to all the fretting about the inadequacy of the trust fund. It would require the introduction of nary a technological marvel and would bring the United States into greater conformity with the other nations of the developed world, many of which assess fuel taxes but few of which dedicate them to highway spending. The major, overriding, and likely insuperable objection is that this would undermine the user-fee concept that has long undergirded US highway policy. No longer would there be even the fig leaf of a user-pay system. Representatives of districts without large concentrations of automobile owners would resist this fiercely. And it would stall innovative toll ideas in their tracks, for if toll fees are not to be dedicated to certain roads and bridges, then their public support would utterly vanish. Finally, anyone who thinks that the House and Senate committees whose purview is transportation would cede these realms without a fight befitting a cornered and feral animal is a political naïf. And this brings us to the *T*-word, which is slowly finding itself removed from the index of prohibited ideas.

For Whom the Road Tolls?

In retrospect, the 1990s were a decade awash in possibilities: the Soviet Union dissolved, the Cold War was over, the "peace dividend" was (supposedly) to be rebated to taxpayers, President Clinton declared that the era of big government was over, and the stifling hand of political correctness had yet to shut off debate in the academy. In the field of transportation, toll roads made a comeback, their first since the turnpike boomlet of the 1940s and 1950s. Unlike the New York State Thruway, these new toll roads were usually run by private groups. It was nowhere near the scale of the nineteenth century, when turnpikes and plank roads ribboned the East, but it augured a revival.

The revolution began in Europe. The French approved private construction and operation of tolled highways in 1955. Spain followed suit in 1972, though several of the motorways in both countries were nationalized due to their unprofitability.[130] Italy had been charging drivers to use certain roads since 1924, when the Milan-Lakes route became "the world's first toll highway."[131] Yet the United States, the land that private enterprise built, lagged. A 2013 study found that only one of the thirty-eight largest firms in the world involved in transportation privatization was based in America.[132] (That outlier was Fluor, in Irving, Texas, which despite its name has nothing to do with metallurgical flux but is rather an engineering and construction firm. Europe is also home to certain privately or partially privately owned airports, such as Heathrow outside London, while American airports are typically government owned.)

Tolls, whether on private roads or public thoroughfares, appeared as a response to both the need for revenue and the aggravating temporal elongation of commuting times. Commuters in the most congested city in the world, Los Angeles, spend an average of 104 peak hours in congestion; three other US cities, New York, San Francisco, and Atlanta, are also among the top ten.[133] The average time of a commute is forty-eight minutes in the United States, as opposed to forty-two minutes in Germany, thirty-eight minutes in Great Britain, and thirty-one minutes in Italy.[134] The transportation analytics company INRIXS estimates the cost of this congestion to US drivers at almost $300 billion annually.[135]

Harmful automobile emissions are exacerbated by traffic congestion, which also results in an estimated three million gallons of gasoline wasted each year.[136] The stop-and-start traffic typical of clogged highways is multiple times more pollution creating than a smooth traffic flow. And it is incredibly stressful, too. Perhaps the only bright side is that it allows drivers the chance to get through more books on tape; the diligent commuter in Southern California ought to be fluent in a dozen languages after a few years of freeway snarls.

The easy and obvious—if taxpayer-burdening—answer is to build more roads. Yet the Fundamental Law of Road Congestion, handed down by Gilles Duranton and Matthew A. Turner in 2011, is that "roads cause traffic."[137] Vehicle miles traveled rise in direct proportion to an increase in available lane miles. The law seems fixed and immutable. Building new highways does not relieve congestion, no matter if the highway lobby may wish it were so.[138]

Congestion, or variable, pricing, on the other hand, is a form of tolling that relieves rather than worsens jammed traffic, raising tolls during peak traffic hours and lowering them at off-peak hours. Variable pricing encourages those with a degree of flexibility to postpone or move up their travels to take advantage of cheaper off-hour rates. Or they find another method of conveyance. Such common pricing is used to set airfares, hotel rates, phone charges, subway fares, etc. Making it cheaper to drive at 1 a.m. than at 3 p.m. also saves night owls and those working the third shift a few bucks. An economic incentive to drive at off-peak hours reduces congestion and lessens the pollution resulting therefrom. And tolls may encourage carpooling as well, which contributes to these salutary outcomes.

Naturally, there are naysayers to every permutation of tolls. For instance, adding tolled lanes to otherwise "free" expressways sometimes elicits objections to a "two-tiered" system in which those who can, or who choose to, pay, will travel at a faster rate than those who do not. The argument has an egalitarian appeal. California State Senator Bill Lockyer laid it out in classic form back in 1991, when he argued against the use of public funds in privately funded highway demonstration projects. In part, Lockyer made the libertarian argument that "It is wrong to provide public subsidies to private investors unable to make investments viable without tax dollars."[139] If such projects cannot attract enough private funding, then we should heed the signal the market is sending and refuse them public support. Fair enough. But Lockyer went on to assert that "toll roads are fundamentally inegalitarian," as they "create a two-tiered system, where people of ordinary means drive on roads that are falling apart while the affluent pay tolls and drive on new or improved highways."[140]

But of course, those traveling via the nontolled lanes are doing so on roads made *less* congested by the existence of the tolled lanes. Moreover, as Robert W. Poole Jr., a longtime privatization advocate who founded the libertarian Reason Foundation, points out, a tiered system obtains in many other government services, as for instance the US Postal Service, which delivers more expensive first-class mail with greater alacrity than it does, say, media mail. And if one wishes that her package arrive the next day, she may choose to send it via next-day air (or via the private firms Federal Express or United Parcel Service) at a sometimes substantially higher cost.[141]

Vastly increased dependence on tolling, though perhaps under a less threatening name—ideally an inscrutable acronym!—seems an inevitability. Although tolls in 1956 meant frequent stops at manned booths and the attendant slowdowns, the days of backups and congestion at tollbooths on the Pennsylvania Turnpike or the New York State Thruway are coming to an end, no matter how fiercely the toll collectors and their union may resist. The last three decades have seen a virtual revolution in the technology of tolling. Electronic toll collection (ETC) was introduced in the 1980s, as motorists driving segments of the interstate such as the Massachusetts Turnpike and the New York State Thruway gained the option of E-ZPass, by which a small transponder mounted on a vehicle's windshield is read by antennae, thus allowing the motorist to bypass the toll collector. She receives a monthly bill for E-ZPass usage. California boasted the nation's first ETC on the Coronado Bridge in San Diego.

Gone, or so it was prophesied, were the stop-and-go, bumper-to-bumper lines at toll booths, as motorists fumbled for loose change to toss into mesh nets or hand to surly attendants. Well, the toll booth was more stubborn, more pertinacious in its determination to resist extinction, than others had thought. It hung on, no matter how many frustrated motorists missed the nets with their tossed quarters, saw their receipts blow out the window, or hit the car in front of them as it hiccuped down the entry lane. Yet the toll booth may soon be as obsolete, if not charmingly obsolete, as the telephone booth. Manual collection is expensive and inefficient, and it wastes gasoline and increases emissions. Recent advances in toll technology have made it possible to obviate the traffic jams at exits.

As the twenty-first century dawned, the age of all-electronic tolling (AET) arrived. (AET: doesn't that sound milder with that harsh and discordant word *tolling* reduced to a single letter?) Under AET, *all* vehicles are tolled electronically, thus scrapping the need for toll plazas, booths, and barriers, as well as well-compensated toll collectors. Those who eschew transponders are tolled via license plate imaging. With AET, backups, congestion, and fender benders due to stop-and-start driving at the tollbooth will be outmoded like the hand-crank engine startup. And reduced labor costs are unwelcome news for the toll collector but good news for everyone else in the form of cheaper tolls.[142] On the flipside, AET denies motorists who prefer to use cash that option. It is another step toward the cashless society that can be viewed as dystopian. The Reason Foundation has anticipated the shift to electronic tolling for decades. It has, in a series of richly detailed reports, explained the case therefor, and the case against continued reliance on motor fuel taxes to fund highway work—for such tolling need not be a supplement to gasoline taxes but a substitute for them.

The cost of motor fuel collection, as engineer, academic, and respected transportation consultant Dr. Daryl S. Fleming writes, is about 5 percent of the tax revenue collected. Studies have pegged the cost of American AET operations at a similar level: "5% of the revenue collected for a $5.00 toll (or 8% of revenue collected for a $2.00 toll)."[143] These figures are not universally accepted; public agencies associated with cash toll collection have published estimates inflating to 30 percent the cost of AET operations against total revenue collection.[144] Such astronomical projections may be taken with the proverbial grain, or vein, of salt. Less outrageous is the FHWA's pegging of the cost of motor fuel tax collection at about 1 percent of revenues. But, offers Fleming in rebuttal, this includes only the direct costs. It ignores the considerable costs to distributors (who now collect the tax that was once collected at the retail level); these are passed along to the retailers and in turn to the customers. It also ignores certain costs associated with tax filing to the IRS. Adding in the cost exacted by fraud and abuse as well as the opportunity costs related to congestion and the inability of the current system to offer innovative solutions such as time-of-day pricing, the cost of motor fuel tax collection could be as high as *20 percent* of revenue.[145]

Significantly addressing a major weakness of motor fuel taxes, AET captures revenue from all vehicles on the road, not just those that use federally and state-taxed motor fuels, so in fact it is, by a substantial margin, a "more cost-effective way of generating revenue for our highway system."[146] AET can vary toll rates in order to manage traffic, hiking them at peak hours and lowering them at off-peak, in order to encourage a smoother traffic flow. If time-of-day pricing reduced peak-hour traffic by just a modest 5 percent, explains Daryl S. Fleming, delays due to congestion would decrease by 10 percent.[147] And for those worried about the government's not-so-venerable but oft-furtive practice of diverting alleged user fees to nonhighway purposes, the tolling system permits motorists and legislators to see just how much revenue each route generates, and makes it that much more difficult for other interests to sneak out a piece of the pie. Even the most fervent toll advocates, such as Robert Poole, admit that rural and mountainous states such Alaska, Montana, and Vermont would likely not be able to capture anywhere near enough revenue from tolling to support interstate maintenance and reconstruction. Unless the states are to go it alone, some federal subsidy is probable in those cases.[148]

A September 2011 study by Poole explained how toll revenue might enable the state of Wisconsin to reconstruct and modernize its 743 miles of interstate highways over a period of thirty years. Though interstates make up less than 1 percent of roadway miles in the Badger State, they carry almost one-fifth (18 percent) of the state's vehicle miles of travel and more than one-fifth (21 percent) of its heavy truck traffic.[149] (This is similar to the nationwide ratio in which rural and urban interstates constitute but 2.52 percent of total lane miles but almost one-quarter—24.4 percent—of vehicle miles traveled.[150]) Using data from the Wisconsin Department of Transportation, Poole estimated the cost of rebuilding and modernizing Wisconsin's interstates at $26.2 billion, which vastly exceeds the state's capacity to pay. Yet the introduction of *value-added tolling*—that is, tolling that would not take effect until the lanes had already been improved—could pay for the entirety of the modernization project on rural interstates, whose rebuilding costs are $12.5 billion, and up to 71 percent of the cost of the necessary work on the interstate system in the southeastern corner of the state, according to Poole. These would be "pure user fees," collected only from those who use the roads, and dedicated only to those roads that are being tolled.[151] The tolls would not be collected in the old style, with motorists queued up at exits as harried toll collectors make change, and drivers further back in line stew and fume and fiddle with the radio dial. There are neither toll booths nor toll plazas in Poole's vision of tomorrow's Wisconsin: just cashless, quick, and easy electronic passes and billing systems.

Poole has done kindred calculations on the ability of tolls to subsidize the reconstruction of the nation's interstate system. Given its half-century design life, nearly all of the interstate lanes will need rebuilding or even widening over the next dozen or so years. Including the expense of transitioning to AET on these roads, Poole in 2014 estimated the cost of reconstructing the entire interstate system at $589 billion, or $148 billion for rural interstates ($1.2 million per lane mile) and $441 billion for urban interstates ($4.78 million per lane mile). Half of this bill, he notes, would be run up in eight states: California, Florida, Georgia, Illinois, Michigan, New York, Pennsylvania, and Texas.[152]

Poole found that "modest" toll rates—that is, rates lower than those on most existing tolled lanes—would be sufficient to cover reconstruction costs in the vast majority of states, with the exceptions of Alaska, Montana, New York, North Dakota, South Dakota, Vermont, and Wyoming, most of which are on the large-state/low-population-and-traffic model that has traditionally nettled toll advocates. New York and Wyoming, he writes, could finance reconstruction by pegging tolls at a somewhat higher, though by no means confiscatory, level—though New Yorkers and Wyomingites have different ideas as to what constitutes confiscatory taxation—and the other states, Alaska excepted, would need to retain a fuel tax. Alaska, the "special case," would almost certainly require federal assistance, though it might be extended grudgingly.[153] (Alaska is always a special case: for instance, in 2015, federal highway funding for the Last Frontier equaled about $657 per Alaska resident, as compared to New York's apportionment of $82 per New Yorker. Unfair? Sure. But then, as Harvard's Edward Glaeser puckishly remarks, low-density states such as Alaska "are remarkably well-endowed with senators per capita."[154])

Absent the introduction of toll financing, the federal gasoline tax would need to be bumped up by 40 to 50 cents per gallon to cover the costs of reconstruction—a boost that even the most tone-deaf and *vox populi*–ignoring politico will concede is about as likely as the emplacement of bike paths along interstate shoulders.[155] As Poole notes, the AET system makes it possible to rebate fuel tax payments to motorists in the event that tolls do not entirely supplant the federal gas tax. For as he knows well, a tax, once enacted, is devilishly hard to snuff.

* * *

Certain reformers urge a shift to levies based on vehicle miles traveled, or VMT. (No issue is really an issue until it has its own acronym.) A VMT system would track the number of miles an automobile travels and tax its owners on that basis, with a likely cents-per-mile charge. As with the federal gasoline tax, states and maybe local governments are expected to piggyback on this tax. Advocates assert that VMT, by measuring miles traveled instead of gasoline bought, is a more accurately calibrated user fee. A motorist cannot escape its sweep by driving a more fuel-efficient, or non–gasoline-powered, vehicle. The gas tax, it is argued, "is too negligible and opaque to influence behavior."[156] When you fill up at the pump, your receipt does not itemize the various taxes that contribute to the sum, and that also induce your weary sighs and roll of the eyes as that sum mounts ever higher. By contrast, a VMT bill every month would quite literally drive home the cost of your motoring. VMT would also be impervious to changing CAFE standards, fuel efficiency, and the introduction of alternative fuels. All that matters is miles driven.

Pilot tests in Oregon suggest that VMT could reduce congestion, though response to this pilot has been "tepid" at best.[157] In 2015, the Evergreen State launched OReGO, advertised as the country's first road usage charge program. Limited to a maximum of five thousand voluntary participants, OReGO imposes what is currently a per-mile charge of 1.7 cents on motorists. You simply plug a mileage-reporting device into your GPS or another outlet and begin paying by miles driven in lieu of the state's (current) 34-cents-per-gallon gas tax. (Drivers still pay the state fuel tax at the pump but receive a credit against their VMT tax.)[158] The program has yet to take off; participation has hovered around one thousand. Just one-fifth of the five thousand available slots have been taken.[159]

But privacy concerns arise. The VMT would require installation of a tracking device in motor vehicles. Who wants Uncle Sam, or his minions burrowed deep in the warrens of the US Department of Transportation or the state departments of transportation, to know when and where she is driving her car? Supporters whisper soothing words to the effect that the federal government would never, ever, misuse such information or abuse the liberties and privacy of American motorists, but Americans are by instinct and experience suspicious of claims of government benevolence. No one this side of a 1950s junior high school social studies textbook writer believes such government assurances. In addition, some charge the VMT with "bias against rural drivers," as a pair of researchers from the Washington, DC–based Bipartisan Policy Center write.[160] They drive further than urban motorists, for the most part, and though the lack of starting and stopping gives them better gas mileage, under a VMT such efficiencies are irrelevant.

Parsing data from the State Farm Mutual Automobile Insurance Company, economists Ashley Langer, Vikram Maheshri, and Clifford Winston argue that a VMT differentiating between urban and rural miles is preferable to a gasoline tax in that it reduces such external costs as congestion and accidents. Whether political realities would permit a heavier taxing of motorists on urban than rural routes is, as usual, a matter of the relative influence of he whose ox is being gored and he who is doing the goring.[161]

For now, the VMT is locked in the garage, awaiting a more propitious time for its introduction. When in 2009 President Obama's transportation secretary Ray LaHood innocently remarked, "We should look at the vehicular miles program where people are actually clocked on the number of miles that they traveled," he was quickly rebuked by the White House press secretary.[162] But then the hyperpolitical White House is usually more sensitive to the winds of public opinion than is a secretary of transportation. For in that same year, 2009, a public opinion survey by the bipartisan infrastructure interest group Building America's Future found that a whopping 81 percent of respondents agreed that VMTs were "not acceptable."[163] Ironically, Secretary LaHood would later cochair Building America's Future with ex–New York City Mayor Michael Bloomberg and ex-Pennsylvania Governor Edward Rendell. LaHood must have learned the VMT lesson. He had certainly learned the cliché-speak of the building class: "America is one big pothole," he declared while secretary of transportation, an observation that suggests LaHood had little acquaintance with the world outside the Beltway of Washington, DC or the mean streets of his hometown of Peoria, Illinois.[164]

(LaHood was no stranger to the gaffe, which Michael Kinsley once defined as a politician accidentally telling the truth. In May 2009, the secretary of transportation was recorded telling an audience at the National Press Club that the Obama administration was looking for ways to "coerce people out of their cars."[165] Honesty, alas, is not a trait highly prized among the governing class.)

* * *

Congress took the first tentative step toward scrapping the ban on interstate tolls with ISTEA in 1991, with further relaxations in the 1998 and 2005 reauthorizations. Actually, the first crack in the toll ban had appeared in 1987, when Congress authorized eight toll demonstration projects in eight different states; the federal government pledged to contribute up to 35 percent of costs, though the facilities had to be publicly owned. Private toll roads, though common in the socialist nations of Europe, were still unthinkable in the United States. A 1991 revision to the law enabled states to build tollways with a 50 percent federal contribution, with the rest an admixture of state funds, bond monies, and private investment. Despite the sporadic and extremely limited relaxation of the ban on interstate tolling, 1,158 miles, or about 2 percent of the IHS, are currently tolled.

Transportation analyst William Newman, a former Conrail executive, has proposed an elegantly simple federal legislative solution: "Any state, to the extent authorized by state law, may toll any federal highway, bridge or tunnel, and approach thereto, including those highways, bridges and tunnels, and approaches, on the Interstate system, whether existing or new."[166] That about covers it. But tolls, though often favored by economists and intellectuals associated with right-leaning think tanks, have yet to gain a public constituency, even among right-leaning voters. In Texas, the state Republican Party convention of 2014, under pressure from Tea Party activists, ended a provision of its platform favoring "the legitimate construction of toll roads in Texas."[167] This was a rebuke to Governor Rick Perry, the Republican under whose fourteen-year tenure the number of toll roads in the state had risen from a handful to twenty-five. The antitoll faction, grouped around an organization calling itself Texans Uniting for Reform and Freedom, spoke of the "enormous amount of toll road fatigue in Texas."[168]

Truckers are a solid phalanx in the antitoll army, as are those who have not accepted recent advances in tolling technology and point to the frequency of accidents in and around toll plazas. (Tolls on the Connecticut Turnpike were removed after a horrific 1983 accident at a toll plaza in Stratford in which seven women and children were killed after the sleeping driver of a semitrailer crashed into a line of cars.[169]) There is also the old chestnut that "the roads are already paid for," so why should Americans be taxed every time they venture out on these allegedly "free" roads?—to which toll advocates reply, sure, the construction has been paid for—largely by previous generations, it might be noted—but these roads don't maintain or reconstruct themselves, y'know![170]

The libertarian analyst Randal O'Toole makes the case for user fees on practical grounds: "The difference between state highways, which are in good condition, local roads, which are in fair condition, and transit systems, which are in poor condition, is simple: State road maintenance is paid for almost entirely out of user fees; local road maintenance is paid for by a combination of taxes and user fees; while transit maintenance is paid for entirely out of taxes."[171] A user fee requires those who use a road to pay for it, which as a method of financing fits a definition of *fairness* and also makes the funding of white-elephant projects far more difficult.

A 2017 Associated Press (AP) story noted that tolls were unpopular, citing a *Washington Post* poll that found that "66 percent of the public opposes granting tax credits to investors who put their money into transportation projects in exchange for the right to charge tolls."[172] And, the AP might have added, 73 percent of respondents had no idea what the question meant. This is far too wordy and obscure a query, and the words *tax credits* and *tolls* are surefire provokers of a hearty *nay!* The reality is murkier. To what extent is the resistance to tolls based in a reluctance to pay for something heretofore "free"—access to a segment of interstate highway—and to what extent is it due to unpleasant experience with toll roads: the slowdowns, the stop-and-start traffic at the plazas, maybe even the truculence of the bored toll collector?

A 1988 survey by the *Urban Transportation Monitor* found 48 percent of respondents expressing a negative opinion about toll roads, though the vast majority (85 percent) believed that their opinion would change if the toll collection were automated.[173] (Sorry, toll collectors.) In their study of public opinion on tolls and road pricing, Johanna Zmud and Carlos Arce of NuStats, LLC, found, contra the expectations of many, that "in the aggregate there is a clear majority support for tolling and road pricing."[174] This came as a surprise; the conventional wisdom has it that toll road advocacy is the third rail of transportation politics: touch it and you're dead, politically. But Zmud and Arce found that it just isn't so. Their data set comprised a literature review of 110 public opinion surveys conducted between the years 2000 and 2007, most of them concerning specific projects that included tolls or road pricing. The locales in which the surveys were taken stretched from the redwood forests to the Gulf Stream waters: from Orange County, California, to the state of Maine; from El Paso, Texas, to the New York City metro area; from the state of North Carolina to Puget Sound, Washington; and everywhere in between.

In 56 percent of these 110 public opinion polls, a majority supported the proposal for tolls or road pricing; majorities opposed tolls or road pricing in 31 percent of the polls. The other 13 percent showed mixed results, with neither side gaining a majority. There were sharp regional differences in opinion. Majority support for tolls or road pricing was found in 84 percent of the surveys in the western United States, with nays constituting a majority in only 13 percent of the polls. Midwesterners also largely supported (64–27 percent), Southerners supported but less so (44–32 percent), and in the Northeast, it was a wash, as yeas and nays each won majorities in 36 percent of the surveys.[175]

As is always the case with polling, the phrasing of the question can determine the answer. Given a choice between tolls and "free" roads, only a masochist (or an economist) would choose the former. But if the tolls are presented as an alternative to fuel taxes or general revenue taxes, the public shifts. As Zmud and Arce write, "Most individuals prefer tolling over taxes."[176] For instance, a 2006 survey commissioned by the Maine Turnpike Authority asked four hundred Maine residents how they would prefer to fund a new highway, bridge, or bypass. Most—56 percent—chose tolls, 16 percent preferred an increase in the state's gasoline tax, and 10 percent favored canceling the project.[177] The authors also quote a Minneapolis man who volunteered, "I like tolls because I wouldn't use them and I wouldn't pay for it. We've got enough taxes."[178]

They conclude that there is an "apparent disconnect between political perceptions of the public attitude toward tolling and actual public opinions."[179] The extent of that disconnect may well be gauged in the near future, for judging from the feebleness of legislative efforts at hiking the federal gas tax, the political will for a major tax increase on motorists is nowhere in sight. We've passed the quarter-century mark since the last increase, which occurred during the first year of Bill Clinton's first term in the presidency, and another big boost seems about as likely as a nonconsecutive third term for President Clinton.

Moreover, the concern over climate change, whatever one may think of the science and politics involved, makes continued dependence on a motor fuel tax less lucrative in an age in which gasoline consumption is likely to be increasingly discouraged. Even the AAA has endorsed certain tolling principles as well as a move from per-gallon gas taxes to per-mile levies. As Robert Poole writes, "The truckers aren't there yet, but they have to come up with a feasible way to pay for the $1 trillion Interstate replacement need that faces us today." He concludes, optimistically, "In the face of a major need, eventually 'something' beats 'nothing.'"[180]

PPPs: Private Advance or Public Subsidy?

Since the 1970s, Robert Poole has been a central figure, a policy guru, in the privatization movement, which seeks to return various functions typically performed today by government, from mail delivery to the protection of natural resources, to the private sector. Poole has been indefatigable in pushing privatization, or at least the injection of market mechanisms into public works. As early as the 1970s and '80s he was evangelizing for tolls and congestion pricing so that those who use the roads are the ones who pay for them.[181] (For a wide-ranging and valuable survey of the prospects and issues involved in the private provision of roads, see the Independent Institute's anthology *Street Smart: Competition, Entrepreneurship, and the Future of Roads*.)

The prospect of a network of private roads latticing the North American continent is remote at present.[182] The transportation historian Bruce Seely points out that "virtually all" of the modern privatization projects receive government subsidy in some form or other, so that they may more properly be called "mixed enterprises."[183] (Internationally, airports lead the way in privatized transportation infrastructure; more than one hundred have been privatized since the late 1990s. The only commercial American airport in private hands is San Juan International in Puerto Rico.[184])

The mixed enterprise that has emerged as a significant alternative to the government highway is the private-public partnership, or PPP, which is "a catchall phrase for an array of contractual relationships between one or more private parties and a public-sector entity."[185] The acronym is new; the concept is not. Toll bridges and turnpikes, typically overseen by private interests working under a state charter and under state regulation, were early examples of this arrangement. The government sets the parameters of a new project and accepts bids from private parties, and the entity submitting the winning bid pays the substantial up-front costs, which it will, it believes, recoup through the imposition of tolls and user fees. As analyst R. Richard Geddes notes, a PPP "transfers to investors the risks that would otherwise be borne by taxpayers."[186]

The first American PPP, says Henry Petroski, was the bridge spanning the Charles River and connecting Boston with Charlestown. The Charles River Bridge Company, incorporated in Massachusetts, built the toll bridge, collected tolls for forty years, and then turned it over to the Commonwealth of Massachusetts.[187] PPPs are not privatization; the government remains the owner of the facility, and the private entity is a lessee or manager of a concession. It receives the right to collect tolls, fees, and the like for a predetermined time period, after which either the government takes control of the enterprise or the contract is extended or renegotiated. The responsibility of designing, running, and maintaining the project is largely on the private partner, which is also saddled with the risk should it invest in the road less traveled. (Which is fine for poets, but not PPPs.) Private entities, not taxpayers, bear the bulk of the risk, and of course reap the rewards, if any.

By linking construction to operation, PPPs provide "incentives to minimize life-cycle costs," as a Brookings Institution study explained.[188] Franchises, or concessions, are granted for periods as long as seventy years in some cases, and the projected toll revenue over these lengthy terms enables the private parties to attract the necessary financing.

PPPs are as public as they are private; in fact, one critic called them "the most corporate welfared-up industry that there is."[189] They sometimes take advantage of loans backed by the US Department of Transportation, which is to say the taxpayer, or receive tax-exempt financing. So, these are not balms to the free-market purist's soul.

Australia, Canada, and Great Britain have staked out a pioneer position on PPPs. One Australian study contrasting twenty-one public-private partnerships with thirty-three conventional infrastructure projects found that "PPPs demonstrate clearly superior cost efficiency over traditional procurement.... PPPs provide superior performance in both the cost and time dimensions, and ... the PPP advantage increases (in absolute terms) with the size and complexity of projects."[190]

A form of PPP came to the interstate highway system in 2005 when the Indiana Toll Road, a 156-mile piece of its interstate over which cars and trucks have been rumbling since 1956, was leased for seventy-five years to an international consortium, which paid $3.8 billion to the state, which in turn financed improvements to state highways. The Indiana Toll Road Concession Company, the new operators, modernized the toll plazas but also jacked up tolls (which hadn't been increased in twenty years), resulting in a serious decline in traffic, as erstwhile Indiana Toll Road sojourners opted for alternate routes. Before a decade was out, the operator had filed for bankruptcy, and the concession was awarded to an Australian concern, Industry Funds Management, for the remaining sixty-six years. These things happen—no investment is guaranteed a healthy return—and vehicles continue to travel the road, which is doing better under the new management.[191] (Worries about foreign PPPs are ill-founded, says R. Richard Geddes, because "transportation assets are by their nature sunk and cannot be physically expropriated by any investor, no matter where they are located."[192])

Ideological foes of anything smacking of privatization seized on the Indiana case as evidence that only under the soothing and paternal hand of government could toll roads thrive, but PPPs advance, no matter the caterwauling.[193] Other US PPPs include the widening of ten miles of I-70 in northeast Denver, a joint venture of the consortium Kiewit Meridiam Partners and the Colorado Department of Transportation. The former, the private partner, pledged $610 million in up-front costs, while the latter, the public partner, is on the hook for $687 million. The four-year project has a target finishing date of 2022; the Colorado Department of Transportation has agreed to pay its private partner for operation and maintenance of the I-70 expansion for a period of thirty years, as well as making annual payments to Kiewit Meridiam for its equity investment.

The South Norfolk Jordan Bridge in Virginia spans the Elizabeth River and connects the cities of Portsmouth and Chesapeake. Built for $142 million by Figg Bridge Developers, it opened in 2012, replacing a privately built bridge that had opened to traffic in 1928, been transferred to the ownership of the city of Chesapeake in 1977, and closed in 2008 for lack of public funding. It charges peak and off-peak prices, which vary by the vehicle's number of axles.[194] Toll revenues should enable the operators to repay investors.

And the LBJ Express, a 13.3-mile project in the Dallas area that offers toll-lane options on I-635 and I-35E, is one of the nation's largest PPPs, as befits size-conscious Texas.[195] Opened in 2015, the LBJ Express, whose lead builder was the Texas-based infrastructure company Cintra, was a means of relieving the congestion on the four-decade-old LBJ Expressway, among the most congested highways in America. While the highway remains "free," with all the user-tax qualifications appertaining thereto, the addition of optional toll lanes enables motorists to avoid the snarled traffic for which the Dallas metro area is famous. The early returns indicate that "congestion is down, speeds are up, and usage is higher" along its corridor.[196] Those early returns are indeed early; the term of concession is fifty-two years.[197] (Texas is a pioneer in this field. In 1994, four scholars from the Center for Transportation Research and the Center for Legal and Regulatory Studies at the University of Texas at Austin, in concert with the US and Texas departments of transportation, explored the potential for highway privatization in the Lone Star State. They concluded that the field was ripe with opportunity.[198])

Trump Time

The elite view of transportation policy and its necessary reformation was presented, in all its peremptory certitude, by the Council on Foreign Relations (CFR) in its January 2016 report *Road to Nowhere: Failing U.S. Transportation Infrastructure*, which was part of the CFR's Renewing America project. The council, historically averse to anything that smacks of nationalism or international competition, nonetheless asserted that the United States was "falling behind" European and other nations with respect to infrastructure quality.[199] Whereas in 2005 the United States ranked fifth in this somewhat ambiguous measure, a decade later it had dropped to sixteenth and been "lapped," to use the CFR's racetrack jargon, by the likes of the United Arab Emirates, Finland, the Netherlands, Austria, Iceland, Japan, France, Portugal, Spain, Luxembourg, and Denmark.[200] While conceding that the United States has the most "paved roads, rail tracks, and airports" in the world, the CFR authors noted darkly that among G7 nations, the United States is tops, quality-wise, only with its airports.[201]

The price of such mediocrity in facilitating mobility can be reckoned in lost hours of productivity. In a fitting example, given its proximity-to-power milieu and cast of mind, the CFR noted that in our nation's capital, "each driver loses eighty-two hours a year in traffic"[202]—hours, we may be sure, that would otherwise have been spent lobbying for more federal funding or in some way aggrandizing power in the center as against the provinces and outlands.

The CFR report accepted PPPs as an arrangement of limited usefulness but reminded readers that "ultimately, the American people will have to pay more for their infrastructure."[203] Yet as Chris Edwards of the Cato Institute reminded Congress in 2014, the private sector shoulders most of the infrastructure-spending burden. Private expenditures on factories, pipelines, cell towers, refineries, and the like are more than four times greater than the total infrastructure spending by federal, state, and local governments combined.[204]

The Business Roundtable, an elite group consisting of no Arthurian knights but just CEOs of the largest US-based companies, also made a great deal of the United States ranking sixteenth in the "quality of overall infrastructure" category in the World Economic Forum's Global Competitiveness Index. This was well below Germany, France, and Japan and, so the alarums suggest, approaches Chad-Paraguay territory.[205] The Roundtable called for "strong leadership—particularly by the federal government" in its 2015 report *Road to Growth: The Case for Investing in America's Transportation Infrastructure.*[206] This demand for the centralization of decision making was decidedly passé: federal spending as a percentage of total public spending on infrastructure had peaked at 38 percent in 1977.[207] Most infrastructure spending today—62 percent of capital expenditures and 88 percent of operations and maintenance of transportation and water projects—is done by state and local governments, as the Founders had intended, post roads clause notwithstanding.[208]

Two centuries after Henry Clay outlined his American System, internal improvements keep their hold on the politically ambitious, particularly labor-connected Democrats and industrial-state Republicans. Vice President Joe Biden, eyeing a 2016 race for the Democratic nomination that he never made (though he made up for it in 2020), lectured a *Washington Post*–sponsored 2014 conference that "it is just *not acceptable* that the greatest nation in the world does not have—across the board—the single most sophisticated infrastructure in the entire world." He paused for a breath, and then repeated, "It is *not acceptable*."[209] There is something amiss when a man who has been in elected federal office since he turned thirty years of age, or for more than four decades, chastises listeners who do not hold federal office for their dereliction of duty with regard to public works. Isn't that *his* job? And lest he play the partisan card, Biden's party has controlled one or both houses of Congress for a longer period of time since 1970 than has the other major party.

Party differences blur, however, when the subject is infrastructure spending. In the early nineteenth century, the distinctions between Federalists and Republicans, or Whigs and Democrats, were clear if not always stark, but even as Democrats and Republicans of the early twenty-first century have become polarized to a greater extent than ever before, when spending for roads and bridges is on the table distinctions tend to melt.

The wild card—or joker, or ace, depending on one's perspective—in this deck was Donald Trump. While the most heavily publicized planks in his 2016 platform had to do with trade and immigration, Trump also emphasized infrastructure spending, which had been a central theme of his sporadic political pronouncements since he first expressed an interest in running for president of the United States in 1987. Canny special interests, noticing Trump's appeal, made their play for public works dollars. Consider the National Association of Manufacturers (NAM), the venerable organization of small and medium-sized US manufacturing firms. Founded in 1895, NAM is regarded in general as an influential lobby on behalf of pro–Main Street business legislation. Though nonpartisan, it has tended to a Republican coloration; whereas the US Chamber of Commerce, which NAM helped to beget in 1912, has an establishment, corporate Republican reputation, NAM cuts a more grassroots conservative profile. It harbors a greater belief in the power of free enterprise than corporate welfare, though it is not, shall we say, dogmatic on the question.

For when the subject is infrastructure, free-market ideals fly out the window. During the 2016 campaign, NAM published *Building to Win*, a Trump-titled call to action. A "substantial investment in modernizing our nation's infrastructure," declared NAM, "would create jobs, boost economic growth, save lives and help secure America's mantle of economic leadership in the world."[210] The moment was there for the seizing, and no boilerplate was left undeployed. Roads, bridges, ports, and such were, NAM said, outdated, congested, unsound, and of course *crumbling*. The implication was that bridges were collapsing, plunging helpless motorists into the icy depths of America's rivers. A demand was made for boldness; so was a renewal of confidence, a restoration of faith in the power of free enterprise ... properly directed free enterprise, of course.

Terms, left undefined, confuse. NAM's references to free enterprise sat uneasily next to calls for huge hikes in government spending. So did paeans to the IHS, forever to be known, apparently, as the greatest public works project in the history of the country, and yet we are informed by NAM that the interstate served as "the arteries of a free market system."[211] Now, the interstate may be salubrious, revolutionary, a boon or a curse or both, but a free-market artery it is not.

NAM's rhetoric could be confused with that of ASCE. References to "an alarming state of disrepair" prefaced statistics on job loss (2.5 million by 2025), the gap between infrastructure needs and current spending, and the cost to families ($3,400 per year), which were identical to those in ASCE publications.[214] In this church, everyone sings from the same hymnbook. NAM even copied a page from Joe Biden's book in calling the condition of America's roads and bridges "completely unacceptable."[213] (In earlier years, the phrase would have been "Third World," but that has since passed into un-PC unacceptability.) This was not, NAM strove to make clear, an argument made from self-interest, or an assertion of debatable points. The time for debate, discussion, disagreement, was past. "Some critics wrongfully contend that such numbers are exaggerated," announced NAM with what one imagines was a weary rolling of the institutional eyes, but these critics were safely ignored. "Rather than debating the scope of the problem, it is time to come together under a 'Building to Win' strategy."[214] So let's stop all the palavering and get down to some serious appropriating!

Whence shall come the funds needed to fund fully highway and bridge work? Historically, NAM members have looked askance at tax increases, and NAM is usually responsive enough to its constituency that it will not come right out and demand a heavier tax burden. So it called for "a reliable, user-based, long-term funding stream so that families, drivers and manufacturers can have the safe, efficient highways they need."[215] This was vague enough to provide plausible deniability should members complain that NAM had been infected with Beltway tax enthusiasm. When it did get around to offering funding options, NAM was careful to state that these were not prescriptions but just possibilities to spark conversation, and that in fact "the best options may not have yet been identified."[216] In other words, we're not taking sides!

The options so cautiously advanced included a one-time gas tax bump of 15 cents per gallon, which would raise an estimated $41.8 billion over five years; indexing the gas tax to inflation, which could raise $16 billion over five years; shifting to a VMT fee, which could bring in $176.5 billion from cars and $70.7 billion from trucks over five years; and imposing a federal vehicle registration fee that is in addition to state registration fees. This last-named could either be in the form of a $100 registration fee on electric vehicles and a $50 fee on hybrids (which would capture revenue foregone by the gasoline tax) or a $20 fee on all vehicles, whether gasoline or electric powered.[217] A federal registration fee would be dead on arrival, politically speaking, though the infrastructure lobby surely would embrace such a proposal were it to develop anything like political legs.

NAM, no doubt conscious of its members' historic aversion to tax increases, may have tiptoed cautiously around the subject, but the US Chamber of Commerce shows no such timidity. Hiking the gas tax, declares the chamber, would be "the simplest, most straight-forward, and most effective way to generate enough revenue."[218] So ardent has its support been that Rep. John Mica, then chairman of the House Transportation and Infrastructure Committee, reproached the chamber in a 2011 letter to its president and CEO, Thomas J. Donohue: "During my years of service on the Transportation and Infrastructure Committee I have seen the National Chamber of Commerce evolve from an Association that would advocate strong infrastructure and responsible fiscal policy on behalf of its members to an organization whose primary purpose in the national infrastructure arena appears to be to lead the lobby for tax increases."[219]

The chamber did fall shy of endorsing a taxpayer-funded National Infrastructure Bank, an idea that enjoyed a brief vogue in the Obama years. Such a bank would finance internal improvements under the aegis of the federal government or a public-private setup. The bank, capitalized by the federal government, would lend money to municipal and private actors for infrastructure projects. (Under President Obama's proposal, the bank would have financed up to half the cost.) Defenders claim that this bank would remove politics from infrastructure spending—a claim so risible that only the most callow op-ed columnist could possibly regurgitate it—and that, more plausibly, it would create a more certain source of long-term funding for large-scale projects. Yet it would also "further centralize transportation decision making in Washington," says Robert Krol, and encourage funding of projects that could not pass muster with private lenders or local governments.[220] Attorney Adam J. White, evaluating the Obama administration's proposal for a National Infrastructure Bank for the *New Atlantis*, wrote that it "would only exacerbate the public's traditional suspicion that government-supported infrastructure is just pork barrel, intended more to benefit the well-connected than the national interest." The bank's directors would be human, not robotic, and well entrenched in the power structure; the idea that they would or could be immune to outside influences is absurd. In addition, it "would do nothing to transform today's regulatory landscape, which offers too many opportunities for environmental activists and others to tie up even environmentally sound projects in interminable litigation."[221]

This last concern is no right-wing fantasy. The National Environmental Policy Act of 1969 required that government give "proper consideration" to the environmental impact of any federal action when the potential of such impact is significant.[222] This act, usually known by its acronym NEPA, has been a useful tool in stalling or defeating large federal expenditures on various infrastructural projects, but it has also boosted the costs of those that leap the NEPA hurdle. With every passing decade, it seems, surmounting the hurdle becomes that much more difficult. In the 1970s, it took an average of 2.2 years to successfully complete a NEPA study; the corresponding figure for subsequent decades has been 4.4 years in the 1980s, 5.1 years in the 1990s, and 6.6 years in the 2000s.[223] The Obama administration, recognizing the dilatory effect of these regulations, exempted close to 200,000 stimulus projects from their strictures, though this does point to a paradox: this law, so often reviled by conservatives and free-marketeers, serves to delay, or even effectively cancel, *government* projects—thus it may actually redound to the benefit of fiscal conservatives.

* * *

In his Election Night victory speech to supporters, Donald Trump promised, "We are going to fix our inner cities and rebuild our highways, bridges, tunnels, airports, schools, hospitals. We're going to rebuild our infrastructure, which will become, by the way, second to none. And we will put millions of people to work as we rebuild it."[224] Trump was not shy—but then when has he ever been shy?—in speeches about comparing his infrastructure proposal to Ike's interstate system. Hillary Clinton, his general election opponent, had called for "the biggest infrastructure investment since Dwight Eisenhower built the interstate highway system," but she mentioned it almost in passing, for the traditional supporters of such spending—males in blue-collar occupations—were not, to put it mildly, a core constituency of hers.[225] Secretary Clinton's five-year plan (a phrase that one would think perished with the Soviet Union; four- or six-year plans, while their numbers lack roundedness, at least sound less Stalinist) envisioned $275 billion in spending, of which $250 billion would be in the form of direct federal investment and the remainder would be put toward the progressive chestnut of a national infrastructure bank.[226] The Trump team tagged the Clinton plan as "Tax America First."[227]

Trump advisers Wilbur Ross, a banker who would later serve as his secretary of commerce, and University of California, Irvine, business professor Peter Navarro delineated the Trump plan in the closing stages of the campaign. It relied heavily on private-sector investment and was, they claimed, revenue neutral, offering instead of large infusions of taxpayer monies a tax credit equaling 82 percent of equity. Private investors would package their own up-front contribution with borrowings in the private bond market; their return would come in the form of user fees.[228] Navarro and Ross anticipated a total private-sector investment of approximately $167 billion. They called it a "bold, visionary plan … in the proud tradition of President Dwight D. Eisenhower," though Ike had raised most of the money for his boldest (and most expensive) domestic initiative through user taxes, with nary a tax credit in sight.[229]

Writing in the *Wall Street Journal*, Princeton University economists Alan S. Blinder and Alan B. Krueger charged that the Ross-Navarro-Trump plan would enable a $3 billion infrastructure deal to be financed with $2.5 billion in municipal bonds, $410 million in federal tax credits, and $90 million in private equity. "This means $90 million in private money winds up controlling a $3 billion asset," they noted. "Mr. Trump likes leverage, but isn't 33–1 a little ridiculous?"[230] Republicans in states with less-than-jampacked highways were skeptical of the broader Trump plan, which implied tolls in order to raise the necessary financing. Charles Bisby, chairman of the transportation committee in the Mississippi House of Representatives, said of the scheme, "I struggle to see how that would fit in a rural state such as Mississippi."[231]

The devil resided, as he always does, in the details. Senate Democrats were quick out of the gate with their own plan to spend a nice round trillion dollars over ten years to fix America's perpetually crumbling infrastructure. They declined to say just where the money would come from; that minor detail could wait for later. But it would be direct federal spending, none of this tax credit legerdemain. The administration did not take the bait. Transportation Secretary Elaine Chao confirmed to a Senate committee that federal tax credits would be an element of any Trump infrastructure plan, though she was careful to say that general revenues would also be a source.[232] Infrastructure adviser Norman Anderson pledged that Trump would reduce the bureaucratic hurdles to government-financed projects so that the average time of approval would be shortened from what he claimed was an average of nine and a half years to just a year and a half.[233] Trump himself pledged to overhaul "the painfully slow, costly, and time-consuming process of getting permits and approvals to build," though his suggested reform—creating a "new council to help project managers navigate the bureaucratic maze"—seemed a hair-of-the-dog cure: birth a new bureaucracy to fight an old bureaucracy.[234]

Through an Executive Order issued in August, 2017, President Trump required that federal agencies coordinate to review projects simultaneously, rather than consecutively, with a joint schedule.[235] The order, known as One Federal Decision, could potentially cut approval time from 10 years to 2 years, according to D.J. Gribbin, and was later incorporated as statute in the 2021 Infrastructure Bill.[236]

About a year into the Trump presidency, the White House released its "Legislative Outline for Rebuilding Infrastructure in America," which provided a jot-and-tittle rendering of a plan it promised would stimulate at least $1.5 trillion in "new investment" over the next decade, and truncate the approval process for federally sponsored projects.[237] This issue, which if not exactly central to Trump's 2016 campaign was certainly not peripheral, never quite achieved liftoff, as the administration was soon embattled and fighting along various other fronts. The bipartisan public works coalition hinted at by some labor-backed Democrats and Trump Republicans did not coalesce early in Trump's term, when such a coalition seemed possible, and by 2020 such an alliance was hopeless.

The Trump team talked the infrastructure talk: White House Press Secretary Sean Spicer used the *C*-word—crumbling—to describe the nation's bridges and roads and ports, and he gravely warned of coming disasters lest Steps Be Taken.[238] The president, during his campaign, had also trafficked in the language of the Crumble, saying with a generous dollop of hyperbole that "we have bridges that are falling down. I don't know if you've seen the warning charts [prepared, no doubt, by ASCE!], but we have many, many bridges that are in danger of falling."[239]

Critics carped that the envisioned federal commitment of $200 billion over ten years was to be raised not by increasing taxes but by snuffing obsolete or ineffective federal programs.[240] This hoary chestnut seems to drop from the trees every election time, though the precise identity of the programs to be abolished is never specified, and in fact said programs endure. Moreover, as the Cato Institute's Randal O'Toole pointed out, tax credits enable private contractors, and not the local or state government, to borrow the money to undertake the projects, yet those governments (read: taxpayers) are obligated to repay the debt, even though the taxpayers never authorized the assumption of that debt via the usual semidemocratic means of approving bonds, whether via referendum or through their elected representatives.[241]

Many Beltway conservatives were uncomfortable with Trump's themes. "Conservatives do not view infrastructure spending as an economic stimulus,"[242] said the Heritage Foundation's Dan Holler, who was echoed by Marc Scribner of the free-market Competitive Enterprise Institute, who denied that "public works projects promote long-term economic growth."[243] Yet the Trump plan was not the same old same old. Privatization guru Robert Poole of the Reason Foundation worked with D. J. Gribbin, the so-called infrastructure czar of the incoming administration, and it showed, at least in the margins of the Trump agenda. For instance, two of Poole's ideas, the repeal of the ban on interstate tolls and the repeal of the ban on commercial service plazas along interstate routes, were included, as were various Poole-generated ideas relating to the privatization of airports.[244] Modification of the ban on interstate tolls has proceeded at a snail's, or perhaps an LA freeway at rush hour, pace. A federal pilot program enacted in 1998 allowed three states to experiment with interstate tolls; Missouri, North Carolina, and Virginia snagged those three berths and over the course of two decades levied nary a toll. As this book went to press, the FHWA was asking for applicants to refill

those three slots, but applicants, perhaps wary of the perceived public sentiment against tolls, were keeping well hidden.[245]

The ban on commercial service plazas on nontolled interstates has endured
due to the vigorous lobbying of the truck stop lobby. (When even truck stops
have a mighty lobby, you know that the scramble for governmental favors
has gotten out of hand.) For the hungry interstate traveler who doesn't want
to leave the road it's vending machines only, unless you're on the New York
State Thruway or another tolled road.

The Next Road?

There is no Albert Gallatin or Henry Clay—compelling and sympathetic
tribunes of an activist internal improvements federal policy—in today's political world. Nor are there visionary Erie Canals or Interstate Highway Systems—paradigm-setting projects to advance commerce and travel by water
or road—on the drawing board. Oh, there are noisy constituencies for greater
and greater spending on infrastructure, most noisily ASCE and the construction trade unions. A president of ASCE, David Mongan, lamented that "we
seem to have lost the vision that existed in the fifties, when Eisenhower signed
the interstate highway bill, where we looked down the road ... to a dream of
having this forty- to fifty-thousand miles system of highways interconnect-
ing all of the states in major urban areas in this country."[246] Americans woke
up from that dream early, to the sound of bulldozers and trucks laden with
asphalt, all paid for by the motorist who might never even use an interstate.
It was a magnificent engineering achievement, but it came with costs, some
bearable, some not so bearable, and ASCE's Mongan is correct in saying that
few outside those industries directly benefiting from massive infrastructure
expenditures desire a reprise. Still, change is inevitable, though its wheels
grind slowly. Governments at the federal, state, and local levels are not about
to allow their roads and bridges to deteriorate sharply, let alone collapse. They
can sell such expenditures to the public, which may grumble but sees such
programs as worthy of public support.

The Highway Trust Fund, born after a false start or two and central to
Dwight D. Eisenhower's great public works accomplishment, the National

System of Interstate and Defense Highways, has easily survived the handful of challenges it has faced during its six and a half decades, from Senator Harry Byrd's objections to President Gerald Ford's failed attempt to divert a substantial portion of its revenue to the general fund, not to mention the eloquent but politically impotent protests of libertarians and poets, nature-lovers and New Urbanists, against what they have seen as its profligacy, its utilitarian unimaginativeness, its wanton destruction of old buildings and settled neighborhoods and organic patterns of life. These latest challenges—cars that do not run on gasoline, toll roads that pay for themselves rather than depending on tax revenue—look to be more formidable than those earlier ones. But those who profit from government-sponsored infrastructure have the means and the motive—in spades—to defend one of their most reliable revenue pools.

Change is inevitable; but those interests will not surrender to radical reforms, whether widespread tolling or privatization, without an epic fight.

Conclusion

THE POET T.S. ELIOT may have been no fan of internal improvements ("And the wind shall say: 'Here were decent godless people: / Their only monument the asphalt road / And a thousand lost golf balls'"),[1] but one of his most famous works ("Little Gidding") supplies a fitting epigraph for our conclusion:

> And the end of all our exploring
> Will be to arrive where we started
> And know the place for the first time.

Two centuries after the foundational debates over the proper method of designating, financing, and administering the construction of (or refusal to construct) roads, bridges, and canals, certain of those earliest questions and themes are being heard once more. No, the matter of the constitutionality of the federal authorization and funding of roads, so contentious in the age of Andrew Jackson, has not been revisited, not even in the age of Donald Trump—and certainly not in the inner councils presided over by Joe Biden and Kamala Harris. We may be the poorer for it, but no one wrangles over the meaning of "post roads" anymore.

Yet the days in which the big and the expensive and the national seemed invariably to hold the upper hand are waning. For one thing, a rejuvenated federalist tendency in American politics, a reaction against overweening and centralizing government, has put on the table the possibility of transferring to the states responsibility for the maintenance and reconstruction of the IHS. The completion of the IHS has diminished its political attractiveness at the federal level; members of Congress are less lionized than they used to be for obtaining lucrative funding for shining new stretches of road. The less political appeal an infrastructure project has, the greater the likelihood that responsibility for it will be devolved to lower, more local levels of government.

Senator Mike Lee's aforementioned Transportation Empowerment Act never really shifted past neutral, let alone into overdrive, but it picked up two cosponsors (Republicans Marco Rubio of Florida and Ted Cruz of Texas) with their eyes on the White House. So the Utah senator's proposal to reduce the federal gas tax, in phases, to 3.7 cents per gallon and turn over responsibility for the nation's highways from the federal government to the states and localities is still roadworthy, awaiting only the turning of a key—or the election of a sympathetic president.

The Highway Trust Fund keeps on truckin', but it is no longer the unstoppable perpetual motion machine of the past. Its aura of invincibility has faded, at least to an extent. On both the populist right and the moderate left, abolition of the fund has been bruited about, though Reason's Robert Poole warns that in the current climate the vanishing of the Highway Trust Fund would not necessarily mean the surcease of federal subsidies for road construction and maintenance. Rather, predicts Poole, federal fuel taxes would "likely be renamed greenhouse gas taxes and the proceeds put into the general fund."[2]

Having scrapped the user-pays principle, the party in power would then direct federal transportation funding to the flavor of the day (or whichever special interests happened to hold sway): high-speed rail, streetcars, subways, Jeff Bezos rocket ships, whatever. Yet in the hope-springs-eternal version of Highway Trust Fund termination, the raising of highway construction and maintenance monies through gasoline taxes would be handed back to the states—or perhaps responsibility for the roads would even be turned over to the private sector. A state function that was arrogated unto itself by the federal government two-thirds of a century ago would be returned where it belongs, constitutionally.

Meanwhile, the wailing and gnashing of teeth by representatives of the government-infrastructure complex over the alleged loss of vision of the American people is likely to intensify. The crumbling infrastructure crowd agrees with Rahm Emanuel that one should never let a good crisis go to waste, but since their public-relations blitz of the early 1980s, they have been unable to generate even a modest level of concern, let alone full-blown hysteria, over any new crisis necessitating large expenditures of federal dollars on their pet programs.

The politicians who profit, or would like to profit, from the support of this infrastructure lobby will try, with predictable regularity, to come up with grand and majestic proposals for massive federal investment—you can be sure they'll use the word *investment*—in infrastructure, à la Eisenhower's IHS. But federal debt as far as the eye can see and a populace that seems less amenable to such projects will be formidable obstacles to overcome. A skepticism born of hard experience has crept into the public mind and generated opposition to the infrastructuralists' appeals; the clumsy and even ruinous excesses of previous generations of internal improvers have left a mark on the collective memory.

There is, of course, one recent and major exception to the long-term tarnishing of infrastructure's reputation, though this is likely to be an anomaly birthed by a confluence of political and economic factors. On August 10, 2021, the Senate approved, by a bipartisan vote of 69–30, the budget-busting $1.2 trillion Infrastructure Investment and Jobs Act, a keystone of President Biden's agenda. (Notice how the bill's title hit all the buzzwords: the only things missing were "national defense" and "children.")

The 2,700-page Infrastructure Investment and Jobs Act, which the Congressional Budget Office estimated would add more than $250 billion to the federal deficit over the next decade, included $550 billion in new spending. (The remainder of the cool trillion-plus had already been authorized.) As has been the fashion in recent years, infrastructure was defined elastically. The bill directed $110 billion toward roads and bridges—which were, of course, described as crumbling, decrepit, and dangerous.

But the bulk of the new spending went to other areas: $66 billion for passenger and freight rail (notably Amtrak's Acela corridor connecting New York City and Boston with Washington, DC, and serving an affluent and power-wielding constituency); $39 billion for public transit (low-emission bus manufacturers hit the jackpot); and $65 billion for broadband access (to buy the votes of legislators representing rural states and districts). Another $65 billion was dedicated to modernizing the electric grid (the rolling blackouts in California did their job); $55 billion went to upgrading water and wastewater facilities; $25 billion was allocated to airports; $17 billion went to port infrastructure; $21 billion went to the cleanup of Superfund and other contaminated sites; and a few billion here and there were marked for whatever other pet projects legislators were able to fund. The Biden plan also included $12.5 billion to promote and facilitate the use of electric cars—a regressive expenditure rivaling NPR funding.[3]

The last-named expenditure was not made any less regressive by the Biden administration's insistence that construction of a network of 500,000 electric vehicle chargers would focus on "rural and disadvantaged communities"—for you can't charge what you don't own.[4]

Among the bill's provisions that were remote from even the slackest definition of infrastructure were an "an unproven new drunk-driving-prevention technology on cars, a vaping ban on Amtrak, and new reporting requirements for cyptocurrency."[5]

President Biden compared the scope of this gargantuan creature to—you guessed it—the Interstate Highway System. In Senate debate, members of the self-proclaimed world's greatest deliberative body waxed mawkish and magniloquent, gushing and goofy. No one quite reached the heights of John C. Calhoun, who had famously pledged to "conquer space," but Virginia Democrat Mark Warner cooed that the bill was "a little balm to the psychic soul of the country."[6]

House debate did not reach the rhetorical heights of the Senate, as progressives had put a damper on infrastructure triumphalism by dismissing the bill as mingy and meager compared to a parallel $3.5 trillion package containing bountiful funding for such "human infrastructure" programs as universal preschool, Medicaid, federally subsidized childcare, climate-change eradication, and other initiatives.

Rep. Peter DeFazio (D-OR), chairman of the House Committee on Transportation and Infrastructure, opened and later closed debate with a hackneyed "crumbling infrastructure" catalogue of "potholes damaging ... cars, failing bridges, decrepit transit, trains that derail, water mains that explode, [and] sewer systems that back up into their basements and that pollute our rivers."[7] It all seemed curiously cursory.

The measure had the flavor of not so much a portent as a swansong, or at least a one-off. About half of the new funding came from federal dollars redirected from COVID-19 relief, making it equivalent to "found money" in the eyes of most politicians. Roads, highways, and bridges—once the mainstay of the infrastructure complex—accounted for barely 20 percent of the funds newly authorized. And the timing, coming shortly after the defeat of Donald Trump and in the waning days of the media honeymoon with Joe Biden, was propitious.

One positive development of the tumult of the previous year was a wider recognition of the damage done to poor and minority communities by previous generations of highway builders. The destruction and depredations of the likes of Robert Moses and the highwaymen seem, thankfully, grim artifacts of the past. They are relics of those years when Americans, conditioned by the stated exigencies of hot wars and a Cold War, were willing to cede extraordinary powers to governmental authorities and were reluctant to challenge them even when they ran riot over the most basic private property rights.

The reckoning of the toll taken by highway construction extends leftward and rightward. In recent years, informed by fresh memories of the damage done by urban renewal and highway construction—and enraged by the US Supreme Court's protection of a particularly outrageous act of property grabbing by government in *Kelo v. City of New London* (2005)—constitutional and private property rights activists have succeeded in launching a determined counterattack against eminent domain. States are erecting barriers against such wanton theft. The crimes of a new Robert Moses against the homeowners and businesspeople of an American community would be far more unthinkable today.

* * *

Just as was the case in the canal-digging era of antebellum America, different forms of public-private partnerships are being explored in this first quarter of the twenty-first century. These may turn out to be special-interest subsidies under more palatable names—corporate welfare dressed up as innovation—or they may be examples, even harbingers, of a shift toward the privatization of what have been, for many decades, governmental functions.

It is with respect to toll roads that things are truly coming full circle, or that we are at least beginning to return to the beginning. Nineteenth-century turnpikes were mostly private enterprises, although in some cases state governments purchased up to 50 percent of the shares issued by those enterprises. After the turnpike boom went to bust, the very concept of tolls, or requiring payment for passage along roads, fell into a general disfavor from which it was rescued, and only partially, by the post–World War II toll road boomlet of which the New York State Thruway was the acknowledged leader. But it is only in the last several years that the eventual widespread tolling of selected roads has come to take on a certain inevitability. The old antitolling arguments, based on ideas of equity and fairness, have lost much of their force. Instead, Adam Smith's contention that "it seems scarce possible to invent a more equitable way of maintaining" highways and bridges than to require users to "pay for the maintenance of those public works exactly in proportion to the wear and tear which they occasion of them" is seen as cogent and just.[8]

In addition, market-sensitive adjustments such as congestion pricing are regarded now as environmentally superior policies. In this area and others, the prospect of a sustained and powerful alliance of fiscal conservatives, libertarians, and ecologically concerned greens is possible.

The work of Gabriel Roth looms large here. A research fellow with the Independent Institute, Roth spent twenty years at the World Bank as a transportation economist and has written widely on the private provision of roads as well as market strategies to reduce congestion. Roth edited *Street Smart: Competition, Entrepreneurship, and the Future of Roads* (2006), a groundbreaking collection of articles laying out a vision of a transportation system that can "relieve congestion, operate roadways more efficiently, and improve the safety of our highways."[9]

"Most U.S. road systems," says Roth, "are like relics of the former Soviet Union: socialist enterprises run by well-intentioned planners with no regard to the pricing and investment criteria that allocate goods and services in free societies."[10] They belong on the ash-heap of history—not unlike the Soviet Union.

For all the technological advances in the mechanical conveyance of persons from one place to another, the limitations inherent to government ownership, operation, and maintenance of the roads have produced a distinctly suboptimal situation.

For instance, in 2021, 47 percent of urban interstates were congested during peak hours.[11] And it's not getting better: American highways have become more congested almost every year since the Texas A&M Transportation Institute began issuing its annual *Urban Mobility Report* in 1982. (The less-congested COVID-19 year of 2020 was a fluke not—we hope—to be repeated.)

Congestion worsened despite the late twentieth-century introduction of heralded HOV (high-occupancy vehicle) lanes in urban areas. Intended to encourage carpooling, HOV lanes were set-asides for vehicles carrying a specified number of passengers. Sometimes the threshold was as low as one driver and one passenger, people who would be traveling together regardless of lane set-asides, which is why these shallow carpools were mockingly referred to as "fam-pools." Or "date-pools." These didn't even rise to the level of mild palliatives for what ailed the road. As Robert W. Poole Jr. and C. Kenneth Orski noted, the growth of HOV lanes coincided with an actual *decline* in carpooling and an increase in single drivers.[12]

And despite improvements in safety designs, traffic fatalities in the United States have taken a sharp and somewhat perplexing upward turn. In 2020, despite a 13 percent decrease in miles driven by Americans, deaths on the highway totaled 38,680, a 7.2 percent increase from 2019. The rate of deaths per one hundred million miles driven rose to 1.37, its highest level since 2006.[13] Globally, more than 1.2 million people die in traffic accidents every year (an average of 3,242 per day), and somewhere between 20 and 50 million people are injured in such fashion annually. According to the World Health Organization, "road traffic crashes rank as the 11th leading cause of death and account for 2.1% of all deaths globally."[14]

There is, to put it mildly, room for reform.

In the matter of highway safety, which is tangential to the scope of this book, John Semmens, a longtime senior planner in the Arizona Department of Transportation, has advocated the privatization of vehicle and driver testing as a means of removing incompetent drivers and unsafe vehicles from the roads.[15] Such a step awaits what surely would be a knock-down, drag-out fight between two of the least-loved institutions in American life: state departments of motor vehicles and insurance companies.

We venture no guesses as to the outcome of such a fight, but the cure, or at least the alleviating solution, for congestion and other road ills also involves a heavy dose of private-sector market discipline.

The possible, if partial, privatization of American highways will be facilitated by the growing ease and acceptance of electronic tolling. Just as is the case today, the private and semiprivate roads of nineteenth-century America depended upon tolls for revenue and sustenance. Their two requisites, which posed formidable challenges, also remain in effect today:

1. devising simple ways to pay for road use, preferably without vehicles having to stop; and
2. ensuring that payments for road use get to the road providers.[16]

Modern tolling methods have greatly advanced the ability of toll roads to meet these challenges. In fact, technology has obviated the main nonpolitical obstacle to tolling. The debate in coming years will focus on the extent to which private providers can or should build, maintain, and own these roads.

The now widespread use of electronic tolling has made the tollbooth an unloved and inefficient artifact of the past. The electronic toll collection market is forecast to jump from $3 billion in 2020 to $5 billion in 2026. The resulting smoother traffic flow, decline in fender-benders caused by tollbooth slowdowns, greater fuel efficiency, and reduction in wasted time combine to make this a growth industry. And it is becoming an integrated network: as of 2021, seventeen states were part of the E-ZPass system, which originated in the Northeast, and thirty-five million vehicles were equipped with E-ZPass devices.[17]

A huge stumbling block to what one analyst calls "de-socializing the roads" is the durable prejudice that "only the government can operate a dependable road network sensitive to the needs of travelers."[18] Overcoming that kind of public suspicion of private roads will take more than a savvy public relations campaign. Drivers are empiricists; they want hard data. As yet, private roads advocates are still amassing sufficient evidence.

The transfer of existing public highways to private owners is likely to bring objections that a public asset, paid for by taxpayers, is being gifted to well-connected private interests. Justified or not, it will be characterized as a rip-off, an act of corporate welfare. If a road becomes newly tolled, as is almost a certainty in the event of its transfer to a private owner (rather than a private contractor who is merely maintaining a government road), complaints will rain down about "double taxation," meaning the one-two punch to the purse of a gas tax and a toll.[19]

John Semmens has suggested that such objections can be countered by "an emphasis on the fact that privatized roadways would eliminate highway-user taxes," though this would apply only in the event that the entire federal highway system were privatized, an exceedingly unlikely prospect at present.[20]

More palatable to the public would be the construction of new highways that would be financed and owned by private firms. A standard objection to tolls—"drivers paid for the road with our taxes; why should we have to pay to drive on it?"—would dissolve. Only those driving on the new highway would be charged for its use. Those driving the existing untolled government roadways would be better off, as they would find them less congested. But as Semmens notes, the financial risk associated with such a large project makes it difficult to find underwriters: "New highways have no established base of traffic. Forecasts of projected toll-paying customers are subject to error. Financiers demand high rates of return in the face of these uncertainties."[21]

Certainly there can be no objections lodged to private roads on constitutional grounds. The post roads language in the US Constitution is, after all, in the nature of a permission; nowhere are such roads proscribed, and as the University of Minnesota's David Levinson has observed, the overshadowed but unrepealed Tenth Amendment, which reads, "The powers not delegated to the United States by the Constitution, nor prohibited by it to the states, are reserved to the states respectively, or to the people," can reasonably be read as barring federal sponsorship of highways.[22] (Of course, "post roads" offered the barest legal opening to federal involvement, but the Good Roads and Interstate Highway advocates barreled through.)

The early returns on the political acceptability of private highways are mixed. California, responding to the crawl-like pace on its freeways, has led the way. Of particular interest to advocates of private roads was the opening in 1995 of the State Route 91 Express Lanes.

SR 91 is an east-west highway in the greater Los Angeles area spanning the fifty-nine miles from Gardena to Riverside. It had been even more congested than most Southern California freeways: prior to the construction of the express lanes, delays in the most heavily traveled ten-mile segment (from Anaheim to the Riverside/Orange County line) typically exceeded half an hour. The state legislature, having exhausted other possibilities, turned to private capital, in the form of the California Private Transportation Company (CPTC), for a solution.

The CPTC designed, built, and operated four express lanes (two in each direction) in the median of SR 91 over that heavily traveled ten-mile stretch. These were high-occupancy toll (HOT) lanes: a driver entered at either terminus point and did not exit until the other one, as there were no intermediate places of ingress or egress. There were no tollbooths along the route; vehicles needed to be equipped with a transponder.

Express-lane tolls in the earliest years of the SR 91 project ranged from $1 to $4, depending upon the time of day. Vehicles with three or more occupants (HOV3+, as the shorthand goes) were and are untolled except at peak hours (now 4 to 6 p.m. eastbound), when they are charged a 50 percent toll. As this book went to press the express lanes had been extended to eighteen miles in length, and the maximum toll had risen to $20.85 at the time of peak demand.

The $134 million project was, writes Edward C. Sullivan, professor of civil and environmental engineering at the California Polytechnic State University in San Luis Obispo, "California's first modern example of private investment to create new urban highway capacity."[23]

The SR 91 Express Lanes can be credited a genuine success but also a partial failure.

Upon the opening of the tolled private lanes, delays in SR 91's free lanes were cut in half or more, from an average of thirty minutes to under ten minutes. Congestion "declined dramatically."[24] These gains were eventually lost due to increased traffic caused by regional economic and population growth. The express lanes, however, have remained free-flowing.

By mid-1998, not even three years in, the California Private Transportation Company was showing a profit, with revenues exceeding $20 million.[25] The path to private roads seemed to have cleared; a tolled future beckoned.

Ah, but the potholes of public opinion gave the CPTC a rude jolt. According to the initial agreement, the CPTC was to operate the express lanes under a franchise agreement for a period of thirty-five years, after which they would revert to the California Department of Transportation, or Caltrans. The agreement included a "noncompete" provision by which the state pledged not to improve competing public highways. This proved a public relations disaster. As Sullivan writes, "It was characterized as giving private companies power to prevent the State and other agencies from making any road improvements, even for safety reasons."[26]

The noncompete provision was a grave political miscalculation. It fed into a caricature of privatization as a cynical scam by heartless corporations in which the rich drive on gleaming superhighways while the proles and helots bump along on crowded, exhaust-reeking boulevards of death and destruction. Less than eight years into the experiment, the Orange County Transportation Authority purchased the SR 91 Express Lanes from the CPTC for $207.5 million.

Foremost among its innovations, SR 91 has from the start set tolls based on the principle of congestion pricing, which holds that "the motorist should pay for all the costs of his trip, including congestion costs." The toll rate is set in response to the volume of traffic, which in turn affects a driver's decision whether to enter the express lane or take the freeway. A motorist may choose not to avail herself of the HOT option, in which case she drives on the untolled SR 91 lanes, presumably at a lower rate of speed than had she entered the tolled lanes. The variability of congestion pricing, and the interplay of the differential toll rates and the choices made by drivers, result "in a more efficient distributing of trip time and places."[27]

A contemporaneous innovative Caltrans project in the Golden State, the I-15 HOT lanes north of San Diego, was positively avant-garde in its setting of toll rates if not in its conventionally public nature. When launched in 1996, these two HOT lanes, running along eight miles in the median of I-15, were open only during rush hour and in one direction at a time: southbound in the a.m., northbound in the p.m. Their great innovation was in the use of "dynamic pricing," under which the toll might change every six minutes in response to demand. As with the SR-91 project, congestion on the untolled portion of the freeway was initially reduced but later rebounded as the surrounding area continued to develop. Traffic still flowed freely in the HOT lanes, however, which have since been lengthened to twenty miles and now operate twenty-four hours a day. Tolls currently range from 50 cents to $8 per trip.[28]

Whatever their hiccups and growing pains, both California projects demonstrated that "commuters will voluntarily pay tolls to enjoy the benefits of reduced travel time, improved driving comfort, and the perception of improved safety"[29]—whether the road is owned, maintained, or leased to private or public interests.

HOT lanes remain a promising strategy for applying market incentives to highways. Though sometimes derided as "Lexus Lanes," with the inference of elitism, they are in fact a user-pays alternative to gas taxes, which grow more regressive by the day, as upper-income drivers increasingly opt for electric cars and lower-income drivers chug away in gas-guzzlers.

The road to reform is long and arduous, but 95 percent of personal trips are taken via road, and despite the dreams of light-rail (or outer space) enthusiasts, this is unlikely to change anytime soon.[30] Efficient electronic tolling has set the stage for a new era of private roads, although given the capital requirements this is likely to begin à la California's SR 91, as private HOT lanes are fitted in the median of existing state or federal highways.

As always, the wisdom of the late Senator Russell Long (D-LA) is relevant: "Don't tax you / Don't tax me / Tax that fellow behind the tree." The regressive nature of the gasoline tax in this age of hybrid cars, and the fact that an increasing portion of the revenue is directed to nonhighway recipients—upward of one-third of road-user revenues are spent on "non-road projects"[31]— ought to fertilize the ground for serious reform, if not outright abolition. The user-pays concept has degenerated into a "you, sir, pays" scheme whereby working-class drivers are taxed to subsidize Prius drivers and mass-transit–riding stockbrokers. Any populist who can't make hay out of this arrangement isn't worthy of the name.

The old strategy of the internal improvements crowd—identifying opposition to their demands as somehow old-fashioned, out of date, and the position of reactionary cranks—has itself become a ridiculous anachronism. The critics of large-scale government infrastructure projects are the forward-thinkers of our day; the ideas, the fresh proposals, and the momentum belong to them.

The infrastructure lobby is no paper tiger. Its battery of trade associations, political action committees, and corporate and union allies are formidable.

If it is no longer cutting edge, or poised on the frontiers of progressivism, as were the leaders of the Good Roads movement, it is entrenched. It is dug in and capable of spending lavishly to defend and extend its privileges. Certainly the Biden administration's Infrastructure Investment and Jobs Act showed that the *I*-word retains a cachet in politics. One underestimates it at one's peril—and at a cost that can be measured in the trillions of dollars.

But perhaps the coming years will find Americans and their political leaders once more debating the wisdom of government sponsorship and direction of large-scale infrastructure projects—and maybe, just maybe, private alternatives thereto will finally reassert their rightful place in the discussion.

It's about time.

Notes

Introduction

1. Frédéric Bastiat, "That Which Is Seen, and That Which Is Not Seen," Mises Institute, December 18, 2019, https://mises.org/library/which-seen-and-which-not-seen.

2. John Moteff, Claudia Copeland, and John Fischer, "Critical Infrastructure: What Makes Infrastructure Critical?", Congressional Research Service, updated January 29, 2003, 14, https://fas.org/irp/crs/RL31556.pdf.

Chapter 1: Internal—or Infernal?—Improvements: A New Nation Confronts Infrastructure

1. Moreover, federal politicians are increasingly regulating state and local governments. See James T. Bennett, *Mandate Madness: How Congress Forces States and Localities to Do Its Bidding and Pay for the Privilege* (Piscataway, NJ: Transaction Publishers, 2014).

2. James Madison, *Notes of Debates in the Federal Convention of 1787 Reported by James Madison*, with an introduction by Adrienne Koch (Athens: Ohio University Press, 1966/1840), 470.

3. Madison, *Notes*, 638.

4. Madison, 638.

5. Madison, 638.

6. Madison, 638.

7. Wayne Wheeler, "History of the Administration of the Lighthouses in America," United States Lighthouse Society, accessed July 30, 2018, https://uslhs.org/history-administration-lighthouses-america.

8. See US Senate Historical Office, "The Lighthouses Act of 1789," US Senate, 1991.

9. R. H. Coase, "The Lighthouse in Economics," *Journal of Law and Economy* 17, no. 2 (October 1974): 357–76.

10. For a counter to Coase, see David E. van Zandt, "The Lessons of the Lighthouse: 'Government' or 'Private' Provision of Goods," *Journal of Legal Studies* 22, no. 1 (January 1993): 47–72. Van Zandt argues that while lighthouses were owned and run by private individuals, there were no instances of "pristine" private ownership unassisted by governmental regulation up to and including the guarantee of monopoly status.

11. Joseph H. Harrison Jr., "'*Sic et Non*': Thomas Jefferson and Internal Improvement," *Journal of the Early Republic* 7, no. 4 (Winter 1987): 339.

12. Harrison, "'*Sic et Non*'," 339.

13. Alexander Hamilton, "Report on the Subject of Manufactures," National Archives Founders Online, accessed July 30, 2018, https://founders.archives.gov/documents/Hamilton /01-10-02-0001-0007.

14. Victor L. Albjerg, "Internal Improvements without a Policy (1789–1861)," *Indiana Magazine of History* 28, no. 3 (September 1932): 169; "Ebenezer Zane," *Ohio History Central*, accessed August 5, 2018, http://www.ohiohistorycentral.org/index.php?title=Ebenezer _Zane&rec=427.

15. US Department of Transportation Federal Highway Administration, *America's Highways, 1776–1976: A History of the Federal-Aid Program* (Washington, DC: US Government Printing Office, 1976), 16. This is an excellent historical survey of US roadbuilding.

16. US Department of Transportation, *America's Highways*, 3.

17. George Rogers Taylor, *The Transportation Revolution, 1815–1860* (New York: Holt, Rinehart, and Winston, 1951), 15.

18. Rensselaer Polytechnic Institute, "Institute History," accessed August 1, 2018, http:// www.rpi.edu/about/history.html.

19. John Lauritz Larson, *Internal Improvement: National Public Works and the Promise of Popular Government in the Early United States* (Chapel Hill: University of North Carolina Press, 2001), 54.

20. Larson, *Internal Improvement*, 54.

21. Thomas Jefferson, "Sixth Annual Message to Congress," The Avalon Project at Yale Law School, accessed August 5, 2018, http://avalon.law.yale.edu/19th_century/jeffmes6.asp.

22. Thomas Jefferson, "Second Inaugural Address," *Inaugural Addresses of the Presidents of the United States from George Washington 1789 to John F. Kennedy 1961* (Washington, DC: US Government Printing Office, 1961), 18 (italics in the original).

23. Larson, *Internal Improvement*, 58.

24. Russell Kirk, *John Randolph of Roanoke: A Study in American Politics* (Indianapolis: Liberty Press, 1978/1951), 105 (emphasis added).

25. John Randolph, "Speech on Surveys for Roads and Canals, January 30, 1824," in Kirk, *John Randolph of Roanoke*, 426.

26. Philip D. Jordan, *The National Road* (Indianapolis: Bobbs-Merrill, 1948).

27. Larson, *Internal Improvement*, 56.

28. Jordan, *The National Road*, 75.

29. Richard F. Weingroff, "'Clearly Vicious as a Matter of Policy': The Fight against Federal-Aid," US Department of Transportation Federal Highway Administration, accessed July 24, 2018, https://www.fhwa.dot.gov/infrastructure/hwyhist01.cfm.

30. Albert Gallatin, *Report of the Secretary of the Treasury, on the Subject of Public Roads and Canals* (Washington, DC: R. C. Weightman, 1808), accessed August 5, 2018, http:// oll.libertyfund.org/titles/gallatin-report-of-the-secretary-of-the-treasury-on-the-subject-of -public-roads-and-canals.

31. Gallatin, *Report*.

32. Gallatin, *Report*.

33. Gallatin, *Report*.

34. Gallatin, *Report*.

35. Gallatin, *Report*.

36. Thomas Jefferson, "First Inaugural Address," The Avalon Project at Yale Law School, accessed August 7, 2018, http://avalon.law.yale.edu/19th_century/jefinau1.asp.

37. Gallatin, *Report*.

38. Gallatin, *Report*.

39. "Federal 1801 Spending by Function," US Government Spending, accessed December 5, 2018, https://www.usgovernmentspending.com/fed_spending_1801USmn.

40. Larson, *Internal Improvement*, 62.

41. Henry Adams, *The Life of Albert Gallatin* (Philadelphia: J. B. Lippincott, 1879), 399.

42. James Madison, "Seventh Annual Message," The American Presidency Project, accessed August 7, 2018, https://www.presidency.ucsb.edu/node/204622.

43. Merrill D. Peterson, *The Great Triumvirate: Webster, Clay, and Calhoun* (New York: Oxford University Press, 1987), 79.

44. Margaret L. Coit, *John C. Calhoun: American Portrait* (Boston: Houghton Mifflin, 1961/1950), 116.

45. Larson, *Internal Improvement*, 66.

46. *Annals of Congress*, 14th Cong., 2nd sess., 178.

47. Adam J. White, "Infrastructure Policy: Lessons from American History," *New Atlantis* 35 (Spring 2012): 17–18.

48. James Madison, "March 3, 1817: Veto Message on the Internal Improvements Bill," UVA Miller Center, accessed August 7, 2018, https://millercenter.org/the-presidency/presidential-speeches/march-3-1817-veto-message-internal-improvements-bill.

49. Norman K. Risjord, *The Old Republicans: Southern Conservatism in the Age of Jefferson* (New York: Columbia University Press, 1965), 173.

50. Larson, *Internal Improvement*, 25.

51. Larson, 28.

52. Jesse Hawley, "Introductory Essay," *Hawley's Essays*, accessed April 25, 2018, http://xroads.virginia.edu/~ma02/volpe/canal/hawley_intro.html.

53. Ronald E. Shaw, *Erie Water West: A History of the Erie Canal, 1792–1854* (Lexington: University of Kentucky Press, 1966), 29.

54. Jack Kelly, *Heaven's Ditch: God, Gold, and Murder on the Erie Canal* (New York: St. Martin's Press, 2016), 8.

55. Shaw, *Erie Water West*, 36.

56. Shaw, 22 (emphasis added).

57. Kelly, *Heaven's Ditch*, 19.

58. Kelly, 28.

59. Shaw, *Erie Water West*, 58.

60. Shaw, 55.

61. Shaw, *Erie Water West*, 73–75; Roger Evan Carp, "The Erie Canal and the Liberal Challenge to Classical Republicanism, 1785–1850" (PhD diss., University of North Carolina, 1986).

62. Shaw, *Erie Water West*, 74.

63. Kelly, *Heaven's Ditch*, 32.

64. Shaw, *Erie Water West*, 67.

65. Carol Sheriff, *The Artificial River: The Erie Canal and the Paradox of Progress, 1817–1862* (New York: Hill and Wang, 1996), 201.

66. Sheriff, *The Artificial River*, 201.

67. Sheriff, 201.

68. Daniel B. Klein and John Majewski, "Plank Road Fever in Antebellum America: New York State Origins," *New York History* 75, no. 1 (January 1994): 60.

69. Kelly, *Heaven's Ditch*, epigraph.

70. "Letter of Thomas Jefferson to Messrs. Riker, Agnew, and Bolton, June 8, 1826," *Niles' Register* 30 (July 1, 1826): 315.

71. Sheriff, *The Artificial River*, 173.

72. Nathaniel Hawthorne, "The Canal Boat," *New England Magazine*, December 1835, accessed April 25, 2018, http://historymatters.gmu.edu/d/6212/.

73. Taylor, *The Transportation Revolution*, 137.

74. See Larson, *Internal Improvement*, 195–224. While 28 percent of the federal monies directed to roads between 1789 and 1861 were spent in the territories and 72 percent in the states, barely 1 percent of the over $2.4 million spent by the federal government on canal construction over that same period was expended in the territories. Albjerg, "Internal Improvements," 170.

75. Ulrich B. Phillips, "Transportation in the Ante-Bellum South: An Economic Analysis," *Quarterly Journal of Economics* 19, no. 3 (May 1905): 443–44.

76. John Bell Rae, "Federal Land Grants in Aid of Canals," *Journal of Economic History* 4, no. 2 (November 1944): 167.

77. Rae, "Federal Land Grants," 168.

78. Taylor, *The Transportation Revolution*, 34.

79. Carter Goodrich, "The Revulsion against Internal Improvements," *Journal of Economic History* 10, no. 2 (November 1950): 145.

80. Sheriff, *The Artificial River*, 99.

81. Glyndon G. Van Deusen, "Some Aspects of Whig Thought and Theory in the Jacksonian Period," *American Historical Review* 63, no. 2 (January 1958): 317.

82. Taylor, *The Transportation Revolution*, 139.

83. Taylor, 53.

84. Gerald Gunderson, "Privatization and the 19th-Century Turnpike," *Cato Journal* 9, no. 1 (1989): 192.

85. Daniel B. Klein and Gordon J. Fielding, "Private Toll Roads: Learning from the 19th Century," University of California Transportation Center, reprint no. 118 (August 1992): 323; originally published in *Transportation Quarterly* 46, no. 3 (July 1992).

86. Klein and Fielding, "Private Toll Roads," 326.

87. Robert F. Hunter, "Turnpike Construction in Antebellum Virginia," *Technology and Culture* 4, no. 2 (Spring 1963): 178, 186.

88. Adam Smith, *The Nature and Causes of the Wealth of Nations*, in *The Works of Adam Smith*, vol. 4 (London: W. Strahan and T. Cadell, 1811), 95–96.

89. David Levinson, "The Political Economy of Private Roads," in *Street Smart: Competition, Entrepreneurship, and the Future of Roads*, ed. Gabriel Roth (Oakland, CA: The Independent Institute, 2006), 81.

90. N. S. Shaler, "The Common Roads," *Scribner's*, October 1889, 475.

91. Shaler, "The Common Roads," 476.

92. Daniel B. Klein and John Majewski, "Economy, Community, and Law: The Turnpike Movement in New York, 1797–1845," *Law & Society Review* 26, no. 3 (1992): 481.

93. Klein and Majewski, "Economy, Community, and Law," 488–89.

94. Klein and Majewski, 470.

95. US Department of Transportation, *America's Highways*, 9.

96. US Department of Transportation, 10.

97. Gunderson, "Privatization," 196.

98. Klein and Majewski, "Economy, Community, and Law," 500.

99. Klein and Fielding, "Private Toll Roads," 326.

100. Klein and Majewski, "Economy, Community, and Law," 481.

101. Klein and Majewski, 494.

102. Klein and Majewski, 495.

103. Klein and Majewski, 484.

104. Klein and Majewski, "Economy, Community, and Law," 497; see also Frederick James Wood, *The Turnpikes of New England and Evolution of the Same through England, Virginia, and Maryland* (Boston: Marshall Jones Company, 1919), 87–89.

105. Gunderson, "Privatization," 199.

106. Klein and Fielding, "Private Toll Roads," 329.

107. Daniel B. Klein and Chi Yin, "Use, Esteem, and Profit in Voluntary Provision: Toll Roads in California, 1850–1902," *Economic Inquiry* 34, no. 4 (October 1996): 678.

108. Klein and Yin, "Use, Esteem, and Profit," 680.

109. Klein and Yin, 681–82.

110. Klein and Yin, 686.

111. Klein and Yin, 691.

112. Klein and Yin, 691.

113. *Annals of Congress*, 15th Cong., 1st sess., 1385 (emphasis added).

114. *Annals of Congress*, 15th Cong., 1st sess., 1386.

115. *Annals of Congress*, 15th Cong., 1st sess., 1138.

116. *Annals of Congress*, 15th Cong., 1st sess., 1138 (emphasis added).

117. Risjord, *The Old Republicans*, 201.

118. *Annals of Congress*, 15th Cong., 1st sess., 1141 (emphasis added).

119. *Annals of Congress*, 15th Cong., 1st sess., 1147–48.

120. Maurice G. Baxter, *Henry Clay and the American System* (Lexington: University Press of Kentucky, 1995), 27.

121. *Annals of Congress*, 15th Cong., 1st sess., 1165.

122. *Annals of Congress*, 15th Cong., 1st sess., 1178.

123. *Annals of Congress*, 15th Cong., 1st sess., 1201.

124. *Annals of Congress*, 15th Cong., 1st sess., 1231.

125. Larson, *Internal Improvement*, 109.

126. Larson, 186.

127. Risjord, *The Old Republicans*, 237.

128. James Monroe, "Veto Message," The American Presidency Project, accessed August 12, 2018, https://www.presidency.ucsb.edu/node/208044.

129. Monroe, "Veto Message."

130. Larson, *Internal Improvement*, 111.

131. *Annals of Congress*, 18th Cong., 1st sess., 1341.

132. *Annals of Congress*, 18th Cong., 1st sess., 1308.

133. Phillips, "Transportation in the Ante-Bellum South," 440. Norman Risjord writes that "growing Southern opposition to internal improvements" after 1820 "was directly related to a fear of the extension of federal power that might free the slaves as well as build roads and canals." Risjord, *The Old Republicans*, 204.

134. Noble E. Cunningham Jr., "Nathaniel Macon and the Southern Protest against National Consolidation," *North Carolina Historical Review* 32, no. 3 (July 1955): 376.

135. Jordan, *The National Road*, 161–62.

136. Larson, *Internal Improvement*, 138.

137. William E. Dodd, *The Life of Nathaniel Macon* (Raleigh, NC: Edwards & Broughton, 1903), 297.

138. Dodd, *The Life of Nathaniel Macon*, 297–98.

139. Cunningham, "Nathaniel Macon," 379.

140. Dodd, *The Life of Nathaniel Macon*, 310.

141. Harry L. Watson, "Squire Oldway and His Friends: Opposition to Internal Improvements in Antebellum North Carolina," *North Carolina Historical Review* 54, no. 2 (April 1977): 117.

142. Watson, "Squire Oldway," 114.

143. Watson, 114.

144. Watson, 110.

145. Watson, 112.

146. Phillips, "Transportation in the Ante-Bellum South," 446. Larson says that North Carolina, in contrast to Erie Canal–era New York, "sank backward into a libertarian malaise that seemed to be ineradicable." Under the spell of the "cult of true republicanism," its backcountry farmers and tidewater planters alike refused to countenance state subsidy of roads, canals, and other improvements. This "grim inheritance," opines Larson, retarded economic and commercial development in the Tar Heel State. Larson, *Internal Improvement*, 73, 98.

147. Goodrich, "Revulsion," 162–63.

148. Goodrich, 162.

149. Goodrich, 163.

150. Goodrich, 163.

151. John Quincy Adams, "First Inaugural Address of John Quincy Adams," The Avalon Project at Yale Law School, accessed August 5, 2018, http://avalon.law.yale.edu/19th_century/qadams.asp.

152. National Park Service, "Chesapeake and Ohio Canal National Historical Park," accessed August 5, 2018, https://www.nps.gov/choh/index.htm.

153. George Washington, "Farewell Address," *The Papers of George Washington*, accessed August 6, 2018, http://gwpapers.virginia.edu/documents_gw/farewell/transcript.html.

154. William Henry Seward, *Life and Public Services of John Quincy Adams, Sixth President of the United States* (Auburn, NY: Derby, Miller, 1849), 221.

155. Carter Goodrich, "National Planning of Internal Improvements," *Political Science Quarterly* 63, no. 1 (March 1948): 30.

156. Albjerg, "Internal Improvements," 173.

157. Albjerg, 35.

158. Albjerg, 29, 36.

159. Dan Monroe, *The Republican Vision of John Tyler* (College Station: Texas A&M University Press, 2003), 51.

160. Monroe, *Republican Vision*, 52.

161. Carlton Jackson, "The Internal Improvement Vetoes of Andrew Jackson," *Tennessee Historical Quarterly* 25, no. 3 (Fall 1966): 263.

162. Andrew Jackson, "May 27, 1830: Veto Message regarding Funding of Infrastructure Development," UVA Miller Center, accessed April 12, 2018, https://millercenter.org/the-presidency/presidential-speeches/may-27-1830-veto-message-regarding-funding-infra-structure.

163. Carlton Jackson, "Internal Improvement Vetoes," 267.

164. Andrew Jackson, "Veto Message."

165. Andrew Jackson, "Veto Message."

166. Carlton Jackson, "Internal Improvement Vetoes," 273–74.

167. Carlton Jackson, 274.

168. Stephen Minicucci, "Internal Improvements and the Union, 1790–1860," *Studies in American Political Development* 18, no. 2 (Fall 2004): 162.

169. Carlton Jackson, "Internal Improvement Vetoes," 266.

170. Taylor, *The Transportation Revolution*, 21.

171. Albjerg, "Internal Improvements," 174.

172. "1844 Democratic Party Platform," PoliTxts, accessed January 22, 2019, http://janda.org/politxts/PartyPlatforms/Democratic/dem.844.html.

173. James K. Polk, "August 3, 1846: Veto Message Regarding Funding Internal Improvements," UVA Miller Center, accessed August 2, 2018, https://millercenter.org/the-presidency/presidential-speeches/august-3-1846-veto-message-regarding-funding-internal.

174. Polk, "Veto Message."

175. Mary Russell, "House Sustains Carter's Veto," *Washington Post*, October 6, 1978.

176. Paul H. Bergeron, *The Presidency of James K. Polk* (Lawrence: University Press of Kansas, 1987), 194.

177. Eugene Irving McCormac, *James K. Polk: A Political Biography* (New York: Russell & Russell, 1965/1922), 684.

178. Michael F. Holt, *Franklin Pierce* (New York: Henry Holt, 2010), 43. See also Larry Gara, *The Presidency of Franklin Pierce* (Lawrence: University Press of Kansas, 1991).

179. Albjerg, "Internal Improvements," 177.

180. Jason Lee, "An Economic Analysis of the Good Roads Movement in the 20th Century" (PhD diss., University of California, Davis, 2012), 52.

181. Henry Clay, "On the Cumberland Road Bill," in *The Life and Speeches of the Hon. Henry Clay*, vol. 1, ed. Daniel Mallory (New York: Robert P. Bixby, 1844), 230.

182. Gerrit Smith, "Speech on the Pacific Railroad," *Speeches of Gerrit Smith in Congress* (New York: Mason Brothers, 1856), 236.

183. Smith, "Speech on the Pacific Railroad," 249.

184. Klein and Majewski, "Plank Road Fever," 41.

185. Klein and Majewski, 47.

186. Taylor, *The Transportation Revolution*, 30–31.

187. Phillips, "Transportation in the Ante-Bellum South," 444.

188. Klein and Majewski, "Plank Road Fever," 58 (emphasis added).

189. Klein and Majewski, 45.

190. Goodrich, "Revulsion," 156.

191. Goodrich, 146.

192. Goodrich, 146.

193. Goodrich, 153. The sentiment in the Empire State persisted after the war: an 1874 amendment to the New York state constitution banned state aid to roads.

194. Minicucci, "Internal Improvements," 161–62.

195. Robert Nisbet, *The Sociological Tradition* (New York: Basic Books, 1966), 128.

Chapter 2: Good Roads—or Here Come the Wheelmen!

1. Gary Allan Tobin, "The Bicycle Boom of the 1890's: The Development of Private Transportation and the Birth of the Modern Tourist," *Journal of Popular Culture* 7, no. 4 (Spring 1974): 839.

2. Tobin, "Bicycle Boom," 840–41.

3. Carlton Reid, *Roads Were Not Built for Cars: How Cyclists Were the First to Push for Good Roads & Became the Pioneers of Motoring* (Washington, DC: Island Press, 2015), 148.

4. Michael R. Fein, *Paving the Way: New York Road Building and the American State, 1880–1956* (Lawrence: University Press of Kansas, 2008), 27.

5. Tobin, "Bicycle Boom," 840.

6. Tobin, 840.

7. Reid, *Roads Were Not Built for Cars*, 158.

8. Reid, 151.

9. Reid, 151.

10. Christopher W. Wells, "The Changing Nature of Country Roads: Farmers, Reformers, and the Shifting Uses of Rural Space, 1880–1905," *Agricultural History* 80, no. 2 (Spring 2006): 149.

11. David R. Wrone, "Illinois Pulls out of the Mud," *Journal of the Illinois State Historical Society* 58, no. 1 (Spring 1965): 61.

12. Franklin Smith, "An Object Lesson in Social Reform," *Popular Science Monthly* 50 (January 1897), 306.

13. Smith, "Object Lesson," 306.

14. Smith, 307.

15. Smith, 307.

16. Smith, 307.

17. Smith, 308.

18. Smith, 310.

19. James Longhurst, "The Sidepath Not Taken: Bicycles, Taxes, and the Rhetoric of the Public Good in the 1890s," *Journal of Policy History* 25, no. 4 (2013): 568.

20. Longhurst, "Sidepath," 557, 560.

21. Longhurst, 562.

22. Fein, *Paving the Way*, 29.

23. Wells, "Country Roads," 148.

24. Wells, 150.

25. Wells, 150.

26. Jason Lee, "An Economic Analysis of the Good Roads Movement in the 20th Century" (PhD diss., University of California, Davis, 2012), 71.

27. Lee, "Economic Analysis," 71.

28. Wells, "Country Roads," 150.

29. Wells, 151.

30. Reid, *Roads Were Not Built for Cars*, 153.

31. Reid, 157.

32. Albert A. Pope, "Automobiles and Good Roads," *Munsey's Magazine*, May 1903, 168.

33. Pope, "Automobiles and Good Roads," 168.

34. Pope, 170.

35. Reid, *Roads Were Not Built for Cars*, 143.

36. Lee, "Economic Analysis," 2.

37. Charles L. Dearing, *American Highway Policy* (Washington, DC: Brookings Institution, 1941), 42.

38. Hal S. Barron, "And the Crooked Shall Be Made Straight: Public Road Administration and the Decline of Localism in the Rural North, 1870–1930," *Journal of Social History* 26, no. 1 (Autumn 1992): 83.

39. N. S. Shaler, "The Common Roads," *Scribner's*, October 1889, 477.

40. Dearing, *American Highway Policy*, 2.

41. Dearing, 221.

42. Barron, "And the Crooked Shall Be Made Straight," 85.

43. Dearing, *American Highway Policy*, 229–30.

44. Dearing, 240.

45. Harold Parker, "Good Roads Movement," *Annals of the American Academy of Political Science* 40, no. 1 (March 1912): 55.

46. Henry Petroski, *The Road Taken: The History and Future of America's Infrastructure* (New York: Bloomsbury, 2017/2016), 39.

47. Wells, "Country Roads," 150.

48. Benjamin F. Alexander, *Coxey's Army: Popular Protest in the Gilded Age* (Baltimore: Johns Hopkins University Press, 2015), 3.

49. Alexander, *Coxey's Army*, 3.

50. Lee, "Economic Analysis," viii.

51. Alexander, *Coxey's Army*, 46.

52. Alexander, 49.

53. Donald L. McMurry, *Coxey's Army: A Study of the Industrial Army Movement of 1894* (Boston: Little, Brown, 1929), 117.

54. McMurry, *Coxey's Army*, v.

55. McMurry, 301.

56. McMurry, 301–2.

57. Dearing, *American Highway Policy*, 233.

58. Richard F. Weingroff, *Portrait of a General: General Roy Stone* (Washington, DC: US Department of Transportation Federal Highway Administration, n.d.), 34, accessed April 26, 2018, https://www.fhwa.dot.gov/infrastructure/stone.pdf.

59. Weingroff, *Portrait of a General*, 36.

60. Wayne E. Fuller, *RFD: The Changing Face of Rural America* (Bloomington: Indiana University Press, 1964), 190–91.

61. Weingroff, *Portrait of a General*, 39.

62. Weingroff, 43.

63. Earl Swift, *The Big Roads: The Untold Story of the Engineers, Visionaries, and Trailblazers Who Created the American Superhighways* (Boston: Houghton Mifflin Harcourt, 2011), 15.

64. Weingroff, *Portrait of a General*, 49.

65. Weingroff, 46.

66. Weingroff, 47.

67. Albert Perry Brigham, "Good Roads in the United States," *Bulletin of the American Geographical Society* 36, no. 12 (1904): 723.

68. Dearing, *American Highway Policy*, 235.

69. Wayne E. Fuller, "Good Roads and Rural Free Delivery of Mail," *Mississippi Valley Historical Review* 42, no. 1 (June 1955): 76.

70. Brigham, "Good Roads," 725.

71. Harry A. Barth, "State Taxation of Passenger Automobiles," *National Municipal Review* 13, no. 11 (November 1924): 650.

72. Brigham, "Good Roads," 726.

73. Brigham, 726.

74. Brigham, 735.

75. Fein, *Paving the Way*, 22.

76. Brigham, "Good Roads," 722.

77. Weingroff, *Portrait of a General*, 55.

78. Weingroff, 60.

79. Brigham, "Good Roads," 730.

80. US Department of Transportation Federal Highway Administration, *America's Highways, 1776–1976: A History of the Federal-Aid Program* (Washington, DC: US Government Printing Office, 1976), 76.

81. US Department of Transportation, *America's Highways*, 76.

82. Weingroff, *Portrait of a General*, 76.

83. Theodore Roosevelt, "Good Roads as an Element in National Greatness," Office of Public Road Inquiries, US Department of Agriculture, Proceedings of the National Good Roads Convention (Washington, DC: Government Printing Office, 1903), 79.

84. Martin Dodge, "Ideas of Clay and Calhoun: A Return to Them Is Now Imperative," *League of American Wheelmen Magazine*, June 1900, 17.

85. US Department of Transportation, *America's Highways*, 47.

86. US Department of Transportation, 50.

87. James J. Flink, *America Adopts the Automobile, 1895–1910* (Cambridge, MA: MIT Press, 1970), 17. See also Robert G. Koch, "George B. Selden's Road Engine," *Crooked Lake Review*, August 1992, http://www.crookedlakereview.com/articles/34_66/53aug1992/53koch.html.

88. Flink, *America Adopts the Automobile*, 29.

89. Flink, 2–3.

90. Flink, 54.

91. Fuller, "Good Roads," 81.

92. Flink, *America Adopts the Automobile*, 64.

93. Flink, 68.

94. Flink, 180.

95. Reid, *Roads Were Not Built for Cars*, 6.

96. Fuller, *RFD*, 178.

97. Flink, *America Adopts the Automobile*, 203, 210.

98. "The Political Economy of Good Roads," *Scientific American* 99, no. 25 (December 19, 1908): 451.

99. "The Political Economy of Good Roads," 451.

100. Smithsonian National Postal Museum, "Frequently Asked Questions: What Is the Postal Service Motto?," accessed August 14, 2018, https://postalmuseum.si.edu/about/frequently-asked-questions/index.html#history10.

101. Fuller, *RFD*, 186–87, 189.

102. Brigham, "Good Roads," 729.

103. Fuller, *RFD*, 192.

104. Lee, "Economic Analysis," 24.

105. Lee, 23.

106. Fuller, "Good Roads," 71.

107. Wells, "Country Roads," 158.

108. US Department of Transportation, *America's Highways*, 80.

109. Richard F. Weingroff, "The Brownlow-Latimer Bill," US Department of Transportation Federal Highway Administration, accessed April 29, 2018, https://www.fhwa.dot.gov/highwayhistory/dodge/09.cfm.

110. Richard F. Weingroff, "'Clearly Vicious as a Matter of Policy': The Fight against Federal-Aid," US Department of Transportation Federal Highway Administration, accessed July 24, 2018, https://www.fhwa.dot.gov/infrastructure/hwyhist01.cfm.

111. US Department of Transportation, *America's Highways*, 60.

112. "Death of Representative Otey," *Good Roads Magazine*, May 1902, 21.

113. Fuller, "Good Roads," 75.

114. Weingroff, "The Brownlow-Latimer Bill."

115. Theodore Roosevelt, "Third Annual Message," The American Presidency Project, accessed May 29, 2018, https://www.presidency.ucsb.edu/node/206201.

116. Weingroff, "The Brownlow-Latimer Bill."

117. Weingroff, "Clearly Vicious."

118. Dearing, *American Highway Policy*, 259.

119. "US Population, 1790–2000," U-S-History.com, accessed June 20, 2018, https://www.u-s-history.com/pages/h980.html.

120. Reid, *Roads Were Not Built for Cars*, 156.

121. Dearing, *American Highway Policy*, 54.

122. Lee, "Economic Analysis," 57, 96.

123. James W. Martin, "The Motor Vehicle Registration License," *Bulletin of the National Tax Association* 12, no. 7 (April 1927): 194.

124. Mark H. Rose and Raymond A. Mohl, *Interstate: Highway Politics and Policy since 1939*, 3rd ed. (Knoxville: University of Tennessee Press, 2012), xi.

125. Martin, "The Motor Vehicle Registration License," 194.

126. Martin, 194–95.

127. For a detailed look at early registration rates, see Barth, "State Taxation," 641–51.

128. James A. Dunn Jr., "The Importance of Being Earmarked: Transport Policy and Highway Finance in Great Britain and the United States," *Comparative Studies in Society and History* 20, no. 1 (January 1978): 29.

129. Dunn, "The Importance of Being Earmarked," 34.

130. Dunn, 38.

131. Flink, *America Adopts the Automobile*, 54, 56.

132. Flink, 78.

133. Reid, *Roads Were Not Built for Cars*, 46.

134. Fein, *Paving the Way*, 32–33.

135. Fein, 33.

136. Fein, 35.

137. Fein, 45, 46.

138. Barron, "And the Crooked Shall Be Made Straight," 89.

139. Fein, *Paving the Way*, 56, 64. By 1912, New York motor vehicle registrations would zoom to 107,262.

140. Rodney O. Davis, "Iowa Farm Opinion and the Good Roads Movement, 1903–1904," *Annals of Iowa* 37, no. 5 (Summer 1964): 321.

141. Davis, "Iowa Farm Opinion," 323.

142. Davis, 332.

143. Davis, "Iowa Farm Opinion," 333–34.

144. Wrone, "Illinois Pulls out of the Mud," 55.

145. Wrone, 61.

146. Lee, "Economic Analysis," 48.

147. Lee, 5.

148. Lee, 77, 88.

149. Peter J. Hugill, "Good Roads and the Automobile in the United States," *Geographical Review* 72, no. 3 (July 1982): 340.

150. Dearing, *American Highway Policy*, 240.

151. Brigham, "Good Roads," 726.

152. Lee, "Economic Analysis," vi, 153.

153. Lee, 123.

154. Lee, 143.

155. Christopher R. Berry and Martin R. West, "Growing Pains: The School Consolidation Movement and Student Outcomes," *Journal of Law, Economics, & Organization* 26, no. 1 (April 2010): 4.

156. Dearing, *American Highway Policy*, 278.

157. Berry and West, "Growing Pains," 1.

158. Berry and West, 1, 24.

159. Berry and West, 2.

160. Alex Lichtenstein, "Good Roads and Chain Gangs in the Progressive South: 'The Negro Convict Is a Slave,'" *Journal of Southern History* 59, no. 1 (February 1993): 86.

161. Lichtenstein, "Good Roads," 87.

162. Lichtenstein, 88.

163. Lichtenstein, 88–89, 93.

164. Lichtenstein, 100.

165. Lichtenstein, 102.

166. Lichtenstein, 101.

167. Lichtenstein, 104.

168. "1908 Democratic Party Platform," The American Presidency Project, accessed May 6, 2018, https://www.presidency.ucsb.edu/node/273198.

169. "Republican Party Platform of 1908," The American Presidency Project, accessed May 6, 2018, https://www.presidency.ucsb.edu/node/273324.

170. "1912 Democratic Party Platform," The American Presidency Project, accessed May 6, 2018, https://www.presidency.ucsb.edu/node/273201.

171. "Progressive Party Platform of 1912," The American Presidency Project, accessed May 6, 2018, https://www.presidency.ucsb.edu/node/273288.

172. Fuller, *RFD*, 193–94.

173. Fuller, "Good Roads," 80.

174. Fuller, *RFD*, 195.

175. Fuller, "Good Roads," 81.

176. Fuller, *RFD*, 196.

177. Weingroff, "Clearly Vicious."

178. Weingroff, "Clearly Vicious."

179. Weingroff, "Clearly Vicious."

180. US Department of Transportation, *America's Highways*, 102.

181. Dearing, *American Highway Policy*, 261.

182. Dearing, 248.

183. Dearing, 259.

184. For a history of Civil War pensions, see James T. Bennett, *Paid Patriotism: The Debate over Veterans' Benefits* (Piscataway, NJ: Transaction Publishers, 2017).

185. Fein, *Paving the Way*, 71.

186. Weingroff, "Clearly Vicious."

187. "1916 Democratic Party Platform," The American Presidency Project, accessed June 18, 2018, https://www.presidency.ucsb.edu/node/273203.

188. "1916 Republican Party Platform," The American Presidency Project, accessed June 18, 2018, https://www.presidency.ucsb.edu/node/273328.

189. "Republican Party Platform of 1920," The American Presidency Project, accessed June 19, 2018, https://www.presidency.ucsb.edu/node/273373.

190. "1920 Democratic Party Platform," The American Presidency Project, accessed June 25, 2018, https://www.presidency.ucsb.edu/node/273205.

191. Flink, *America Adopts the Automobile*, 116.

192. "The Automobile in War," *Motor Age*, October 11, 1900.

193. "The Automobile in War," *Motor Age*, October 11, 1900.

194. Dearing, *American Highway Policy*, 137.

195. US Department of Transportation, *America's Highways*, 101.

196. Dearing, *American Highway Policy*, 138.

197. H. L. Bowlby, "Distribution of Surplus War Materials for Road Building," *Public Roads* 2, no. 24 (April 1920): 23.

198. Bowlby, "Distribution," 23.

199. Bowlby, 26.

200. Pete Davies, *American Road: The Story of an Epic Transcontinental Journey at the Dawn of the Motor Age* (New York: Henry Holt, 2002), 6.

201. Davies, *American Road*, 41.

202. Dwight D. Eisenhower, *At Ease: Stories I Tell to Friends* (Garden City, NY: Doubleday, 1967), 157.

203. Eisenhower, *At Ease: Stories I Tell to Friends*, 157–58.

204. Petroski, *The Road Taken*, 42.

205. Eisenhower, *At Ease*, 166–67.

206. John Chynoweth Burnham, "The Gasoline Tax and the Automobile Revolution," *Mississippi Valley Historical Review* 48, no. 3 (December 1961): 440.

207. Burnham, "Gasoline Tax," 444.

208. Burnham, 446.

209. Dearing, *American Highway Policy*, 101.

210. Barth, "State Taxation," 648.

211. On making the gasoline tax more progressive, see Richard W. Lindholm, "Note on the Benefits Justification of the Gasoline Tax," *Southern Economic Journal* 17, no. 1 (July 1950): 55–58.

212. Burnham, "Gasoline Tax," 454.

213. Burnham, 454–55.

214. US Department of Transportation, *America's Highways*, 124.

215. Wrone, "Illinois Pulls out of the Mud," 70.

216. Mary Rowland, "Kansas and the Highways, 1917–1930," *Kansas History* 5, no. 1 (Spring 1982): 33.

217. Frederic L. Paxson, "The Highway Movement, 1916–1935," *American Historical Review* 51, no. 2 (January 1946): 243.

218. Rowland, "Kansas," 35.

219. Rowland, 39.

220. Rowland, 39.

221. Rowland, 39.

222. Rowland, 50.

223. Rowland, 46.

224. Rowland, 46–47.

225. Wells, "Country Roads," 144.

226. Barron, "And the Crooked Shall Be Made Straight," 82.

227. Harry L. Watson, "Squire Oldway and His Friends: Opposition to Internal Improvements in Antebellum North Carolina," *North Carolina Historical Review* 54, no. 2 (April 1977): 111.

228. US Department of Transportation, *America's Highways*, 41.

229. Wells, "Country Roads," 160.

230. Dearing, *American Highway Policy*, 50.

231. Dearing, 51.

232. Fein, *Paving the Way*, 15.

233. Dearing, *American Highway Policy*, 61.

234. Weingroff, *Portrait of a General*, 56.

235. Swift, *The Big Roads*, 13.

236. Davies, *American Road*, 12.

237. Davies, 16.

238. Swift, *The Big Roads*, 31.

239. Hugill, "Good Roads," 342.

240. Davies, *American Road*, 18.

241. Hugill, "Good Roads," 347.

242. Davies, *American Road*, 33.

243. Davies, 34.

244. Davies, 36.

245. Davies, 37.

246. Davies, 222.

247. James Lin, "Lincoln Highway: A Brief History," accessed May 9, 2018, http://www.lincolnhighway.jameslin.name/history.

248. US Department of Transportation, *America's Highways*, 83.

249. "King of the Lincoln Highway," accessed September 11, 2018, https://web.archive.org/web/20180903033753/http://lincoln-highway-museum.org/Miller/Miller-Index.html. See

also Max J. Skidmore, "Restless Americans: The Significance of Movement in American History (With a Nod to F. J. Turner)," *Journal of American Culture* 34, no. 2 (June 2011): 171.

250. Gary T. Schwartz, "Urban Freeways and the Interstate System," *California Law Review* 49 (1976): 413.

251. Swift, *The Big Roads*, 81.

252. See Stanley Mallach, "The Origins of the Decline of Urban Mass Transportation in the United States, 1890–1930," *Urbanism Past & Present* 8 (Summer 1979): 1–17.

253. Mallach, "Origins," 9.

254. Mallach, 7.

255. Edward Glaeser, "Spending Won't Fix What Ails US Infrastructure," *Bloomberg*, February 13, 2012, https://www.bloomberg.com/opinion/articles/2012-02-14/spending-won -t-fix-what-ails-u-s-transport-commentary-by-edward-glaeser.

Chapter 3: Ike's Autobahn: The National System of Interstate and Defense Highways

1. Jason Scott Smith, *Building New Deal Liberalism: The Political Economy of Public Works, 1933–1936* (New York: Cambridge University Press, 2006), 90, 95.

2. Mark H. Rose and Raymond A. Mohl, *Interstate: Highway Politics and Policy since 1939* (Knoxville: University of Tennessee Press, 2012), 10. For an argument that New Deal public works programs were "a strikingly effective method of state-sponsored economic development," see Smith, *Building New Deal Liberalism*, 22.

3. James M. Bickley, "The Federal Excise Tax on Gasoline and the Highway Trust Fund: A Short History," Congressional Research Service, September 7, 2012, 2.

4. Smith, *Building New Deal Liberalism*, 250–51.

5. Smith, 257.

6. David A. Ripple, "History of the Interstate System in Indiana," School of Civil Engineering, Joint Highway Research Project, vol. 1, accessed February 1, 2019, https://archive .org/stream/historyofinterst7526ripp/historyofinterst7526ripp_djvu.txt.

7. Pete Davies, *American Road: The Story of an Epic Transcontinental Journey at the Dawn of the Motor Age* (New York: Henry Holt, 2002), 93.

8. Earl Swift, *The Big Roads: The Untold Story of the Engineers, Visionaries, and Trailblazers Who Created the American Superhighways* (Boston: Houghton Mifflin Harcourt, 2011), 55.

9. Tom Lewis, *Divided Highways: Building the Interstate Highways, Transforming American Life* (New York: Viking, 1997), 5.

10. Lewis, *Divided Highways*, 92.

11. A. W. Brandt, "Shaping Our Highway Program for National Defense," *American Highways* 19, no. 1 (January 1940): 19.

12. Brandt, "Shaping Our Highway Program," 19.

13. US Department of Transportation Federal Highway Administration, *America's Highways, 1776–1976: A History of the Federal-Aid Program* (Washington, DC: US Government Printing Office, 1976), 144.

14. Rose and Mohl, *Interstate*, 19.

15. Rose and Mohl, 20.

16. Gary T. Schwartz, "Urban Freeways and the Interstate System," *California Law Review* 49 (1976): 424.

17. Smith, *Building New Deal Liberalism*, 252.

18. Rose and Mohl, *Interstate*, 102.

19. Thomas H. MacDonald, "The Case for Urban Expressways," *American City*, June 1947, 92.

20. MacDonald, "Urban Expressways," 92.

21. MacDonald, 92.

22. David St. Clair, "The Automobile Industry's Interests in Interstate Highway Legislation, 1930–1956," in *Essays in Economic and Business History: Selected Papers from the Economic and Business Historical Society*, vol. 3, ed. Edwin J. Perkins (Los Angeles: Economic and Business Historical Society, 1984), 164.

23. Henry Petroski, *The Road Taken: The History and Future of America's Infrastructure* (New York: Bloomsbury, 2017/2016), 155.

24. Schwartz, "Urban Freeways," 419.

25. William A. Bresnahan, "Who Should Pay How Much of Highway Costs?," *Commercial Car Journal*, July 1952, 51.

26. Rose and Mohl, *Interstate*, 34.

27. Bresnahan, "Who Should Pay," 52.

28. Rose and Mohl, *Interstate*, 33.

29. New York State Thruway Authority, "Overview of the Thruway System," accessed November 26, 2018, https://www.thruway.ny.gov/oursystem/overview.html.

30. Michael R. Fein, *Paving the Way: New York Road Building and the American State, 1880–1956* (Lawrence: University Press of Kansas, 2008), 177.

31. Fein, *Paving the Way*, 181.

32. Fein, 197.

33. Fein, 185, 196.

34. Fein, 203.

35. Fein, 209.

36. Swift, *Big Roads*, 148.

37. Fein, *Paving the Way*, 2.

38. Swift, *Big Roads*, 5.

39. William G. Wing, "The Concrete Juggernaut," *Audubon*, July–August 1966, 268.

40. Rose and Mohl, *Interstate*, 95.

41. Petroski, *The Road Taken*, 227.

42. Lewis, *Divided Highways*, 99.

43. Dwight D. Eisenhower, *Mandate for Change, 1953–1956* (Garden City, NY: Doubleday, 1963), 548.

44. Richard M. Nixon, "Address by Honorable Richard M. Nixon," *Proceedings of the Governors' Conference* (1954): 90–91.

45. Nixon, "Address," 91.

46. Nixon, 92.

47. Nixon, 92.

48. Raymond A. Mohl, "Ike and the Interstates: Creeping toward Comprehensive Planning," *Journal of Planning History* 2, no. 3 (August 2003): 254.

49. Richard F. Weingroff, "General Lucius D. Clay—The President's Man," US Department of Transportation Federal Highway Administration, accessed June 26, 2018, https://www.fhwa.dot.gov/infrastructure/clay.cfm.

50. Weingroff, "General Lucius D. Clay."

51. Schwartz, "Urban Freeways," 439–41; "Interstate Frequently Asked Questions," US Department of Transportation Federal Highway Administration, accessed December 29, 2018, https://www.fhwa.dot.gov/interstate/faq.cfm.

52. Dwight D. Eisenhower, "Special Message to the Congress Regarding a National Highway Program," The American Presidency Project, February 22, 1955, accessed January 25, 2021, https://www.presidency.ucsb.edu/node/233952.

53. US Department of Transportation, *America's Highways*, 127.

54. Eisenhower, "Special Message."

55. Swift, *Big Roads*, 179.

56. Eisenhower, "Special Message."

57. Lewis, *Divided Highways*, 108.

58. Lewis, *Divided Highways*, 152.

59. Raymond Moley, "The Clay Highway Plan," *Newsweek*, March 21, 1955.

60. Weingroff, "General Lucius D. Clay."

61. "The President's Highway Program," special issue, *Congressional Digest*, May 1955, 160.

62. Rose and Mohl, *Interstate*, 79.

63. "Address of Senator Richard L. Neuberger," March 15, 1955, in "The President's Highway Program," special issue, *Congressional Digest*, May 1955, 155.

64. John J. Martin Jr., "Proposed Federal Highway Legislation in 1955: A Case Study in the Legislative Process," *Georgetown Law Journal* 44 (1956): 223.

65. "Statement of Mr. Triggs, Assistant Legislative Director of the American Farm Bureau Federation," February 23, 1955, in "The President's Highway Program," special issue, *Congressional Digest*, 157.

66. "Statement of Mr. Triggs," 159.

67. Martin, "Proposed Federal Highway Legislation," 238.

68. "Statement of the Hon. Sinclair Weeks," March 10, 1955, in "The President's Highway Program," special issue, *Congressional Digest*, May 1955, 150.

69. "Republican Party Platform of 1952," May 1955, The American Presidency Project, accessed May 19, 2018, https://www.presidency.ucsb.edu/node/273395.

70. James A. Dunn Jr., "The Importance of Being Earmarked: Transport Policy and Highway Finance in Great Britain and the United States," *Comparative Studies in Society and History* 20, no. 1 (January 1978): 47.

71. New York State Thruway Authority, "Overview."

72. "Statement of the Hon. Joseph Campbell," March 28, 1955, in "The President's Highway Program," special issue, *Congressional Digest*, May 1955, 149.

73. "Statement of the Hon. Joseph Campbell," 151.

74. Richard F. Weingroff, "Senator Harry Flood Byrd of Virginia—The Pay-as-You-Go Man," US Department of Transportation Federal Highway Administration, accessed May 15, 2018, https://www.fhwa.dot.gov/infrastructure/byrd.cfm.

75. "Statement by Hon. Harry F. Byrd, of Virginia, Relative to the Clay Commission Highway Report," January 18, 1955, US Department of Transportation Federal Highway Administration, accessed September 10, 2018, https://www.fhwa.dot.gov/infrastructure/byrdstm.cfm.

76. "Statement by Hon. Harry F. Byrd," January 18, 1955.

77. "Statement by Hon. Harry F. Byrd," January 18, 1955.

78. "Statement by Hon. Harry F. Byrd," January 18, 1955.

79. "Statement of Hon. Walter J. Kohler," March 2, 1955, in "The President's Highway Program," special issue, *Congressional Digest*, May 1955, 156.

80. "Statement of the Hon. Harry F. Byrd," March 18, 1955, in "The President's Highway Program," special issue *Congressional Digest*, May 1955, 145.

81. "Statement of the Hon. Harry F. Byrd," March 18, 1955, 147.

82. "Statement of the Hon. Harry F. Byrd," March 18, 1955, 145.

83. Martin, "Proposed Federal Highway Legislation," 268.

84. Martin, 234.

85. "Statement of the Hon. George Humphrey," March 22, 1955, in "The President's Highway Program," special issue, *Congressional Digest*, May 1955, 144.

86. Eisenhower, *Mandate for Change*, 548.

87. Eisenhower, 501.

88. Eisenhower, 501.

89. Weingroff, "General Lucius D. Clay."

90. Martin, "Proposed Federal Highway Legislation," 221.

91. Eisenhower, *Mandate for Change*, 548.

92. "Statement of Hon. Herbert Brownell," March 22, 1955, in "The President's Highway Program," special issue, *Congressional Digest*, May 1955, 150.

93. "Construction Ahead," *New Republic*, May 16, 1955.

94. Martin, "Proposed Federal Highway Legislation," 241.

95. Martin, 221.

96. Schwartz, "Urban Freeways," 434.

97. Martin, "Proposed Federal Highway Legislation," 262.

98. American Trucking Associations, "Reports, Trends, & Statistics," accessed June 27, 2018, http://www.trucking.org/News_and_Information_Reports.aspx.

99. Martin, "Proposed Federal Highway Legislation," 262.

100. Eisenhower, *Mandate for Change*, 502.

101. Rose and Mohl, *Interstate*, 89.

102. Ben Kelley, *The Pavers and the Paved* (New York: Donald W. Brown, 1971), 33.

103. Karl Detzer, "Our Great Big Highway Bungle," *Reader's Digest*, July 1960, 45.

104. Lewis, *Divided Highways*, 121.

105. "13-Year Highway Program," *CQ Almanac 1956*, accessed June 26, 2018, https://library.cqpress.com/cqalmanac/document.php?id=cqal56-1349098.

106. David R. Levin, "Federal Aspects of the Interstate Highway Program," *Nebraska Law Review* 38, no. 2 (1959): 393.

107. For a look at the effect of interstate exchanges on rural development, specifically in Appalachia, see Henry E. Moon Jr., "Interstate Highway Interchanges Reshape Rural Communities," *Rural Development Perspectives* 4, no. 1 (October 1987): 35–38.

108. Schwartz, "Urban Freeways," 479–80.

109. Daniel P. Moynihan, "New Roads and Urban Chaos," *Reporter*, April 14, 1960, 14.

110. Daniel P. Moynihan, *Coping: On the Practice of Government* (New York: Vintage, 1975/1974), 276–77.

111. J. B. Jackson, "Abolish the Highways!," *National Review*, November 29, 1966, 1213.

112. Swift, *Big Roads*, 220.

113. For an account of Route 66—the way it was and the ways in which we choose to remember it—see Peter B. Dedek, *Hip to the Trip: A Cultural History of Route 66* (Albuquerque: University of New Mexico Press, 2007).

114. Dedek, *Hip to the Trip*, 48.

115. Dedek, 61.

116. Rickie Longfellow, "Back in Time: The National Road," US Department of Transportation Federal Highway Administration, accessed June 24, 2018, https://www.fhwa.dot.gov/infrastructure/back0103.cfm.

117. Nathaniel Baum-Snow, "Did Highways Cause Suburbanization?," *Quarterly Journal of Economics* 122, no. 2 (May 2007): 775–805.

118. Rose and Mohl, *Interstate*, 96.

119. "Bertram D. Tallamy," US Department of Transportation Federal Highway Administration, accessed June 13, 2018, https://www.fhwa.dot.gov/infrastructure/50tallamy.cfm.

120. Lewis, *Divided Highways*, 193.

121. Robert A. Caro, *The Power Broker: Robert Moses and the Fall of New York* (New York: Vintage, 1975/1974), 21.

122. Robert Moses, "Slums and City Planning," *Atlantic*, January 1945.

123. Anthony Flint, *Wrestling with Moses: How Jane Jacobs Took On New York's Master Builder and Transformed the American City* (New York: Random House, 2009), xii.

124. Lewis Mumford, "The Skyway's the Limit," *New Yorker*, November 14, 1959, 173.

125. Mumford, "The Skyway's the Limit," 176.

126. Raymond A. Mohl, "Stop the Road: Freeway Revolts in American Cities," *Journal of Urban History* 30, no. 5 (July 2004): 678.

127. "Build Expressways through Slum Areas," *American City*, November 1951, 125.

128. J. S. Bragdon, "Memorandum for the Record," November 30, 1959, US Department of Transportation Federal Highway Administration, accessed June 29, 2018, https://www.fhwa.dot.gov/infrastructure/113059.cfm.

129. "Eisenhower's Meeting with General Bragdon, 4/6/60," US Department of Transportation Federal Highway Administration, accessed June 29, 2018, https://www.fhwa.dot.gov/infrastructure/bragdon2.cfm.

130. Mohl, "Ike and the Interstates," 255.

Chapter 4: We're Not Going to Take It Anymore: Americans Revolt against the Freeway

1. Gary T. Schwartz, "Urban Freeways and the Interstate System," *California Law Review* 49 (1976): 408–9.

2. Daniel P. Moynihan, "New Roads and Urban Chaos," *Reporter*, April 14, 1960.

3. Raymond A. Mohl, "Ike and the Interstates: Creeping toward Comprehensive Planning," *Journal of Planning History* 2, no. 3 (August 2003): 246.

4. Raymond A. Mohl, "Ike and the Interstates," 246.

5. Richard A. Miller, "Expressway Blight," *Architectural Forum* 111 (October 1959): 159.

6. Gabriel Roth, "Why Involve the Private Sector in the Provision of Public Roads?," in *Street Smart: Competition, Entrepreneurship, and the Future of Roads*, ed. Gabriel Roth (Oakland, CA: The Independent Institute, 2006), 4.

7. Lewis Mumford, "The Highway and the City," *Architectural Record*, April 1958, 179.

8. Mumford, "Highway," 179.

9. Mumford, 182.

10. Mumford, 179, 181.

11. "Fighting the Freeway," *Newsweek*, March 25, 1968, 64.

12. Jerry L. Mashaw, "Legal Structure of Frustration: Alternative Strategies for Public Choice Concerning Federally Aided Highway Construction," *University of Pennsylvania Law Review* 122, no. 1 (November 1973): 71.

13. Moynihan, "New Roads."

14. Moynihan, "New Roads."

15. Alan Finder with Daniel Patrick Moynihan, "Westway, a Road That Was Paved with Mixed Intentions," *New York Times*, September 22, 1985.

16. Alan Finder with Daniel Patrick Moynihan, "Westway, a Road That Was Paved with Mixed Intentions."

17. Moynihan, "New Roads," 13.

18. Moynihan, 17.

19. Karl Detzer, "Our Great Big Highway Bungle," *Reader's Digest*, July 1960, 48–49.

20. Detzer, "Highway Bungle," 45.

21. Detzer, 48.

22. Jason Scott Smith, *Building New Deal Liberalism: The Political Economy of Public Works, 1933–1936* (New York: Cambridge University Press, 2006), 164.

23. Detzer, "Highway Bungle," 50.

24. Peter B. Dedek, *Hip to the Trip: A Cultural History of Route 66* (Albuquerque: University of New Mexico Press, 2007), 33.

25. Tom Lewis, *Divided Highways: Building the Interstate Highways, Transforming American Life* (New York: Viking, 1997), 128.

26. C. W. Enfield, "Right-of-Way Acquisition for the National Interstate System," *Better Roads*, June 1957, 35.

27. On the velvet glove—or brass knuckles—common to both urban renewal and urban transportation, see William H. Claire, "Urban Renewal and Transportation," *Traffic Quarterly* 13, no. 3 (July 1959): 414–22.

28. "The Great Uprooting," *Time*, March 24, 1958.

29. "Great Uprooting."

30. "Great Uprooting."

31. Russell Kirk, "The Bureau of Public Roads, Devastator," *National Review*, February 21, 1967, 202.

32. Kirk, "Bureau," 202.

33. Brian Ladd, *Autophobia: Love and Hate in the Automobile Age* (Chicago: University of Chicago Press, 2008), 129.

34. George F. Kennan, *Around the Cragged Hill: A Personal and Political Philosophy* (New York: W. W. Norton, 1993), 161.

35. Juan Cameron, "How the Interstate Changed the Face of the Nation," *Fortune*, July 1971, 81.

36. Ben Kelley, *The Pavers and the Paved* (New York: Donald W. Brown, 1971), 169–70.

37. Robert Moses, "Slums and City Planning," *Atlantic*, January 1945.

38. Richard J. Whalen, "The American Highway: Do We Know Where We're Going?," *Saturday Evening Post*, December 14, 1968, 64; Bruce L. Benson, "Do Holdout Problems Justify Compulsory Right-of-Way Purchase and Public Provision of Roads?," in *Street Smart: Competition, Entrepreneurship, and the Future of Roads*, ed. Gabriel Roth (Oakland, CA: The Independent Institute, 2006), 43–77.

39. A. Q. Mowbray, *Road to Ruin* (Philadelphia: J. B. Lippincott, 1969), 103.

40. Mowbray, *Road to Ruin*, 103–4.

41. Rose and Mohl, *Interstate*, xi.

42. Kelley, *Pavers*, viii.

43. William G. Wing, "The Concrete Juggernaut," *Audubon*, July–August 1966, 267.

44. Wing, "The Concrete Juggernaut," 270–71.

45. "Fighting the Freeway," 64; Richard Starnes, "Mortgaged to the Road Gang," *Field & Stream*, January 1969, 14.

46. Moynihan, "New Roads," 19.

47. Kelley, *Pavers*, 16.

48. Richard Hebert, "How the AAA Uses Its Members to Pave the Way for More Freeways," *Washingtonian*, June 1970, 36.

49. Lewis, *Divided Highways*, 220.

50. Albert R. Karr, "The Highway Lobby Aims to Prove There Is No Highway Lobby," *Wall Street Journal*, February 17, 1972.

51. Karr, "Highway Lobby."

52. Karr, "Highway Lobby,"

53. Kelley, *Pavers*, 17.

54. Kelley, 18.

55. Marvin G. Cline, "Urban Freeways and Social Structure," in *Transport Sociology: Social Aspects of Transport Planning*, ed. Enne de Boer (Oxford, UK: Pergamon Press, 1986), 44.

56. Cline, "Urban Freeways," 45.

57. Mowbray, *Road to Ruin*, 34.

58. Lewis, *Divided Highways*, 163.

59. Daniel Hapgood, "The Highwaymen," *Washington Monthly* 1, no. 2 (March 1969): 4.

60. John Steinbeck, *Travels with Charley in Search of America* (New York: Penguin, 2017/1962), 220.

61. Homer Bigart, "US Road Plans Periled by Rising Urban Hostility," *New York Times*, November 13, 1967.

62. Schwartz, "Urban Freeways," 486.

63. Mowbray, *Road to Ruin*, 33.

64. "The Revolt against Big-City Freeways," *US News & World Report*, January 1, 1962, 48.

65. Raymond A. Mohl, "Stop the Road: Freeway Revolts in American Cities," *Journal of Urban History* 30, no. 5 (July 2004): 679.

66. William Issel, "'Land Values, Human Values, and the Preservation of the City's Treasured Appearance': Environmentalism, Politics, and the San Francisco Freeway Revolt," *Pacific Historical Review* 68, no. 4 (November 1999): 627–28.

67. Griffin Estes, "The Panhandle Freeway and the Revolt That Saved the Park," *Hoodline*, March 29, 2015, https://hoodline.com/2015/03/panhandle-freeway-revolt.

68. Rose and Mohl, *Interstate*, 108.

69. Patricia A. House, "Relocation of Families Displaced by Expressway Development: Milwaukee Case Study," *Land Economics* 46, no. 1 (February 1970): 76.

70. Mohl, "Stop the Road," 683, 685, 687.

71. Whalen, "The American Highway," 22, 24. See also "An African American Community's Fight over I-40," Tennessee 4 Me, accessed November 29, 2018, http://www.tn4me.org/sapage.cfm/sa_id/248/era_id/8/major_id/12/minor_id/9/a_id/172.

72. Kelley, *Pavers*, 104.

73. Priscilla Dunhill, "An Expressway Named Destruction," *Architectural Forum* 126 (March 1967): 54, 56.

74. Tom Lewis has an absorbing account of this battle of New Orleans in *Divided Highways*, 179–210.

75. Earl Swift, *The Big Roads: The Untold Story of the Engineers, Visionaries, and Trailblazers Who Created the American Superhighways* (Boston: Houghton Mifflin Harcourt, 2011), 230.

76. Mohl, "Stop the Road," 689.

77. Mohl, 692.

78. "Hitting the Road," *Time*, April 9, 1965.

79. Marian Morton, "The Clark, Lee and Heights Freeways," Cleveland Heights Historical Society, accessed February 1, 2021, http://www.chhistory.org/FeatureStories.php?Story=BadIdeas&View=Freeways&section=1.

80. Mark H. Rose and Bruce E. Seely, "Getting the Interstate System Built: Road Engineers and the Implementation of Public Policy, 1955–1985," *Journal of Policy History* 2, no. 1 (January 1990): 37.

81. Kevin Fox Gotham, "Political Opportunity, Community Identity, and the Emergence of a Local Anti-Expressway Movement," *Social Problems* 46, no. 3 (August 1999): 344.

82. Suzanne Hogan, "Highway 71 and the Road to Compromise," KCUR-89.3, June 3, 2014, http://www.kcur.org/post/highway-71-and-road-compromise#stream/0.

83. Mowbray, *Road to Ruin*, 227.

84. "Fighting the Freeway," 64–65.

85. Elisheva Blas, "The Dwight D. Eisenhower National System of Interstate and Defense Highways: The Road to Success?," *History Teacher* 44, no. 1 (November 2010): 134.

86. Kelley, *Pavers*, 120.

87. Kelley, 112.

88. Whalen, "The American Highway," 58. For a look at the biracial nature of the Washington, DC activists, see Rice Odell, "To Stop Highways Some Citizens Take to the Streets," *Smithsonian* 3 (April 1972): 24–29.

89. Rose and Mohl, *Interstate*, 138.

90. Mowbray, *Road to Ruin*, 10.

91. Lewis, *Divided Highways*, 242.

92. Mowbray, *Road to Ruin*, 138.

93. Mowbray, 140.

94. "Fighting the Freeway," 64.

95. Kelley, *Pavers*, 111.

96. Rose and Mohl, *Interstate*, 110.

97. Rose and Mohl, 140.

98. Alan Boyd, interview by Zachary Schrag, October 2, 2001, accessed May 18, 2018, https://archive.org/stream/ms2214_s02_transcript_alan_boyd/ms2214_s02_transcript_alan_boyd_djvu.txt.

99. Alan Boyd, interview by Zachary Schrag. For an equivocal look at the debate in Baltimore, see Michael P. McCarthy, "Baltimore's Highway Wars Revisited," *Maryland Historical Magazine* 93, no. 2 (Summer 1998): 137–57.

100. Kelley, *Pavers*, 8.

101. Rose and Mohl, *Interstate*, 155–56.

102. Cameron, "How the Interstate Changed the Face of the Nation," 124.

103. Mowbray, *Road to Ruin*, 34. For Moynihan's role in the Nixon administration, see John Osborne, "Moynihan at Work in the White House," *New Republic*, March 22, 1969, 11–13.

104. Mowbray, *Road to Ruin*, 54, 58.

105. Federal-Aid Highway Act of 1968, Pub. L. No. 80-495, §508.

106. Kelley, *Pavers*, vii.

107. Cameron, "How the Interstate Changed the Face of the Nation," 124.

108. James A. Dunn Jr., "The Importance of Being Earmarked: Transport Policy and Highway Finance in Great Britain and the United States," *Comparative Studies in Society and History* 20, no. 1 (January 1978): 47.

109. Dunn, "The Importance of Being Earmarked," 50.

Chapter 5: Crumbling Infrastructure or Focus-Group Buzzwords?

1. "Infrastructure (n.)," Online Etymology Dictionary, accessed May 14, 2018, https:// www.etymonline.com/word/infrastructure.

2. US Department of Transportation Federal Highway Administration and Federal Transit Administration, *2015 Status of the Nation's Highways, Bridges, and Transit: Conditions and Performance* (Washington, DC: US Department of Transportation, 2016), https://www .fhwa.dot.gov/policy/2015cpr/pdfs/2015cpr.pdf.

3. Chris Edwards, "Who Owns US Infrastructure?," Cato Institute Tax & Budget Bulletin no. 78 (June 1, 2017), 2, 3.

4. Ronald D. Utt, "Infrastructure 'Crisis' Is about Socialism," Heritage Foundation, December 13, 2011, https://www.heritage.org/transportation/commentary/infrastructure -crisis-about-socialism.

5. Pat Choate and Susan Walter, *America in Ruins: The Decaying Infrastructure* (Durham, NC: Duke Press Paperbacks, 1983).

6. Randall Rothenberg, "The Idea Merchant," *New York Times Magazine*, May 3, 1987.

7. Rothenberg, "The Idea Merchant."

8. Choate and Walter, *America in Ruins*, 1.

9. Edward M. Gramlich, "Infrastructure Investment: A Review Essay," *Journal of Economic Literature* 32, no. 3 (September 1994): 1176–77.

10. Choate and Walter, *America in Ruins*, xi–xii.

11. Choate and Walter, xi, 9.

12. Choate and Walter, 69, 88.

13. John Herbers, "Nationwide Renewal of Public Works Urged," *New York Times*, April 5, 1981.

14. Melinda Beck, "The Decaying of America," *Newsweek*, August 2, 1982.

15. Center for an Urban Future, *Caution Ahead: Overdue Investments for New York's Aging Infrastructure* (New York: Center for an Urban Future, March 2014), 4, 8, https:// nycfuture.org/pdf/Caution-Ahead.pdf.

16. Martin Finucane, "Financier Ferber sentenced to 33 Months," AP News, December 19, 1996, https://www.apnews.com/5b6ef72f8272a572112561d895eafado.

17. Beck, "Decaying of America."

18. William F. Shughart II, "Katrinanomics: The Politics and Economics of Disaster Relief," *Public Choice* 127, no. 1-2 (2006): 32.

19. William F. Shughart II, "Disaster Relief as Bad Public Policy," *Independent Review* 15, no. 4 (Spring 2011): 523.

20. George F. Will, "Not All Infrastructure Is 'Crumbling,'" *Washington Post*, February 15, 2018.

21. American Society of Civil Engineers, *2017 Infrastructure Report Card: A Comprehensive Assessment of America's Infrastructure* (Reston, VA: ASCE, 2017), 2.

22. American Society of Civil Engineers, *2017 Infrastructure Report Card*, 6.

23. American Society of Civil Engineers, 7.

24. American Society of Civil Engineers, 7–8. The Congressional Progressive Caucus, backed by several economists of like bent, has endorsed a $2 trillion "investment" in in-

frastructure. See also "Economists in Support of a Substantial Increase in Infrastructure Investment," Economic Policy Institute, accessed May 12, 2018, https://www.epi.org/economists-in-support-of-a-substantial-increase-in-infrastructure-investment/.

25. American Society of Civil Engineers, *2017 Infrastructure Report Card*, 9.

26. Robert L. Reid, "The Infrastructure Crisis," *Civil Engineering* 78, no. 1 (January 2008): 43.

27. American Society of Civil Engineers, *2017 Infrastructure Report Card*, 31, 42, 54, 84.

28. American Society of Civil Engineers, 27–28.

29. Ryan Bourne, "Would More Government Infrastructure Spending Boost the US Economy?," Cato Institute Policy Analysis no. 812 (June 6, 2017), 18.

30. American Society of Civil Engineers, *2017 Infrastructure Report Card*, 29.

31. Business Roundtable, *Road to Growth: The Case for Investing in America's Transportation Infrastructure* (Washington, DC: Business Roundtable, September 2015), 5.

32. American Society of Civil Engineers, *2017 Infrastructure Report Card*, 9, 30.

33. American Society of Civil Engineers, 76.

34. American Society of Civil Engineers, 77.

35. Reid, "The Infrastructure Crisis," 45.

36. Reid, 46, 63.

37. Adam J. White, "Infrastructure Policy: Lessons from American History," *New Atlantis* 35 (Spring 2012): 5.

38. Debra Knopman et al., *Not Everything Is Broken: The Future of US Transportation and Water Infrastructure and Financing* (Santa Monica, CA: RAND Corporation, 2017), ix.

39. Knopman et al., *Not Everything Is Broken*, x.

40. David T. Hartgen, M. Gregory Fields, and Elizabeth San Jose, "Are Highways Crumbling? State and US Highway Performance Trends, 1989–2008," Reason Foundation Policy Study 407 (February 2013), 5, 7; David T. Hartgen, Baruch Feigenbaum, and M. Gregory Fields, "22nd Annual Highway Report," Reason Foundation, September 22, 2016, https://reason.org/policy-study/22nd-annual-highway-report-south-carolina-south-dakota-and-kansas-have-the-nations-most-cost-effective-state-highway-systemsalaska-ranks-last-just-ahead-of-new-jersey-and-hawaii/; M. Gregory Fields, Baruch Feigenbaum, and Spence Purnell, "Ranking the Best, Worst, Safest, and Most Expensive State Highway Systems—The 23rd Annual Highway Report," Reason Foundation, February 8, 2018, https://reason.org/policy-study/23rd-annual-highway-report.

41. Jeffrey R. Campbell and Thomas N. Hubbard, "The State of Our Interstates," *Chicago Fed Letter*, no. 264 (July 2009): 2.

42. Robert Krol, "America's Crumbling Infrastructure?," InsideSources, June 26, 2015, https://insidesources.com/opinion-americas-crumbling-infrastructure/. See also Robert Krol, "America's Infrastructure Isn't Crumbling: Some Facts on Highway, Road, and Bridge Conditions in the United States," Mercatus Center, May 16, 2017, https://www.mercatus.org/publications/urban-economics/america's-infrastructure-isn't-crumbling.

43. Henry Petroski, *The Road Taken: The History and Future of America's Infrastructure* (New York: Bloomsbury, 2017/2016), 193–94.

44. Hartgen, Fields, and San Jose, "Are Highways Crumbling?," 13; Fields, Feigenbaum, and Purnell, "Ranking the Best, Worst."

45. Hartgen, Fields, and San Jose, "Are Highways Crumbling?," 15; Fields, Feigenbaum, and Purnell, "Ranking the Best, Worst."

46. "US DOT Announces 2017 Roadway Fatalities Down," US Department of Transportation National Highway Traffic Safety Administration, October 3, 2018, https://www.nhtsa.gov/press-releases/us-dot-announces-2017-roadway-fatalities-down.

47. Fields, Feigenbaum, and Purnell, "Ranking the Best, Worst."

48. Josh Bivens, "The Short- and Long-Term Impact of Infrastructure Investments on Employment and Economic Activity in the US Economy," Economic Policy Institute Briefing Paper 374 (July 1, 2014), 15.

49. Elizabeth C. McNichol, "It's Time for States to Invest in Infrastructure," Center on Budget and Policy Priorities, August 10, 2017, 3.

50. Stephen Goldsmith and Jill Jamieson, *Tapping Private Financing and Delivery to Modernize America's Federal Water Resources*, Cambridge, MA: Ash Center for Democratic Governance and Innovation, Harvard Kennedy School, January 2017, 1.

51. Meagan Clark, "Aging US Power Grid Blacks Out More Than Any Other Developed Nation," *International Business Times*, July 17, 2014.

52. James Pethokoukis, "Driverless Cars Are as Much an Infrastructure Challenge as a Tech One," AEI, May 19, 2017, https://www.aei.org/economics/driverless-cars-are-as-much-an-infrastructure-challenge-as-a-tech-one/.

53. National Transportation Safety Board, *Collapse of I-35W Highway Bridge, Minneapolis, Minnesota, August 1, 2007* (Washington, DC: National Transportation Safety Board, November 14, 2008), xiii.

54. Gerald F. Seib, "In Crisis, Opportunity for Obama," *Wall Street Journal*, November 21, 2008; Reid, "The Infrastructure Crisis," 41.

55. "A Bridge Collapses," *New York Times*, August 5, 2007.

56. Lawrence Summers, "The Next President Should Make Infrastructure Spending a Priority," *Washington Post*, September 11, 2016.

57. Reid, "The Infrastructure Crisis," 44. The bridge had been rated "structurally deficient" and was slated for replacement in 2020. Matthew E. Kahn and David M. Levinson, "Fix It First, Expand It Second, Reward It Third: A New Strategy for America's Highways," The Hamilton Project, Discussion Paper 2011-03 (February 2011), 10.

58. "Collapse of the Interstate 5 Skagit River Bridge Following a Strike by an Oversize Combination Vehicle," National Transportation Safety Board, accessed September 19, 2018, https://www.ntsb.gov/investigations/AccidentReports/Pages/HAR1401.aspx.

59. Randal O'Toole, "The Truth about Infrastructure," *US News & World Report*, March 25, 2015.

60. Daniel Bier, "Throwing Money at Bridges Will Not Fix the Problem," Reason Foundation, June 17, 2013, https://reason.org/commentary/throwing-money-at-bridges-will-not/.

61. Robert Puentes et al., *The Way Forward: A New Economic Vision for America's Infrastructure* (New York: KKR, May 2014), 3, https://www.kkr.com/sites/default/files/KKR_New.Economic.Vision.for_.Americas.Infra_052014.pdf.

62. National Association of Manufacturers, *Building to Win*, 2016, 8.

63. Ronald D. Utt, "Infrastructure Stimulus Spending: Pandering to Organized Labor," Heritage Web Memo no. 3003 (September 8, 2010), 1.

64. Andrew Garin, "Putting America to Work, Where? The Limits of Infrastructure Construction as a Locally-Targeted Employment Policy," accessed May 12, 2018, https://scholar.harvard.edu/garin/publications/putting-america-work-where-limits-infrastructure-construction-locally-targeted. See also Edward L. Glaeser, "If You Build It ... Myths and Realities about America's Infrastructure Spending," *City Journal*, Summer 2016, https://www.city-journal.org/html/if-you-build-it-14606.html. For a paper arguing that US public highway spending "positively affects GDP" at two points—during the first two years of spending and then in the six- to eight-year frame—see Sylvain Leduc and Daniel Wilson, "Roads to Prosperity or Bridges to Nowhere? Theory and Evidence on the Impact of Public Infrastructure Investment," *NBER Macroeconomics Annual 2012* 27 (May 2013): 134.

65. Clifford Winston, "We Don't Need Another 'Bridge to Nowhere,'" *Boston Globe*, April 13, 2014.

66. Howard J. Shatz et al., *Highway Infrastructure and the Economy: Implications for Federal Policy* (Santa Monica, CA: RAND Corporation, 2011), 50.

67. Wilbur Ross and Peter Navarro, "Trump versus Clinton on Infrastructure," press release, October 27, 2016.

68. Andrew Fieldhouse, "Restore Full Employment with a Massive Infrastructure Program," Economic Policy Institute, December 14, 2012, https://www.epi.org/publication/restore-full-employment-massive-infrastructure/.

69. Veronique de Rugy and Matthew D. Mitchell, *Would More Infrastructure Spending Stimulate the Economy in 2017?* (Arlington, VA: Mercatus Center, January 2017), 9–10.

70. Stephen J. Entin, Huaqun Li, and Kadri Kallas-Zelek, "Evaluating the Economic Impact of Additional Government Infrastructure Spending," Tax Foundation Fiscal Fact no. 535 (January 2017); Frédéric Bastiat, "That Which Is Seen, and That Which Is Not Seen," Mises Institute, December 18, 2019, https://mises.org/library/which-seen-and-which-not-seen.

71. Robert Krol, "Public Infrastructure and State Economic Development," *Economic Development Quarterly* 9, no. 4 (November 1995): 337.

72. Atif Ansar et al., "Does Infrastructure Investment Lead to Economic Growth or Economic Fragility? Evidence from China," *Oxford Review of Economic Policy* 32, no. 5 (2016): 385.

73. Ansar et al., "Infrastructure Investment," 360.

74. James Pethokoukis, "The Dodgy Economics of Infrastructure Spending on 'Megaprojects,'" AEIdeas, June 2, 2015, https://www.aei.org/economics/the-dodgy-economics-of-infrastructure-spending-on-megaprojects/.

75. US General Accounting Office, "The Davis-Bacon Act Should Be Repealed," April 27, 1979.

76. Tracy Miller and Megan Hansen, *How to Fix Roads and Bridges without Increasing the Fuel Tax: Reform Federal Highway Policy and Use the Savings for Roads* (Arlington, VA: Mercatus Center, July 2015), 4.

77. Mike Clark, "The Effects of Prevailing Wage Laws: A Comparison of Individual Workers' Wages Earned on and off Prevailing Wage Construction Projects," *Journal of Labor Research* 26, no. 4 (Fall 2005): 732.

78. Miller and Hansen, *How to Fix Roads and Bridge*s, 2.

79. Robert Krol, *Political Incentives and Transportation Funding* (Arlington, VA: Mercatus Center, July 2015), 10.

80. Krol, *Political Incentives and Transportation Funding*, 4.

81. Martin Wachs, "When Planners Lie with Numbers," *APA Journal* 55, no. 4 (Autumn 1989): 477.

82. Bent Flyvbjerg, Mette Skamris Holm, and Soren Buhl, "Underestimating Costs in Public Works Projects: Error or Lie?," *Journal of the American Planning Association* 68, no. 3 (Summer 2002): 279.

83. Flyvbjerg, Holm, and Buhl, "Underestimating Costs," 283, 286.

84. Flyvbjerg, Holm, and Buhl, 279.

85. Flyvbjerg, Holm, and Buhl, 288, 290.

86. Flyvbjerg, Holm, and Buhl, 279.

87. "Reinventing Michigan's Infrastructure: Better Roads Drive Better Jobs," A Special Message from Governor Rick Snyder, State of Michigan Executive Office, October 26, 2011, 1.

88. "Reinventing Michigan's Infrastructure," 2.

89. David Eggert, "Higher Fuel, Vehicle Taxes Start Sunday in Michigan," *Crain's Detroit Business*, December 31, 2016.

90. Robert S. Kirk, William J. Mallett, and David Randall Peterman, "Transportation Spending under an Earmark Ban," Congressional Research Service, January 4, 2017, 6.

91. Alison Acosta Fraser and Jonathan Swanson, "Federal Highway Spending Jumps the Shark," Heritage Foundation, August 4, 2004, https://www.heritage.org/budget-and-spending/report/federal-highway-spending-jumps-the-shark; Gian-Claudia Sciara, "Peering Inside the Pork Barrel: A Study of Congressional Earmarking in Transportation," *Public Works Management & Policy* 17, no. 3 (2012): 218.

92. Sciara, "Peering Inside the Pork Barrel," 219.

93. R. Richard Geddes, *The Road to Renewal: Private Investment in US Transportation Infrastructure* (Washington, DC: AEI Press, 2011), 2–3.

94. "End Sought for 'Bridge to Nowhere,'" *New York Times*, September 22, 2007; White, "Infrastructure Policy," 6.

95. Diane Whitmore Schanzenbach, Ryan Nunn, and Greg Nantz, *If You Build It: A Guide to the Economics of Infrastructure Investment* (Washington, DC: The Hamilton Project/Brookings Institution, February 2017), 7; Kirk, Mallett, and Peterman, "Transportation Spending," 1.

96. Pengyu Zhu and Jeffrey R. Brown, "Donor States and Donee States: Investigating Redistribution of the US Federal-Aid Highway Program 1974–2008," Boise State University ScholarWorks, January 1, 2013, 3.

97. Zhu and Brown, "Donor States and Donee States," 8–9.

98. Brian Knight, "Parochial Interests and the Centralized Provision of Local Public Goods: Evidence from Congressional Voting on Transportation Projects," *Journal of Public Economics* 88, no. 3-4 (March 2004): 845.

99. Zhu and Brown, "Donor States and Donee States," 4. Minimum apportionment was no twenty-first-century innovation; the 1921 Federal-Aid Highway Act guaranteed each state at least half of one percent of the funds spent.

100. Zhu and Brown, 30.

101. Knight, "Parochial Interests," 865.

102. Patrick J. Sellers, "Fiscal Consistency and Federal District Spending in Congressional Elections," *American Journal of Political Science* 41, no. 3 (July 1997): 1024–41.

103. Emily Goff, "How to Fix America's Infrastructure," Heritage Foundation, June 2, 2014, https://www.heritage.org/transportation/commentary/how-fix-americas -infrastructure.

104. Petroski, *The Road Taken*, 233. Several, mostly western, state legislatures, among them Arizona and Colorado, have over the years passed resolutions asking that the federal government turn over federal fuel tax monies to the states in which they are collected. See Gabriel Roth, "Liberating the Roads: Reforming US Highway Policy," Cato Institute Policy Analysis no. 538 (March 17, 2005), 17.

105. Senator Mike Lee, "The Transportation Empowerment Act," press release, July 13, 2018.

106. Aaron M. Renn, "Beyond Repair: America's Infrastructure Crisis Is Local," Manhattan Institute Issue Brief, October 22, 2015, 7.

107. Jeremy Kutner, "Downtown Need a Makeover? More Cities Are Razing Urban Highways," *Christian Science Monitor*, March 2, 2011.

108. Robert A. Peck, "The Fall and Rise of Public Works," in *Daniel Patrick Moynihan: The Intellectual in Public Life*, ed. Robert A. Katzmann (Washington, DC: Woodrow Wilson Center Press, 1998), 80.

109. ISTEA authorized responsible officials to designate about 150,000 miles of American road part of a "National Highway System," consisting of the interstates as well as other "roadways important to the nation's economy, defense, and mobility." "National Highway System," US Department of Transportation Federal Highway Administration, accessed May 18, 2018, https://www.fhwa.dot.gov/planning/national_highway_system/.

110. Intermodal Surface Transportation Efficiency Act of 1991, Pub. L. No. 102-240, § 1105(a)(1).

111. Randal O'Toole, "ISTEA: A Poisonous Brew for American Cities," Cato Institute Policy Analysis no. 287 (November 5, 1997), 1.

112. Council on Foreign Relations, *Road to Nowhere: Failing U.S. Transportation Infrastructure* (New York: Council on Foreign Relations, January 2016), 7.

113. Veronique de Rugy and Tracy Miller, *Improving Funding and Management of Surface Transportation Infrastructure* (Arlington, VA: Mercatus Center, 2017), 7.

114. Kate Miller-Wilson, "How Many Miles Do Americans Drive Per Year?," LoveToKnow .com, accessed November 27, 2018, https://cars.lovetoknow.com/about-cars/how-many -miles-do-americans-drive-per-year.

115. O'Toole, "ISTEA," 28.

116. Raymond A. Mohl, "The Expressway Teardown Movement in American Cities: Rethinking Postwar Highway Policy in the Post-Interstate Era," *Journal of Planning History* 11, no. 1 (2012): 92. See also Jack Skelley, "Tear Down That Freeway!," *Urban Land*, April 20, 2011, https://urbanland.uli.org/sustainability/tear-down-that-freeway/.

117. Nicole Gelinas, "Lessons of Boston's Big Dig," *City Journal*, Autumn 2007, https://www.city-journal.org/html/lessons-boston's-big-dig-13049.html.

118. Lew Powell, "How Terry Sanford Greenlighted the Big Dig," *North Carolina Miscellany*, October 12, 2016, https://blogs.lib.unc.edu/ncm/2016/10/12/divide-hightways/.

119. Noah Bierman, "No Big Dig Copycats," *Boston Globe*, March 4, 2008.

120. Bierman, "No Big Dig Copycats."

121. Federation of Tax Administrators, "State Motor Fuel Tax Rates," accessed May 14, 2018, https://www.taxadmin.org/assets/docs/Research/Rates/mf.pdf.

122. William F. Shughart II and Kristian Fors, "California's Soaring Gas Taxes Aren't Even Going to the Roads," Foundation for Economic Education (FEE), January 14, 2018, https://fee.org/articles/californias-soaring-gas-taxes-arent-even-going-to-the-roads/.

123. "Raise the Gas Tax to Fix America's Roads," *New York Times*, January 10, 2015.

124. "Raise the Gas Tax."

125. R. Richard Geddes and Brad Wassink, "Bring Highway Funding Up to Speed," *Wall Street Journal*, June 17, 2014.

126. Reid, "The Infrastructure Crisis," 64.

127. Mary Lunetta, "Don't Be Fooled: Annual Fees on Electric Vehicle Drivers Are Not 'Fair,'" Sierra Club, April 2, 2018, https://www.sierraclub.org/compass/2018/04/don-t-be-fooled-annual-fees-electric-vehicle-drivers-are-not-fair.

128. Lunetta, "Don't Be Fooled."

129. Council on Foreign Relations, *Road to Nowhere*, 12.

130. For more on the French experience, see Alain Bonnfous, "The Economic Regulation of French Highways: Just How Private Did They Become?," *Transport Policy* 41 (2015): 33–41.

131. Mike Allen Euritt et al., "An Overview of Highway Privatization," Research Report 1281-1, Center for Transportation Research, University of Texas at Austin, February 1994, 41.

132. Chris Edwards, "Take the Public-Private Road to Efficiency," *Wall Street Journal*, February 19, 2013.

133. Chad Lonski and Baruch Feigenbaum, "Solving Regional Traffic Congestion through Pricing," Reason Foundation, March 14, 2017, https://reason.org/commentary/solving-regional-traffic-congestion/.

134. Business Roundtable, *Road to Growth*, 5.

135. Robert W. Poole Jr., "Examining the Claims about America's Crumbling Infrastructure," Reason Foundation, March 6, 2017, https://reason.org/commentary/examining-the-claims-about-americas-crumbling-infrastructure/.

136. Geddes, *The Road to Renewal*, 1.

137. Leighton Walter Kille, "Fundamental Law of Road Congestion: Evidence from U.S. Cities," *Journalist's Resource*, Harvard Kennedy School, November 17, 2014,

https://journalistsresource.org/studies/environment/transportation/fundamental-law-road-congestion-evidence-u-s-cities.

138. Gilles Duranton and Matthew A. Turner, "The Fundamental Law of Road Congestion: Evidence from US Cities," *American Economic Review* 101, no. 6 (October 2011): 2616–52.

139. Bill Lockyer, "Public Funds Should Not Be Used to Build Toll Roads," *Los Angeles Times*, March 19, 1991.

140. Bill Lockyer, "Public Funds."

141. Robert W. Poole Jr., "Resolving Gridlock in Southern California," *Transportation Quarterly* 42, no. 4 (October 1988): 520.

142. See Baruch Feigenbaum, "Widening of Alabama Bridge Shows Private Infrastructure Ownership Works," Reason Foundation, July 21, 2017, https://reason.org/commentary/widening-of-alabama-bridge-shows-private-infrastructure-ownership-works/.

143. Daryl S. Fleming, "Dispelling the Myths: Toll and Fuel Tax Collection Costs in the 21st Century," Reason Foundation Policy Study 409 (November 2012), 48.

144. Fleming, "Dispelling the Myths," 1.

145. Fleming, 18–19, 23.

146. Fleming, Executive Summary.

147. Fleming, 23.

148. Robert W. Poole Jr., "How and Why to Toll the Interstates that Need Reconstruction," Reason Foundation, June 9, 2017, https://reason.org/commentary/how-and-why-to-toll-the-interstates-that-need-reconstruction/.

149. Robert W. Poole Jr., "Rebuilding and Modernizing Wisconsin's Interstates with Toll Financing," Reason Foundation and Wisconsin Policy Research Institute Policy Study 398 (September 2011), 2.

150. Robert W. Poole Jr., "The Feasibility of Modernizing the Interstate Highway System via Toll Finance," *Research in Transportation Economics* 44 (2014): 12.

151. Poole, "Rebuilding and Modernizing," 2.

152. Poole, "Feasibility," 14. See also Robert W. Poole Jr., "Interstate 2.0: Modernizing the Interstate Highway System via Toll Finance," Reason Foundation Policy Study 423 (September 2013), 14.

153. Poole, "Interstate 2.0," 15, 19.

154. Glaeser, "If You Build It."

155. Poole, "Interstate 2.0," 26.

156. Joshua Schank and Nikki Rudnick-Thorpe, "End of the Highway Trust Fund? Long-Term Options for Funding Federal Surface Transportation," *Transportation Research Record*, no. 2221 (2011): 4.

157. Daniel C. Vock, "Aging Infrastructure," *Sage Business Researcher*, February 13, 2017.

158. "Welcome to OReGO!," Oregon Department of Transportation, accessed November 19, 2018, https://www.myorego.org/.

159. Vock, "Aging Infrastructure."

160. Schank and Rudnick-Thorpe, "End of the Highway Trust Fund?," 5.

161. Ashley Langer, Vikram Maheshri, and Clifford Winston, "From Gallons to Miles: A Disaggregate Analysis of Automobile Travel and Externality Taxes," *Journal of Public Economics* 152 (2017): 41.

162. Schank and Rudnick-Thorpe, "End of the Highway Trust Fund?," 5.

163. Schank and Rudnick-Thorpe, 5.

164. Chris Edwards, "Crumbling Infrastructure?" *National Review Online*, March 20, 2013, https://www.nationalreview.com/2013/03/crumbling-infrastructure-chris-edwards/.

165. Randal O'Toole, "Secretary of Behavior Modification," Cato at Liberty, May 28, 2009, https://www.cato.org/blog/secretary-behavior-modification.

166. William Newman, "It's Time to Allow Tolling on All Federal-aid Highways," Reason Foundation, May 3, 2017, https://reason.org/commentary/its-time-to-allow-tolling-on-all-federal-aid-highways/.

167. Aman Batheja, "A G.O.P. Shift against Toll Roads in Texas," *Texas Tribune*, July 3, 2014.

168. Batheja, "A G.O.P. Shift."

169. Jesse Gosselin, "Crash Survivor Recalls Accident That Removed Connecticut's Tolls," WTNH.com, April 24, 2015, https://www.wtnh.com/news/politics/crash-survivor-recalls-accident-that-removed-connecticuts-tolls/.

170. Ed Regan and Steve Brown, "Building the Case for Tolling the Interstates," *Tollways*, Spring 2011, 4.

171. Bourne, "Would More Government," 20.

172. Joan Lowry, "Senate Democrats Propose $1 Trillion Infrastructure Plan," Associated Press, January 24, 2017.

173. Euritt et al., "Overview," 27.

174. Johanna Zmud and Carlos Arce, *Compilation of Public Opinion Data on Tolls and Road Pricing* (Washington, DC: Transportation Research Board, 2008), 1.

175. Zmud and Arce, *Compilation*, 41, 45.

176. Zmud and Arce, 3.

177. Zmud and Arce, 17.

178. Zmud and Arce, 47.

179. Zmud and Arce, 2.

180. Poole, "How and Why to Toll."

181. See Poole, "Resolving Gridlock in Southern California," 499–527.

182. One seldom-discussed advantage of private ownership of roads—at least an advantage to the exchequer and to other property owners—is that the private owners would be assessed property taxes, which presumably would result in lower tax burdens for others in the same jurisdiction. For an examination of the revenue potential of privatization in Minnesota, see Jason Junge and David Levinson, "Property Tax on Privatized Roads," *Research in Transportation Business & Management* 7 (2013): 35–42.

183. Bruce Seely, "A Republic Bound Together," *Wilson Quarterly* 17, no. 1 (Winter 1993): 39.

184. Robert W. Poole Jr. and Austill Stuart, "Federal Barriers to Private Capital Investment in U.S. Infrastructure," Reason Foundation Policy Brief 138 (January 2017), 2.

185. Geddes, *The Road to Renewal*, 6.

186. Geddes, 25.

187. Petroski, *The Road Taken*, 263.

188. Quoted in Chris Edwards, "Rethinking Federal Highway and Transit Funding," Cato Institute, May 6, 2014, https://www.cato.org/testimony/rethinking-federal-highway -transit-funding.

189. Petroski, *The Road Taken*, 268.

190. Edwards, "Rethinking Federal Highway and Transit Funding." For an examination of the Mexican experience with PPPs, which has proceeded through stages of high optimism, discouragement, nationalization, and then a renewed privatization and profitability, see Samuel Carpintero and Jose A. Gomez-Ibañez, "Mexico's Private Toll Road Program Reconsidered," *Transport Policy* 18, no. 6 (November 2011): 848–55.

191. Robert W. Poole Jr., "Indiana Can Serve as a Model for Private Infrastructure Investment," Reason Foundation, August 14, 2017, https://reason.org/commentary/indiana -can-serve-as-a-model-for-private-infrastructure-investment/; see also Robert W. Poole Jr., "Annual Privatization Report 2016: Surface Transportation," Reason Foundation, April 2016, 8, https://reason.org/wp-content/uploads/2016/08/apr-2016-surface-transportation .pdf.

192. Geddes, *The Road to Renewal*, 73.

193. For responses to the most common criticisms of PPPs, see Robert W. Poole Jr., "Toll Concession Public Private Partnerships: Frequently Asked Questions," Reason Foundation, October 5, 2016, https://reason.org/faq/toll-concession-public-private-partnerships -frequently-asked-questions/.

194. "South Norfolk Jordan Bridge," accessed September 19, 2018, http://www.snjb.net/.

195. "LBJ Express Project," LBJ TEXPress Lanes, accessed September 25, 2018, https:// www.lbjtexpress.com/about-us/lbj-express-project; "LBJ Highway in Dallas, Texas," Ferrovial, accessed September 25, 2018, https://www.ferrovial.com/en-us/business/projects /lbj-expressway/.

196. Bill Hethcock, "LBJ Express 'Lexus Lanes' Seem to Be Working," *Dallas Business Journal*, September 16, 2016, https://www.bizjournals.com/dallas/news/2016/09/16/lbj -express-lexus-lanes-seem-to-be-working.html.

197. "LBJ Express," accessed September 25, 2018, https://cintra.us/ourprojects/lbj -express/.

198. Euritt et al., "Overview." The Dulles Greenway, familiar to motorists near the nation's capital, is not really a PPP. It's a thirteen-mile privately built and financed (to the tune of $350 million) but state-regulated toll road in the suburbs of Washington, DC, that opened in 1995. Geddes compares it to a "facility built under a nineteenth-century toll road charter." He also notes that unlike government roads, the land for which is often confiscated by eminent domain, the investor-owners of the Dulles Greenway negotiated with landowners and paid them market price. Under the original agreement, the road was to become property of the state of Virginia in 2036, but this was extended to 2056. See Geddes, *The Road to Renewal*, 36.

199. Council on Foreign Relations, *Road to Nowhere*, 5.

200. Council on Foreign Relations, 5.

201. Council on Foreign Relations, 6.

202. Council on Foreign Relations, 6.

203. Council on Foreign Relations, 3.

204. Edwards, "Rethinking Federal Highway and Transit Funding."

205. Business Roundtable, *Road to Growth*, 4.

206. Business Roundtable, 13.

207. Business Roundtable, 11.

208. George F. Will, "Infrastructure Spending Won't Transform America," *Washington Post*, February 15, 2018.

209. Emily Badger, "Joe Biden Is Very Angry at Us for Scrimping on Our Infrastructure," *Washington Post*, October 21, 2014.

210. National Association of Manufacturers, *Building to Win*, 5.

211. National Association of Manufacturers, 5.

212. National Association of Manufacturers, 6, 8–9.

213. National Association of Manufacturers, 11.

214. National Association of Manufacturers, 15.

215. National Association of Manufacturers, 16.

216. National Association of Manufacturers, 29.

217. National Association of Manufacturers, 28.

218. Renn, "Beyond Repair," 2.

219. James M. Bickley, "The Federal Excise Tax on Gasoline and the Highway Trust Fund: A Short History," Congressional Research Service, September 7, 2012, 9.

220. Robert Krol, *Can a Federal Public Infrastructure Bank Improve Highway Funding?* (Arlington, VA: Mercatus Center, January 2017), 4.

221. White, "Infrastructure Policy," 30–31.

222. "Summary of the National Environmental Policy Act," Environmental Protection Agency, accessed September 19, 2018, https://www.epa.gov/laws-regulations/summary -national-environmental-policy-act.

223. Chris Edwards, "Removing Barriers to Infrastructure Investment," Cato at Liberty, January 9, 2017, https://www.cato.org/blog/removing-barriers-infrastructure-investment.

224. "Transcript: Donald Trump's Victory Speech," *New York Times*, November 9, 2016.

225. Hillary Clinton, "Remarks on Investing in Infrastructure during the First 100 Days in Office," press release, May 25, 2016.

226. Adie Tomer and Joseph W. Kane, "Short- and Long-Term Strategies to Renew American Infrastructure," Brookings Big Ideas for America, October 26, 2016, https://www .brookings.edu/research/short-and-long-term-strategies-to-renew-american-infrastructure/.

227. Ross and Navarro, "Trump Versus Clinton."

228. Ellen Brown, "Trump's $1 Trillion Infrastructure Plan," *Web of Debt Blog*, November 14, 2016, https://ellenbrown.com/2016/11/14/trumps-1-trillion-infrastructure-plan -lincoln-had-a-bolder-solution/.

229. Kathryn A. Wolfe and Lauren Gardner, "Conservatives vs. Trump's Infrastructure Plan," *Politico*, November 11, 2016, https://www.politico.com/story/2016/11/conservatives-vs -trumps-infrastructure-plan-231221.

230. Alan S. Blinder and Alan B. Krueger, "Trump's Infrastructure Mistake," *Wall Street Journal*, December 19, 2016.

231. Vock, "Aging Infrastructure."

232. Melanie Zanona, "Chao Commits to Multiple Funding Tools for Trump's Infrastructure Plan," *The Hill*, January 11, 2017, https://thehill.com/policy/transportation/313814 -chao-commits-to-multiple-funding-tools-for-trumps-infrastructure-plan.

233. Julia Limitone, "Taxpayers Off the Hook with Trump's Infrastructure Plan," *Fox Business*, January 16, 2017, http://www.foxbusiness.com/features/taxpayers-off-the-hook -with-trumps-infrastructure-plan.

234. Jay Landers, "Trump Administration Highlights Need for Infrastructure Spending, Permitting Reform," *Civil Engineering* 87, no. 7 (July/August 2017): 13.

235. "Executive Order 13807 of August 15, 2017, Establishing Discipline and Accountability in the Environmental Review and Permitting Process for Infrastructure Projects," *Code of Federal Regulations*, title 3 (2017): 40,463–69, https://www.federalregister.gov/documents /2017/08/24/2017-18134/establishing-discipline-and-accountability-in-the-environmental -review-and-permitting-process-for.

236. Mary Salmonsen, "One Federal Decision will save time, money in infrastructure permitting," *Construction Dive*, Dec. 15, 2021, https://www.constructiondive.com/news /one-federal-decision-construction-save-time-money-environmental-review-infrastructure -permit/611559/.

237. The White House, "Legislative Outline for Rebuilding Infrastructure in America," February 12, 2018.

238. Bourne, "Would More Government," 17.

239. Wolfe and Gardner, "Conservatives."

240. Robert W. Poole Jr., "Assessing the White House Infrastructure Plan," *Surface Transportation Innovations*, no. 172 (February 2018).

241. Randal O'Toole, "The Trouble with Trump's Infrastructure Ambitions," *New York Daily News*, November 30, 2016.

242. Wolfe and Gardner, "Conservatives."

243. Wolfe and Gardner, "Conservatives."

244. David Nott, email to the author, "Trump's Infrastructure Plan: Privatization, Deregulation, and More," February 14, 2018. Poole has insisted that any interstate toll revenue be dedicated solely to the capital and operating costs of the roads themselves and not be put to nongermane uses. Robert W. Poole Jr., "Removing Barriers to Public-Private Partnership Infrastructure Projects," Reason Foundation, February 9, 2017, https://reason.org/commentary/removing-barriers-to-public-private-partnership-infrastructure-projects/.

245. "FHWA Seeks Applicants for Failed Tolling Pilot Program," NATSO, accessed May 22, 2018, https://www.natso.com/articles/articles/view/fhwa-seeks-applicants-for-failed -tolling-pilot-program.

246. Reid, "The Infrastructure Crisis," 65.

Conclusion

1. T. S. Eliot, *The Rock: A Pageant Play, Written for Performance at Sadler's Wells Theatre 28 May–9 June 1934 on Behalf of the Forty-Five Churches Fund of the Diocese of London* (New York: Harcourt, Brace), 1934.

2. Robert Poole, "Don't Abolish the Highway Trust Fund," Reason Foundation, June 5, 2015, https://www.reason.org/commentary/dont-abolish-the-highway-trust-fund.

3. Mary C. Jalonick, "What's Inside the Senate's Bipartisan Infrastructure Bill," AP News, August 11, 2021, https://apnews.com/article/joe-biden-business-bill.

4. "Fact Sheet: President Biden Announces Support for the Bipartisan Infrastructure Framework," The White House, June 24, 2021, https://www.whitehouse.gov/briefing-room /statements-releases/2021/06/24/fact-sheet-president-biden-announces-support-for-the -bipartisan-infrastructure-framework/.

5. Peter Suderman, "The Bipartisan Infrastructure Bill Is a Sham," *Reason*, August 10, 2021, https://reason.com/2021/08/10/bipartisan-infrastructure-1-trillion-sham -reconciliation-bill/.

6. Lisa Mascaro, "Big Win for $1T Infrastructure Bill: Dems, GOP Come Together," AP News, August 10, 2021, https://apnews.com/article/senate-infrastructure-bill-politics -joe-biden-a431f8c9f3f113b661cb3526512fc4e0.

7. House Committee on Transportation and Infrastructure, "Chair DeFazio Closes House Floor Debate on the Infrastructure and Jobs Act," News release, September 28, 2021, https://transportation.house.gov/news/press-releases.

8. Adam Smith, *The Nature and Causes of the Wealth of Nations*, in *The Works of Adam Smith*, vol. 4 (London: W. Strahan and T. Cadell, 1811), 95–96.

9. Mary E. Peters, foreword to *Street Smart: Competition, Entrepreneurship, and the Future of Roads*, ed. Gabriel Roth (Oakland, CA: The Independent Institute, 2006), xv.

10. Gabriel Roth, "Toll Roads to the Rescue," Independent Institute, October 24, 2007, https://www.independent.org/news/article.asp?id=2056.

11. "Interstate Highway System Fact Sheet—June 2021," TRIP (The Road Information Program), https://tripnet.org/reports/interstate-highway-system-fact-sheet-june-2021.

12. Robert W. Poole Jr. and C. Kenneth Orski, "HOT Networks: A New Plan for Congestion Relief and Better Transit," in *Street Smart: Competition, Entrepreneurship, and the Future of Roads*, ed. Gabriel Roth, 452.

13. David Shepardson, "U.S. Traffic Deaths Soar to 38,680 in 2020; Highest Yearly Total since 2007," Reuters, June 3, 2021, https://www.reuters.com/world/us/us-traffic-deaths-soar -38680-2020-highest-yearly-total-since-2007-2021-06-03/.

14. "World Report on Road Traffic Injury Prevention," World Health Organization, accessed August 12, 2021, https://www.who.int/violence_injury_prevention/publications /road_traffic/world_report/main_messages_en.pdf.

15. John Semmens, "Improving Road Safety by Privatizing Driver Testing and Licensing," in *Street Smart: Competition, Entrepreneurship, and the Future of Roads*, ed. Gabriel Roth, 97–113.

16. Gabriel Roth, "Why Involve the Private Sector in the Provision of Public Roads?" in *Street Smart: Competition, Entrepreneurship, and the Future of Roads*, ed. Gabriel Roth, 14.

17. "North America Electronic Toll Collection (etc) Market—Growth, Trends, CO-VID-19 Impact, and Forecasts (2021-2026)," Mordor Intelligence, accessed August 16, 2021, https://www.mordorintelligence.com/industry-reports/north-america-electronic-toll-collection-market.

18. John Semmens, "De-Socializing the Roads," in *Street Smart: Competition, Entrepreneurship, and the Future of Roads*, ed. Gabriel Roth, 35.

19. David Levinson, "The Political Economy of Private Roads," in *Street Smart: Competition, Entrepreneurship, and the Future of Roads*, ed. Gabriel Roth, 93.

20. Semmens, "De-Socializing the Roads," 39.

21. Semmens, "De-Socializing the Roads," 37. For more on how a private highway system might work in practice, see Gabriel Roth, "Senate Finance Committee Testimony on Financing Infrastructure," US Senate Committee on Finance, Hearing on Financing 21st-Century Infrastructure, May 17, 2011, https://www.finance.senate.gov/hearings/financing-21st-century-infrastructure.

22. Levinson, "The Political Economy of Private Roads," 87.

23. Edward C. Sullivan, "HOT Lanes in Southern California," in *Street Smart: Competition, Entrepreneurship, and the Future of Roads*, ed. Gabriel Roth, 189.

24. Sullivan, 199.

25. Sullivan, 197.

26. Sullivan, 216–17.

27. Gopinath Menon, "Congestion Pricing: The Singapore Experience," in *Street Smart: Competition, Entrepreneurship, and the Future of Roads*, ed. Gabriel Roth, 117.

28. "FasTrak: San Diego Region," accessed August 17, 2021, https://511sd.com/fastrak511sd/fastrakhome.

29. Sullivan, "HOT Lanes in Southern California," 218.

30. Peter Samuel, "The Way Forward to the Private Provision of Roads," in *Street Smart: Competition, Entrepreneurship, and the Future of Roads*, ed. Gabriel Roth, 503.

31. Gabriel Roth, "Who Should Pay for Highways?" *Sacramento Bee*, December 28, 2011.

Index

A

lAAA (American Automobile Association), 76, 100, 126, 130, 134, 157–58, 218

AASHO (American Association of State Highway Officials), 76, 91, 137

AASHTO (American Association of State Highway and Transportation Officials), 76

Adams, Henry Carter, 14, 24

Adams, John Quincy, 3, 38–42

Adams, Louisa, 39

AET (all-electronic tolling), 210–13

African Americans: negative impact of highway building on, 162–63, 165; roads built by, 88–90

airports, 207, 219, 222, 236; *see also* aviation

Alaska: Bridge to Nowhere, 34, 194–95; fuel tax in, 213

Albert, Carl, 136

Albjerg, Victor L., 44

all-electronic tolling (AET), 210–13

Allen, Henry J., 102

Allis-Chalmers, 125

Altshuler, Alan, 148–49

America in Ruins (Choate and Walter), 174–75

American Association of State Highway and Transportation Officials (AASHTO), 76

American Association of State Highway Officials (AASHO), 76, 91, 137

American Automobile Association (AAA), 76, 100, 126, 130, 134, 157–58, 218

American Concrete Institute, 116

American Dream, 130

American Farm Bureau Federation, 129–30

American Institute of Certified Planners, 190

American Motor League, 71

American Petroleum Institute, 100, 126

American Railroad Journal, 37–38

American Recovery and Reinvestment Act (2009), 187

American Road Builders Association, 76, 167

American Society of Civil Engineers (ASCE), 178–82, 184, 185–86, 204, 225, 231

American System, 24, 31–32, 223

American Trucking Association, 117–18

Ames, Fisher, 28

Ansar, Atif, 188

Arce, Carlos, 217–18

Arizona Department of Transportation, 239

Army of the Commonweal of Christ (Coxey's Army), 61–63

ASCE (American Society of Civil Engineers), 178–82, 184, 185–86, 204, 225, 231

asphalt, 60

Asquith, Herbert, 81

Aswell, James B., 93

Atlanta, traffic congestion in, 208

Austin, Archibald, 32

Autobahn, 113, 122, 129

Automobile Association of America, 91

automobiles, 56, 71–73, 75–76, 84, 105; alternative-fuel vehicles, 204; deaths and injuries caused by, 122, 127, 183, 239; electric vehicles, 204, 205–6, 236; fuel efficiency and emissions, 204–5; licensing fees, 101; in Los Angeles, 117; military, 95; Model A/Model T, 107; ownership of, 86; private testing of, 239; registration fees for, 80–82, 225–26; in the Roaring '20s, 109; self-driving, 184–85; used for mail delivery, 75

automotive taxes, 114–15; *see also* fuel taxes; taxation

aviation, 179, 194; *see also* airports

About the Author

JAMES T. BENNETT is Eminent Scholar, the William P. Snavely Chair of Political Economy and Public Policy in the Department of Economics, and Director of the John M. Olin Institute for Employment Practice and Policy at George Mason University. He received his Ph.D. in economics from Case Western Reserve University, and he has been a McKinsey Scholar at Columbia University, Ford Motor Company Scholar and Federal Reserve Bank of Cleveland Fellow; and he has specialized in research related to public policy issues, the economics of government and bureaucracy, labor unions, and health charities.

Co-editor of the books, *Information and Technology and the World Bank* (with Daphne Gottlieb Taras and Anthony M. Townsend) plus *What Do Unions Do? A Twenty-Year Perspective* and *The Future of Private Sector Unionism in the United States* (both with Bruce E. Kaufman), he is the author of *Corporate Welfare: Crony Capitalism That Enriches the Rich*; *The Doomsday Lobby: Hype and Panic from Sputniks, Martians, and Marauding Meteors*; *Health Research Charities: Image and Reality*; *The History and Politics of Public Radio: A Comprehensive Analysis of Taxpayer-Financed U.S. Broadcasting*; *Information Technology and the World of Work*; *Mandate Madness: How Congress Forces States and Localities to Do its Bidding and Pay for the Privilege*; *Not Invited to the Party: How the Demopublicans Have Rigged the System and Left Independents Out in the Cold*; *Paid Patriotism? The Debate over Veterans' Benefits*; *Patterns of Corporate Philanthropy: Ideas, Advocacy, and the Corporation*; *The Politics of American Feminism: Gender Conflict in Contemporary Society*; *Stifling Political Competition: How Government Has Rigged the System to Benefit Demopublicans and Exclude Third Parties*; *Subsidizing Culture: Homeland Security Scams*; *Intercollegiate Athletics, Inc.*; *Taxpayer Enrichment of the "Creative" Class*; *Tax-funded Politics*; *They Play, You Pay: Why Taxpayers Build Ballparks, Stadiums, and Arenas for Billionaire Owners and Millionaire Players*; *Unhealthy Charities: Hazardous to Your Health and Wealth*; and *Unsustainable: The History and Politics of Green Energy*.

He is co-author of *Better Government at Half the Price: Private Production of Public Services* and *Political Economy of Federal Government Growth* (both with Manuel H. Johnson) and co-author with Thomas DiLorenzo of *Cancer-Scam: Diversion of Federal Cancer Funds to Politics*; *Destroying Democracy: How Government Funds Partisan Politics*; *The Food and Drink Police: America's Nannies, Busybodies and Petty Tyrants*; *From Pathology to Politics: Public Health in America*; *The History and Politics of Public Radio: A Comprehensive Analysis of Taxpayer-Financed U.S. Broadcasting*; *Official Lies: How Washington Misleads Us*; *Public Health Profiteering*; *Underground Government: The Off-Budget Public Sector*; and *Unfair Competition: The Profits of Nonprofits*.

Founder and Editor of the *Journal of Labor Research*, he is a contributing author to seventeen books and has published more than 130 articles and reviews in scholarly journals. And his popular articles have appeared in the *Wall Street Journal, Society, Alternatives in Philanthropy, Consumers' Research, Tax Notes, Federal Reserve Bank of Atlanta Review, Inc., Inquiry, Intercollegiate Review*, and *The Bureaucrat*.

Independent Institute Studies in Political Economy

THE ACADEMY IN CRISIS | *edited by John W. Sommer*

AGAINST LEVIATHAN | *by Robert Higgs*

AMERICAN HEALTH CARE | *edited by Roger D. Feldman*

AMERICAN SURVEILLANCE | *by Anthony Gregory*

ANARCHY AND THE LAW | *edited by Edward P. Stringham*

ANTITRUST AND MONOPOLY | *by D. T. Armentano*

AQUANOMICS | *edited by B. Delworth Gardner & Randy T Simmons*

ARMS, POLITICS, AND THE ECONOMY | *edited by Robert Higgs*

A BETTER CHOICE | *by John C. Goodman*

BEYOND POLITICS | *by Randy T Simmons*

BOOM AND BUST BANKING | *edited by David Beckworth*

CALIFORNIA DREAMING | *by Lawrence J. McQuillan*

CAN TEACHERS OWN THEIR OWN SCHOOLS? | *by Richard K. Vedder*

THE CHALLENGE OF LIBERTY | *edited by Robert Higgs & Carl P. Close*

THE CHE GUEVARA MYTH AND THE FUTURE OF LIBERTY | *by Alvaro Vargas Llosa*

CHINA'S GREAT MIGRATION | *by Bradley M. Gardner*

CHOICE | *by Robert P. Murphy*

THE CIVILIAN AND THE MILITARY | *by Arthur A. Ekirch, Jr.*

CRISIS AND LEVIATHAN, 25TH ANNIVERSARY EDITION | *by Robert Higgs*

CROSSROADS FOR LIBERTY | *by William J. Watkins, Jr.*

CUTTING GREEN TAPE | *edited by Richard L. Stroup & Roger E. Meiners*

THE DECLINE OF AMERICAN LIBERALISM | *by Arthur A. Ekirch, Jr.*

DELUSIONS OF POWER | *by Robert Higgs*

DEPRESSION, WAR, AND COLD WAR | *by Robert Higgs*

THE DIVERSITY MYTH | *by David O. Sacks & Peter A. Thiel*

DRUG WAR CRIMES | *by Jeffrey A. Miron*

ELECTRIC CHOICES | *edited by Andrew N. Kleit*

ELEVEN PRESIDENTS | *by Ivan Eland*

THE EMPIRE HAS NO CLOTHES | *by Ivan Eland*

THE ENTERPRISE OF LAW | *by Bruce L. Benson*

ENTREPRENEURIAL ECONOMICS | *edited by Alexander Tabarrok*

FAILURE | *by Vicki E. Alger*

FINANCING FAILURE | *by Vern McKinley*

THE FOUNDERS' SECOND AMENDMENT | *by Stephen P. Halbrook*

FUTURE | *edited by Robert M. Whaples, Christopher J. Coyne, & Michael C. Munger*

GLOBAL CROSSINGS | *by Alvaro Vargas Llosa*

GOOD MONEY | *by George Selgin*

GUN CONTROL IN NAZI-OCCUPIED FRANCE | *by Stephen P. Halbrook*

GUN CONTROL IN THE THIRD REICH | *by Stephen P. Halbrook*

HAZARDOUS TO OUR HEALTH? | *edited by Robert Higgs*

HOT TALK, COLD SCIENCE | *by S. Fred Singer*

HOUSING AMERICA | *edited by Randall G. Holcombe & Benjamin Powell*

JUDGE AND JURY | *by Eric Helland & Alexander Tabarrok*

LESSONS FROM THE POOR | *edited by Alvaro Vargas Llosa*

LIBERTY FOR LATIN AMERICA | *by Alvaro Vargas Llosa*

LIBERTY FOR WOMEN | *edited by by Wendy McElroy*

LIVING ECONOMICS | *by Peter J. Boettke*

Independent Institute Studies in Political Economy

INDEPENDENT INSTITUTE

100 SWAN WAY, OAKLAND, CA 94621-1428

For further information:

510-632-1366 • orders@independent.org • http://www.independent.org/publications/books/